THE BEST OF KITCHEN BASICS

Jenifer Lang is one of the most distinguished graduates of the Culinary Institute of America, which she attended to add food knowledge to her journalism skills in order to become a food writer. She was the American editor for the latest version of the definitive food encyclopedia, *Larousse Gastronomique* [Crown Publishers, 1988]. As a practicing mother, she also wrote a cookbook for feeding babies and children, *Jenifer Lang Cooks for Kids* [Harmony Books, 1993], which equally pleased children and parents. *The Best of Kitchen Basics* is an outgrowth of a column Ms. Lang wrote in *The Washington Post* called "The Resolute Shopper."

Since 1990, Jenifer Lang has been Managing Director of the celebrated 3-star Café des Artistes in New York City, which she owns with her husband, the prominent writer and restaurateur George Lang. The Langs, including children Simon and Gigi, live in Manhattan.

THE BEST OF KITCHEN BASICS

Completely Revised and Updated

JENIFER LANG

WINGS BOOKS
New York • Avenel, New Jersey

Grateful acknowledgment is made for permission to use the following recipes:

Simca's Herbes de Provence from *Herbs* by Emelie Tolley. Photographs by Chris Mead. Text copyright © 1985 by Emelie Tolley. All rights reserved. Used by permission of Clarkson N. Potter, Inc.

Tuna and Pistachio Terrine by Helen McCully from *The Great Cooks Cookbook* by James Beard *et al.* Copyright © 1974 by The Good Cooking School, Inc. Reprinted by permission of Doubleday & Company, Inc.

Espresso Ice Cream from *Italian Country Cooking* by Judith Gethers. Copyright © 1984 by Judith Gethers. Reprinted by permission of Villard Books, a division of Random House, Inc.

To Stabilize Yogurt from *A Book of Middle Eastern Food* by Claudia Roden. Copyright © 1968, 1972 by Claudia Roden. Reprinted by permission of Alfred A. Knopf, Inc.

Salmon Gravlax with Mustard-Dill Sauce from *The Café des Artistes Cookbook* by George Lang. Text copyright © 1984 by George Lang. Used by permission of Clarkson N. Potter, Inc.

Tea Cream from *European Cookery* by Jane Grigson. Copyright © 1983 by Michael Joseph. Reprinted with the permission of Atheneum Publishers, Inc.

Shaker Flank Stead from *The Best of Shaker Cooking* by Amy Bess Miller and Persis Fuller. Copyright © 1970 by Shaker Community, Inc. Reprinted with permission of Macmillan Publishing Company.

Homemade Ketchup from *Make Your Own Groceries* by Daphne Metaxas Hartwig. Copyright © 1979 by Daphne Hartwig. Reprinted with permission of Macmillan Publishing Company.

Shaker Herb Soup from *The American Table* by Ronald Johnson. Copyright © 1984 by Ronald Johnson. Reprinted by permission of William Morrow & Company.

Chocolate Oblivion Truffle Torte by Rose Levy Beranbaum. Copyright © 1984 by Rose Levy Beranbaum. All rights reserved. Used by permission of Rose Levy Beranbaum.

Elizabeth David's Homemade Yogurt from *Masterclass: Expert Lessons in Kitchen Skills* by Elizabeth David. Copyright © 1982 by Elizabeth David. Used by permission of Jill Norman and Hobhouse, Limited.

Herbes de Provence from *The Wonderful Food of Provence* by Jean-Noel Escudier and Peta J. Fuller. Copyright © 1968 by Houghton Mifflin Co. Reprinted by permission of Houghton Mifflin Co.

Chocolate Mousse and "Original" Original Nestlé Toll House® Cookies are reprinted with the permission of the Nestlé Foods Corp.

Originally titled *Tastings: The Best from Ketchup to Caviar*

This 1996 edition is published by Wings Books,
a division of Random House Value Publishing, Inc.,
40 Engelhard Avenue, Avenel, New Jersey 07001,
by arrangement with the author.

Random House
New York • Toronto • London • Sydney • Auckland

Printed and bound in the United States of America

Library of Congress Cataloging-in-Publication Data
Lang, Jenifer Harvey.
The best of kitchen basics / by Jenifer Lang. — Completely rev. and updated.
p. cm. — (Wings great cookbooks)
Rev. ed. of: Tastings—the best from ketchup to caviar. c1986.
Includes bibliographical references and index.
ISBN 0-517-14704-1 (hardcover)
1. Food—Sensory evaluation. 2. Cookery. I. Lang, Jenifer Harvey.
Tastings—the best from ketchup to caviar. II. Title. III. Series.
TX546.L34 1995
641.3—dc20 95-35872
CIP

Design by Milton Glaser

10 9 8 7 6 5 4 3 2 1

CONTENTS

CANNED FOODS

HERBS AND SPICES

BEVERAGES

BAKING GOODS AND SWEETS

LUXURY FOODS

SOURCES

ACKNOWLEDGMENTS

Over the years that I worked on this book, several people assisted me with the research and organization of the tastings. Mark Umbach was the first "associate" in Jenifer Harvey Associates, before he changed directions and became a successful fine art dealer. Lori Longbotham did a great job in the initial stages of research. Before moving back to Paris and La Varenne, Charles Pierce proved an able backup and was particularly helpful when we needed a slow, southern drawl to talk to experts below the Mason-Dixon line. Mindy Heiferling provided invaluable creative research. My friend, Melissa Marek Babb, lent a month of her time and helped to keep the balls in the air. Allison Shuker gathered together the bits and pieces of my jumbled life throughout the last two years. Howard Solganik was a great help years ago in Washington, when I first began holding these kinds of tastings.

Barbara Kafka was most generous with her time and advice, going over the manuscript and giving unerring direction, proving to me once again that she has one of the best minds in the business. Irena Chalmers lent her sense of humor and marketing skill to the search for a good title.

Pamela Thomas, my editor, proved a dear and considerate midwife for this book, full of patience and good sense, and just the right questions.

Nach Waxman, who was the book's first editor, helped enormously to shape the list of foods to be included.

Amanda Urban, my agent, supported me and the project with professional advice, as well as being the first one to say, "I *need* a book like this!"

Harvey-Jane Kowal at Crown seemed to spend almost as much time with the manuscript as I did, but found many more of its inconsistencies. Erica Marcus spent hours on the book's behalf and claims to have "permissions" tattooed on her forehead.

Milton Glaser made the book a visual masterpiece with his design; also I was grateful that he didn't ask, "How's the book?" every time we saw each other during the four-year period of its creation.

My parents, John Lonergan and Kathlyn Free, *did* ask, "How's the book?" at regular intervals, and I appreciated them every bit as much as everyone else who graciously *didn't* ask. I suppose that their enormous interest in food and good living, combined with boundless energy, inspired me to do something like this in the first place.

My good friend Eva Pusta knows that in reality this entire book is dedicated to her, "without whom it would have been finished two years earlier!"

Last I thank the fine editor Bill Rice, because he was the first one to come up with the idea when he asked me to do the "Resolute Shopper" column in the *Washington Post*, which set me on the road to *Tastings: The Best from Ketchup to Caviar*, now called *The Best of Kitchen Basics.*

FOREWORD

by Morley R. Kare, Ph.D., M.D.,
the late Director of the Monell Chemical Senses Center

Your sense of taste was inherited, but it has subsequently been modified by experience. Because of these genetic, environmental, and other factors, there is enormous diversity in individual sense of taste. Taste is both chemical specific and concentration dependent. For example, not everyone perceives a bitter component in saccharin; however, this ability is specific only for this compound and does not reflect the individual's total taste capability. Similarly, one person may find that a single teaspoon of sugar in a beverage provides a sweet sensation, whereas another individual may require four times as much sugar for the same effect. In any population, these differences pose a challenge in deciding on the flavor for mass-produced foods and beverages.

When most people speak of taste, they mean all the sensations experienced with the ingestion of a food or beverage. These include odor, thermal information, pain or irritation, and mouth feel or texture, plus a variety of other factors. People speak of the taste of wine, but most of those sensory qualities actually relate to smell. Even visual qualities can affect taste perception; for example, would black-yolked eggs be acceptable?

The functions of taste and smell in foods relate to ingestion, digestion, and metabolism. The mouth serves as a gatekeeper, determining what enters the digestive tract and also alerting the digestive system precisely on how to prepare for the nutrients about to arrive. A small amount of sugar in the mouth will almost immediately initiate the release of insulin. Exactly how the mouth copes with the variety of sweeteners currently in soft drinks has yet to be determined. From animal experiments we know that the sensory quality of food can dramatically influence the release of digestive enzymes. Food that is introduced directly into the stomach by tube may be processed differently from food that is tasted. Only recently has the physiological importance of flavor in food been scientifically described.

One's sense of taste is not constant. Although the newborn responds to sugar in much the same way as an adult does, an infant is largely indifferent to salt in the early months of life. In the same person, after extensive exercise, when energy stores in the body have been partially depleted, the response to sugar can be altered to complement this need. Some medications can alter taste. Also, the fourth dessert probably has a taste different from the first. Nutritive state can affect taste response, and dramatic changes in taste occur with deficiencies of some vitamins and minerals. Exposure to an aroma or taste can change our perception of it. These and many other factors impact on our judgment of flavor.

How our taste and smell receptors work is only now being explained. In the coming decades we will begin to understand how to use this information to potentiate and modify the flavor of food, even as it grows. The behavioral information collected in this book will become even more useful for supplementing and effectively applying new discoveries of research on our sense of taste and of smell.

Jenifer Lang's book provides a unique opportunity for all of us to compare our chemical senses with those of an educated panel. Our taste preference for slight rancidity or a unique texture may contradict the preferences of a trained palate. However, each of us lives in his or her own sensory world, and it is interesting to discover whether—and why—we differ from experts in our perceptions of quality.

AN EXPLANATION OF HOW WE TASTE

by Julia Wesson, President of Palatex,
a sensory evaluation, testing, and consulting firm in New York City

Tasting, as most people mean it, is a complex sensory experience. When food or liquid is taken into the mouth and prepared for swallowing, the total perception is a combination of smell, taste, feel, sight, and sound.

SMELL

When we lift a fork to our mouth, rip open a package of nuts, or stir a cup of coffee, we develop expectations from the aroma we experience. This can prove to be an important stimulus to eat or an early warning to prevent us from swallowing something unfit for consumption. When the food or beverage is actually in the mouth, smell is again important. A major portion of our "taste" experience (sometimes estimated at 80 to 90 percent of the total sensory experience, though it is impossible to make an accurate estimate) is the perception of aroma stimulated by the release of volatile compounds in the mouth as a combined result of chewing, warming up cold foods, cooling down hot foods, and mixing food and drink with saliva. The same sensory organ, the olfactory bulb, is the receptor for smelling materials inside as well as outside the mouth. The mode of entry is different (the nostrils from the outside, the nasal cavity behind the mouth from the inside), and the environmental conditions are changed, but the sense is the same.

TASTE

In the context of physical tasting, the definition of "taste" is very narrow. It refers to the basic tastes accepted by most experts: sweet, sour, salty, and bitter. The receptors for these sensations are the taste buds, which are specialized for each basic taste, and which are situated on visible structures called *papillae*. Taste buds are scattered all over the mouth, the soft palate and the bottom side of the tongue included, but perception of each basic taste is concentrated on areas of the top side of the tongue: sweetness is perceived primarily on the tip, saltiness on the front sides, sourness on the back sides, and bitterness on the back.

FEEL

This encompasses two types of feelings in the mouth: *textures* perceived by the kinesthetic or muscle sense and the tactile sense; and *chemical irritations* of the nerve endings producing some feelings which are, in fact, mild pain sensations.

Texture is the perception of structure or substance. The kinesthetic sense, which perceives the heaviness of a weight held in the hand or the force of a punch to the stomach, also perceives texture sensations like the hardness of French bread and the brittleness of a potato chip. The tactile sense is essential in the perception of the fibers in celery, flakes in fish, beads in tapioca, and the tiniest grain of sand in a spinach salad.

Chemical sensations like heat from red pepper, the astringency of tea, the prickle from carbonation, or the harshness from alcohol are essential aspects of the integrated "taste" experienced.

Although these sensations are clinically classified as pain, they can be the differentiating sensory aspects of foods and beverages, imparting key elements of pleasure to many products.

SIGHT

In recent years, scientific study has demonstrated what we have always believed about the importance of appearance on the perception of the "taste" of food and beverages. The simplest examples are studies of the relationships between the intensities of added colors on the perception of flavor—the stronger the color, the stronger the perceived flavor. For example, a fruit-flavored candy may pass as "grape" simply on the basis of purple color, even if the flavoring is not actually very grapelike. For many people, the key difference between perception of peppermint and spearmint is the sight of pink for peppermint as opposed to green for spearmint.

Sight is also very important in the perception of texture. In fact, the appearance of the structure or substance of a product is, by definition, part of texture. Just as the appearance of wood grain or velvet is an important part of sensation before you actually touch the surface, so is the appearance of a frothy milkshake or crunchy peanut butter an important part of taste before you actually eat or drink.

SOUND

The sense of hearing can be important to perception of foods with "active" textures, like hardness, crunchiness, and brittleness. The crunchy sounds associated with eating a thick, hard pretzel, or the sound from bursting corn kernels on the cob certainly reinforce the "taste" sensations inherent to these foods.

Because tasting involves all of the senses, and infinite combinations of flavor, texture, and appearance exist in foodstuffs, it is very difficult to communicate about the sensory characteristics. It is no wonder that we have traditionally focused very little attention on the most critical aspect of enjoyment in eating—the way products taste. In spite of the neglect of sensory descriptions in popular food writing and everyday expression about food, consumers do, of course, care about how products taste. Consumers respond negatively to unexpected sensory changes in their favorite products and positively to the increasing refinement in the better-tasting foods available in today's supermarkets.

The food and beverage industry understands the importance of taste (that is, the integrated sensory experience) in consumer acceptance. However, it has only been in recent years that a discipline has evolved—called *sensory evaluation* —to describe and quantify the flavor, texture, and appearance characteristics of products. Most companies utilize sensory testing methods, together with consumer acceptance testing, in the development of new products. In progressive companies manufacturing large volumes of food or beverages, sensory evaluation is also applied to controlling product quality. As consumers become more discriminating about what they buy, and as the competition for grocery-shelf space increases, sensory evaluation technology is becoming more important to the success of food and beverage manufacturers.

Although communication and understanding about taste has improved within the industry, there is still little communication with consumers about this most critical aspect of value for the money. That is why I was thrilled to see the manuscript of this book, the first consumer guide to the plethora of products on the grocery shelf. Jenifer Lang has not only provided useful information about products in the important categories of packaged foodstuffs, but committed herself to the difficult task of rating products according to the taste criteria of food experts. The book will serve as a valuable reference for homemakers, shoppers, and cooks, and as an excellent impetus for making better buying decisions based on the way products taste. I am sure that Jenifer Lang is on the forefront of a new consumer trend for more discriminating choices at the store.

A STATEMENT OF PURPOSE AND A BIT OF CLARIFICATION

by Jenifer Lang

few years ago, a tomato paste manufacturer ran a television commercial that went something like this: "We want you to do something that you've probably never done before—taste your tomato paste right out of the can," and then they showed Typical Housewife taking a spoonful of their brand of tomato paste out of the can and tasting it, and then smiling and nodding when she found that it was good. Even though this seems like a reasonable thing to do, the thought was really quite revolutionary. How many of us, professionals and home cooks alike, buy a brand of tomato paste, or any other food that we use only to cook with, because our mothers bought it, or because we are familiar with the company? The reasons could go on: we buy it because it's imported from Italy, or because it's made from plum tomatoes and we read in a cookbook somewhere that they're the best, or because a friend told us that this brand is particularly good. Very few cooks buy a brand of tomato paste, or any other packaged food, because they have tried several brands at one time and found one to be the best-tasting.

I have been involved with this kind of comparison and assessment all of my professional life. About 20 years ago, when I met with William Rice and Marian Burros, then the co-food editors of the *Washington Post*, I was given the assignment of beginning a "Resolute Shopper" column. For my first column, I covered olive oil, purchasing every brand available in the Washington, D.C., area and holding a blind controlled professional tasting to find which ones were excellent, which were ordinary, and which were unacceptable. I applied wine-tasting methods to the procedure, including using an amended version of the University of California at Davis scoring system—a 20-point scale taking into consideration taste, color, aroma, and so on. From olive oil, the column progressed to chocolate, mustard, tea, and on down the line to give a pretty fair picture of the quality and range available to someone shopping for basic foods in the nation's capital.

This kind of investigation appeals to my innate aversion to sham (I have a very literal mind), and also to the fact that I like to pamper my palate with the best food. These proclivities of mine led to four years of active hard work on *Tastings: The Best from Ketchup to Caviar*, now re-published as *The Best of Kitchen Basics*. To my surprise, my editor Pamela Thomas suggested that, instead of writing a turgid treatise on the physiological nature of the process of tasting, I should simply tell readers *why* I wrote this book. The simplest answer is that I wanted to provide readers with the real information they wanted in order to buy and cook with the best foods.

After conducting scores of blind tastings, with food professionals with trained palates and a library of taste memories—food writers, professional chefs, manufacturers, buyers, importers, wholesalers, editors, restaurateurs—the real answer to why I wrote this book became vividly obvious to me. Very few of even these top professionals had ever done this kind of comprehensive assessment before, and the results of the tastings were *always* a revelation to the participants. It became clear that my instincts were correct: it was time that someone put together a book stating how to judge the foods we eat and which foods actually taste the best.

For the past two decades, more and more time and money have been spent on food by a greater proportion of the population, but in the midst of all this activity, true benchmarks for taste have not been established. The cooks of this generation have honed their basic skills, learned about various major and minor cuisines of the world, and acquired a *batterie* of the proper equipment. But apart from reading labels, which even the most casual shopper does today, these sophisticated home cooks have not really learned about basic raw ingredients. Sharp discriminating lines between truly *good* foods and the trendy/unusual/boutique/well-packaged foods have not been established.

The more consumers allocate for food from their disposable incomes, the more brands appear on our supermarket and speciality-food-store shelves. When confronted with an array of 55 different brands of mustard in a store such as Zabar's in New York City or Macy's Cellar in San Francisco, even a food expert is bewildered. Do I buy the cheapest brand, or the most expensive, or the one imported from France, or the domestic mustard, or the one in a fancy package, or the one with a no-frills label, or the one I've read so much about lately? This kind of dilemma can't be solved by logical thinking, and so many of us end up buying a tried-and-true brand, such as Grey Poupon, because at least we know that one is not *bad*, or perhaps we reason that it must be at least acceptable to have stayed around for so long, even though a truly great mustard may be on the shelf right next to it.

In many areas of life, art, and science, the law of the fittest is alive and well, but in packaged foods this unfortunately is not the case. Extinction or survival is not necessarily a logical process. Often it is the result of clever marketing techniques or simply inherited tradition. This book is a series of unsentimental investigations in search of facts that may or may not coincide with the best-selling products.

The profit motive and total disclosure of practical information make uneasy bedfellows, and so generally we cannot rely on much helpful information from manufacturers except, of course, that which they are required by law to give, such as ingredient labeling. I spent four years cajoling large and small food producers into giving much more specific information than they have ever revealed to consumers before—information about how their foods are manufactured, which specific ingredients are used and why, demographic information about their products, and methods for manufacturers' own tastings.

To use business-school vocabulary, *intrinsics* are fast becoming more important than *extrinsics* when consumers decide why to buy this product or that. An intrinsic reason for purchasing a food is that it tastes good and we like it. An extrinsic reason for buying a food is that we like the image it conveys; Crabtree & Evelyn products are beautifully packaged and presented, and thus make terrific gifts, no matter how they taste. (Sometimes good, sometimes not so good, according to my tastings.)

With basic pantry foods, the swing is going to the opposite way. The American public is beginning to be too sophisticated to buy Dannon yogurt simply because the company makes commercials showing that it is soothingly cerebral. We have grown up and away from Dannon, and have discovered other brands that taste better and please us more.

Not only were these blind horizontal tastings (one brand against another) a new experience for the professionals on my panels, but they also marked the first time experts from many food-related disciplines were brought together in one place to taste various foods. A specialty-food store owner and a couple of his knowledgeable employees might get together on a regular basis to try two or three brands of a food to decide which one to buy for the store, but rarely had the same owner met with a professional chef, a food writer, a wine expert, and a manufacturer, to judge the value of those same brands.

My hope is that the book adds up to an educational tome on the most basic foods in the American pantry, one that will stand as a guide for many more years. It is not meant to be complete, as not even a good-size book on each food could accomplish that, but it contains the salient facts needed to outfit a basic pantry with necessary items.

When this book was first published, it contained tasting charts of all (or nearly all) of the national brands of each of the pantry basics under consideration. To assess the foods, I assembled about ten people, a different panel for each food group, gathering food writers such as James Beard, professional chefs such as Jacques Pepin, restaurateurs such as Barry Wine, retailers such as Giorgio DeLuca. I also included those who were experts in the specific food being tasted; for example, a chocolate expert from Nestlé was present at the chocolate tasting. All of the tastings were blind—none of the brands was identified.

For this book's re-issue, I decided to excise the tasting charts. Not only have the available brands changed in the last decade, but also the number of food products has expanded geometrically, making proper assessment of all national brands daunting, if not impossible.

However, in the "Conclusions and Suggestions" segment of each chapter, I have made my recommendation for the best of class in each of the categories, partly based on the original tastings—if the information is still correct—and also based on my 20 years of expertise in this field.

That being said, I believe one of the most useful sections in the book is "How to Judge . . ." For the first time anywhere, I have set down the industry rules for how to assess the qualities of each food in the book. These sections contain everything from how the mechanics of a tasting are orchestrated (why vinegar is tasted from sugar cubes, for example), to what qualities to look for while tasting. This is a how-to guide for those who may want to conduct tastings on their own at home. For example, if you wanted to try three different brands of Darjeeling tea to see which one you like the best, or to educate your palate about the characteristics of Darjeeling tea, you would simply look up the "How to Judge Tea" section and find how to brew the tea properly for tasting, which is different from how to brew it for drinking; at what temperature to taste it; what to use to clear your palate, and what qualities to look for in good and bad Darjeelings. Even if brands change as new ones are imported and old ones go off the market, this information will always be current and useful.

In any case, few words are more illusive or pliable than "best." Perhaps the closest to an objective definition, one that has guided me throughout my professional life, is the statement made by the late Fernand Point (the most influential chef of our time) of La Pyramide restaurant in Vienne, France, who said, "Foods should taste and look like what they are."

After all of this, *you* may still like Heinz, of course, as some foods are chosen for emotional reasons (I know, you have been eating Heinz ketchup ever since your very first hamburger). Neither my panels of experts nor I can argue with you, nor would we want to change your mind. But even if you're a dyed-in-the-wool Heinz lover, maybe we can help you in the mustard department, to guide you through the maze of brands with which you aren't familiar and help you to find one you'll be just as loyal to as your ketchup.

The "Dash of History" section in each chapter is just that—a bit of background about the food in question simply to satisfy our curiosity. The suggestions on how to cook with (or simply to cook) the food may be obvious to some, but I hope I give tips that are new to many.

The "Handling and Storage" information is vital, largely because many cooks mishandle their ingredients and then blame the manufacturers for their poor quality. For example, super premium ice cream does not last more than a few days in a home freezer, and mustard has a very short shelf life, even if kept in the refrigerator, where it belongs. I've even answered that burning question that has plagued generations of American cooks: "Should ketchup be kept in the refrigerator or at room temperature in the pantry?"

The recipes are meant to show off the foods to their best advantage. They are all thoroughly tested and favorites of mine; none, I hope, is run-of-the-mill. Standard recipes using any of the foods in this book can be found in a good basic cookbook, such as the *Doubleday Cookbook, Joy of Cooking,* or *Fannie Farmer.* I deliberately selected recipes that are unusual enough and/or good enough to merit the ink and paper on which they are printed.

Musicians have been able to agree on an exact international pitch, setting A at 440 vibrations per second, so that orchestras the world over can play on the same pitch. Wine tasters have also quantified their impressions, by accepting the Wine Aroma Wheel developed by the American Society of Enology and Viticulture in Davis, California. The wheel divides wine aromas into 10 primary, 27 secondary, and 95 tertiary aromas. Similar vocabularies are available for taste, body, and color of wine. In the food world we are not so lucky, as tastes are rarely measurable by a scientific or even a quasi-scientific gauge (although salinity and spicy-hotness can be computed with some degree of consistency). The only method we have within our power is to gather a goodly number of profession experts of good standing and record, and sort out and interpret their opinions, which were formed through blind and strictly controlled tastings. We can also provide benchmarks for honing our own tastebuds and making our own judgements. More we cannot achieve in the field of assessing the quality and taste of basic ingredients at this time, but at least I hope that this book, its approach, and techniques are the right step in that direction.

This book is dedicated to
Simon and Gigi, my two
favorite kids in the
whole wide world!

with love from Mommy

GRAIN PRODUCTS

FLOUR

heat, milled into flour and made into bread, is the principal food staple in 45 countries, including ours. The rest of the world eats rice as a staple. In spite of flour's important status in the world, its use in the American kitchen has been declining since the 1950s. More and more meals are eaten outside the home these days, which means that less food is cooked at home; smaller family size also accounts for less home baking, and homemakers are no longer counted on, as they once were, to provide bread for their families. In 1900, 95 percent of the flour sold in America was bought by home bakers; today the figure is closer to 5 percent. Because of the enormous popularity of bread machines, bread flour sales grew 96 percent between 1990 and 1992. It is the only type of consumer flour that is showing an increase in sales.

Today, most home bakers use all-purpose bleached flour about 60 percent of the time. Unbleached and whole-wheat flours account for 11 percent of the remaining market. Six percent is bread flour, 17 percent is self-rising, and "other" (such as rye) is 5 percent. Curiously, most of the flour we use at home goes into bread, then cookies. The highest per capita consumption in the nation is in the Southeast, where most of the flour is made into biscuits.

Almost nothing in our pantry is more basic than flour, and yet it is characterized by less uniformity from brand to brand and region to region than any other commercial manufactured food we use. This fact is not widely known among home cooks, and so many baking disasters are blamed on technique or equipment rather than on the flour, which may be performing differently from previous batches of the same brand.

A professional baker can open up a new sack of flour, pick up a fistful, and squeeze it together to assess its properties. Like a scientist, he can mentally calibrate all of his or her standard recipes to adjust for the moisture and gluten content of this particular batch of flour. Most professional bakers perform this important task every time a new sack of flour arrives in his or her bakeshop!

A DASH OF HISTORY

The history of flour spans recorded time. Man has been making bread from ground wheat for thousands of years, first in the form of a wheat-and-water gruel that was dried out to make a flat cake. Mexican tortillas are just one example of this ancient flat bread that has survived to the modern era. As refinements in the milling process occurred and natural leavening was discovered, the puffy loaves we commonly consider "bread" came into the diet of Europeans.

The ancient Greeks had developed techniques to refine their wheat enough to distinguish between white and brown (whole-wheat) flours. All over the world throughout the subsequent hundreds of years, those who could afford to eat bread from white flour were considered superior to those who ate coarser, brown bread made from less-refined, and thus cheaper, flour. Marie Antoinette's immortal line, "Let them eat cake," is more correctly translated as "Let them eat brioche," a particularly rich form of bread native to France.

Only since the 1960s have the health-giving properties of bread made from the entire wheat kernel become widely known and accepted, and thus tables have completely turned. Instead of poor people eating brown bread and rich people eating white bread as in centuries past, educated people with knowledge of food and nutrition are eating whole-grain breads, which are often more expensive than breads made from refined flour.

In the last 200 years, with the inventions of the steam engine and the roller mill system—an improvement on the relatively inefficient stone grinding method—flour milling has become sophisticated. Millers are no longer dependent on sources of natural power, such as wind and water. The big business of making flour really got under way around the turn of this century, and "Down by the Old Millstream" became a nostalgic anthem.

HOW FLOUR IS MADE

It's easier to understand the manufacturing process by knowing a little about the construction of a kernel of wheat. The three main components are the *bran,* which is $14^1/_2$ percent of the total kernel; *endosperm,* 83 percent; and *germ,* $2^1/_2$ percent. White flour is made from the endosperm only, while whole-wheat flour is made from all three components of wheat.

The bran is the tough outer layer and contains most of the fiber (cellulose) of the wheat, as well as many nutrients. The endosperm is the bulk of the kernel, covered up by the bran layer. The germ contains most of the fat of the kernel and, in the case of white flour, is removed so that the flour doesn't turn rancid and spoil quickly.

The Milling Process

The six top wheat-growing states in the country in order of highest volume produced are Kansas, North Dakota, Montana, Oklahoma, Washington State, and Minnesota. Wheat is shipped from farms to huge mills and blended with the wheat from other growing areas to achieve standardization. Then it is cleaned and washed. To clean the wheat, it is passed through a vibrating screen that removes bits of straw and other coarse materials, then the grains move across another screen while air sucks off dust and lighter particles. The grain moves to a scourer, where beaters throw the wheat against a drum, buffing each kernel and breaking off the beard, or tiny hairs that grow off the top of the kernel. During this process, air currents carry off the dust and bran coating. Next, the grain goes to a magnetic separator that pulls off iron and steel particles (nuts, bolts, and rivets that may have come loose from machinery). High-speed rotators then spin the wheat in a water bath, where excess water is thrown out by centrifugal force.

After it is cleaned, the wheat is *tempered* or soaked in water to toughen the outer bran layer and soften the endosperm so that they can be separated easily. The wheat kernels are then ground through corrugated rollers that become successively smoother to make smaller and smaller particles. These particles are sifted through several screens, like giant sifters, until about 72 percent of the wheat is extracted as flour. The remains of the ground kernel, called shorts, are used for cattle feed.

At this point, flour is classified into grades of refinement that are important for the professional baker, but do not apply to the flour used by the home baker. The generic name for all grades of flour mixed together and the kind sold in the supermarket for home use is *straight flour.* When the flour is broken down into separate grades for sale to professionals, straight flour becomes (from highest quality to lowest):

Long Patent
Medium Patent
Short Patent
First Patent
Extra Short or Fancy Patent
First Clear
Fancy Clear
Second Clear

The quantity of each grade produced from various wheat crops depends on the particular crop of wheat, the region in which it is grown, and the way it is milled.

Flour is naturally a yellowish color, due to a pigment in the wheat. Traditionally, after milling, it is stored for about 2 months so that the yellow turns white because of exposure to the oxygen in the air. This aging also develops the proteins in the flour *(gliadin* and *glutenin),* strengthening them so that, on contact with liquid, they connect with each other more solidly to create *gluten,* the protein in flour that allows bread to rise. Thus, flour that has been aged will make dough with more strength and elasticity.

Because storage time is expensive—and variable, depending on each particular crop of wheat—a chemical shortcut called *bleaching* was invented to speed up the process. After milling, chlorine is added to flour to simulate the effects of long aging: to turn it white and to develop the proteins.

Because many people object to the chemicals added to bleached flour, naturally bleached (called *unbleached)* flour has become increasingly available. Even if flour is unbleached, however, sometimes part of the aging process is artificially simulated with the addition of potassium bromate; if potassium bromate is added, the flour is called "bromated" on the label.

Manufacturers also include small amounts of malted (sprouted) barley or wheat in some flours, which provide certain natural enzymes essential for the proper fermentation of yeast; it is not required that these additions be stated on the label.

After milling and bleaching, the flour is enriched. Because many of the nutrients are lost when the bran and germ are separated from the endosperm of the wheat, a law was passed in 1941 requiring that some of these vitamins be replaced in white flour. As a result, three B vitamins, 2.9 mg of thiamine, 1.8 mg of riboflavin, 24 mg of niacin, as well as 20 mg of iron, must be added to every pound of enriched flour. This law harks back to a time when Americans gained more of their sustenance from bread than we do today, and this enrichment was vital.

VARIETIES OF WHEAT AND FLOUR

Wheat changes its character depending on the geography of the place where it is grown, the climate, the season in which it is planted, and the variety of the plant itself. The two main classifications of wheat are *winter wheat* and *summer wheat.* Winter wheat is sown in the fall and harvested in the summer; summer wheat is sown in the spring and harvested in the fall. Different varieties of wheat are planted in each season, based on their ability to withstand the particular climatic conditions.

Although the botanical varieties of the wheat plant may vary, each is classified as *hard wheat* or *soft wheat.* Hard wheats have a 10 to 13 percent protein content, and the kernels are literally hard and tough. Soft wheats have a 6 to 10 percent protein content and are softer and more starchy than hard wheat. *(Durum* wheat is another type of wheat altogether, even tougher than "hard wheat," and is primarily used to make pasta; see Pasta, page 11.)

The two most important proteins in wheat are gliadin and glutenin, and when flour comes into contact with a liquid these proteins combine to make the all-important protein, *gluten.* Gluten fibers form a network; when dough is kneaded, these fibers become more and more elastic. With bread, enzymes are produced by the action of the yeast and these enzymes ferment the natural and added sugars in the dough. This fermentation process releases carbon dioxide, causing the dough to "rise." The carbon dioxide inflates the fibers of gluten, and when baked, these stretched fibers stiffen as a result of the heat, giving bread the texture of a sponge. In pastry making, gluten provides strength for the many layers of flour, liquid, and fat (such as butter), assuring flakiness.

Without gluten, flat breads like crackers or matzohs would be the only breadstuffs known to man. The gluten found in wheat is the only protein in any grain that is strong enough to trap and hold up the carbon dioxide gas bubbles released in the dough by the fermenting action of yeast (or other leavener) on the sugars in the dough. Gluten allows anything made with wheat flour to "rise" and stay risen after cooking. Flour made from any other grain, such as rice, has no gluten and thus can't make puffy loaves of bread.

Breads need a lot of gluten in their flour to withstand the action of the yeast and high rising. Flours containing much less gluten and a higher percentage of starch are needed to make foods that are meant to be tender and light yet not so high-rising, such as cookies, cakes, and crackers. In fact, too much gluten can toughen such delicate products. Certain kinds of pastries, such as puff pastry and croissants, need a moderate amount of gluten in order to provide structure for their many layers and to absorb their large proportions of butter.

When wheat is brought into a mill, it is first analyzed to gauge its protein content. Generally, *hard spring flour* comes from the northernmost sections of the United States, and it has a large amount of high-quality gluten. *Hard winter flour* comes from the Central Plains and has gluten that is less strong. *Soft winter flour* comes from the South and the Midwest and has a small amount of weak gluten.

After these major classifications, flour can be further categorized in the following ways:

All-Purpose Flour

In the past, flour was ground in local mills from the wheat grown nearby, and so bakers worked with whatever kind of flour was available. This explains why biscuits are a tradition in the South, and tall loaves of crisp-crusted bread are more indigenous to the North. Because of the humid climate, southern flour is "soft" and low in gluten, and northern flour is "hard" and high in gluten.

With the industrialization of the milling process, big companies began to package flours that were a blend of hard and soft wheats transported from all over the country. These are called *all-purpose flours,* meant to be suited to any and all home baking purposes. Because no federal standard for all-purpose flour (sometimes called "family flour") exists, it can be a blend of 40 percent hard wheat and 60 percent soft wheat, vice versa, or any other combination. Several decades ago, when flour packagers noticed that Americans weren't baking as much bread at home as they used to, many of the all-purpose blends became predominately soft wheat and lower in gluten to accommodate today's more popular baking needs, such as flour for cookies and cakes. Generally, all-purpose flour has about a 10 percent protein content.

For home cooks, it is helpful to know that southern brands of all-purpose flour are made primarily of soft wheat, and northern and mid-western brands have a higher proportion of hard wheat. So, when a recipe calls for "all-purpose flour" and the gluten content of the flour is crucial, such as in a bread recipe, results might differ, depending upon the brand of flour used.

Professional bakers can be very specific about the flour they require for separate baking tasks, but home cooks are stuck with the ubiquitous all-purpose flour that isn't really good for either breads *or* pastries, but is simply adequate for all household and cooking tasks, including breading fried chicken and making Christmas tree ornaments. Also, because all-purpose flour has been available for several decades, virtually all modern recipes call for it and are adjusted to its properties. Even if a home baker is resourceful enough to seek out professional-quality flours or the specialty flours mentioned farther along in this chapter, he has to have the mind of a chemist and enormous perseverance to figure out the best way to use them. Some flours absorb more liquid than others, depending on whether the wheat was grown during a rainy season or a dry one; some have weak gluten; some are not finely milled; the variations are endless. A sophisticated baker needs to test and blend different flours for his needs. This kind of experimentation appeals to some people, especially those who always bake their own bread and are looking for a foolproof recipe with proper ingredients. Because commercial bakers can get flours that are much more specialized than those available in the supermarket, and because many of these flours need heavy-duty machinery to knead and develop their doughs, many of us rely on factory-made bread and pastries for our everyday needs because, frankly, it is easier.

Cake Flour

Cake flour is made entirely from soft wheat, sometimes with the addition of cornstarch to heighten the starch content. If you squeeze a handful of cake flour, the flour will stick together in a clump because of its high starch content. The protein content of cake flour is around 6 percent. It is more finely milled and more heavily bleached than all-purpose flour.

"High-ratio" cakes, those supersweet commercial products that contain more sugar than flour, can only be baked with bleached cake flour. The heavy bleaching perforates the starch granules in the flour and allows it to begin absorbing water even before the batter goes into the oven. Since sugar becomes a liquid with the heat of baking, the bleached cake flour can absorb more sugar than unbleached. In countries where bleached flour is against the law, such as Japan, these sweet, rich, moist cakes don't exist. High-ratio cakes are also those made from packaged cake mixes; they can be distinguished by the fact that their batters are pourable.

When using cake flour, add 1/8 teaspoon of baking soda for every cup of flour in the recipe. This neutralizes the acidity in the flour caused by the bleaching; otherwise your cakes and pastries can be gummy.

Pastry Flour

Pastry flour (also called *cookie flour* or *cracker flour)* has a slightly higher protein content than cake flour, usually about 8 percent, and is also not as heavily bleached. Both cake flour and pastry flour are more finely milled than other flours.

Bread Flour

This is white flour made from hard wheat, which has a higher protein content, about 14 percent, than all-purpose flour and is thus best suited to making bread. It is the closest thing to the hard wheat flours milled and packaged for professional bakers, and bread made from it rises high and has an airy texture, reminiscent of factory-made bread. Soft wheat flour has a better taste than hard wheat flour. Some bread bakers are willing to sacrifice a good-looking loaf for flavor, so they use flour with less gluten, such as all-purpose. This flavor distinction is the reason why French bread tastes so good; French flour is made primarily of soft wheat, and French bakers have developed a type of loaf suited to this flour, which also happens to taste delicious.

Gluten Flour

This is white flour from which almost all of the starch has been removed. It is often used by people who are required to go on low-starch diets. Its protein content is between 13 and 15 percent. When making bread, the best use for gluten flour is to add a tablespoon of it for every cup of flour that is naturally low in protein, such as whole-wheat flour or rye flour. This will help the bread made from these flours rise a little higher than they would without the amplification, although too much gluten flour added to a bread recipe will result in a loaf that tastes like cardboard.

Whole-Wheat Flour and Graham Flour

These two flours are technically the same, flour ground from the germ, endosperm, and bran of the wheat kernel, rather than just the endosperm, which is the only part used for white flour. Both whole-wheat and graham flours are beige rather than white because they contain the entire wheat kernel; sometimes whole-wheat flour is called *entire flour.* Little brown flecks, the ground germ and bran, are visible. Although the government doesn't make a distinction between the two, graham flour is usually more coarsely ground than whole-wheat flour. The term comes from Reverend Sylvester Graham, an American advocate of nutrition who, in 1837, preached the health-giving properties of whole-wheat flour.

Whole-wheat flour has less gluten than white flour because the germ and the bran of the wheat make up part of the bulk of the flour, and thus reduce the proportion of other components. This makes whole-wheat flour perform differently in recipes. Foods made with whole-wheat flour tend to be heavier, coarser, and smaller than those made with white flour. Therefore, unless you are a stickler for nutrition, it's a good idea to mix whole-wheat flour with all-purpose flour. When making whole-wheat pancakes, waffles, doughnuts, and crêpes, substitute whole-wheat flour for about three quarters of the white flour, and at the same time increase the liquid content slightly. In pastry recipes, mix whole-wheat and white flours about half and half; before kneading, allow the dough to rest for about 5 minutes.

Breads and pasta can be made with 100 percent whole-wheat flour, but they will be difficult to handle; to compensate, add more water and an extra egg yolk, and let them rest for a few minutes before kneading or rolling out. Knead for an extra few minutes as well.

Stone-Ground Flour

To make stone-ground flour, large stones are used to crush kernels of wheat, which is the same method that was used for thousands of years before the technological advances of the nineteenth century. Advocates feel that stone-ground flour contains more nutrients because the wheat is not heated as much during the milling process. Whether or not it is a better-quality flour, stone-ground flour is always coarser than factory-ground, which accounts for the rough texture of food made with it—a texture preferred by most of those who use it.

If you prefer to use stone-ground flour but don't like its heavy coarseness, you can give it a slightly more conventional texture by adding 3 tablespoons of cornstarch for every cup of *all-purpose* stone-ground flour, or by adding 1/3 cup of cornstarch for every cup of *whole-wheat* stone-ground flour.

Rye Flour

Rye flour comes from rye, a different grain from wheat, one that contains very little gluten. Since gluten allows bread to rise, most rye breads contain large amounts of wheat flour to make a puffy, commercially acceptable loaf.

Rye flour is often classified as light, medium, or dark, depending on how finely ground it is and how much of the germ and bran it contains. The darker the rye used, the darker the bread. Medium rye is the one most available in our supermarkets, but light and dark ryes can also be found, generally in health-food stores.

Pumpernickel Flour

Pumpernickel flour is to rye flour what whole-wheat flour is to white flour. In other words, the flour contains the entire rye kernel—the germ, bran, and endosperm. In commercial pumpernickel breads, molasses and unsweetened cocoa powder are usually added to make them dark and tasty. In addition, as with rye bread, high proportions of white flour can be added. The clue to the amount of genuine pumpernickel flour in bread is the size of the loaf; the greater the percentage of pumpernickel flour in a product, the smaller the volume and the more compact its texture.

Triticale Flour

Triticale is a relatively new kind of grain, developed in the last 20 years as a hybrid of wheat and rye. It contains more protein (but not gluten protein) than either wheat or rye flours, and so it is used to make foods for third-world nations, and to make a specialty flour usually sold in health-food stores to discriminating Americans.

The gluten content of triticale flour is very low, and so it should be used in combination with other flours, such as white flour or gluten flour; one third triticale flour to two thirds all-purpose flour is a good combination. If it is combined with whole-wheat flour, it creates a bread (or other food) with a very dense texture.

Self-Rising Flour

Self-rising flour is packaged with about 1 1/4 teaspoons of double-acting baking powder and a pinch of salt for every cup of flour. It is generally made with soft wheat and is suitable for biscuits and pancakes; in fact, commercial pancake mix is an example of a type of self-rising flour. Use it only for recipes that call for it specifically.

If all you have on hand is self-rising all-purpose flour and you want to make bread, compensate for the chemically leavened taste by adding 2 tablespoons of sugar for every 4 cups of flour.

Granulated Flour (also called Instant Flour)

The commercial product Wondra is the prime example of granulated flour. Developed about 30 years ago, it flows freely, like sugar, and dissolves much more quickly in liquids than other flours. It is best used for sauces and gravies, but is not usually suitable for baking. Nevertheless, some professional bakers use a small proportion of granulated flour (about 10 percent of the total) when making puff pastry and croissants. Because it absorbs liquid readily, it helps to make a crisp crust.

TIPS FOR USING ALL TYPES OF FLOUR

Many professionals rely on a baking test to gauge the qualities of a batch of flour. Using a standard bread recipe, they bake a few loaves and then calculate such attributes as water absorption, "oven spring," elasticity, and taste. Using a similar technique, the best way to judge flour at home is to make your favorite bread, cake, or pastry recipe several times with different kinds of flour (following the general rules of thumb listed under the specific varieties above), and then to stick with the flour that performs the best.

To determine easily the amount of gluten in any flour, look for the nutrition label printed on the package. About 85 percent of the protein listed on this label is the gluten content of the flour. If you are looking for a flour to make bread, choose one that has a high protein content (13 percent or over); if you are looking for a flour to make a cake, choose one with a low protein content (11 percent or under).

In general, whenever a recipe calls for sifted flour, take the direction seriously. One cup of

COMMON BRANDS OF ALL-PURPOSE FLOUR AND THEIR PROPERTIES

FLOUR (where distributed)	PROTEIN CONTENT	% SOFT VS. HARD WHEAT	BEST USED FOR
White Lily *(Southeast)*	*8.5–9%*	*100% soft wheat*	*pastry, cakes, biscuits, quick breads, sauces*
Martha White *(Southeast)*	*10%*	*mostly soft wheat*	*pastry, cakes, biscuits, quick breads*
Robin Hood *(North Central)*	*12%*	*100% hard wheat*	*yeast breads, pastry dough*
Gold Medal *(Nationwide)*	*10 1/2%*	*100% low protein hard wheat*	*average results in all home cooking tasks: yeast breads, quick breads, cakes, cookies, biscuits*
Pillsbury *(Nationwide)*	*10 1/2%*	*mostly hard wheat*	*breads, quick breads, cakes, cookies, biscuits*
Heckers* *(Northeast)*	*15%*	*mostly hard wheat*	*yeast breads, pastry dough*

* Also sold under the *Sarasota* label in the Chicago and Milwaukee areas

sifted flour weighs 30 percent less than 1 cup of unsifted flour, and so the quantities will be out of balance unless directions are followed carefully. If you don't feel like sifting flour even though the directions call for it, measure the flour and then subtract 2 tablespoons per cup.

Flours can vary in density by as much as 30 percent, which means that 1 cup of flour may weigh anywhere from 4 to 5 ounces. So, depending on how firmly your flour is packed and the brand you are using, you could be adding a different amount each time you measure. Because of this inexactitude, professional bakers and professional recipes never use measuring cups, but always rely on scales, which are much more accurate; a quarter pound of flour is always a quarter pound of flour, while 1 measuring cup of flour may or may not always equal 4 ounces.

If you're using a recipe that calls for a cup measurement of flour, to be as accurate as possible use a measuring cup that you can dip into the flour and then level off with the dull side of a knife, in order to get an exact amount. Never use a glass measuring cup, which is meant for measuring liquids.

If you substitute cake flour for all-purpose flour in a recipe that calls for a cup measurement, add 2 tablespoons of cake flour for each cup of flour you are using. Conversely, if you substitute all-purpose flour for cake flour in a recipe that calls for a cup measurement, subtract 2 tablespoons of the all-purpose flour for every cup of flour used.

Since gluten is heavier than starch, all-purpose flour is heavier than cake flour; in other words, 5 ounces of cake flour has greater volume than 5 ounces of all-purpose flour. In a recipe that calls for ounce measurements, if you are making a substitution of one type of flour for the other, simply add an equal weight of the flour you have on hand. The fact that cake flour will have greater volume than an equal weight of all-purpose flour will not affect the final product.

Bleaching weakens the gluten in flour, and some bakers claim that food made with unbleached flour has a better, firmer texture because of its slightly higher protein content, and that unbleached flour absorbs more liquid than bleached. I find that the difference between the performance of the two, for almost all cooking tasks, is minimal. For bread baking, however, when high protein content is important, unbleached flour does a slightly better job. For delicate pastries, such as piecrust, unbleached flour is *not* good, unless a little more liquid is added to the recipe to compensate for the higher gluten content. Two common brands of unbleached flour are Heckers and Sarasota.

HANDLING AND STORAGE

Flour absorbs odors, so it should be stored in airtight containers. White flour can last up to a year, if it is stored in cool, dry conditions. Generally, however, it's not a good idea to keep it past about 3 months; although it wouldn't seem spoiled, it would not perform as well as when it was fresh. If it smells musty, flour has gone bad and should be discarded.

Whole-wheat flour, because it contains the oil in the germ, goes rancid much more quickly and should be stored in the refrigerator or freezer, where it will last about 2 months as long as it is packed completely airtight. Old whole-wheat flour smells like rancid oil. Just before using whole-wheat flour, bring it to room temperature, since it will have absorbed some moisture, which should be evaporated.

Self-rising flour will keep no longer than about 2 months, because the baking powder it contains will lose its strength.

If you store an unwrapped stick of peppermint gum or a bay leaf in your flour, you will protect it from weevils, the tiny bugs that proliferate in humid conditions. These unsavory bugs are not dangerous; they can be easily removed by freezing the flour overnight and then sifting the bugs out. I prefer to throw infested flour away and buy a new bag. Refrigerating flour can help prevent weevils, but not always. Storing flour airtight doesn't prevent weevils, since most flour contains their eggs.

RECIPES

A few years ago, when I was working in the test kitchen of *Redbook Magazine,* I did an article that offered one master white bread recipe and gave directions for making minor changes to create all different types of loaves: French bread, raisin bread, whole-wheat bread, dinner rolls, hamburger buns, potato bread. After days of testing to find the best white bread recipe to use as the master, the hands-down favorite of all of the home economists and food professionals was my grandmother's bread, one she made every day of her married life! Needless to say, I was very proud and am happy to offer the recipe here.

My Grandmother's Basic White Bread

One batch of this can be made into 4 regular loaves, or 4 braided loaves, or 28 hamburger buns, or 40 dinner rolls, or about 7 dozen bread sticks. Or you can bake a variety of shapes and sizes.

9–10 cups bread flour or all-purpose flour (bread flour will give you a slightly higher loaf)
1/4 cup sugar
2 envelopes active dry yeast
1 tablespoon salt
1 quart hot milk, about 125°F.
1 large egg (optional)

1. In the large bowl of a heavy-duty electric mixer, mix 3 cups of the flour, the sugar, yeast, and salt. Gradually add hot milk to flour mixture and beat at medium speed for 2 minutes, scraping bowl occasionally with a rubber spatula. Add egg and 2 more cups of the flour. Beat at high speed for 2 minutes, scraping bowl occasionally. Stir in 3 to 4 more cups of the flour (by hand if your mixer isn't strong enough), enough to make a stiff dough.

2. Turn out dough onto a floured surface and knead for 8 to 10 minutes, until dough is smooth and elastic, adding only as much of remaining flour to surface as needed to prevent dough from sticking. Shape dough into a ball and place in a greased bowl. Turn dough to bring greased side up. Cover with a damp dish towel or clear plastic wrap and let rise in a warm place (top of the refrigerator or in an unlit oven with a pilot light with the door ajar are good places). Dough should rise until double in volume, about 90 minutes at 80°F.

3. Grease 4 bread pans $8^1/_2 \times 4^1/_2 \times 2^1/_2$ inches. Divide dough into 4 equal pieces (about 22 ounces each, if you have a scale). Shape each piece into a loaf and place in prepared pans. Cover with a dry dish towel and let rise in a warm place until dough has risen just above the rims of the pans, about 1 hour at 80°F.

4. Uncover pans, put into oven, and turn on oven to 400°F. Bake for about 45 minutes, or until bread sounds hollow when tapped with your knuckles on the top and bottom. Remove from pans and cool on wire racks or place loaves diagonally across tops of pans to cool.

Whole-Wheat Bread

To make whole-wheat bread from the basic recipe, substitute whole-wheat flour (or graham flour, if you like coarser bread) for half of the all-purpose flour. Reduce kneading time to 5 minutes. Expect slightly smaller loaves, because of the lower gluten content in the flour.

Triticale Bread

Follow method for whole-wheat bread, but use triticale flour in place of the whole-wheat flour.

Potato Bread

Follow original recipe, adding 1 cup mashed potatoes with the egg. Just before baking rub each loaf with 1/4 teaspoon white flour.

PASTA

n the last 20 years Americans have fallen in love with pasta. Always a popular staple, pasta has now become chic. Small stores selling fresh pasta have opened in many American cities, in much the same way as pasta shops abounded in Italian neighborhoods in the early part of the century.

In 1981, Americans consumed 2 billion pounds of pasta, or about 10 pounds per person. In 1994, the National Pasta Association estimated that the average American now eats almost 20 pounds of pasta per year. This figure shows no sign of decreasing; in fact, of all foods consumed in the U.S., only soft drinks have grown faster than pasta in the past five years. Nearly 74 percent of adults eat a pasta meal for dinner at home at least once every two weeks.

Pasta has become so popular in this country that between 1970 and 1981 big food corporations bought up almost all of the small pasta-producing companies. Foremost-McKesson bought Mueller's; American Beauty, La Bella Rosa, Delmonico, and Skinner are owned by Hershey Foods; Borden owns Creamette; Ronzoni is owned by General Foods Corporation, which in turn is owned by Philip Morris. Twenty years ago, 200 small regional pasta companies existed, and now 5 large corporations control over half of the American pasta industry. For decades, pasta manufacturing has been an entirely regional business, but now it is becoming part of a larger American food picture. This can be compared with Italy today, where 238 pasta manufacturers produce over a ton of pasta every day.

According to Morton I. Sosland, publisher of *Milling and Baking News,* "Pasta has become big business and the food giants that have moved in are trying to hold down costs because they are in an increasingly bitter struggle among themselves for market shares, and they also face competition from rising imports from Italy."

Despite these increases, Americans still eat less pasta per capita than the Italians, who eat an astonishing 60 pounds per person annually. This statistic is decreasing, but Italians still eat twice as much as the next largest consumers, the Venezuelans, who eat 30 pounds per capita annually, and the Swiss, who eat 20 pounds per year. The French eat 15 pounds per year, while the Germans eat 10 pounds per year.

In 1980, imported pasta accounted for about 2 percent of the eastern United States pasta market, where imports make the biggest impact. By 1994, that figure had grown by over ten times.

The largest-selling type of pasta in the United States is spaghetti, together with other "long pastas," such as linguine and spaghettini, which account for 36 percent of all pasta sales. The next most popular shape is elbow macaroni and other short pastas, which makes up 35 percent of the market. Egg noodles have a 17 percent share of the market, and the "specialty" shapes (a category that includes shells, fettuccine, bow ties, and so on) make up only 12 percent of the pasta-buying market.

A DASH OF HISTORY

Pasta has been around since the beginning of recorded history. One Etruscan tomb has a wall painting of a rolling pin and a kneading board where pasta was worked, and even a cogged cutting wheel for making curly edged noodles.

In ancient Rome, pasta was called *laganum* and was said to be adored by Cicero. In the late 1200s the first macaroni was made in Sicily. Marco Polo is often credited with introducing pasta to Italians upon his return from China in the fifteenth century, but records of Italians eating pasta exist long before then. Historians report that by the year 1500, the daily fare of Italy included lasagne, tagliatelle, and vermicelli. During the sixteenth century, Italian pasta was served with both savory and sweet sauces, which sounds odd to us today, although some recipes for modern sweet pasta dishes appear occasionally, such as *bocconotti,* a dish from the Apulia region of Italy, which is sweet baked ravioli filled with custard cream and cherry jam, and *calciuni,* a Christmas dish also from Apulia, which is deep-fried ravioli filled with chestnut purée, chocolate, rum, almonds, and spices.

Thomas Jefferson was responsible for introducing pasta to America, together with many other culinary delights, such as rice, figs, dates, almonds, and ice cream. In 1788, Jefferson's secretary was in Naples and ordered a copper pastamaker for use at Monticello. In 1789, Jefferson himself brought macaroni back to the United States from the port of Le Havre in France and continued to order pasta from his agent in Marseilles. An undated letter of Jefferson's states, "the best Maccaroni *[sic]* in Italy is made with a particular sort of flour called semola, in Naples."

Pasta began to be sold commercially in the United States in 1848 by the Zerega Company in New Jersey, but didn't become widely popular until around the turn of the century. In 1898, durum wheat, essential for making good pasta, was introduced from Russia by Dr. Mark Carleton, who was sponsored by the United States Department of Agriculture. Some companies that began production around the turn of the century were Mueller, Prince, Ronzoni, La Rosa, Skinner, and Creamette. When European imports of pasta were cut off during World War I, American production got under way in earnest.

Just after World War II, from mid-1944 to around the end of 1947, American pasta companies flourished because they sent pasta to Europe for the American army and for war-torn European countries governed by the Marshall Plan. By 1949, pasta companies realized that they needed to make a big marketing push in the United States to keep their industry healthy and growing, and so Americans' acceptance of pasta on a large scale dates from that time.

HOW PASTA IS MADE

Basically two main varieties of pasta exist, with several categories within each variety:

Fresh Homemade Pasta

Fresh pasta is called in Italy *pasta fresca* (fresh pasta) or *pasta all'uovo* (pasta with egg). This is pasta made outside of a factory, either at home or in a small shop. It is generally made with eggs; with flour from common wheat *(Triticum aestivum)*, the ordinary flour used in home kitchens; and sometimes with the addition of water or oil. It can be made by hand, in the old-fashioned way, by making a dough and kneading it, rolling it out with a long rolling pin, and cutting it into simple shapes with a big knife. It can also be made partially or completely by a small pasta machine. These machines, whether hand-cranked or electric, can knead, roll, and cut flat pasta shapes; some also extrude dough into pasta shapes, such as spaghetti or macaroni.

Many purists are vociferously opposed to pasta machines; nevertheless, fresh pasta sold in gourmet groceries is often made by machines larger than the ones available for home use. Pasta made by machine is still authentically "fresh" if it is made in small batches with flour moistened primarily with eggs and little or no water.

Pasta does not have to have been "just made" to be considered fresh. It can be dried and kept for as long as a month if it is kept in an airtight container. As long as it is made by hand, or by hand-cranked or electric machine, with eggs and ordinary flour and put up, it is considered "fresh." Some pasta companies make fresh pasta and package it so it will keep for up to 3 months. These pastas are sometimes packaged in plastic boxes. It is slightly dried, with a moisture content of 15 percent compared to 25 percent for fresh pasta just after it has been made, and 12 percent for dried commercial pasta. Commercial stuffed pasta shapes, such as tortellini and cappelletti, come in one of 4 ways: fresh, stuffed with fresh ingredients and sold within a day or two of being made, such as at Raffetto's in New York City; the same version which is frozen; dried and filled with bread crumbs and dried cheese (among other filling ingredients), such as the Bertagni brand; and frozen, defrosted, sold in bulk, such as the Fini brand. Many companies, by the way, pasteurize their nonfrozen packaged pasta, both stuffed and flat shapes, to keep it fresh in the package for up to 35 days.

Dried Commercial Pasta

Dried pasta is called in Italy *pasta secca* (dry pasta). This kind is made with flour and water in a factory, where conveyor belts supply the ingredients to machines, which mix and knead them together, each machine processing as much as 1,500 pounds per hour.

The dough is extruded through dies on machines that operate continuously, or rolled on large rolling machines and cut into long noodles of various widths. The pasta, which has a moisture level of about 30 percent at this point, is blown with air as it comes out of the extruding or cutting machines, then it is put into rooms filled with a carefully controlled amount of dry heat so that it dries slowly. Then the pasta is put into humid ovens, where the drying process is completed. Depending on the type of machinery used, the drying time for long pastas, such as spaghetti and linguine, is about 24 hours; for short pastas, such as macaroni, about 10 hours. The moisture level of finished factory-made dried pasta must be at least as low as 12 percent in order to prevent spoilage. The dried pasta is then packaged for distribution.

The "Chemistry" of Factory-Made Pasta

The best dried pasta is always made of durum wheat. Durum wheat, *Triticum durum,* is different from the strain of wheat used for bread (see "Durum Wheat," page 14); it is the hardest of the hard wheat strains. Durum wheat flours have more gluten, and a stronger type of gluten, than flour made from soft wheat or from other strains of hard wheat. Gluten is a protein that makes pasta resilient. Dried pasta made with durum wheat stretches and has more "give"; it does not tear or break easily as does pasta made with ordinary flours. The gluten acts as a shell for the starches in the pasta, allowing the pasta to be cooked to a firmer consistency, which is desirable for good, Italian-style dried pasta. Italians call this firmness *al dente* or "to the tooth." Durum wheat is amber and translucent, instead of cream-colored and opaque like ordinary common wheat, and it is milled into three different forms:

• *Durum Semolina* Semolina is "chunks" (a technical term) of endosperm, the inner part of a grain of wheat. Durum semolina has the consistency of sand or granulated sugar. Federal regulations require that semolina can contain only 3 percent "flour," the powdery residue from the milling process. The best dried pasta is made from durum semolina.

• *Granular Durum* Granular is the same as semolina, except that it contains 3 to 10 percent flour. It is a low-quality form of durum wheat. Dried pasta made from granular is not as good as dried pasta made from semolina.

• *Durum Flour* Flour is the powdery substance that remains from the processing of semolina; this is the lowest-quality level of durum wheat milling. It makes dried pasta inferior to that made with durum semolina. It appears on labels of dried pasta as "durum flour" or "durum wheat flour," and sometimes erroneously as "semolina flour."

Any type of dried commercial pasta made from grain other than durum semolina tends to cook to a gluey, slimy mass unless it is carefully handled, and even then the results are not predictable. Some inferior factory-made dried pasta (called *scotta* in Italy) is made of one of the following rather than durum semolina: granular durum wheat, durum flour, farina (a granular form of common hard wheat), common hard-wheat flour, or soft-wheat flour. If a label reads simply "semolina," then the pasta was not made with durum wheat, but with a softer flour; it will also be inferior. A careful reading of the label will determine what kind of wheat has gone into the pasta. During cooking, dried pasta made of cheaper, softer flours will exude great quantities of foam, which will rise to the surface of the cooking water, evidence that the soluble starches of the soft flour are leaching out.

The milling of durum wheat into semolina for dried pasta is a more expensive process than the milling of other flours, largely because durum wheat kernels are extremely hard; in fact, the shell of the kernel has the consistency of cork. It is impossible to use durum wheat to make fresh pasta at home; it is so hard that it needs the pressure of the large machines used in factories to process it. Durum wheat is milled by about 10 companies across the United States, who use extra-hard steel rollers.

When durum wheat is milled into flour for pasta, the shell of the wheat kernel is ground into *bran* to be used in other food products, while the center of the kernel, the *endosperm,* will be ground to make semolina. (See "Flour," page 2, for a complete explanation of the milling process.) The semolina may be sifted as many as 9 times to remove the bran from the grain.

The innermost portion of a kernel or "grain" of wheat is the *germ,* where many of the nutrients lie. Most semolina does not contain the germ of the wheat because the germ contains oil and increases the risk of the flour becoming rancid; it is usually sold to wheat germ companies.

COMMON WHEAT
(the wheat used to make flour for home use)

Farina*

This is the powdery substance commonly known as "flour," the kind used in home kitchens.

Semolina

When common wheat is milled to a texture resembling sand, it is called "semolina."

DURUM WHEAT
(the hardest of the hard-wheat flours)

Semolina†

Semolina is "chunks" (a technical term) of endosperm, the inner part of a grain of durum wheat. Federal regulations require that semolina can contain only 3 percent "flour," the powdery residue from the milling process.

---

* Common wheat flour is used to make fresh pasta.

† The best dried pasta is made from durum wheat semolina. To save money, some pasta manufacturers make pasta from lower grades of durum wheat or from common wheat.

Granular

Granular is the same as *semolina,* except that it contains 3 to 10 percent flour. It is a low-quality form of durum wheat.

Flour

Flour is the powdery substance that remains from the processing of semolina; this is the lowest level of quality of durum wheat milling.

Additives

Sometimes, one or more of the following additives are put into factory-made pasta:

• *Disodium phosphate* is a "buffering texturizer" that helps pasta to cook more quickly. Federal regulations require that it be not less than .5 percent nor more than 1 percent of the weight of the pasta.

• *Gum gluten* is a protein added to hold together the ingredients in pasta. It is not allowed to be more than 13 percent of the pasta.

• *Glyceryl monostearate* prevents pasta from foaming too much during cooking. It cannot exceed more than 2 percent of the pasta.

• *Egg white* is often used in "light" pasta. The outside of the pasta is coated with a film of egg white that allows the pasta to absorb more water. This results in a pasta with one third fewer calories, the federal stipulation for the label designation "light."

• *Vitamins* are sometimes added to pasta. It is enriched with the same B-complex vitamins as bread, but twice as much is used because the product is water-soluble and thus vitamins leach out into the cooking water.

• *Food coloring* is sometimes added to egg noodles that are made with pasteurized liquid eggs; the pasteurization makes the noodles pale, and so a small amount of color is needed to make the product more appealing to consumers.

VARIETIES OF PASTA

Egg Pasta

Another type of factory-made dried pasta is called in Italian *pasta all'uovo,* or egg noodles. Small amounts of egg are added to pasta shapes that traditionally require them, such as fettuccine. In Italy, the law is that egg noodles must be made with 4 eggs per 2.2 pounds (1 kilo) of flour. In the United States, egg noodles must legally contain 5.5 percent egg solids.

Whole-Wheat

Dried whole-wheat pasta is buff-colored with a slightly stronger and nuttier flavor than regular pasta, but only mildly so; on the other hand, fresh whole-wheat pasta has a distinctive whole-wheat flavor.

Vegetable

An enduring food rage seems to be pastas flavored and colored with vegetables: spinach, tomato, mushroom, carrot, broccoli. They are made in both fresh and dried versions, and usually with eggs. Whether fresh or dried, most of the time the pastas are flavored with dried vegetable powders rather than puréed fresh vegetables as they would be at home.

The dried vegetable pastas have very little if any of the flavor of the vegetables used to make them. They are simply colorful and a change from the ordinary white pasta. Fresh pastas sometimes have a very slight taste of vegetables, but not enough to stand out through the flavor of a sauce. Again, they provide a colorful variety but little nutrition or flavor.

Buckwheat

Pizzocheri are hearty buckwheat noodles traditionally used in the Valtellina region of Italy. They have recently become available in the United States in dried versions. They are rustic and full of buckwheat flavor.

HANDLING AND STORAGE

If kept in an airtight container, factory-made pasta with eggs will keep for up to 6 months. Some experts recommend that factory-made pasta without eggs be kept only 1 year, some suggest it will last at least as long as 5 years, since it is a dehydrated product and cannot spoil. The United States Army's limit for storing pasta is 2 years. After a long time in storage, however, dried pasta will become brittle and will break apart when cooked.

Fresh pasta, whether made at home or bought in a store, can be used right away or dried for several hours, spread out on a paper towel on a flat surface, like a kitchen counter. It will then keep for up to a month if it is put in an airtight container, such as a tightly closed plastic bag. According to one of America's preeminent Italian food experts, Marcella Hazan, fresh pasta should never be refrigerated or frozen. This goes against the practices of many, if not most, of the fresh pasta shops in the country, where pasta is refrigerated and freezing is recommended. Since drying fresh pasta and keeping it on the pantry shelf is so easy, I have always treated it that way, whether it's fresh pasta I have made myself or fresh pasta I have bought in a store.

Any type of pasta will absorb extraneous odors and flavors, so it should always be stored absolutely airtight and away from strong-smelling substances. Pasta should also be stored in a cool, dry place, because excess humidity will cause it to fall apart.

HOW TO JUDGE PASTA

Tasting Media

By following the package directions for cooking the pastas, the textures of the various pastas can be judged by their own manufacturers' standards. Many manufacturers give a range of cooking time, which allows you to choose *al dente* or soft, depending on your preference. Choose the same shape for all brands, in order to be consistent.

In all professional pasta tastings, pasta is tasted hot and plain, with no embellishment.

Color/Eye Appeal

The quality of a factory-made pasta can be determined before it is cooked. The best pasta is not only translucent before cooking but also a bright yellow color; this is a good indication that it was made with hard-wheat flour.

A "checked" appearance indicates that it was made improperly (probably with soft-wheat flour), dried improperly, or is old. Checking, tiny white lines throughout the pasta, indicates a fracturing of the wall of the pasta. Checked pasta will literally fall apart in the cooking water at the points where the white lines appear.

Pasta made with soft-wheat flour may also be flecked with white spots or have a grayish tinge.

Pasta flecked with tiny brown spots may have been made (or "padded," to use the industry parlance) with the bran of the wheat. Pasta with black spots may contain "extraneous matter" (to use another industry term), which may include insect fragments and animal hairs. If you're looking for the black spots, the best method is to put the pasta in front of a light and use a magnifying glass. Once the pasta has been boiled these spots won't hurt you, but they are certainly unsavory.

In addition to being translucent and a fine yellow, the best pasta is smooth and shiny before being cooked. Boxes that contain broken pasta may be old and stale. Before cooking, the best pastas are elastic and will bend without breaking; they are not stiff and brittle.

Taste/Aroma

When tasting pasta you should detect no foreign flavors. Pasta should taste fresh and ever-so-slightly sweet and nutty, with a faint smell of wheat.

The best pasta is the blandest. It should be a neutral vehicle for the sauce served with it, even if the sauce is simply butter and cheese.

Consistency

A good pasta cooks uniformly with the outside cooking at the same rate as the inside. Many pastas made with soft-wheat flour are mushy on the outside when the inside is still raw.

Aftertaste

Because the best pasta is bland, it should also have no discernible aftertaste.

CONCLUSIONS AND SUGGESTIONS

Of all of the tastings I have ever conducted, pasta showed the least amount of difference among the foods being sampled. Most of the brands were very close in flavor and quality. This is good news, because it means that you can shop for price, and not have to worry about quality differences.

That being said, however, the major difference among pastas is not in taste, which was generally very bland, but in texture. Some pastas became quite mushy, indicating that they were not made with durum wheat semolina, notably American Beauty, Mueller's and Creamette (which, by the way, is the only national brand of pasta).

Many imported brands are also inferior in texture, including Spigadoro, De Cecco and Del Verde. De Cecco is a favorite gourmet-store brand, and costs about twice as much as supermarket brands, but it seems that you're not getting what you pay for.

The highest rated pastas in *Consumer Reports'* most recent pasta assessment were supermarket brands. My advice would be to search the labels for the words "durum semolina" and then buy by price.

Fresh Pasta versus Dried Pasta

Some parts of the American acceptance of pasta are healthy, both figuratively and literally, while others are quite pointless. As with any food fad, there is a great deal of interest in the subject along with some misinformation. Stores that sell so-called fresh pasta, pasta supposedly made with eggs, often sell inferior noodles, made with second-rate ingredients, badly cut. Perhaps because Americans think that fresh is always best, and perhaps because many shopkeepers are ignorant, much of this fresh pasta is refrigerated, which ruins it. Some of it is even frozen. Any Italian knows that fresh pasta made with eggs may be dried and kept in an airtight container for as long as a month, but it must *never* be refrigerated.

The renowned and influential California chef Jeremiah Tower (who put the restaurant Chez Panisse on the map and is now owner of his own place, Stars, in San Francisco) characterized Americans' attitude toward pasta when he said in *Cook's* magazine that he was against "the tyranny of fresh pasta." He feels that restaurants are using it haphazardly, "like the kitchen sink, just dumping anything on it."

The best pasta out of a box can be delicious, if it's prepared properly, and certainly much better than an inferior fresh product. Most Italians cook with both fresh and dried pasta, depending on the needs of the dish they are making. Some dishes require fresh pasta, especially those of Emilia-Romagna origin, and some must be made with dried pasta. The Italians, by the way, are making their own fresh pasta at home less these days.

The prosperous North of Italy specializes in fresh pasta, simply because it is a more expensive product and the northerners can afford it. The southern Italians, who are on the whole not as wealthy as their northern cousins, usually eat factory-made pastas because they are made of flour and water and are cheaper.

These geographical differences also dictate the kinds of sauces used on pasta. Factory-made pasta is usually served with oil- and tomato-based sauces, rather than creamy sauces made with butter. One reason for this is that olive oil is the main cooking fat in the South. (It's cheaper to grow olive trees than to raise cows for butter and milk.) Pasta made with eggs (or fresh pasta) is traditionally served with sauces made with butter and cream; in the North of Italy, the pasturage is richer, and, therefore, butter and cream are readily available.

Some experts feel that because of the high

moisture content in even the best homemade pasta, as well as the soft-wheat flour it contains, it can never be cooked to as firm a degree as dried commercial pasta. When pasta is made in a factory, it is dried until it contains only 10 to 12 percent moisture (see "How Pasta Is Made," page 12). Homemade pasta contains approximately 25 percent moisture; even if it is dried for up to 2 days, the moisture content will never get below 15 to 18 percent. This affects the cooking quality of the pasta, and unless it is handled very carefully, it can easily become mushy. The fact that fresh pasta is so often made with soft-wheat flour and flour other than semolina also contributes to its tendency to become pasty.

The price considerations can also be persuasive when deciding whether to use fresh or dried pasta. When you buy an 8-ounce package of dried pasta for 69 cents, you actually get a pound (16 ounces) of cooked pasta for that price; because dried pasta is dehydrated, it expands to almost double its size during cooking. When you buy 8 ounces of fresh pasta for $2.50 you are paying $5 for a pound, since fresh pasta doesn't expand much at all and the price you pay is the actual price of the pasta.

These facts do not broach the subject of taste. Pasta made at home with ordinary flour and eggs will have a different flavor—and for some cooks, a better flavor—than pasta made with semolina and water and perhaps a bit of egg. Nevertheless, perhaps a lesson can be learned in the experience of one of the most popular and prestigious restaurants in New York City, known for its fine cuisine. After making his own pasta for many years, the French chef decided to cook with Ronzoni fettuccine because, being dried and factory-made, it was easier to handle. Two years later, not one customer has noticed the switch. The chef's pasta dishes continue to get raves from critics and customers.

In an experimental blind tasting of the best homemade-style fettuccine in New York City against dried fettuccine, our panelists found that the dried fettuccine was thicker and had more bite to it. The texture was vastly superior to the fresh fettuccine. We could only detect a flavor difference when the noodles were eaten without any sauce whatsoever; then the fresh fettuccine tasted of the fresh eggs of which it was made.

Many commercial brands of fresh pasta, however, such as Contadina and Di Giorno, have a sulfur taste that comes from using stale eggs.

COOKING PASTA

The names of various pastas can be enormously confusing, owing to the fact that 600 different shapes exist, by some reliable estimations. Sometimes the same pasta has three or four names, depending on the region of Italy where it's being served. Pasta companies, to confuse matters even further, use their own fanciful names for pasta shapes, which do not correspond with other companies' names for the same shapes. The Italians, as in other matters as well, are not very fussy about the exactitude of pasta lexicon. In fact, to try to make a comprehensive guide to the subject of pasta names is to defy reason.

In general, however, some basic rules exist in Italy for matching specific pasta shapes with sauces. Long, thin pasta, such as spaghetti, linguine, and vermicelli, should be dressed with smooth, oil-based sauces, such as a tomato sauce, or with light seafood sauces. Chunky sauces shouldn't be put onto long pastas, because the chunks in the sauce slide off the pasta and end up at the bottom of the serving bowl. Flat noodles, such as fettuccine, tagliatelle, and pappardelle, call for richer sauces based on meat or stock, butter, cheese, or cream, thick, creamy sauces that can coat the flat surfaces of the pasta. Pasta with holes, grooves, and indentations, such as ziti, rigatoni, penne, and bucatini, are served with substantial sauces containing chunks of meat and vegetables. The convoluted shapes of the pasta will catch the pieces and hold them to the pasta. These elaborately shaped pastas are also good for baked pasta dishes. Very small pasta shapes (called in Italian *pastina),* such as *acini di pepe* and *stelline,* are traditionally served in broth. Hearty pastas, such as whole-wheat pasta and buckwheat pasta *(pizzocheri* in Italian), call for rustic ingredients. The traditional *pizzocheri alla*

Valtellina contains Swiss chard, potatoes, butter, and fontina cheese.

Whatever kind of pasta they're cooking, Italians on the whole use much less sauce than Americans do. The sauce on Italian pasta is a flavoring rather than the main event. Think of pasta sauce as performing the same function as salad dressing, simply to coat the noodles. A sauce (or a salad dressing) should not pool in the bottom of the bowl.

In the 1950s, because of a shortage of durum wheat in this country, many pasta manufacturers began to make their products with common wheat. As a result, Americans developed a taste for mushy pasta, which is now just beginning to change. Nevertheless, although our collective American taste for pasta is conforming more to that of the Italians and more domestic manufacturers are making their pasta with durum wheat, it seems that the recommended cooking times on boxes of pasta, especially American-made pasta, have not changed with it. Therefore, subtract a couple of minutes from the recommended cooking times on the packages and begin to taste for "doneness" at that point. If you decrease the suggested cooking time, you will have a better chance of getting your pasta *al dente,* or "to the tooth," with a little bit of bite to it.

When cooking pasta, gauge 1 gallon of water for every pound of pasta, and add salt to the water, if you wish. Salt delays the boiling of water, so if you're in a hurry, don't add salt to the water until after it has come to a boil. Add the pasta only when the water has come to a full rolling boil and stir immediately. After adding the pasta, cover the pot just until the water comes back to a full boil. Stir the pasta well a couple of times during the cooking time. When testing for doneness, the pasta should be firm, but not stiff or white inside when you break it with your fingernail or a fork.

As soon as the pasta is done (and maybe a little before, since it will continue to cook even after it's taken off the heat), drain it well in a colander and return the pasta to the empty cooking pot. At this point you might like to reserve a cup or so of the cooking water in case you need to dilute the sauce for the pasta.

Drizzle a little olive oil or a tablespoon or two of butter, depending on the cooking fat used in the recipe for the sauce, over the pasta in the cooking pot and toss it well. Then place the pasta in a serving dish and top with the sauce. In general, you can count on 8 ounces of box spaghetti making 5 cups of cooked pasta, enough to serve 2 people for a main course, or 4 for a first course, Italian-style. One pound of fresh pasta serves 2 people as an entrée, or 4 as a first course.

RECIPES

How to Make Your Own Fresh Pasta

You can make homemade pasta entirely by hand, or in a machine. I always make it by machine, and that way dinner can be on the table within half an hour of starting to make the pasta. (Serves 4 to 6 for a first course)

Pasta Made by Hand

3 cups all-purpose flour, approximately
4 large eggs

1. Mound the flour on a flat, sturdy surface and make a well in the center of the mound. Break the eggs into the well.

2. With a table fork, begin to stir the eggs, incorporating bits of flour into the eggs as you proceed. Continue stirring until you have incorporated as much of the flour into the eggs as you can with a fork. Then begin to work the dough with your hands, incorporating more of the flour so that the dough is no longer sticky, but pliable. With a dough scraper, remove all extra bits of flour from the counter. Knead the dough for 5 to 10 minutes, until it begins to have some "give" and is very smooth. Cover with plastic wrap or put into an airtight container and let dough rest at room temperature for 15 minutes.

3. Working with one quarter of the dough at a time and leaving the rest of the dough in the airtight container, begin to roll it out with a rolling

pin. The dough is thin enough when you can see your hand through it when you hold it up. Roll up the sheet of dough and cut into noodles of any width you prefer.

4. Shake out the noodles and lay over the back of a chair on which you have placed a clean dish towel, or on a pasta-drying rack. Dry for 15 to 20 minutes before cooking. Homemade pasta takes only about 60 seconds to cook; be sure not to overcook.

Pasta Made with a Machine

3 cups all-purpose flour
4 large eggs

1. Put the flour into the bowl of a food processor and break in the eggs. Process for a few seconds, until dough has formed a ball. Remove dough from food processor and knead for about 15 seconds.

2. Working with one quarter of the dough at a time and covering the rest of the dough with plastic wrap or putting it into an airtight container, feed the dough into the smooth rollers of an electric or hand-cranked pasta machine, with the rollers set at the widest setting. Continue to feed the dough into the machine at this setting until it feels pliable and very smooth, 6 or 7 times. Set the rollers at one setting narrower and feed the dough through once. Continue until you have reached the narrowest setting on the machine. Put the cutting attachment onto the machine and cut sheet dough into noodles.

3. Shake out the noodles and lay over the back of a chair on which you have placed a clean dish towel, or on a pasta-drying rack. Dry for 15 to 20 minutes before cooking. Homemade pasta takes only about 60 seconds to cook; be sure not to overcook.

Pasta with Roasted Garlic and Broccoli

(Serves 6 for a main course, 12 for a first course)

1 whole bulb of garlic
3/4 cup olive oil
1 bunch of broccoli
3/4 cup fresh basil leaves
1/2 cup heavy cream
salt and freshly ground pepper
1 1/2 pounds pasta
3/4 cup freshly grated Parmesan or Romano cheese, or to taste

1. Peel the outside skin from the bulb of garlic and place in a small, heatproof dish. Pour 1 tablespoon olive oil over the garlic and bake in a 325°F. oven until the garlic begins to brown, about 1 hour. Allow to cool slightly and remove the inside from each clove of garlic; reserve.

2. Cut the stems from the broccoli florets; chop the stems roughly and blanch both the florets and stems in boiling water for about 6 minutes.

3. In a food processor, place the blanched broccoli, the basil leaves, and the peeled baked garlic. Process quickly, on and off, adding the remaining oil through the tube of the food processor until a thick, coarse consistency is reached. Add heavy cream and process briefly. (You may want to leave the sauce in the food processor and add some of the cooking liquid from the pasta, if you need it to achieve a proper consistency.) Add salt and pepper to taste.

4. Bring 6 quarts of water to a boil and cook the pasta *al dente*. Drain, turn back into the cooking pot, and add the cheese. Toss well. Turn into a serving bowl and top with the sauce.

RICE

More than half the people on earth eat rice as the mainstay of their diet; in fact, rice makes up 80 to 90 percent of the total diet of that (mostly Asian) population. The rest of the world eats wheat as a staple, which accounts for only about 50 percent of the diet where it predominates.

Rice is so important to some cultures that the very word means "food" or "meal," in such languages as Japanese and Thai. In China, the phrase for quitting a job is to "break your rice bowl." No matter how much food he has eaten, a Japanese or a Chinese does not feel full until he has eaten some rice. It is also a symbol of fertility in many cultures; even Americans throw rice at a newly married couple to wish the bride and groom good luck.

Since more than half of all the rice in the world is eaten within five miles of where it is grown, 93 percent of the world production of rice comes from Asia; only 2 percent comes from the United States, and even with that we export over two thirds of our rice crop to over 100 countries.

In spite of our minor contribution to the world's rice market, we are the third-largest rice-producing country in the world. As with staple carbohydrates of other countries (pasta, for example), we have lately begun to appreciate rice better. American consumption figures bear this out: from 1981 to 1991 there was a 65 percent increase in the per capita consumption of rice in the United States, and the national consumption has increased by about 5 percent in each year since. Today we eat about 18 pounds of rice per person per year. If you count in all the rice used in beer brewing, that figure increases to over 22 pounds. The per capita consumption of rice is highest in the United States in areas near where rice is grown: the people in the area 200 miles inland from Charleston, South Carolina, eat 40 pounds yearly, compared to people in the rest of South Carolina, who eat 4 pounds yearly. Per capita consumption of rice in Louisiana is 26 pounds per year, but citizens of southern Louisiana eat 50 pounds per year.

To put these figures in perspective, it must be noted that the Japanese eat about 1/2 pound of rice per person per day, and the average Chinese eats 1 pound!

A DASH OF HISTORY

References to rice appear as far back as 2800 B.C., when it was written that a Chinese emperor established a ceremonial ordinance for its planting. The cultivation of rice may be much older than that. Perhaps because it is so ancient, historians are not sure whether rice originated in China, India, or even Thailand; clearly, it has been an important crop in those countries for thousands of years. From the Far East, the cultivation of rice spread to the Middle East, where it was cultivated in the Euphrates Valley in 400 B.C.

Rice first appeared in Europe around A.D. 900, when the Moors took it from North Africa to Spain. A few hundred years later, in 1475, rice spread to Italy. One of the earliest European recipes using rice was "rys Lonbarde," a dish that obviously emanated from Italy and was made with spices and hard-cooked egg yolks. In 1574 the Italians adopted the new grain for *risotto alla Milanese,* a creamy rice dish flavored with saffron and broth, for which the city of Milan is still famous.

Rice is mentioned in one of the earliest cookbooks ever written, *Le Viandier* by Taillevent, which was published in France in the fourteenth century. In spite of this early reference, the French disliked rice so much that during the famine of 1870 in Paris, when the zoo animals were slaughtered to feed the starving populace, great stores of rice remained untouched. These days, of course, the French are more open-minded about rice, and they serve it with or in many of their dishes, such as *blanquette de veau* and *riz à l'impératrice.*

The first time rice appeared in America was in 1671, when it was planted in Virginia by Dr. Henry Woodward; the doctor didn't know how to clean the rice, so it was thought of as a curiosity until 1694, when a Dutch ship bound from Madagascar to England ran into a storm, went off course, and landed at Charleston in the Carolinas for repairs. The grateful ship's captain gave the colonists a bag of rough rice, which was then planted and cleaned properly. By 1698, 60 tons of rice were exported from the Carolinas to England. The great success of the rice crop in this part of the New World was due to the fact that the marshy land and the climate provided the perfect growing conditions. In addition, rice is a labor-intensive crop, and the plantation owners of the Carolinas were able to supply the slaves to grow the grain. It is from this time that the term "Carolina rice" emanates; the term "golden rice" was also used in the eighteenth century to describe this high-quality rice.

Until the Civil War, rice was the most important crop in South Carolina. Several factors converged to change things, among them a series of hurricanes, the decline of the slave-based economy, and competition from western states. Even though very little rice comes from South Carolina today, the name still connotes quality because of this past association. Ninety-nine percent of the rice in the United States is now grown primarily in six states; in order of production they are Arkansas, California (where it was first grown in the nineteenth century to feed the Asian population), Louisiana, Texas, Mississippi, and Missouri.

HOW RICE IS MADE

Two major botanical varieties of rice exist: *indica,* which grows in colder climates and is a hard-cooking, long-grain type of rice, and *japonica,* which grows in warmer climates, is short-grained, and cooks up soft.

Because the rice crop needs a great deal of water—it takes 300 gallons to produce 1 finished pound—it obviously grows best in areas where water is plentiful, along the shores of rivers or tidal basins, or where long rainy seasons are common. Wherever it's cultivated, the method is essentially the same: the seeds are sown in the spring, and after a few weeks the seedlings are transplanted to paddies, or rice fields, which are flooded with water.

In third-world countries, the growing of rice is a labor-intensive and backbreaking job. The rice is planted by hand in prepared beds, and about a month later the seedlings are transplanted one by one to paddies. In most primitive countries, the flooding of the rice paddies is left to chance, and farmers wait for monsoons to come at just the right time. After the plant reaches about four feet in height, it is harvested, again by hand.

By contrast, rice growing in the more advanced countries of the world is a highly mechanized process with air-conditioned tractors to prepare the land, airplanes to sow the seeds, and a complicated permanent system of dams and channels to irrigate the fields.

In the fall the paddies are drained by mechanical means, or by nature (when the monsoons stop), and the rice is harvested. About two weeks before harvesting, the fields are drained. The soil dries out a bit, but the rice plant retains a high moisture content of 19 to 22 percent. The rice is harvested by power combines, which cut and thresh at the same time. At this stage, before milling, rice is called *paddy* or *rough* rice.

The first step in the processing of rice is to clean it, removing pieces of mud, leaves, and stalks. Next, the nonedible hull is removed in shelling machines, and at this stage it becomes brown rice, with the tan-colored bran layer intact surrounding the kernel.

To make white rice, the brown rice is milled by machines that rub the grains together under pressure to remove the bran layers by abrasion. As technologically advanced as this process is, 15 percent of the grains of rice break during milling and cannot be marketed. The remaining whole-grain rice is called *head rice* by processors and is called *fancy* on labels of packaged rice. Broken kernels are often sold to breweries, which use them to make beer; in fact, Anheuser-Busch is the largest single user of rice in the United States.

White rice processed in the United States used to be coated with talc and glucose to make it more attractive to consumers, which is why in the past every recipe included washing of the rice before cooking, but now such coatings are illegal in this country. Rice labeled "enriched" has been coated with a mixture of alcohol and a corn protein, then treated with calcium, iron salts, and synthetic vitamins. Six states in the United States—Arizona, California, Connecticut, Florida, New York, and South Carolina—require that all rice sold there be enriched and it must be labeled as such. However, because it is inexpensive and very easy for mills to enrich rice, over 90 percent of all rice produced in the U.S. is enriched. Enriching doesn't seem to affect the flavor of rice, but washing enriched rice removes many of these added nutrients. Cooking rice in more water than it can absorb also removes some of the nutrients.

Processing

Whether long, medium, or short grain, rice is processed into four forms for the American market:

• *Brown Rice* This is rice in its most natural form, with the bran layer intact. It has a nutty flavor and a chewy texture, as well as added nutrients from the bran. Brown rice takes twice as long to cook as white rice, because the bran layer makes it more difficult for the grains to absorb water. Only 3 percent of the rice consumed in the United States is brown rice.

Generally, large rice mills sell brown rice to health-food companies, who repackage the rice under their own labels. Almost all of the brown rice found in health-food stores is the same as the rice in supermarkets.

• *White Rice* When the hulls, bran layer, and germ are removed, the result is the familiar and ubiquitous white rice, sometimes called *polished* rice. It has a bland flavor.

• *Converted Rice* Another name for converted rice is *parboiled*. The term "Converted" is a trademark of Uncle Ben's. Long-grain rice is soaked in water or subjected to steam while it's still in the shell in order to gelatinize the grain to make it harder, as well as drive some of the vitamins into the center of the grain; then the rice is milled in the normal fashion. It has a smoother surface than regular rice, a slightly darker color when raw, and fewer broken grains. After cooking, converted rice is less sticky and the grains more separate than ordinary white rice. It takes almost twice as long to cook converted rice as ordinary rice.

Converted rice was invented before World War II in the Philippines to combat beriberi, since this process leaves vitamin B_1 in the grain.

• *Instant Rice* Instant rice is also sometimes called *precooked* rice. First it is cooked, then all the moisture is removed from it by flash freezing. To prepare instant rice, it only needs to be reconstituted in boiling water. It was developed for wartime use by General Foods and is now sold under several brand names, such as Minute Rice. Instant rice costs about four times as much as regular rice.

VARIETIES OF RICE

By various botanical estimates, there are anywhere from 4,000 to 7,000 varieties of rice in the world; twenty of them are grown in the United States. The better-known varieties break down roughly as follows:

Long Grain

The kernels of long-grain rice are four to five times as long as they are wide, and when cooked they are separate and fluffy. Long-grain rice is popular in the United States and it accounts for 71 percent of the rice consumed here. This type is best used for pilaf, paella, curries, and elegant dishes where dry, fluffy grains are important for the "look" of the dish.

The most important varieties of long-grain rice are Lebonnet, Bluebelle, Labelle, and Starbonnet. These are words sometimes seen on packages of long-grain rice.

• *Aromatic Rice* Included in the category of long-grain rice are aromatic rices, which includes *basmati* rice, a thin, long-grain rice grown in the foothills of the Himalayas in the north of India that has a nutty-milky perfumed flavor and a spongy texture *(basmati* means scented in the Hindi language). Imported basmati rice is available in Indian markets and can be quite expensive, especially if it is aged for a year or two, which is said to enhance the flavor.

Dean & DeLuca sells their own brand of brown basmati rice, which has the strongest, nuttiest flavor of all aromatic rices. Its mealy, husky texture is reminiscent of kasha.

Many new strains of American aromatic rices have come on the market in the last decade, all descended from a variety of rice that came from Indochina at the beginning of the century. Thus, they all taste somewhat similar.

One of these new American aromatic rices is *Texmati.* Grown in Texas, Texmati is a cross between basmati and American long-grain rice. It doesn't taste as strongly perfumed as Indian basmati rice, but it has more flavor than American white rice. Texmati comes in white and brown versions; the white Texmati tastes slightly nutty and the brown has a little more nutty flavor.

The Farms of Texas brand of Texmati rice (the kind most often seen in a blue and white box) is inferior to the Thomas Garraway brand, which seems to have a stronger flavor.

Another new strain of aromatic rice is *Wild Pecan Rice,* which is grown in New Iberia, Louisiana (near where Tabasco sauce is made), and is available in specialty-food stores. It contains neither wild rice nor pecans, but is a botanical hybrid, milled with about 80 percent of the bran layer left on the grains. It tastes nutty, and smells something like popcorn when cooked.

Wehani (sometimes spelled *Wehoni)* rice is yet another new American aromatic rice, a brown basmati-type rice grown in California. It tastes like a combination of brown, white, and wild rice, with a nutty flavor.

Ellis Stansel's Rice is another brand of American aromatic rice, with perhaps the plainest flavor of them all.

Popcorn Rice is yet another of this ilk; it tastes mild—only slightly aromatic—and not much like popcorn.

• *Wild Rice* Wild rice is a classic misnomer, since it is not really a rice at all, but the seed of a water grass that grows wild in the Great Lakes region of the United States and in the bordering provinces of Canada. It is sometimes called "the caviar of grains" because it is so delicious and so expensive. Ninety percent of the truly *wild* wild rice in this country is harvested by Chippewa Indians on their reservation in Minnesota. These days, however, 80 percent of the entire crop of wild rice grown in this country is cultivated, not really wild but grown on farms. In the last few years, several farms in California and some in Minnesota have begun to grow cultivated wild rice. While it is less expensive than the truly *wild* wild rice, it is not quite as tasty; it has a milder flavor.

Over 60 percent of the wild rice grown in this country is boxed with mixtures of long-grain white rice and is usually sold in supermarkets.

Wild rice shouldn't be used for any kind of ordinary rice recipe, but should be enjoyed for its unique nutty flavor and texture. Many people find that it has a fermented, earthy flavor that is quite strong. Perhaps like many other exquisite foods it is an acquired taste. To tame the flavor and the price, wild rice can be cooked and combined with cooked brown or white rice.

Medium Grain

This type of rice is about three times as long as it is wide, and tends to stick together a little more than long-grain rice. It accounts for 27 percent of the rice consumed in the United States and can be used for the same dishes as long-grain rice.

The most important varieties of medium-grain rice are Nato, Saturn, Nova, Vista, and Calrose. These are the words sometimes seen on packages of medium-grain rice.

Short Grain

Sometimes called *round* or *pearl* rice, this type of grain is almost as wide as it is long, and is the stickiest of all; unlike the other varieties of rice it becomes creamy when cooked. (The rule of thumb is that the shorter the grain, the stickier the rice.) The Japanese and natives of the Caribbean prefer this rice precisely *because* the grains stick together. Because short-grain rice accounts for only 2.5 percent of the rice market, it isn't very easy to find in American stores except in Asian or Puerto Rican neighborhoods. Most of it in this country goes to make puffed rice cereals. It's the best rice to use for *sushi,* or dishes that need binding and a creamy consistency, such as rice pudding.

Pearl and Nortai are the most common varieties of short-grain rice.

• *Glutinous Rice* Also called *sweet, sticky,* or *waxy* rice, glutinous rice is made up of little round grains that are plump and exceptionally sticky, yet still chewy, used to make sweet Oriental dishes as well as *congee,* the savory rice gruel eaten by the Chinese for breakfast. It can be found in Oriental markets and shouldn't be used in any recipes except those that call for it.

• *Arborio Rice* Arborio rice is one of many varieties of short-grain rice from Italy; it is the one most often imported into the United States. It can tolerate long cooking, absorb a great deal of liquid, and still retain the *al dente* ("toothy") quality prized by Italians for risotto. It is easily identified by a little bright white opaque dot on one side of the grain. Arborio rice contains a lot of starch, and so can become creamy rather than dry after a long simmer over low heat.

Italians categorize their rice according to size, and Arborio is in the largest category, called *superfino.* These days, you can find other *superfino* rice in the United States, notably Carnaroli, which Italians prefer for risotto over Arborio.

In the fall of 1995, a U.S.-grown arborio rice was introduced into the market.

HANDLING AND STORAGE

Uncooked white rice will keep indefinitely in a cool, dry place. Glutinous rice, on the other hand, becomes stale in just a few months and should be kept in the refrigerator. Aromatic rice also goes stale more quickly than white rice and will last only about 6 months unless it is kept in the refrigerator, where it will last a couple of months longer.

Uncooked brown rice is more prone to rancidity and should be kept on the shelf for only 6 months or so. As with many less refined foods, such as whole-wheat flour, refrigeration will extend the shelf life of brown rice for another couple of months or so, up to 8 or 9 months altogether.

Covered tightly, cooked brown or white rice can be refrigerated for up to 7 days, and frozen for up to 4 months. Any kind of rice is best reheated by steaming it over simmering water, which is also a good way to keep rice warm if you've made it ahead of time for dinner.

As a general rule, rice grown in America does not need to be picked over (to look for stones or hulls), nor should it be washed. Washing removes nutrients from rice and also removes surface starch, which prevents the grains from sticking together when cooked. Rice that is imported, on the other hand, should be inspected carefully for any suspicious objects as well as washed. To wash rice, place it in a bowl and cover the rice with cold water; swirl the water around with your hand and drain. Repeat this process until the water is clear.

HOW TO JUDGE RICE

Tasting Media

In order to assess the properties of different brands of rice, put the uncooked rice into a saucepan with the proper amount of water (see "How to Cook Rice," page 27) and bring to a boil; do not add salt. Stir the rice, cover the pan, turn the heat to its lowest setting and cook until tender. (See pages 28–9 for general guidelines for cooking times for rice varieties.) Take the pot off the heat and leave covered for 10 minutes.

Taste the rice plain, warm, and then at room temperature, so that the true flavor of the grains can be detected.

Color/Eye Appeal

The grains of the best rice are uniform in size, and true to the variety (long, medium, or short grain), with no broken grains. The color should be uniform and not splotchy. (On arborio rice, the white dots on the grains are characteristic of that variety and not splotches.) All raw long- and medium-grain white rice kernels should be translucent and free from chalkiness or discoloration of any kind, including pink spots. If raw rice is opaque, this indicates that it contains too much natural moisture. Short-grain rice should look chalky, and the chalkier it is the stickier it will be when cooked.

Taste/Aroma

The best rice exhibits what is called in the trade a "typical rice flavor," true to its variety. (See "Varieties of Rice," page 24, for details.) Grassy flavor is an example of a defect in the taste of brown rice. White rice should be bland, with no obvious faults.

Consistency

Long-grain rice should have separate, dry grains; medium-grain rice has stickier grains, but it should be pleasantly moist without being cloying. Short-grain rice is the stickiest of all. Many lesser-quality rices are rubbery, gummy, too chewy, or pasty.

Long-grain rice from California is made up partly of the *japonica* strain and will be a little softer than long-grain rice from the southern United States.

Aftertaste

Starchy, dry, bitter, or waxy aftertaste are defects in rice.

CONCLUSIONS AND SUGGESTIONS

While many people in Middle America buy either Carolina (also called Mahatma) or Uncle Ben's rice, scores of regional rice companies also exist all over the country. These rice companies sell fine, sometimes superior products and it is time for a change from the standard brands. Carolina is an acceptable rice, but no more. And Uncle Ben's is an odd rice—its grains are completely separate and not sticky, because it is parboiled. American taste has made these two the standard by which other rices are judged, even those that are not parboiled. But other white rices have more flavor and more texture. While I say this, I am very much aware that Uncle Ben's contains more vitamins than regular white rice, and because of my children I often use Uncle Ben's for that reason.

Different cultures value foods in their own way, ranging from barely-disguised boredom to unearthly reverence. Although some parts of the Western world appreciate rice and its preparation with what almost amounts to ritual, Americans still haven't gotten to the point where the extraordinary differences among types and quality of rice are a serious consideration in their diet.

I am not trying to proselytize like a native of Bali, where children's canine teeth, when they come of age, are filed to a point in order never to mash a grain of rice, because each and every grain is thought to contain a small particle of God. But I do hope that we will get to the point where a shopper will not indiscriminately pick up a box of rice in the supermarket, regardless of whether he or she is planning to cook risotto, make a rice torte, or cook rice for a gumbo.

Many of us don't have a big choice about the brand of standard, everyday white rice we use; only one or two regional brands are available in our local supermarkets, barring, of course, converted rice and instant rice, which are for sale everywhere. We do, however, have a choice about the *type* of rice we use. For many occasions, short-grain rice is perfectly appropriate and in fact much more flavorful than long-grain rice. Brown rice may add more interest to some dishes than white rice. For special occasions (because it costs more money), aromatic rice can provide an exotic addition to a meal. But some of the new brands of aromatic rice, the so-called gourmet rices, smack of the emperor's new clothes: the white Texmati and Ellis Stansel's Rice varieties are really quite bland; once dressed with butter and salt and/or sauce I don't believe they are worth the extra money spent on them. The other American aromatics, however, such as Wehani and Wild Pecan Rice, are quite delicious and interesting, and a welcome addition to my pantry.

HOW TO COOK RICE

Depending on the variety, rice expands to about three times its volume when cooked. No two batches of rice are alike, however, and so exacting recipes can be misleading. The age of a rice, for example, affects the way it absorbs water: freshly harvested rice absorbs less water and cooks more quickly than rice that was harvested months before. Cultural preferences vary widely: Indians age their best rice varieties for many years, but in Japan new rice is highly prized. The best way to cook rice is to follow a recipe, but then during cooking continually test for doneness rather than accepting a printed cooking time. Overcooked rice turns into mush, but it can be frozen and used for stuffings, in a meat loaf, or as part of a pancake batter.

Some cooks feel that all rice should be washed before cooking, but although washing might remove some surface starch and make the grains less sticky, it also tends to remove many nutrients from rice. My feeling is that unless it comes from a third-world country where processing is not very mechanized, rice does not need to be washed.

Some cooks also soak their rice before cooking. Although soaked rice cooks more quickly (the soaking prevents the grains from absorbing as much water), it is really not necessary. The pot used to cook rice should not be too small, otherwise the rice on top will compress the rice on the bottom and make it soggy and overcooked. The cooked rice should not fill more than half the pot.

Perhaps the easiest method to use for cooking rice (and the best method to use for low-quality, sticky rice) is to boil it in a large quantity of salted water, as you would cook pasta. Test for doneness, drain thoroughly, and, if necessary, dry the grains in a big frying pan over high heat.

The following chart gives specific information about quantities to cook for different purposes:

HOW MUCH UNCOOKED RICE TO GAUGE PER SERVING	
First course	*½ cup*
Salad	*3 tablespoons*
Side dish	*¼ cup*
Main accompaniment to a dish (such as curry or jambalaya)	*6 tablespoons*
Dessert (such as rice pudding)	*2 tablespoons*
As one of the dishes on a buffet	
For 25 people	*2 pounds*
For 50 people	*4 pounds*
For 100 people	*8 pounds*

Long-Grain White Rice

Perfect Rice

This recipe produces the kind of rice you get in a French restaurant. This is practically the only way I make it when I am preparing rice as a side dish; it's really a classic pilaf. It can be halved or doubled if necessary. (Makes 8 side-dish servings)

1/2 cup minced onion
3 tablespoons unsalted butter
2 cups long-grain white rice (not converted)
1 1/2 cups chicken broth
1 1/2 cups water
1 bay leaf
salt
freshly ground white pepper, or black pepper if that's all you have
2 tablespoons chopped fresh parsley (optional)

1. In a heavy-bottomed saucepan, sauté the chopped onion in the butter for about 5 minutes, until onion is wilted.

2. Add the raw rice and stir for about 2 minutes, until grains are translucent; this step helps to keep the rice grains separate after they're cooked.

3. Add chicken broth, water, bay leaf, salt, and pepper to taste. Give everything one good stir and bring to a boil on the top of the stove; immediately cover tightly and reduce heat to its lowest setting. Cook on top of the stove without uncovering for 15 minutes. All of the liquid should be absorbed and the grains should be tender. Take the pot off the heat and leave it covered for at least 10 minutes before serving; it should stay warm for about 45 minutes if you're not serving it right away. Be sure to remove the bay leaf. If you like, sprinkle the parsley over the rice when you serve it.

NOTES: If you prefer, after bringing rice to a boil in step 3, you can bake the rice in a preheated 400°F. oven for the same amount of time.

You can vary about one third of the liquid content by substituting, for either the water or the broth, orange juice, carrot juice, tomato juice, milk, or unsweetened coconut milk. Select the flavor of the liquid to enhance the other flavors in the meal.

Add variety and flavor with the addition of any of the following ingredients, which should be added at the beginning of the cooking time (amounts listed are appropriate for the proportions in the recipe above): a pinch of saffron; 1 teaspoon whole cumin seeds; 2 tablespoons chopped fresh (or 1 tablespoon dried) herbs, such as mint, chives, basil; 1 teaspoon grated fresh gingerroot; 1/3 cup raisins with 2 tablespoons chopped almonds and 1 teaspoon curry powder; 1/2 cup diced red sweet pepper, added along with the onion; 10 ounces frozen peas, defrosted (stir in after rice is cooked).

Nutty-tasting *Feathered Rice* can be made by first toasting the rice: spread the raw rice on a cookie sheet and place it in a 375°F. oven; stir the rice occasionally until it is light golden brown, about 15 minutes. Proceed with the basic recipe, using the toasted rice.

Medium-Grain White Rice

If you're using medium-grain rice for the Perfect Rice recipe above, or for any other purpose, it will take longer to cook than long-grain rice, approximately 4 or 5 minutes longer.

Short-Grain White Rice

Short-grain rice takes less water to cook than medium- and long-grain rices. The easiest method to cook plain short-grain white rice is to put it into a saucepan with slightly more water than rice (1 cup rice takes 1 1/4 cups water; 1 1/2 cups rice takes 2 cups water; 2 cups rice takes 2 3/4 cups water) and a bit of salt. Bring to a boil, stir, cover the pan, and turn heat to its lowest setting. Cook for 15 minutes, or until rice is tender. Take the pot off the heat and leave it covered for at least 10 minutes before serving.

Converted (Parboiled) Rice

Converted rice expands a little more than ordinary white rice when cooked, so you don't need quite as much raw rice per person. It also takes almost twice as long to cook; for example, in the Perfect Rice recipe, converted rice needs 25 minutes of cooking versus 15 minutes for ordinary white rice.

Brown Rice

Brown rice can be made in just the same way as white rice, keeping two things in mind: it takes about three times as long to cook and needs twice as much liquid as rice, rather than 1 1/2 times as for white rice. Therefore, to make the Perfect Rice recipe, add 2 cups chicken broth and 2 cups water, and cook it for 45 minutes.

Brown rice also expands a little more than ordinary white rice, so you don't need to measure as much raw rice per serving.

Italian Rice

A risotto is a tricky dish to make, especially if you didn't have an Italian grandmother who taught you at her own stove. Like most difficult cooking tasks, however, all it takes is practice. The following recipe is a basic one and can be made without the mushrooms, or with the addition of diced fresh vegetables added halfway through the cooking time.

Risotto with Dried Mushrooms

(Makes 4 generous first-course servings)

1/2 cup dried mushrooms, approximately
3 cups beef or chicken broth
2 cups water
1/2 cup minced onion
5 tablespoons unsalted butter
2 tablespoons olive oil
2 cups arborio rice
salt and freshly ground pepper
1/2 cup freshly grated Parmesan cheese, or to taste

1. Pour 3/4 cup extremely hot tap water over the mushrooms and soak for about 30 minutes while preparing the rest of the ingredients; strain the soaking liquid through a clean dish towel or cheesecloth and cut mushrooms into small pieces, reserving liquid and mushrooms for step 5.

2. Put the broth and water in a saucepan on the stove over moderate-low heat and have a ladle handy nearby.

3. In a heavy-bottomed saucepan, sauté the minced onion in 3 tablespoons of the butter and the olive oil for about 5 minutes, until onion is wilted. Add the raw rice and stir for about 2 minutes, until grains are translucent.

4. Adjust heat to moderate, add a ladleful of the simmering broth to the rice, and stir until liquid has been almost completely absorbed. Continue adding broth in these small quantities and stirring constantly, adjusting the heat so that the liquid is not absorbed too fast nor too slowly. Throughout this process, do not stop stirring for even a few seconds. (Marcella Hazan tells her students to ignore the telephone if it rings while making a risotto.)

5. After the risotto is half cooked, after about 10 minutes, add the mushrooms with their soaking water along with a ladleful of broth. Add salt and pepper to taste.

6. After about 20 minutes, taste a grain of rice. It should be tender, but still a little *al dente.* If still too hard, continue to add broth and stir until rice is cooked; it may take up to 10 minutes more. The final texture of a good risotto should be creamy but not too soupy. You may not need to use all of the broth you have prepared. Take risotto off heat and stir in remaining 2 tablespoons butter and the Parmesan. Serve immediately.

Basmati

Unlike American rice varieties, basmati rice should be washed thoroughly to remove the surface starch so that the cooked rice isn't sticky. It should also be soaked for 30 minutes before cooking in twice the amount of water as there is rice, further to prevent the grains from sticking together.

Julie Sahni, the renowned Indian chef, formerly of Nirvana Restaurant in Manhattan, and author of *Classic Indian Cooking* and *Classic Indian Vegetar-*

ian and Grain Cooking, recommends steaming basmati rice by the following method:

Put the drained soaking water into a large, heavy-bottomed pan with a tight-fitting lid and bring it to a boil. Add the soaked rice, and stir carefully with a fork, until the water comes to a second boil. Reduce heat to low and simmer, partially covered, until most of the water is absorbed and the surface of the rice is full of holes, about 10 to 15 minutes. Cover the pan tightly, reduce the heat to its lowest level and raise the pan about an inch away from the source of the heat (use a wok ring or Flame-Tamer) and let rice steam for 10 more minutes. Take the pan off the heat and let rice rest for 5 minutes without peeking. Remove the cover and fluff the rice gently with a fork, being careful not to break the grains.

Julie also explains that in India the smell of cooked basmati rice is a good way to see if one's servants are doing their work properly: the lazy way to cook basmati rice is over a very low temperature for a long time, but this method gives the rice a "barnyard" smell.

Wild Rice

Although wild rice is expensive, it is less so when you consider that it quadruples in volume when cooked, giving about 22 half-cup servings per pound. One cup of raw rice serves about 6 people. Although there are many methods for cooking wild rice (for years, I dutifully followed the traditional method of pouring successive pots of boiling water over the rice and soaking it), the following is pretty foolproof and bound to make wild-rice lovers out of those who have disdained it in the past:

Place the rice in a strainer and run cold water through it for a minute or two, moving the rice around with your hands to make sure all the grains are clean.

Put the rice into a heavy-bottomed saucepan, and add three times as much chicken or beef broth as rice (or water, if the rice is to be used for a sweet dish), plus some salt if you wish. In other words, 1 cup rice takes 3 cups liquid. Bring to a boil, then cover and reduce temperature to its lowest setting. Simmer the rice without removing the cover for 30 minutes. Test a grain of rice to see if it is cooked. Almost all of the grains should be split and puffed to show a white interior, and it should taste tender, not tough. If the rice isn't done, continue to cook and test every few minutes. Because each batch of rice is different, no exact cooking times can be given. When the rice is finished, take the saucepan off the heat and leave covered for at least 10 minutes, to soften the grains further.

Although the rice can certainly be drained and served at this point, I like to drain it completely and then, just before serving, sauté it in butter or olive oil with diced onions and maybe some chopped pecans.

If I've cooked the rice in water, I make some extra to eat as a delicious cereal the next morning, cold with heavy cream and maple syrup on top.

Raw wild rice can also be popped like popcorn, although not in an electric popcorn popper but in a saucepan on top of the stove.

RECIPES

Pearl Balls

This is a version of Chinese dim sum from Shanghai, from Eileen Yin-Fei Lo's book The Dim Sum Book. *The pearl balls are very pretty and would make a delightful first course, served on a small decorative plate with a little shredded fresh ginger and coriander leaves on the side. I've also served them as part of an Asian buffet. (Makes 20 pieces)*

1 cup raw glutinous rice
1 pound ground pork
4 fresh water chestnuts, peeled, washed, dried, and cut into 1/8-inch dice (optional)
2 scallions (green ends discarded), washed, dried, and finely sliced
1 1/2 teaspoons minced fresh ginger

1	**large egg, beaten**
$1^1/_2$	**tablespoons cornstarch mixed with 2 tablespoons cold water**
$1^1/_4$	**teaspoons salt**
$2^1/_2$	**teaspoons sugar**
1	**teaspoon sesame oil**
2	**teaspoons light soy sauce**
$1^1/_2$	**teaspoons white wine**
	pinch of white pepper
2	**tablespoons peanut oil**

1. Wash the rice and soak it in a bowl for 1 hour. Drain. Allow the rice to dry in the strainer for 2 hours.
2. Combine all the ingredients in a bowl except the rice. Mix in one direction with a wooden spoon or your hands until it becomes soft, thoroughly mixed, and all ingredients stick together.
3. Wet your hands and form 1-inch balls of the mixture; if the mixture sticks to your hands, wet them again and as often as necessary. Place all the balls on a baking sheet lined with wax paper. Refrigerate balls for 1 hour, if possible.
4. On a second sheet of wax paper, smooth the raw rice into a thin layer. Roll each pork ball through the rice so that it receives a single coating of kernels.
5. Line a Chinese bamboo or stainless steel steamer with green lettuce leaves. (If you don't have a Chinese steamer, you can use a collapsible stainless steel steamer in a pot with a small amount of water in the bottom and a tight-fitting lid.) Place pearl balls on lettuce and steam for 15 to 20 minutes, or until rice becomes translucent and pork cooks through. Serve immediately.

Rice Ice Cream

This requires an ice-cream maker, either electric or hand-cranked. (Makes 8 servings)

$^1/_2$	**cup raw short-grain rice**
$3^1/_2$	**cups milk**
1	**vanilla bean**
9	**tablespoons granulated sugar**
	pinch of salt
4	**egg yolks**
2	**cups heavy cream**
1	**tablespoon confectioners' sugar**

1. Put the raw rice in a heavy saucepan and add 3 cups milk, the vanilla bean, 3 tablespoons granulated sugar, and pinch of salt and bring to a boil. Cover and simmer over very low heat for 12 minutes. Remove from the heat and let rice cool completely.
2. Pour the contents of the pan into a sieve and allow rice to drain thoroughly, for about 30 minutes. Remove the vanilla bean.
3. In a small heavy saucepan, place the egg yolks and 6 tablespoons of granulated sugar and stir until a smooth paste is formed. Pour in remaining $^1/_2$ cup milk and set saucepan over low heat, stirring constantly, until custard thickens, but make sure it doesn't boil. Take off heat and transfer to a small bowl to cool custard to room temperature.
4. Mix the cooled and drained rice with the cooled custard. Add heavy cream and confectioner's sugar and mix well. Place this ice-cream mix into an ice-cream maker, and follow manufacturer's directions for freezing.

DAIRY PRODUCTS

BUTTER AND MARGARINE

The Hatter was the first to break the silence. "What day of the month is it?" he said, turning to Alice: he had taken his watch out of his pocket and was looking at it uneasily, shaking it every now and then, and holding it to his ear.

Alice considered a little, and then said, "The fourth."

"Two days wrong!" sighed the Hatter. "I told you butter wouldn't suit the works!" he added, looking angrily at the March Hare.

"It was the best *butter," the March Hare meekly replied.*

This little scene from *Alice in Wonderland* is being repeated in homes all over America, only the modern version deals with the fact that butter might not suit the works all the time, but if it's the *best* butter, it's worth the sacrifice.

Thirty-five years ago, Americans ate just about as much butter as margarine; each of us ate 9.4 pounds of margarine and 7.5 pounds of butter per year. Today Americans eat more than twice as much margarine as butter: annual per capita intake is 4.6 pounds of butter and 10.8 pounds of margarine. As these figures show, our overall consumption of table spreads hasn't changed, but we have made a big shift to margarine.

In 1900, the average American consumed 20 pounds of butter.

Most of the unsalted butter in the United States is sold in New York, partly because of the foreign population of the city (one third of New York City's inhabitants were born in foreign countries), who are used to unsalted butter from their homelands. Another reason is that unsalted butter has been traditionally sold on the East Coast, and as pioneers moved west they began to salt their butter to keep it fresh longer; as a result, Westerners developed a taste for salted butter, and Easterners for unsalted.

A DASH OF HISTORY

The ancient Greeks and Romans used butter as an external medicine for skin injuries and sore eyes. Since then, butter has been valued as a hair ointment, a poultice to erase wrinkles, and a means for buying a wife. The ancient Mongolians and Tibetans drank tea to which melted butter was added, a custom still practiced in northern China. For centuries, butter was one of the only ways known to preserve milk.

The word "butter" comes from the Greek—*bous,* which means cow, and *tyros,* which means cheese. The expression "to butter" meant to flatter as early as 1850, but didn't become "butter up" until the late 1930s.

Margarine was developed in 1869 by a French

chemist in response to the prize offered by Napoleon III for a substitute for butter; the first margarine was made of suet and milk, although nowadays it is made of vegetable oil. It was originally called *oleomargarine,* from the Latin *oleum,* which means oil, and the Greek *margaron,* which means pearl, because it had the pearl-like luster of a glyceride erroneously thought to be an ingredient. After World War II, it began to be called *margarine.*

Because of the well-founded fears of the dairy industry, many impediments were put in the way of the development of margarine in its early days in the United States. Its sale was restricted, and later a heavy tax was placed on it that was not lifted until 1950; it was also required to be labeled by its full imposing name, "oleomargarine," and restaurants had to serve it in triangles instead of the squares used for butter. Its natural color is white, reminding consumers of lard, and many states did not allow manufacturers of margarine to dye it yellow; a little packet of dye was included in every package to be mixed in at home. During the 1930s, margarine manufacturers began to make margarine from oils produced in the United States rather than the imported oils that had been used previously. As a result, American cottonseed and soybean farmers began to support the margarine industry, a crucial step to the acceptance of margarine in this country. Margarine has survived, probably partly because of the fact that it has often been cheaper to buy than butter, and now, as has been stated, it surpasses butter, two to one, in popularity in the United States.

HOW BUTTER AND MARGARINE ARE MADE

Most butter today is made by a continuous churning process, which transports pasteurized cream through an enormous machine and turns out butter at the other end.

Milk comes into the plant within 18 hours after the cows have been milked; it is hauled on trucks each carrying over 3,000 gallons and tested for milkfat content (called *butterfat* by the layman) and checked for flavor characteristics and bacteria count. After a short time in holding tanks, the milk is put into separators, where 61,000 pounds of milk an hour are divided into cream and skim milk. About 9 percent of the milk comes off as cream, with a 40 to 45 percent milkfat content, and it is this cream that is churned into butter. The remaining 91 percent of the milk—skim milk—is dried and made into nonfat dried-milk powder, which is sold separately.

The cream is then pasteurized at 180°F. for about 15 seconds, cooled to 40°F., and then sent to a giant continuous churning cylinder, which is made of either metal or wood. The machinery in the churn agitates the cream and this motion separates the milkfat from the buttermilk in a matter of minutes; then the butter is extruded out of the other end of the churn in a wide ribbon. The liquid that remains after the butter is pumped out of the churn is buttermilk, and it is also dehydrated into powder for use as an additive in food processing. Salt (if the butter is to be salted) and additional water are added in the form of a 14 percent saline solution. The butter is pressed into one-pound blocks (called *prints* in the industry) and quarter-pound sticks. All in all, it takes about 11 quarts of milk to make 1 pound of butter.

By government edict, all butter must have not less than 80 percent milkfat. A butter maker must walk a fine line, says an old-time expert in New York, "If he makes butter with 78 percent milkfat, he is arrested; if he makes it with 82 percent, he's fired because he's cost his boss too much money!"

The remaining 20 percent of butter is made up of 18 to 18½ percent water and 1 to 2 percent curd (milk solids), depending on how much salt is added to the butter. Salt is added to most American butter, in an average proportion of 2.15 percent; most of American unsalted butter is sold in New York. Sometimes an artificial or natural coloring, a synthetic carotene or annatto, yellow color extracted from a seed, are added to compensate for seasonal variations in the color of the milk. Unsalted butter, however, is never colored.

Margarine nowadays is always made from vegetable oil, generally soy or corn oil. First the seeds are pressed for the oil, which is purified, hydrogenated, and fortified with some of the nutrients present in butter, such as vitamins A and D. Then it is colored using the same artificial or natural colorings used for butter. Depending on the brand and type of margarine, emulsifiers, salt, and preservatives are also added. It is the hydrogenation of margarine that makes it solid at room temperature, more or less, depending on what type is being made (see "Varieties of Butter," below). Margarine is also required by the government to contain at least 80 percent fat.

GRADES OF BUTTER

U.S.D.A. grading of butter, symbolized by a shield on the side of a package, is voluntary, not compulsory. Government standards are based on flavor, body, color, and salt content. The numbers 93, 92, and 90 refer to the minimum number of points out of 100 that butter can receive when being rated for quality by government experts. The three grades available for consumers are:

U.S. Grade AA or 93 Score

In official language, this butter possesses "a fine and highly pleasing flavor." It is delicate and sweet, and has a smooth, creamy texture with good spreadability. The salt is completely dissolved in the butter and blended consistently throughout.

U.S. Grade A or 92 Score

This butter has a "pleasing and desirable butter flavor," but can have, to a slight degree, such flavors as aged, astringent, or acidic. It will taste slightly less fresh than AA butter, but, according to the American Dairy Association, "it will please even discriminating consumers." The texture is fairly smooth.

U.S. Grade B or 90 Score

U.S. Grade B butter is made from soured or "ripened" cream. Active lactic-acid cultures with flavor-producing bacteria are introduced to the cream (similar to culturing yogurt), resulting in a butter with more aromatic flavor.

In European countries this kind of cream is favored to make butter in order to create a tangy flavor. In addition, less salt (about 1 percent) is added to the European versions, while more salt (about 3 percent) is added to American. The reason "ripened" butter is downgraded here is that our American palates are accustomed to the blander taste of butter made from fresh cream, labeled "sweet cream" butter to distinguish it from ripened cream butter. Many Europeans feel American butter has no flavor because it is so much blander than what they get in their home countries.

VARIETIES OF BUTTER

Sweet Cream

Sweet cream butter is made from sweet (as opposed to cultured or ripened) cream. Salt is almost always added as a flavoring agent. Originally it was added as a preservative, and it will mask any off-flavors of a lower-quality butter.

Because the salt will keep it tasting fresh even if it is not, salted butter can be stored longer by the producer without detection by the consumer. Since consumers are paying high butter prices for the salt contained in butter, it makes sense to buy unsalted butter and add salt at home. Virtually all professional cooks buy unsalted butter.

Sweet

This is a term usually used for unsalted butter. The label of this kind of butter reads "unsalted sweet butter."

Cultured

This is a version of butter between sweet cream and ripened cream butter. Active lactic-acid cultures have been added directly to the butter, in a concentration of 1 to 3 percent, and a flavor reminiscent of ripened cream butter is produced.

Whipped

Whipped butter is a product that has been whipped to incorporate air to increase its volume and make it easier to spread. Because it contains 30 to 50 percent air, whipped butter should be weighed and not measured when it is used for baking.

European

Some butters from Europe, especially France and Denmark, are sold in gourmet shops in the United States. In many cases, they have a higher milkfat than ours, and so they are higher-quality butters. But often they are spoiled by the time we get them to our tables, as the shipping and holding times can be lengthy.

Light Butter

Water and/or skim milk are added to regular butter to cut the calories and fat. An example of this new type of butter is Land O Lakes Country Morning Blend Light. Some are quite salty and have nearly as much fat as regular butter, so read labels carefully.

VARIETIES OF MARGARINE

Stick

This type of margarine is semisolid at room temperature, although some brands are harder than others. It is softer and more spreadable than butter at room temperature and can be used as a substitute for butter in cooking and baking. Prominent national brand examples are Parkay and Blue Bonnet. Both brands are excellent, but Parkay is slightly superior because it lacks the greasiness of other margarines.

Soft or Tub

These are margarines that are perpetually soft because they have been made with a high proportion of polyunsaturated oil. Their fat content and volume are equal to stick margarines. Prominent brand examples are Parkay Soft and Soft Fleischmann's. Fleischmann's, despite a pronounced saltiness, has a good texture and no characteristic artificial margarine aftertaste, which makes it the superior soft brand.

Whipped

Like whipped butter, these are margarines that have been whipped to incorporate air and make them more spreadable. They do not melt as evenly as regular margarines, so they should not be used for cooking. A brand example is Kraft Miracle.

Liquid

This margarine, of which Squeeze Parkay is the main example, comes in plastic bottles and is liquid at room temperature in order to make it easier to cook with. It is exceptionally salty and greasy; it tastes like the artificial butter used on popcorn at the movies.

High-Polyunsaturate

These come in all forms—stick, tub, and liquid. Some contain more water and less fat than regular margarine. Prominent brand examples are Promise and Fleischmann's Light. Promise has a cloying and very salty taste, while Fleischmann's Light, although a bit too salty, is a better brand because it tastes cleaner and fresher.

Diet

Like the high-polyunsaturates, these margarines substitute water for some of the fat in regular margarine; their fat content is about 40 percent, or half of regular margarine. They should not be used in cooking or baking. Brand examples are Diet Parkay, Diet Mazola, Weight Watchers, and Country Crock. None of them is very good, but the best of the lot is Diet Mazola.

Sprinkles

Not really a margarine, shakeable butter substitutes are made mostly of maltodextrin, which comes from corn. Brand examples are Butter Buds, Molly McButter and Best O'Butter. These products are very high in sodium and don't taste much like butter, but they are low in fat.

BUTTER/MARGARINE COMBOS

Some products are combinations of butter and margarine, usually 40 percent butter and 60 percent margarine. They are usually better-tasting than margarine, but not up to snuff if you have butter in mind.

HOW TO JUDGE BUTTER

Tasting Media

The temperature of the butter when it is being tested should be between 40° and 50°F., and the temperature of the room in which the tasting is conducted should be about 70°F. and not lower than 60°F. Take butter samples with plastic spoons; the warmth of the tasters' mouths melts the butter and frees its volatile aromas so that its taste and smell can be perceived.

Color/Eye Appeal

The best butter is even and uniformly colored throughout. It is considered defective if it is *wavy* or *mottled,* which results from an uneven distribution of salt and moisture; *speckled,* which comes from small particles of coagulated casein or coloring; *streaked,* which comes from faulty churning or churns that have not been cleaned.

In the winter, cattle eat dry feed, which results in butter that is lower in carotene, the coloring agent of butter; therefore, winter butter is paler than summer butter and needs to be colored by the butter manufacturer.

Taste/Aroma

The best butter has a pronounced smell that is pleasant. Lower-quality butter has no smell at all.

Butter is no better and no worse than the cream from which it was made. The very best butter is sweet and delicate and tastes like the high-quality cream used, whether it was sweet cream or ripened cream.

Some of the negative flavor characteristics for butter include *aged,* from the butter being stored for long periods; *barny,* which smells like a barn and results from contamination during milking; *bitter; cooked,* a scalded milk taste from high-temperature during pasteurization; *flat; metallic,* from keeping milk in tin containers on the farm; *musty,* from cream held in a dank cellar; *sharp salt,* from too much salt added to the butter; *weed, wild onion,* or *garlic,* from the feed that cows eat; *woody,* from new wooden churns not properly treated.

Consistency

Butter is not made up of only one kind of milkfat (sometimes called *butterfat),* but several different kinds of fat, each with its own consistency. Each of these fats has a different melting point: some (called *hard fats)* remain solid at warm temperatures, even at 100°F. and higher; but some (called *soft fats)* remain liquid at temperatures far below the freezing point, 32°F. So no matter whether it's warm or cold, or even frozen, butter is always a mixture of solid and liquid fats.

If you leave several sticks of butter out at room temperature, for instance, some will be very soft and some will remain rather hard. The reason is that each stick of butter is made up of different proportions of hard and soft fats; these proportions vary among brands and even from batch to batch.

Another factor that affects the consistency of butter is the season in which it is made. In the summer, because of the type of feed given to the cows, butter contains more liquid fat and tends to be softer, while in the winter, butter contains more solid fat and tends to be harder.

A good butter maker can gauge the makeup of

a batch of cream (he can determine the kinds of fat it contains) and churn it properly to make a butter of the desired consistency. In other words, if a certain batch of cream has a great deal of liquid fat, the butter maker can still make butter from it with a good firm consistency by varying the temperatures at which the cream is processed, thus compensating for the unbalanced makeup of the cream.

The best butter has a consistency that is uniformly firm with a waxy body and good spreadability. It cuts cleanly when sliced.

Some of the negative characteristics in the consistency of butter are *crumbly,* from a large amount of fat crystals associated with higher-melting-point fats; *gritty,* from too much salt added to the butter; *gummy,* from a high percentage of high-melting-point fats; *leaky,* sweating resulting from insufficient incorporation of the water or an uneven salt distribution; *sticky,* from the cattle eating dry feeds.

Aftertaste

Butter should not have a greasy aftertaste.

WORRIES ABOUT MARGARINE

A few years ago, a couple of studies were published that found alarming links between trans-fatty acids—one of the major compounds in margarine—and a rise in cholesterol. Specifically, a diet high in trans-fatty acids raised LDL cholesterol, the so-called "bad" cholesterol, and lowered HDL cholesterol, the "good" cholesterol.

Margarine manufacturers feel that the deductions are premature, and caution that further work needs to be done in order to verify the conclusions.

No matter what the scientific community concludes, the bottom line for consumers will remain the same: For health purposes, even if margarine raises cholesterol, butter is still worse because of its high saturated fat. The softer the margarine, by the way, the lower the content of trans-fatty acids.

CONCLUSIONS AND SUGGESTIONS

I have conducted several butter tastings over the years, and the best was always Breakstone's, a brand which is available in the East. The only national brand of butter is Land O Lakes, a company representing a cooperative of butter producers; this brand is consistently good throughout the nation.

Depending on the type of margarine, butter and margarine cost about the same, so there is usually no financial incentive to using margarine.

When considering health concerns, I prefer to use smaller amounts of (unsalted) butter rather than larger amounts of margarine, for the sake of quality. Even the best margarine—which I believe is Mazola Premium—doesn't measure up to the taste of butter.

HANDLING AND STORAGE

Some people are intolerant of the taste of butter that has been left out at room temperature for a day or more, and some people like it because they find the taste of chilled American butter quite bland. The "gamy" taste, resulting from exposure to the air, can be pleasant in butter, but too much oxidation turns butter rancid.

Butter or margarine can go bad due to exposure to air, light, or warm temperatures, or by being stored next to strong-smelling foods, such as onions, cabbage, or apples. When either butter or margarine has gone rancid, each will taste strongly acidic and gamy.

If butter and margarine are stored in a covered dish in the refrigerator (not in the butter compartment on the door), they will last for several weeks without becoming rancid. The butter compartment in the refrigerator should not be used for butter or margarine unless you are going to use it within 3 or 4 days, since it is set at a higher temperature than the rest of the refrigerator to ensure spreadability, and thus hastens rancidity.

Salted butter and margarine are likely to go

bad more quickly than unsalted, because they may have been stored by the distributor or the producer for a longer period of time. The reason is that salt in butter acts as a preservative and masks rancidity, and manufacturers and distributors like to take advantage of the ability to store salted butter longer than unsalted. The American Dairy Association recommends keeping unsalted butter in the refrigerator for only 1 or 2 weeks.

If frozen in its original package, butter and margarine will last for 1 month without going rancid. If wrapped with an outerwrap of aluminum foil so that it is airtight, either will keep in the freezer for 6 to 9 months.

The larger the piece of butter, the longer it takes for it to go rancid, so if you are planning to freeze or hold butter for a long time, buy it in 1-pound blocks.

COOKING WITH BUTTER

By law, all butter is made up of a minimum of 80 percent fat, 18 to 18½ percent water, and 1 to 2 percent milk solids; therefore, all butter has roughly the same water content. Many professional bakers, however, claim that the water content in different butters varies greatly and this variation affects their baked goods. This theory is, in fact, incorrect. The texture of butter varies, not due to water content, but due to changes in the consistency of the fat from season to season. In the winter, because the fat in butter is mostly hard, it "sweats" more than in the summer. For instance, if a stick of winter butter is cut in half, little beads of water begin to form on the cut edge. In the summer, on the other hand, the fat in butter is slightly softer.

Using cold rather than warm butter in baking recipes will counteract these seasonal variations in its consistency. Keep butter chilled right up to the moment when adding it to the other ingredients, especially in the summer when butter is likely to be soft. If the butter is too soft when added to the other ingredients in a baking recipe, it's likely to make a batter or dough soft and runny and as a result it won't bake properly.

In other words (as explained under the heading "Consistency" above), a number of fats combine to make butter, each fat with its own melting point. The majority of the fats melt between 60° and 70°F. It's important to make sure that the butter used for baking is not warmer than 70°F. If the fat has become too soft (perhaps because it has been left out in a warm kitchen), the result will be an inferior baked product, such as greasy flat cookies, for instance.

Therefore, in spite of many recipe directions, it is not a good idea to let butter sit out at room temperature for more than about 10 minutes before adding it to a dough or batter. Instead, before creaming butter, cut it into small pieces so it's easier to work with. Or, if your kitchen is not too warm (in the winter, for example), let the butter sit out for 10 minutes or so before adding it to a recipe. Also, if you're making a large number of

HOW TO SUBSTITUTE BUTTER FOR CREAM

If you are in the middle of a baking spree and find yourself at home with no cream in the house, you can make the following substitutions in bread, pastry, and cake recipes:

IF THE RECIPE CALLS FOR	YOU CAN SUBSTITUTE
1 cup heavy cream	*⅔ cup skim milk and ⅓ cup unsalted butter*
1 cup light cream	*⅘ cup skim milk and ⅓ cup unsalted butter*
1 cup half-and-half	*1 cup minus 2 tablespoons skim milk and 2 tablespoons unsalted butter*

cookies, keep the dough in the refrigerator while each batch is in the oven.

An easy way to soften frozen butter is to fill a bowl with boiling water, pour out the water and invert the bowl over the butter; the butter will be thawed in minutes.

To coat cookie or baking sheets easily, save the wrappers from sticks or blocks of butter to wipe across the pans. Keep the wrappers in the refrigerator until you need them.

To cut butter into neat pats, use one of two methods: dip the knife into hot water and wipe it dry each time you cut a pat, or wrap the knife in wax paper (or the wrapper from the stick) and cut the pats.

Clarifying Butter

Clarified butter is butter that has been melted to separate the fat from the water and milk solids. The reason for clarifying butter is to remove the milk solids, which burn readily when fried or sautéed and give the butter and the food being cooked a bitter, burned taste. When all of the milk solids are removed, a pure fat that is a clear liquid when melted results, which can be heated to a very high temperature for frying. Many classical French recipes call for clarified butter, which is ideal for frying dishes like breaded veal cutlets or other foods in which a buttery flavor is desired.

I make clarified butter in a very simple way: I put a pound or half a pound of butter in a glass measuring cup and put the cup over the pilot light on the stove. The butter melts very slowly

it takes a couple of hours. After skimming the foam off the top of the butter, I put the measuring cup in the refrigerator. After a few hours the water and the milk solids remain liquid in the bottom of the cup, while the fat has solidified; I pick up the solid fat with a sturdy fork and pour off the water and milk solids. Then, whenever I need some clarified butter I simply dig out a piece with a spoon.

Clarified butter can be kept in the refrigerator for several weeks or in the freezer for several months, as long as it is kept covered in an airtight container.

Measuring Butter

To measure butter, use the water displacement method: Fill a glass measuring cup halfway with water (say, to the one-cup mark in a 2-cup measuring cup) and add pieces of butter until the water has elevated to the level of the measurement you need. For example, if you need 3/4 cup butter, fill the measuring cup with 1 cup water, and add butter until the water measures 1 3/4 cups. Then simply pour off the water.

For even measurements, it's easy to remember that 1 cup of butter equals 2 sticks, 1/2 cup equals 1 stick, and 1/4 cup equals 1/2 stick.

RECIPES

Scandinavian Egg Butter

(Makes about 1 cup)

- **1/2 cup (1 stick) unsalted butter**
- **1/2 teaspoon salt**
- **freshly ground pepper**
- **3 hard-cooked eggs, peeled**

Whip the butter until fluffy. Add salt and pepper to taste. Separately mash eggs with a fork and fold together with butter. Serve on warm toast.

Greek Butter Cookies

This is my version of Kourambiedes, a buttery Greek cookie. (Makes about 4 1/2 dozen cookies)

- **1 pound (4 sticks) unsalted butter**
- **3/4 cup sifted confectioners' sugar**
- **1 egg yolk**
- **1 tablespoon Ouzo (Greek licorice-flavored liquor, available in most well-stocked liquor stores)**
- **1 teaspoon pure vanilla extract**
- **4 1/4 cups sifted all-purpose flour**
- **1 teaspoon baking powder**

1/4 cup finely chopped blanched almonds
confectioners' sugar for sprinkling on finished cookies
candied violets

1. Beat together butter and 3/4 cup confectioners' sugar until light and fluffy. Add egg yolk, Ouzo, and vanilla.

2. Sift together flour and baking powder and add to butter-sugar mixture; mix just until blended. Stir in almonds. Chill dough for at least 1 hour.

3. Using your hands, shape dough into 1 1/2-inch balls, using about 1 tablespoon of dough for each ball. Place balls about 2 inches apart on an ungreased cookie sheet.

4. Bake cookies at 350°F. for 15 minutes, or until cookies are a very light brown. Remove from the oven and immediately sprinkle with confectioners' sugar, through a sieve or a sugar sifter. Press 1 candied violet onto the top of each cookie. Remove cookies to wire racks to cool.

ICE CREAM

ce cream is the most popular food in America. *The School Food Service Journal* reports that nine out of ten children prefer ice cream to all other foods, and according to the International Association of Ice Cream Manufacturers, 56 percent of adults choose ice cream as their favorite dessert.

Most ice cream is eaten between 9 and 11 P.M. (perhaps in front of the TV?) and more is downed on Sunday than on any other day of the week. (Food sociologists with lots of time on their hands can possibly make something out of the curious fact that less ice cream is eaten on Tuesday than on other days.) Eighty-four percent of Americans buy ice cream at least once a month, and 10 percent can't let a day go by without eating at least a dip or two.

New Englanders eat an average of about 24 quarts of ice cream per year, the most of any region, while the nation as a whole averages about 13 quarts per capita, down from 15 quarts 10 years ago. Black people eat more than white people; well-educated people eat more than those who are not. Those under the age of 17 and—surprise!—over the age of 45 are the two largest ice-cream consumer groups.

In buying all this ice cream, Americans spend about $10 billion per year (including frozen desserts, as well), while ice-cream manufacturers use nearly 10 percent of our nation's milk supply.

California produces more ice cream than any other state in the United States, followed by Pennsylvania, Ohio, Texas, and New York. Americans eat far more ice cream than citizens of any other country, the next largest consumers being Australians, followed by Canadians, New Zealanders, and Swedes.

A DASH OF HISTORY

It is impossible to pinpoint the origin of ice cream because it was probably "invented" in many places around the world at about the same time.

The Chinese, for example, have been making water ices, the precursor to ice cream, since before history was recorded. Sicilians, who are famous for their delicious ice cream even today, learned the skill from the Saracens, who migrated from the Eastern Mediterranean to Sicily in the ninth century, and Sicilians figure prominently in the history of ice cream from that time forward. The Arabs also have a very long history of making water ices.

In the thirteenth century Marco Polo brought some recipes for Chinese ices back to Italy, and some of his recipes included milk, which makes them similar to today's sherbet.

The first mention of ice cream appeared in print in England in the fifteenth century, when it was written that King Henry V served *crême frez* at his coronation banquet.

For centuries Italians have carried recipes for their ice cream around the world. Catherine de Médici brought the knowledge and skill of making it with her when she married the future king of France in the sixteenth century. A different flavor of ice cream was served on each of the 34 days of their marriage festivities.

"Iced creams" were first served to the public (as opposed to the privileged classes) sometime after 1686 in Paris in the Café Procope, which was owned by a Sicilian who had changed his name from Procopio. Soon after that, many other Parisian cafés began to serve ice creams and water ices. Most of these establishments were also owned by Italians. By the end of the eighteenth century most fashionable French dinners were ended with a *bombe glacée,* an elaborate terraced structure made of ice cream.

It was not long before the recipe for ice cream found its way to the New World. In 1744, a guest who had attended a dinner at the home of Governor Bladen of Maryland wrote about a "curious" dessert: "some fine ice cream which, with strawberries and milk, eat most deliciously." George Washington loved ice cream; he spent $200 for it in New York over the summer of 1790. Dolley Madison, whose name has unfortunately become attached to a mediocre brand of ice cream, glamorized this dessert when she served a huge pink ice-cream creation as the centerpiece of her husband's second inaugural banquet in 1813.

In America, ice-cream manufacturing on a large scale really got under way in 1851, when a Baltimore milk dealer began to make ice cream to use up his surplus cream. Five years earlier, an ice-cream freezer had been invented, which mechanized the manufacturing process and set the stage for mass production.

Ice cream became extremely popular in the late nineteenth century in America, and ice-cream parlors were popular gathering places. In this century, ice cream became "America's typical food," according to the industry's prose. Although ice cream was dispensed from wagons, drugstores, and lunch counters, it was the soda fountain where most of it was eaten. These fountains, sometimes decorated quite elaborately, symbolized America's youth at its best, through the 1940s.

With the steady decline of the soda fountain as an institution, today more and more ice cream is sold in retail packages. Eighty percent of all ice cream is now sold in supermarkets, grocery stores, and convenience stores.

Two significant changes have occurred in the ice-cream industry in the last few decades: because of long-distance distribution and longer periods of storage, ice cream is now made with increasing amounts of stabilizers, and to keep the supermarket ice-cream prices low, *overrun* (air pumped into ice cream during manufacture) has been increased. A whole generation grew up in the fifties and sixties without tasting high-butterfat, homemade-type ice cream. It is only in the last several years that the "super premium" brands of the eighties have brought that flavor back to America.

HOW ICE CREAM IS MADE

Ice cream is divided by its manufacturers into four subgroups that sound like designations for gasoline, but that have to do only with the subjective quality of the product. These designations are not mandatory or government-regulated; an ice-cream manufacturer can claim that his ice cream falls into any category he likes. Objective criteria for these categories do exist, however, and are outlined below. It is the first two of the following categories that are addressed in this chapter.

Ice Cream Grades

• *Super Premium* Super premium ice cream, which represents 11 percent of the market, is a recent development that is a boon for connoisseurs because it is so delicious. It is made with all-natural ingredients; it has a high fat content for richness, between 16 and 18 percent milkfat (also known as *butterfat)* content; it contains relatively little air (up to 80 percent overrun), which makes it almost as dense as hand-packed ice creams, and it generally contains no additives or preservatives. Super premium ice cream is usually sold in round pint-size containers and costs about $3 or more per pint, while lower-quality ice creams are usually available in rectangular boxes and cost much less. Häagen-Dazs is an example of super premium ice cream.

Commercially available super premium ice creams come very close to the flavor and texture of homemade; they are just as dense and the flavors are natural as opposed to artificial, as well as accurate, and pronounced.

Although consumption of desserts, including most types of ice cream, has fallen off a bit in recent years, the super premium ice-cream market has been increasing dramatically: by 17 percent in 1980, 26 percent in 1981, 70 percent in 1982, 15 percent in 1983, and 15 percent in 1984. Many new brands of super premium ice cream are being introduced to compete with the success of Häagen-Dazs, which claims to have 80 percent of the super premium market.

• *Premium* Premium ice cream represents 24 percent of the entire ice-cream market; examples of this category are Sealtest and Breyers. Premium ice cream contains about 14 percent milkfat (also known as *butterfat)* and up to 85 percent overrun. It is always made with natural flavorings and costs around $4 or more per half gallon.

• *Regular* Regular ice cream, which makes up the largest chunk of the ice-cream market with a 52 percent share, is largely represented by store brands, such as A & P and Kroger's. It contains at least 12 percent milkfat (also known as *butterfat)* and up to 100 percent overrun, the maximum amount allowed by law, which makes for a very light and airy ice cream. Regular ice cream costs about $4 per gallon.

• *Economy* Economy ice cream, which has 13 percent of the total ice-cream market, is not necessarily made with the highest quality in mind; generic brands fall into this category. Manufacturers aim for value, at a very low price point. Economy ice creams are made with artificial flavorings and stabilizers, and a minimum amount of added fruit and nuts.

Ingredients

The manufacture of high-quality ice cream in a commercial plant approximates homemade methods, but on a much larger scale.

The main component of ice cream, whether homemade or commercial, is milk and/or cream. When ice cream is made commercially, the milk (or cream) is broken down into its three main parts: *milkfat, nonfat milk solids,* and *water.* These ingredients are then added separately to the "mix" (an industry term for a batch of ice cream before it is frozen) so that proportions can be controlled and seasonal variations minimized. The mix also contains *sweeteners, flavorings, additives, egg yolks,* and so on, depending on the manufacturer.

The following are the main ingredients in a finished vanilla ice cream. (I've used vanilla as the example because it accounts for 35.1 percent of all sales, or about three times as much as any other flavor.)

• *Milkfat* Milkfat (called *butterfat* by the layman) is the fatty component of milk, and it is also the "good stuff" in ice cream, the ingredient that makes it creamy and rich-tasting. Milkfat gives ice cream a smooth texture and helps it to resist melting.

The best ice cream gets its milkfat content from fresh cream. Other sources are frozen cream, dried cream, butter (which is reconstituted into cream with skim milk), buttermilk, plastic cream (concentrated milkfat with an 80 percent fat content, therefore solid or "plastic"), and a blend of condensed milk and cream.

Since milkfat is expensive and is one of the most important ingredients in ice cream, the government, in order to keep manufacturers honest, requires that ice cream must have a minimum of 10 percent milkfat. The amount of milkfat above 10 percent in a brand of ice cream varies from flavor to flavor; in other words, the milkfat of Brand X's vanilla ice cream may be lower than Brand X's chocolate ice cream because the fat content of the added chocolate amplifies the fat content of the ice cream. Super premium ice creams have well above the 10 percent minimum, generally in the range of 15 to 18 percent.

Although increasing amounts of milkfat are being added to super premium ice creams in order to make them richer (Godiva's 20 percent is the highest I've seen), this can become too much of a good thing. If an ice cream contains over a certain amount of milkfat, around 18 percent, it tastes heavy, pasty, and slick, called *buttery* by the industry. Eating some of the high milkfat ice creams can taste like licking a stick of flavored butter!

• *Nonfat Milk Solids* Nonfat milk solids are similar to powdered milk products sometimes "forced" on small children. When water and milkfat are removed from milk or cream the nonfat milk solids, a powdered substance, is what remains. The milk from which the powder is extracted can be cream, whole milk, skim milk, condensed milk, or any of the forms of cream listed under "Milkfat" above. The best ice cream is made with nonfat milk solids that have been taken from cream and whole milk. Look for the words "cream" and "milk" on a label.

Nonfat milk solids give a dairy flavor to ice cream, and assure a smooth and compact texture. Ice cream is required to have at least 20 percent nonfat milk solids. The more solids in an ice-cream mixture, the less cold it will be because it will contain less water that will have turned into ice crystals. At the same time, if too many solids are added, the ice cream will seem heavy and soggy.

• *Water* The water that is used in ice cream is turned into ice during the freezing process, which helps to stabilize the mix. The higher the water content of ice cream, the "colder" it will be.

• *Sweeteners* Ice cream would not be the popular "sweet" it has always been without the sugar that goes into it. However, it must contain a particularly high percentage of sweetener, about 15 percent, because it is eaten at such a low temperature. Foods taste best when they are in a range between 60° and 100°F. Ice cream, obviously, is much colder than that, usually between 0° and 20°F., and so it numbs the taste buds, making them less sensitive. Manufacturers put twice as much sugar in ice cream as they would if they were making a food meant to be served at room temperature, so that it will be perceived as sweet.

The most commonly used sweetener is sucrose, or plain white table sugar, made from beets or cane. In making ice cream, sucrose is mixed with water and used in a liquid form. Corn syrup (dextrose), maple sugar, honey, fructose, and invert sugar (a mixture of half fructose and half glucose) at times are also used in addition to or instead of sucrose.

Although the best ice cream is made with sucrose, many brands, especially those in the regular and economy categories, are made with a mixture of sucrose and corn syrup, a measure taken by some manufacturers to save money. Corn syrup gives body to ice cream and, perhaps most important for the manufacturer, prolongs shelf life. Corn syrup is cheaper than sucrose, but can give an unpleasant and easily identifiable "syrupy" flavor to ice cream.

Another reason some kinds of sugar are used is to lower the freezing point of ice cream; without sugar the ice cream would not freeze at all. Corn syrup lowers the freezing point more than other sugars. That is why brands of ice cream made with corn syrup are softer, less solidly frozen, than those with sucrose.

• *Egg yolks* Egg yolks mellow the taste of ice cream and add richness, without burdening it with the overly intensive buttery flavor that results from using too much milkfat. In the words of noted ice-cream consultant Dr. Wendell Arbuckle, egg yolks "add life" to an ice cream, as well as help to make it smooth by acting as a natural emulsifier. Egg yolks also improve the whipping ability of an ice-cream mixture so that more air can be incorporated. Fresh eggs make the best ice cream, but powdered eggs are also used, which sometimes results in a characteristic stale and tallowy flavor in the end product.

By legal definition, a product labeled "ice cream" can contain no more than 1.4 percent egg yolk. If it contains more, the product must be labeled "frozen custard," "French ice cream," or "French custard ice cream."

Although Easterners generally like their ice cream with more egg in it than the rest of the country, Philadelphia ice cream, made without eggs, has been famous since before the United States became a nation. The traditional Philadelphia-style ice cream is an assembly of basics: cream, sugar, and flavoring.

• *Salt* Some manufacturers add up to 1 percent salt to their ice cream to round out the flavor, to add bulk, and to stabilize the mix.

Additives

Although super premium and premium ice creams have very few additives, some of the following stabilizers and emulsifiers are found:

• *Stabilizers* help prevent ice crystals from forming by coating the particles of milkfat, as well as prevent the ice cream from melting too fast. According to government regulations, an ice cream can contain a maximum of 0.5 percent stabilizers. These also include alginates, cellulose gum, carrageenin, modified geltin and gelatin, guar gum, carob gum, locust bean gum, and pectin.

• *Emulsifiers* help to make ice cream smooth, to incorporate air. (Egg yolks also act as natural emulsifiers.) Only 0.2 percent emulsifiers, not including egg yolks, are allowed. These include mono- and di-glycerides, lecithin, and polysorbate 80.

Ice-Cream Flavorings

The most popular ice creams in order of preference are vanilla, chocolate, nutmeats, chocolate chip, and strawberry. In the super premium brands, vanilla sells more than in the lower-quality types of ice cream.

Depending on how they are flavored, the industry breaks down its products into three categories:

• ALL TRUE (NATURAL) FLAVORS
• A COMBINATION: NATURAL FLAVORS FORTIFIED WITH NATURAL OR SYNTHETIC SUBSTANCES
(to save money)
• ALL SYNTHETIC FLAVORS
(to save even more money)

The label of a container of ice cream gives clues to the natural and synthetic ingredients contained within. If it is labeled "vanilla ice cream," it is flavored naturally; "vanilla flavored ice cream" is flavored with more natural than artificial ingredients; if it is called "artificially flavored vanilla ice cream," it has more artificial than natural ingredients.

• *Vanilla* Not enough real vanilla is produced in the world to supply all the vanilla ice cream made in America; therefore, much vanilla ice cream is flavored with artificial vanilla, called vanillin.

The extract made from natural vanilla owes its flavor largely to vanillin, which is one of the components of the natural flavor. Yet when vanillin is used alone, whether obtained from natural or synthetic sources, it does not duplicate a true complex vanilla flavor in an ice cream.

Since manufacturers of super premium ice cream aim toward pronounced flavors by using all natural ingredients, they attempt to get obvious vanilla flavor without using synthetic vanillin, so often they employ a natural way to heighten the flavor of ice cream by creating a caramel taste through longer pasteurization. This is known as a "cooked" flavor, which tastes something like caramel and has traditionally been deemed undesirable by manufacturers and consumers alike. It seems, however, that times and tastes are changing and now this caramel flavor, at least in the new breed of ice creams, is accepted by consumers.

• *Chocolate* Chocolate ice cream is flavored either with cocoa powder or chocolate liquor (see "Chocolate," page 191) or a combination of both. Cocoa powder, although it is cheaper than chocolate liquor, leaves a burning, acidic aftertaste in ice cream.

Chocolate liquor (which has nothing to do with alcohol but is in its most raw state a combination of cocoa butter and cocoa solids) is first dissolved in a sugar solution to make it liquid and then added to the ice-cream mix before pasteurization and homogenization. If cocoa powder is used, it is added to the ice-cream mix in the pasteurizing vat. Cheaper ice creams make just one mix and add various flavorings just before freezing; high-quality ice-cream companies make both a chocolate mix and a "white" mix in order to vary the flavoring to suit the various flavors.

• *Fruit and Nut* Fruit ice creams, such as strawberry, are best made with fresh or fresh-frozen fruit. The syrup from the fruit is also added to the mix, just before freezing, while the whole pieces of fruit and/or nuts are added after the freezing process and just before the final hardening.

Manufacturing

After the mix is made to the manufacturer's specifications, it is pasteurized to destroy bacteria and to dissolve the ingredients. The pasteurization is accomplished by one of two methods. The first, *short timing,* used by most major companies, requires that the mix be heated to 175°F. for 25 seconds; the second method, *vat pasteurizing,* requires that the mix be heated to about 155°F. for 30 minutes.

The higher temperature method is often employed by manufacturers who are not using the highest-quality ingredients. Ice cream made from the best raw ingredients benefits from the lower temperature pasteurization because the natural flavors of the products are better preserved. This is true of pasteurization of all dairy products, by the way. Most heavy whipping cream on the market today is *ultra-pasteurized* rather than simply pasteurized. Ultra-pasteurization is similar to short-timing pasteurization for an ice-cream mix; both methods result in a "cooked" flavor, which can be compared to the flavor of milk that has been boiled and cooled.

After the mix is pasteurized, it is *homogenized.* About 2,000 pounds of pressure are applied to force the mix through a screen with very tiny holes, to break up milkfat globules into particles ten times smaller to make the ice cream smooth. During this process, the proteins from the milk solids form a film around the milkfat globules. The mixture is then cooled to about 40°F., where it is held for about 4 hours.

Next, the mix is partially frozen to a semisoft stage. Blades, giant copies of the small dashers of a home ice-cream machine, whip air into the ice cream while it is being frozen. The faster the ice cream is frozen, the smoother it will be because the ice crystals that are formed quickly are smaller than those that are formed slowly. In the *continuous freezer* method, which takes only a few seconds, the ice-cream mix is processed in a steady flow through the machinery. In the *batch freezer* method, which takes about 10 minutes, single quantities of mix are frozen one by one.

The air that is incorporated into ice cream during freezing is called *overrun,* a popular buzzword these days among ice cream aficionados, and is limited by law to 100 percent, or the equivalent in volume to the mix itself. Therefore, 20 ounces of ice cream with a 100 percent overrun would still weigh 20 ounces, but it would occupy twice the amount of space as an ice cream with no overrun. Most super premium ice creams have about 20 percent overrun. Since all ice cream is sold by volume (pint, half gallon) and not by weight, you are paying partly for air when you are buying ice cream, and the higher the overrun (as in regular and economy ice creams), the more air you are buying.

The amount of overrun in ice cream is crucial to its texture. An ice cream with no air whipped into it at all would be a solidly frozen buttery mass and not very good to eat. On the other hand, an ice cream with the maximum amount of allowed overrun is light and almost foamy, the texture we have come to associate with the cheapest brands. Low overrun makes heavy, fudgelike ice cream, a texture that is considered desirable in this new generation of ice cream, exemplified by Häagen-Dazs and Frusen Glädjé.

In addition to limiting the amount of overrun in a brand of ice cream, another government control of overrun requires that a gallon of finished ice cream must weigh not less than 4.5 pounds and contain at least 1.6 pounds of food solids.

The final two steps in the making of ice cream are filling the containers and freezing completely to a hard stage. The filled containers are put into the freezers used for hardening, which vary from –20° to –50°F.; at these temperatures the ice cream freezes solidly in an hour or so.

HANDLING AND STORAGE

On the average, it takes about three weeks from the time of manufacture for ice cream to reach the home freezer. Once at home, if ice cream is kept completely airtight at 0°F., it will last for about 2 months. If you don't have a thermometer in your freezer, you can tell that the temperature is as low as 0°F. if the ice cream is so solidly frozen that a spoon bends in it when you try to scoop it out. To soften the ice cream, transfer it to the refrigerator for a few minutes. From 0°F., it takes about 20 minutes in the refrigerator for a half gallon (or 10 minutes for a pint) of ice cream to reach serving temperature of 5°F.

Nuts in ice cream get mushy after a short time, and so ice cream containing nuts doesn't last as long in a home freezer as other flavors, only about a month and a half after it is brought home from the supermarket.

After opening a carton of ice cream, place a piece of plastic wrap over the exposed surface of the ice cream before replacing the lid of the container, and place the container in a sealed plastic bag to help prevent freezer burn.

If ice cream is allowed to thaw partially and then is refrozen, it will form large unpleasant ice crystals throughout. Ice-cream parlor ice cream often contains icy crystals because the dipping cabinet is allowed to stay open for long intervals, bringing up the temperature of the freezer. Since most home freezers today are the frost-free type, their temperatures fluctuate a great deal, which can cause the ice cream to form crystals or scum, turn gritty, or dehydrate slightly. Manufacturers recommend that ice cream be kept in a frost-free freezer for only 1 week.

Super premium ice cream, which is made without stabilizers and emulsifiers, suffers during shipping and storage to the supermarket and to the home. Unless it is eaten while fresh, it will not be in peak condition. Therefore, it's probably best to buy only the amount you will eat at one meal, from a store with rapid turnover. Unfortunately, the probabilities of getting stale ice cream from a store are high.

HOW TO JUDGE ICE CREAM

Tasting Media

The ice cream should be served from the freezer in shallow bowls, one at a time. The tasters should sample each ice cream at least three times, directly from the freezer at 0°F. and at least two more times as they become a bit warmer, up to 10°F.

Ice-cream professionals first temper their ice cream overnight at 5° to 6°F. They taste the ice cream by taking a sample directly from a carton with one spoon and transferring the ice cream to a second spoon. They use apples or unsalted crackers to rinse their palates. After tasting a particularly poor ice cream, ice-cream professionals sometimes clear their palates by going back to a good ice cream, a testing dictum I find particularly interesting.

Color/Eye Appeal

A good vanilla ice cream should be attractive and pleasing in color. It is defective if it looks chalky, dull, gray, streaky, uneven, or unnatural looking. Some of the variations in color have to do with fluctuations in the seasons, which affect the color of dairy products.

A fine-textured ice cream is whiter than coarse ice cream.

Taste/Aroma

The best vanilla ice cream tastes fresh and natural; ice-cream professionals say that a good ice cream tastes "typical" and pleasant. It is defective if it tastes salty, slightly rancid, bitter, metallic, of cardboard, or oily (from oxidation), tallowy (from frozen cream or butter), sour, musty, stale (from having been stored too long or from powdered egg yolks), "cooked" (which can be likened to the taste of milk that has been boiled), too sweet, of gelatin, or artificial.

Consistency

As mentioned earlier, there is a wide divergence of opinion among ice-cream experts as to the proper consistency of ice cream. Some people favor the rich, dense super premium ice creams, while others feel that the texture of these is a violation of long-standing manufacturing practices. Nevertheless, most experts agree on the major defects in the consistency of ice cream: poor ice cream is coarse, icy, snowy, or flaky (from high overrun), sandy (from milk-sugar crystals or from temperature fluctuations in manufacturing), buttery, sticky, gummy, pasty, crumbly or brittle (this happens when it roughens as a spoon is drawn across the surface), foamy (from too many eggs or high overrun), melts to a thin liquid (from a low nonfat milk-solids content), has a low melting resistance, elastic (springs back when pressed with the back of a spoon (from too many stabilizers), retains its shape on melting (also from too many stabilizers).

Aftertaste

The major reason for an unpleasant aftertaste in ice cream is the quantity of synthetic flavorings and the manner in which they are used. They can leave an artificial taste in the mouth.

CONCLUSIONS AND SUGGESTIONS

The two top ice creams in the country, to my mind, are Häagen-Dazs and Howard Johnson's, and they represent very different styles. Both have a high milkfat content; Howard Johnson's is actually a bit higher at 16 percent versus Häagen-Dazs' 15.4 percent. This makes them both creamy and rich-tasting, which is what most of us look for in a commercial ice cream. The main difference between the two front-runners is texture. Häagen-Dazs is the epitome of a super premium ice cream, with 20 percent overrun, which is very low. That makes it richly dense and intensely flavored. Howard Johnson's, on the other hand, has a 50 percent overrun, which produces a lighter, more airy texture.

Howard Johnson's ice cream is also made with stabilizers, while Häagen-Dazs is not, and considering the reality of distribution systems around the country, this gives Howard Johnson's the advantage of lasting longer in the supermarket as well as in the home freezer.

ADDENDUM: LOW-FAT ICE CREAMS AND OTHER ALTERNATIVES

In the past few years, low-fat ice creams and nondairy frozen desserts have become extremely popular, especially among upscale urbanites who may have switched from Häagen-Dazs and its ilk as they got older. Another impetus is new labeling regulations that now allow these products to be called "ice cream" with a qualifier ("light ice cream") rather than unappetizing-sounding names such as ice milk and frozen dairy dessert.

(Ice milk, by the way, was first introduced during the Depression as a low-cost alternative to ice cream.)

The new rules that apply to ice cream as well as all other foods are:

- *Reduced fat* means at least 25 percent less fat than the typical product.

- *Light* means at least one-third fewer calories or 50 percent less fat.

- *Low fat* means 3 grams of fat or less per serving.

- *Non fat* or *Fat free* is less than 1/2 gram of fat per serving.

Sherbets are somewhere between low-fat and nonfat, but they may not be low in calories, since they are usually more dense than ice cream. They contain between 1 and 2 percent milkfat and weigh not less than 6 pounds per gallon.

Ices and sorbets have no dairy ingredients and very little or no fat. They are generally lower in calories than sherbet. By law, water ice contains no dairy ingredients and weighs not less than 6 pounds per gallon.

Americans buy close to a half billion dollars a year of frozen yogurt, often under the mistaken notion that it is better for them than ice cream. In fact, much frozen yogurt has almost as many calories as ice cream, and a great deal of fat as well. Also, the "good" bacteria—those that are believed to fight diarrhea—are mostly killed by the freezing process.

YOGURT

In its basic form, yogurt is a simple food. According to the U.S. government, it is a mixture of cream, milk and/or skim milk, and lactic acid-producing bacteria. The result is a milk custardlike product with some of the tang of sour cream.

When you go beyond the basics, yogurt gets more complicated. Although it is thousands of years old, Americans did not begin to eat it in quantity until the 1960s. Yogurt fit perfectly into the new obsessions with health and body consciousness. Some believed yogurt would put us into a karmic balance of good health and well-being; others went so far as to tout yogurt's ability to help us live into our second century.

In the nineties, yogurt has settled into our life-style quite comfortably. We've become more realistic about yogurt's health benefits. It's a tasty way to eat a dairy product. And yogurt is easy to eat; it's one of the few foods we can eat acceptably right from the carton.

Two thirds of all yogurt eaters consume their yogurt at lunch. The profile of the average yogurt user is a woman between the ages of 13 and 19 or 35 and 44 who lives in a suburb on the Pacific Coast, in New England, or Mid-Atlantic cities. She has some higher education and an income greater than $20,000 per year.

Overall, the average consumption of yogurt in 1990 was 4.1 pounds annually—four times as much as in 1970.

A DASH OF HISTORY

People in much of the world have been eating yogurt for thousands of years. Romantic folk tales have always been told about the origins of yogurt, but it was probably discovered by accident in many different places at many different times.

One story has it that in preparation for a journey across the desert, a nomad packed his milk in a goatskin bag and slung it across the back of his camel. When he settled down around the campfire for his evening meal and attempted to drink his milk, he discovered that it had turned into a custardlike substance. The nomad's milk had interacted with the bacteria in the goatskin bag, creating yogurt. The process was completed by the body warmth of the camel, the heat of the sun, and the rapid drop in the desert temperature at night.

Evidence of yogurt has been found in the writings of the ancient Egyptians, Greeks, and Romans. Genghis Khan not only fed yak's-milk yogurt to his army to strengthen it for battle, but also used it as a marinade to preserve meat while traveling with his troops.

Despite the importance of yogurt to a large part of the world, it was not introduced to Western Europe until the sixteenth century. When François I of France was laid low with an intestinal ailment, fearful court physicians sent for a healer from Constantinople. After a regimen of goat's-milk yogurt the king's health improved. François dubbed yogurt *le lait de la vie eternelle,* the milk of eternal life, which may also have marked the beginning of yogurt's reputation as a miracle food.

The earliest scientific study of yogurt dates to the turn of this century. A Russian bacteriologist named Ilya Metchnikoff, a Nobel Prize winner who was director of the respected Louis Pasteur Institute in France, traced to yogurt the secret of longevity. After discovering that many Bulgarians who live past the age of 100 ate a great deal of yogurt, Metchnikoff isolated a bacterium in yogurt and called it *Bulgarian bacillus* (the name was later changed to *Lactobacillus bulgaricus).* This miracle-working "good" bacterium, he proposed, chased putrefying "bad" bacteria out of the large intestine for Bulgarian centenarians and was the secret to long life. Ironically, Metchnikoff's followers were somewhat disillusioned when he died at the age of 71 in 1916. His theories were later disproven further when scientists discovered that Bulgarians didn't keep good birth records at that time, and reports of advanced ages were probably exaggerated.

Nevertheless, Metchnikoff's research had made it possible to make yogurt commercially in large quantities. A Spaniard named Isaac Carasso used some of Metchnikoff's bacteria to begin to make yogurt in Barcelona. His company was called Danone, after his son Daniel. A few years later, in 1931, an Armenian family named Columbosian started the first commercial yogurt dairy in the United States, in Andover, Massachusetts. The name of their product was Americanized to Colombo. At the end of World War II the Danone company moved to New York where *their* name was changed to Dannon. Although these two businesses flourished for the next couple of decades, practically the only Americans eating yogurt were those of Middle Eastern descent. In 1946, Dannon made yogurt history by mass-producing a fruit-flavored yogurt, strawberry, to be exact, creating "the ice cream without the guilt." Today Dannon has captured 25 percent of the American yogurt market, which is more than all local and regional brands put together.

HOW YOGURT IS MADE

Yogurt is a cultured milk product, as are buttermilk, cottage cheese, and sour cream. It's made by taking pasteurized milk—cow's milk, goat's milk, buffalo milk, or even soy milk—and adding *Streptococcus thermophilus* and *Lactobacillus bulgaricus.* These bacteria multiply and change the milk sugar, called *lactose,* into lactic acid. The milk curdles and the yogurt becomes tart, thick, and creamy.

Another strain of yogurt bacteria is acidophilus culture *(Lactobacillus acidophilus),* added to some yogurts sold in health-food stores. It is also sold in tablet or capsule form. The acidophilus culture is considered by some to be more healthful than the other forms of yogurt bacteria, although this has not been proven conclusively.

In a commercial yogurt plant, the milk (almost always cow's milk in this country) is a blend. Each company uses its own combination of nonfat dry-milk powder, partially skimmed milk, skim milk, whole milk, and cream.

First, the milk is homogenized. (In the few cases where the milk is *not* homogenized, as in Brown Cow yogurt on the East Coast, a layer of yogurt cream can be found on top of the yogurt.) If the yogurt will have fruit flavoring, granulated sugar or some other form of sweetener is added to the milk.

The milk is then pasteurized, cooled to about 110°F., and the bacteria are mixed in. It takes only about 1 ounce of the two primary strains of bacteria to make 408,000 cups of yogurt. In some yogurt formulas, the bacteria are freeze-dried; in others they are frozen and concentrated. Some yogurt is pasteurized both before and after the bacteria is added. This extends the shelf life of the product, but it kills the bacteria and negates all of their intestinal benefits. By law, if yogurt has been pasteurized the label must say "heat-treated after culturing."

In the *can set,* also called *stirred* or *pudding-style* method, the mixture is put into 40-quart stainless-steel vats and held at 110°F. for about 3 to 6 hours, while the bacteria multiply and the proper amount of acidity is reached. According to government stipulations, the final acidity level must not be less than 0.9 percent. At this point, the vats of yogurt are refrigerated and cooled to 40°F. in order to halt the development of the bacteria. After the cooling period, the yogurt is stirred to make it into fluid again (about the texture of light sour cream), and fruit, flavorings, and additives, where applicable are added. Then it is put into retail containers. Yoplait is a brand of yogurt produced by this method.

In the *container set* or *set* method, the yogurt is fermented in the cups in which it will be purchased. It is placed in the retail containers just after the bacteria (as well as fruit, flavorings, and additives) have been added. The containers are kept at 110°F. until the bacteria have developed properly, and then the containers go into the refrigerator. An example of this kind of yogurt is Dannon, with its firm, gelatinous texture.

In both methods, if the yogurt is made sundae-style, with the fruit on the bottom of the container, the fruit and/or preserves are pumped into the container before the yogurt is poured on top.

VARIETIES OF YOGURT

The milkfat of each of the three varieties of yogurt is specified by government regulations and is always listed on the labels:

YOGURT, which is made from whole milk containing at least 3.25 percent milkfat;
LOWFAT YOGURT, which is made from milk that is at least .5 percent but not more than 2 percent milkfat;
NONFAT YOGURT, which is made from milk that is less than .5 percent milkfat.

Lowfat yogurt is by far the most popular variety. However, don't be fooled into thinking that if the yogurt is made with less milkfat it is less fattening. Many yogurt manufacturers lower the milkfat content of their yogurt in order to compensate for the added calories of the fruit, preserves, and sugar, resulting in a yogurt that is, in fact, higher in calories. Most yogurt brands list calories on the containers. On the other hand, 1 cup of plain, unflavored yogurt made with whole milk has 108 fewer calories than a cup of cottage cheese.

Although these designations aren't always listed on the labels, yogurt can also be broken down this way:

Plain

Plain yogurt contains no flavorings or sweeteners; it is pure yogurt.

Flavored

Flavored yogurt contains such additions as lemon, coffee, chocolate, vanilla, etc., and usually sugar, but no fruit.

Fruit-Flavored

This yogurt, America's favorite, contains a combination of fruit and preserves, and is sold in various styles:

• *Sundae-style* In sundae-style yogurt, the fruit preserves are placed in the bottom of the container and the yogurt is poured on top. Dannon is made this way. Most people eat this type of yogurt by first stirring it up. In western states, a type of sundae-style yogurt has been developed that not only has fruit preserves on the bottom of the container, but also syrup on the top.

• *Swiss-style* In Swiss-style yogurt, the fruit and the yogurt are already mixed together. Swiss-style yogurt must be made with additives, natural and/or artificial, in order to keep the fruit suspended in the yogurt. Light n' Lively is an example of Swiss-style yogurt.

• *French-style* In French-style yogurt, the fruit and the yogurt are blended together, but without stabilizers, so it is thinner than Swiss-style. Yoplait is a French-style yogurt. French-style yogurt usually comes in 6-ounce containers rather than

8-ounce, so although it lists less calories, its lighter count is due only to the fact that less yogurt is in the container.

Over 30 flavors of yogurt are available in this country, but the most popular five flavors enjoy 60 percent of the market: strawberry, raspberry, blueberry, peach, and cherry.

Over 90 percent of the yogurt made in the United States is flavored.

FAT CONTENT

By law, whole-milk yogurt must contain 3¹/₄ percent milkfat; lowfat yogurt must contain ¹/₂ to 2 percent milkfat; nonfat yogurt (made from skim milk) must contain less than ¹/₂ percent milkfat.

HEALTH BENEFITS

Even though it's far from a miracle food, yogurt *is* good for you. Because yogurt is made from milk, it has the same nutritional benefits, including high-quality protein, calcium, and phosphorus. Yogurt has at least one advantage over milk. Many adults (most Asians and Blacks and a large percentage of Caucasians) are afflicted with lactase deficiency, which means they have trouble digesting foods containing lactose, such as milk. Since the lactose, also called *milk sugar,* in yogurt has been mostly turned into lactic acid by the fermentation process, those with this problem can digest yogurt more easily.

It has been discovered, however, that when nonfat dry milk is added to yogurt, the lactose concentration increases, making it almost as difficult to digest for a lactose-intolerant person as a glass of milk. On the other hand, an advantage to the addition of nonfat dry milk to yogurt is the additional protein, vitamins, and minerals without the extra fat. All yogurt labels specify if nonfat dry milk has been added.

Because it has been through the fermentation process, yogurt is 90 percent digested within an hour after eating it, compared to 30 percent for milk, giving you a quicker burst of energy than if you had had milk. It is also thought that the bacteria increase yogurt's B-vitamin content slightly.

Many doctors recommend yogurt to their patients who are taking antibiotics, believing that the bacteria in yogurt, which amount to 500 to 800 million cells per milliliter, will replace the beneficial intestinal bacteria that are usually killed by strong antibiotics. Because of this, yogurt has been shown to relieve the diarrhea that is often associated with antibiotic therapy.

Research has also shown that if you eat a pint of yogurt a day for *several* weeks before going on a trip abroad, your resistance against the bacteria that cause "Montezuma's Revenge" will increase. The yogurt implants healthy bacteria in your intestines that help fight off foreign bacteria. To reinforce the effect, you should also eat yogurt daily during your trip. Yogurt is available in tablet form from health-food stores.

To take best advantage of the health benefits of yogurt, eat the brands that contain live bacteria (sometimes called *active cultures).* Some commercial yogurts are pasteurized twice to extend shelf life and thus the healthful bacteria have been killed off. Check the label to make sure it says "live bacteria" or "active cultures."

HANDLING AND STORAGE

If you eat yogurt too long after it's been made, the bacteria will have died off and any benefits you seek from them are gone.

In the first day or two after its manufacture, the bacteria in yogurt continue to increase, even after the yogurt has been packaged and refrigerated. Then the bacteria content levels off and after just 7 days the healthful benefits begin to decline. After 35 days the bacteria begin to decrease significantly, and from 40 to 50 days after manufacture the bacteria have almost completely died.

The older a yogurt gets, the more tart it becomes. Although a small amount of liquid whey on the top of a container of yogurt is normal, yogurt that is past its peak has a greater amount of separation. In either case, the liquid can simply be stirred back into the yogurt.

Unopened fruit-flavored yogurt can be frozen successfully for as long as 6 weeks. It will separate a bit, lose some of its creaminess, and may also become more acidic. To defrost it properly, let it stand at room temperature for about 3 hours.

Different brands of yogurt specify expiration dates anywhere from 21 to 90 days after production; yogurt will be fresh for at least a week beyond the date indicated on the container. Keep in mind, however, that any yogurt that is expected to be fresh for more than about 30 days has to have been pasteurized after fermentation and this has killed off all of the bacteria.

One way to make sure you are getting fresh yogurt is to buy only that which is made close to your home, rather than a brand that has to have been shipped for days before it gets to your store. The *best* way to get ultrafresh yogurt, of course, is to make your own (see "Making Yogurt at Home," page 57).

HOW TO JUDGE YOGURT

Tasting Media

The yogurts should be spooned into shallow glass bowls and tasted with plastic spoons because metal spoons interfere with yogurt's flavor.

Color/Eye Appeal

A small amount of liquid whey is normal on the top of a container of yogurt.

Preservatives and chemicals are rampant in yogurts that are glossy with a uniform color. Yogurt without additives is usually milky white, with the fruit preserves at the bottom of the container, except in the case of French-style and Swiss-style yogurt, in which the fruit is suspended throughout. The color of some yogurts is violent and unnatural, a decidedly unappetizing factor.

Taste/Aroma

Plain yogurt should have a clean, dairy flavor with some tartness from the yogurt bacteria. It should be slightly astringent, but not sour.

Yogurts made with whole milk are creamier and richer-tasting than those made with skim or lowfat milks. Yogurt made with cream tastes even more rich, and less tart.

With fruit-flavored yogurts, you should be able to identify the prevailing fruit without seeing it. More often than not, if you close your eyes while eating a fruit-flavored yogurt, you can't tell which kind of fruit is in it. That's because in many cases fruit preserves are added rather than whole fruit pieces.

Flavored and fruit-flavored yogurt should not be overly sweet, but it often is. Sweetener is often added to the yogurt itself as well as being a substantial part of the preserves. The yogurt flavor itself is often lost, which is a defect.

The aroma of yogurt should be subtle.

Consistency

Yogurt should be creamy and smooth, with no lumps; the texture should be uniform. Yogurt with stabilizers and artificial and natural thickeners can be gelatinous and thick to the point of repulsion. On the other hand, a pudding-like consistency can be pleasant, if it is not exaggerated.

Aftertaste

No bitter, chemical aftertaste should be present, nor should the fruit and sugar seem cloying.

CONCLUSIONS AND SUGGESTIONS

Yogurt is different everywhere around the world. In the Middle Eastern countries, yogurt is thick and strong; in Russia it's effervescent and alcoholic; in Scandinavia it is a drink, and often slimy. In America, we happen to eat yogurt that is most often sweetened and flavored with fruit preserves, while our plain yogurt is relatively mild and innocuous.

As far as I'm concerned, yogurt should taste the way *you* like it. Some people like their yogurt strong and tart, some like it mild and custardy; some like it thin and runny and some like it so thick that it won't fall out of the container when it's turned upside down. The many brands of yogurt on the market cater to all different tastes. On the other hand, some basic guidelines emerge for perceiving the overall quality of yogurt, whatever type it is. For example, any yogurt, whether it is thick or thin, should be smooth and not lumpy. If it is made with fruit, it should taste like the particular fruit, and not simply sugary. Any yogurt, whether it is flavored or plain, should taste like a dairy product and not overprocessed cardboard.

Flavored yogurt fits into my life in the same way that ice cream does. When it's a good brand, it's a high-calorie treat, sweet, creamy, and delicious. Even though, like ice cream, it has some of the nutritional benefits of a dairy product—it supplies some calcium and protein—I don't view it as an everyday food, but as a luxury "sweet" or dessert food because of the fruit and preserves it contains. The few times I have tried to eat only yogurt for a meal, I became hungry again an hour later and so soon abandoned the idea of using yogurt as a low-calorie breakfast or lunch substitute.

Plain yogurt fits into my life much more comfortably. For years my morning breakfast has consisted of plain yogurt, lowfat cottage cheese, and toast and tea, and sometimes fresh fruit. Plain yogurt is tasty as a topping for a fresh fruit dessert and indispensable in Middle Eastern cooking. The East Indians make a delicious condiment called *raeta* or *raita,* which acts as a fire extinguisher for hot curries; the yogurt is simply mixed with chopped cucumbers, salt, and sometimes fresh mint. All in all, plain yogurt is an important part of my cooking and eating habits. My favorite brand of yogurt, plain or flavored, is Colombo.

TIPS FOR COOKING WITH YOGURT

In Hot Dishes

Much has been said about the advantages of substituting yogurt for sour cream in a cooked recipe. Although you certainly save calories—1 cup of plain yogurt has about 150 calories compared to 1 cup of sour cream at 454 calories—it's a bit tricky to keep the yogurt from curdling and you should keep the following points in mind:

- After adding the yogurt to a dish, continue to cook it at a low temperature; fast high heat will make most dairy products separate.

- Cook the dish for a short period of time after adding yogurt. Better yet, stir in the yogurt after the dish is off the heat.

- Alternately, add the yogurt at the very beginning of a long cooking process to allow it to warm up slowly to prevent its curdling and to allow it to meld with all of the other ingredients.

- Shaun Nelson-Henrick, the author of *The Complete Book of Yogurt* (Macmillan, 1980), recommends that "stabilized yogurt" be used for cooking. Here is his recipe:

Stabilized Yogurt for Cooking

(Makes about 4 cups)

4 cups yogurt
1 egg white, lightly beaten, or 1 tablespoon cornstarch mixed with 1 tablespoon cold water
3/4 teaspoon salt

Beat yogurt in a large saucepan until liquid. Add the egg white, or the cornstarch mixed to a light paste with the cold water, and the salt. Stir well with a wooden spoon. Slowly bring to a boil, stirring constantly in one direction only, then reduce the heat to as low as possible and let the yogurt barely simmer, uncovered, for about 10 minutes, or until it has acquired a thick, rich consistency. After simmering, the yogurt can be mixed and cooked with other ingredients, such as meat or vegetables, with no danger of curdling.

Mr. Nelson-Henrick also recommends adding 1/2 teaspoon of baking soda for each cup of yogurt intended for use in baking as a substitute for cream, buttermilk, sour cream, or milk, in order to counteract the acidity in the yogurt.

In Cold Dishes

• If you use yogurt in cold dishes as a substitute for mayonnaise, you will also save a lot of calories: 1 cup of mayonnaise has 1,616 calories to yogurt's 150. The flavor of yogurt is not nearly as rich as mayonnaise, but the texture of foods made with yogurt is smooth and satisfying.

• When you mix yogurt with other ingredients, such as in a dip, it will become thinner. To avoid this, fold instead of stir the yogurt into the dish, then chill the dish to bring it back to its original firmness.

• If you're calorie-conscious, try using half yogurt and half mayonnaise in your favorite chicken or tuna salad recipe, or as a spread for sandwiches.

• As an excellent substitute for cream cheese, make yogurt cheese by following this simple method:

Yogurt Cheese

Take any amount of plain yogurt and place in a colander lined with 2 layers of moistened cheesecloth. Let drain over a plate for 1 hour. Draw up the corners of the cheesecloth and hang from the spigot over the sink for at least 8 hours, or overnight, until the cheese is as thick as you like.

You can use this yogurt cheese any way you would use cream cheese. I like to add minced fresh herbs and pepper to make a boursin-like cheese dip for vegetables and crackers.

MAKING YOGURT AT HOME

There are many recipes for making your own yogurt, but I think Elizabeth David's is by far the most logical and the simplest.

Elizabeth David's Homemade Yogurt

Start with 1 pint of fresh whole, skim, or low-fat milk. Bring the milk to a simmer very slowly, stirring frequently. Reduce the milk to under three quarters of the original amount. Bring to a boil.

Take the milk off the heat and leave it until it reaches 130°F. Use a thermometer here. Stir in a heaping tablespoon of commercial plain yogurt or some left over from your previous batch of homemade yogurt, if this isn't the first time you've made yogurt. Pour into a Thermos or another brand of insulated jug and close the top tightly. In 4 to 6 hours you will have yogurt.

Mrs. David makes her yogurt in the evening and leaves the Thermos on the kitchen counter until the morning.

Mrs. David also suggests the following convenience tip when you are unable to wait for the milk to cool down to the proper temperature:

Boil the milk in advance, put it into the refrigerator until you are ready to make yogurt, and then quickly warm it up to the proper temperature of 130°F. to begin the process.

The important thing to remember about Mrs. David's method is that reducing the milk by simmering it makes a firmer yogurt than most other homemade yogurt recipes; it will be much more like the kind you buy in the store.

If you find that your homemade yogurt is a little thinner than you like, your starter culture is probably weak and it's time to buy another container of plain yogurt to use as a starter. If the yogurt still turns out a little thin, it's possible that the commercial yogurt was too old when you bought it. In that case, you should simply use more of it, or better, buy another, fresher, container of plain yogurt.

RECIPE

Yogurt Milk Soup

This is based on a common Hungarian soup, tejleves, and is really quite delicious, especially for a friendly lunch. (Makes 4 servings)

1 1/2 tablespoons unsalted butter
1 onion, sliced thin
2 cups plain yogurt
2 cups milk
1 cup chicken stock
2 tablespoons sugar
1/2 teaspoon salt
16 tiny new or red-skinned potatoes, unpeeled and cooked (cut the potatoes into quarters after cooking, if they are too large)

1. In a heavy saucepan, melt the butter and add the sliced onion. Cook the onion very slowly in the butter until golden brown, about 10 minutes.

2. Add to the saucepan the yogurt, milk, chicken stock, 1 cup water, the sugar, and salt. Bring to a boil and simmer slowly for 10 minutes, stirring occasionally. Add the cooked potatoes and simmer for 3 more minutes.

NOTE: You can use homemade or store-bought noodles instead of the potatoes. This is a good recipe for using up leftover broken pieces of uncooked spaghetti and fettuccine. Add 1 cup (or about 1/4 pound) of noodles at the beginning of the 10-minute simmering and cook the soup until the noodles are done.

CONDIMENTS

KETCHUP

We put it on hamburgers, mostly, and French fries. Some ketchup finds its way onto cottage cheese (President Nixon's favorite), scrambled eggs, and into meat loaf. Russian gymnast Olga Korbut even put it on her pancakes.

Ketchup is our most important condiment. In 1993, Americans bought the equivalent of 786 million 14-ounce bottles of it; that's 3 bottles for every man, woman, and child. It can be found in 97 percent of all American homes, and the average household uses approximately one 14-ounce bottle per month.

Although everyone seems to use a great deal of it, the profile of the average adult ketchup-user is a person who is politically conservative, has an income of more than $15,000 per year, is between 25 and 54 years old, and lives in a household of three or more people. Residents of North Carolina, South Carolina, and Virginia use twice the national average of ketchup. Women eat ketchup more often than men—four times per week on average. More than four out of five American children eat ketchup at least twice a week, while the average teenager eats ketchup once a day.

It's spelled *ketchup* by Heinz and the Associated Press style book, *catsup,* by Hunt's and Del Monte, and *catchup* or *catch-up* by some cutesy health-food manufacturers. The federal government accepts all of these names.

A DASH OF HISTORY

The origins of our ketchup are somewhat cloudy, although most scholars agree that its distant ancestors are from Asia, where one finds many salty, fish-based sauces with names similar to "ketchup."

A Chinese condiment called *koe-chiap* or *ketsiap* exists that would seem to have been a likely inspiration for ketchup, but at the same time, the Malaysians have a version called *kechap,* a name derived from the native word for "taste." A popular condiment in Indonesia is a very sweet soy sauce called *katjap* or *ketjap*. Western reference to ketchup appears as early as 1690, and legend has it that a taste for the sauce first arrived with an English seaman who had traveled to Singapore.

When these Far Eastern sauces made their way to our part of the world, they metamorphosed into salty, spicy condiments based not on fish brine but on vinegar and such diverse foods as walnuts, mushrooms, oysters, or cucumbers. These sauces were devised and widely used as ways to preserve the foods of which they were made and to add interest to daily fare.

Many eighteenth- and nineteenth-century cookbooks and guides to housekeeping contain varied recipes for "kitchup" or ketchup. One of the best known of these books, *Isabella Beeton's Book of Household Management,* published in 1861: "This flavouring ingredient, if genuine and well-prepared, is one of the most useful store sauces to the experienced cook, and no trouble should be spared in its preparation." Her book included recipes for mushroom, oyster, and walnut ketchups.

On the United States' one-hundredth birthday, Henry J. Heinz began to produce ketchup commercially. The American addition to the ketchup formula was the tomato, possibly because of influence from Mexico and the Spanish West Indies. Nowadays, of course, ketchup generally means tomato ketchup the world over. And no American coffee shop counter would be the same without it.

HOW KETCHUP IS MADE

Ketchup is a manufactured product and by law must be made of tomatoes, vinegar, sugar, spices, flavorings, onions or garlic, and salt.

It takes less than 1 day to process ketchup from picking to bottling. First, the tomatoes—a special strain bred to have more viscosity—are picked when they are very ripe and contain the most natural sugars. There are good and bad years for ketchup tomatoes, just as there are good and bad years for wine grapes. For example, 1983 was considered a banner year for ketchup tomatoes.

The tomatoes are brought into the plant where the seeds and stems are removed. Next the tomato pulp is cooked in a large stainless-steel vat at a boil to evaporate the water. The temperature is lowered so that the color of the tomatoes is preserved during the reduction process. It takes over 5 pounds of tomatoes to make a 32-ounce bottle of ketchup.

When the tomatoes are cooked to the desired thickness, the remaining ingredients—sugar, vinegar, salt, spices, and flavoring—are added. Generally, the spices added to ketchup are mustard seeds, celery seeds, cayenne pepper, nutmeg, mace, cloves, ginger, and pepper, while onion and/or garlic make up the most common flavoring added to ketchup. The standard recipe may be varied by taking out the salt, as long as "no salt added" is clearly visible on the label. If there is no sugar (or sucrose, dextrose, glucose syrup, or corn syrup) in the formula, the ketchup must be labeled "imitation." Many "imitation" products *are* sweetened with honey, however. Those with no sweetener in them at all must be labeled with the word "unsweetened" in the same size lettering as the word "ketchup" or "catsup."

The average amount of sweetener in ketchup is 20 percent, or the equivalent of one fifth of the total (not one third, as is popularly believed). Most brands of ketchup contain about 70 percent water, which comes from the tomatoes.

The top of every ketchup bottle bears a few letters and/or numbers, which are a code to the manufacturing data. The two top-selling brands of ketchup, Heinz and Hunt's, have given me the following information to decipher their codes:

Heinz S M 1 2 4 5

year (1995)

production day (124th day of the year)

which plant produced ketchup*

hour of the day ketchup was produced (A is the first hour of the day and subsequent hours follow letters of the alphabet; S = the nineteenth hour of the day)

*M – Muscatino, Iowa T – Tracy, California
F = Freemont, Ohio

Hunt's F 5 T 9 5

day (5th day of month)

month (September)

plant data

year (1995)

plant data

HANDLING AND STORAGE

Some manufacturers recommend a maximum storage time for ketchup (after the bottle is opened) of 3 to 4 months at room temperature, although it will be safe to eat for much longer. If it is stored longer than 4 months, ketchup will gradually darken and lose some of its sharp, lively flavor. Other manufacturers say their ketchup will never go bad, even after decades of storage; I tend to agree with the first group.

In their article on ketchup, *Consumer Reports* magazine reported that no visible signs of deterioration or mold growth appeared in ketchup samples stored for 50 days at room temperature and none in those stored in the refrigerator for the same amount of time. Ketchup can be stored in either the refrigerator or at room temperature. It is safe to say most of us keep it where our mothers did.

HOW TO JUDGE KETCHUP

Tasting Media

The ketchup should be tasted from shallow glass bowls with spoons.

Color/Eye Appeal

The proper color of a good ketchup is a brilliant red. Darker colors indicate age or poor quality. A pale ketchup can be an indication of wateriness or poor-quality tomatoes.

Taste/Aroma

The taste of ketchup should be sharp and lively; it is a sweet/sour condiment. In essence, ketchup is a sweet/sour relish that has turned into a purée after a long cooking time. The taste of fresh, ripe tomatoes is not as important as the balance of sweet and sour flavors. In fact, the tomatoes are probably simply a vehicle for the other flavors in a ketchup. A good balance of flavors marks a good ketchup; you should not be able to identify distinctly the sugar, vinegar, or cayenne.

Consistency

Ketchup is primarily used for such foods as French fries and hamburgers, so it must be thick enough to adhere to the food without running off. It should also be smooth, without lumps. Some ketchups separate so that the water runs off in a pink stream all over the plate, which can be unpleasant and is considered a defect. Some ketchups are so thick (Heinz, Farm Product) that they are almost cloying.

Aftertaste

Ketchup should not leave a sharp, vinegary, astringent sensation in your mouth, nor should it have a candy-sweet aftertaste.

CONCLUSIONS AND SUGGESTIONS

I have always thought that in a blind tasting everyone would automatically recognize and prefer the ketchup he or she grew up with. Since Heinz has 55 percent of the ketchup market, Hunt's has 9 percent and Del Monte has 9 percent, I thought tasting results would mirror those numbers, but not so.

As I traveled around the country when this book was first published, I held televised ketchup tastings in many cities, and invariably the host of the program would begin by saying that he or she loved Heinz and would pick that one for sure. Almost always, the tasters picked Del Monte, to much chagrin.

I like Del Monte the best because it seems to embody all that a ketchup should be: sweet and pungent at the same time, without being too sour; a hint of tomato flavor, not too salty. Industry scuttlebutt has it that Del Monte is made with pineapple vinegar, and that could be just the touch that makes it taste best. The texture is just right, thick enough to mound nicely next to a pile of French fries for dipping, with no watery runoff.

RECIPES

Homemade Ketchup

I tried many recipes for homemade ketchup, and while they made nice sauces, they didn't come very close to what we think of as standard ketchup. This recipe is adapted from Make Your Own Groceries *by Daphne Metaxas Hartwig (Bobbs-Merrill, 1979). It comes the closest to real ketchup flavor and isn't too difficult to make, since you start with tomato sauce rather than whole tomatoes. Since many of our tasters felt it was a little too spicy, I have toned down the spices for this version. (Makes about 2 average [14-ounce] bottles)*

- **1/4 cup sugar**
- **1 1/2 teaspoons salt**
- **1/2 teaspoon black peppercorns**
- **1/2 teaspoon mustard seeds**
- **1/4 teaspoon celery seeds**
- **pinch of cayenne pepper**
- **3 3/4 cups (30 ounces) canned tomato sauce**
- **2 tablespoons minced onion**
- **1 garlic clove, minced**
- **4 tablespoons plus 2 teaspoons light corn syrup**
- **4 tablespoons plus 2 teaspoons cider vinegar**
- **2 tablespoons plus 1 teaspoon fresh lemon juice**

1. In a dry blender or food processor, place the sugar, salt, peppercorns, mustard seeds, celery seeds, and cayenne. Process until the mixture is almost completely powdered.

2. Put the tomato sauce into a blender or food processor and blend for a minute or two, until completely smooth. Pour into a nonaluminum pot. Add the powdered spice mixture.

3. Add to the pot the minced onion and garlic. Simmer slowly for about 30 minutes, stirring frequently. When the sauce is thick enough to make loose mounds, about the consistency of spaghetti sauce, remove from the heat and add the corn syrup, vinegar, and lemon juice.

4. Strain the sauce through a fine mesh strainer. When cool, pour into clean ketchup bottles and refrigerate.

Shaker Flank Steak

This is a delicious pot roast which is very easy to put together. This version is adapted from The Best of Shaker Cooking *by Amy Bess Miller and Persis Fuller (Macmillan, 1970). I like to serve it with homemade mashed potatoes and Brussels sprouts, which I have taken apart, leaf by leaf, and stir-fried in butter with a touch of fresh lemon juice. (Makes 6 servings)*

- **2 1/2 pounds beef bottom round, about 1 1/2 inches thick**
- **flour for coating beef**
- **3 tablespoons vegetable oil**
- **1 cup chopped onion**
- **salt and freshly ground pepper**
- **1/3 cup chopped celery**
- **1/3 cup chopped carrot**
- **1/4 cup chopped green pepper**
- **1 garlic clove, minced**
- **3/4 cup ketchup**
- **2 tablespoons fresh lemon juice**

1. Score both sides of the beef diagonally at about 2-inch intervals. Coat both sides of the meat completely with flour and shake off excess.

2. Heat the oil in a large skillet or flameproof casserole and brown the meat well on both sides. After turning the meat to brown the second side, sprinkle chopped onion into the skillet and cook, stirring, until onion is light golden brown and the second side of the meat is browned. Season with salt and pepper to taste and add all of the remaining ingredients.

3. Cover skillet tightly with a lid or with a piece of aluminum foil and put into a 350°F. oven. Cook for 1 to 1 1/2 hours, until meat is tender but not overcooked.

4. To serve, slice the meat and place it on a platter in a warm place. Purée the contents of the skillet to make a smooth sauce, or serve the sauce as is, without puréeing. I prefer the latter way.

MAYONNAISE

ayonnaise is one of those quintessentially French foods, such as the croissant, that have been taken over by Americans. Can you imagine a tuna fish salad without mayo, for example? Or potato salad, or a B.L.T.? In fact, mayonnaise is the largest-selling sauce in the United States. Each of us eats the equivalent of 3 big jars, or 2.9 pounds, of commercial mayonnaise per year.

Americans in the West and the Southeast eat more mayonnaise than those in other parts of the country. Just about half the commercial mayonnaise sold in the United States is made by one company, which sells under the Hellmann's label east of the Mississippi and the Best Foods label in the West. Since Westerners prefer stronger-tasting foods, Best Foods mayonnaise is tangier than Hellmann's.

Sixty-five percent of the commercial mayonnaise sold in this country goes on sandwiches. Twenty-one percent is used for "blended salads," such as chicken salad or tuna salad (some put on bread for sandwiches), and 14 percent of the mayonnaise in the United States makes dressings for green salads.

A DASH OF HISTORY

Controversy abounds about when and where French mayonnaise first made an appearance. It's probably safe to say that it was invented in France some time in the eighteenth century. Some historians claim mayonnaise was first served at the table of the Duc de Richelieu in 1756 after he captured Port Mahon, on the Mediterranean island of Minorca, from the British. The great French chef Carême wrote adamantly that mayonnaise should actually be spelled *magnonnaise* because the name comes from the French verb *manier,* which means "to work" or "to stir." Still others believe the word comes from the old French term for egg yolk, *moyeu.* Since so many French dishes are named after places, others like to believe that mayonnaise is derived from *bayonnaise,* and is taken from the southern French town near the border of Spain called Bayonne.

Even though it was elevated to a level of greatness by the French, mayonnaise, or a form of mayonnaise, was probably made by peasants in several Mediterranean countries long before it was "discovered" in France. For example, the Spanish *ali-oli* is a garlic mayonnaise made with olive oil, used long before the eighteenth century.

Even though the word "mayonnaise" first appeared in print in English in 1841, it did not become a popular sauce in the United States until the twentieth century. In 1912, a New York delicatessen owner named Richard Hellmann began to bottle and sell his popular mayonnaise. Within just a couple of years, the mayonnaise was selling so well that Hellmann bought a truck to distribute his product; then, in 1916 he built a factory in Queens, New York, to accommodate his growing business.

In 1923, a company called Best Foods began to sell mayonnaise in California, and in 1932 the Hellmann's and Best Foods companies merged to form one nationwide mayonnaise company, now owned by a major food corporation called CPC International.

By 1933, in the depth of the Depression, mayonnaise had become a luxury food for most Americans. A low-priced substitute was invented by Kraft, which called the new product Miracle Whip after the new Miracle Whip machine that was used to produce it. Miracle Whip is a starch-thickened "spoonable dressing," made with a 36-percent water content, compared with commercial mayonnaise, which contains 17 percent water.

HOW MAYONNAISE IS MADE

The federal government requires that a product labeled "mayonnaise" must contain at least 65 percent vegetable oil by weight, at least $2^1/_2$ percent vinegar and/or lemon (or lime) juice, and some egg yolk. Commercial mayonnaise may also contain salt, sweetener, spices or natural flavorings, monosodium glutamate, preservatives, and citric acid. It must not contain any colorings or artificial flavorings.

By comparison, commercial "salad dressing"—which means, primarily, Miracle Whip, since it is by far the largest-selling in the country—must have at least 30 percent vegetable oil by weight, 4 percent egg yolk, and cooked starch. All other optional and required ingredient specifications are the same as for mayonnaise, although commercial salad dressing is usually spicier and sweeter, since it contains more flavoring ingredients.

The mayonnaise manufacturers were reluctant to divulge processing information about their products. However, CPC International finally sent the following short explanation:

"Hellmann's and Best Foods mayonnaise is made with soybean oil and partially hydrogenated soybean oil, whole eggs, vinegar, water, egg yolks, salt, sugar, lemon juice, natural flavors, and calcium disocium EDTA (to protect flavor). In Best Foods' plants where mayonnaise is produced, the process begins with measuring the vinegar, soybean oil blend, and egg-spice blend. The ingredients are then blended in a stainless-steel mixer and transferred to a mill. The mill blends and homogenizes the oil and vinegar mixture to produce the creamy mayonnaise. The mayonnaise is then guided into filler machines and into jars, topped with lids and labeled."

STORAGE AND HANDLING

Manufacturers of mayonnaise feel that it will last "forever" on a pantry shelf, if unopened. Once opened, mayonnaise should be refrigerated only to preserve the flavor, not to prevent it from "going bad." Practically, an unopened jar of mayonnaise should last for at least a year; after it is opened, mayonnaise should stay fresh in the refrigerator for at least 2 months.

More importantly, the old wives' tale that says that mayonnaise is responsible for food spoilage has recently been disproven by thorough scientific studies. It turns out that commercial mayonnaise contains so much salt and acidity that it actually *inhibits* foods from growing bacteria. Whereas mayonnaise has always been blamed for causing foods to spoil, it is actually the high-protein foods with which it is usually mixed that spoil quickly: eggs, chicken, ham. Foods made with these ingredients, whether or not they are mixed with mayonnaise, are prone to growing bacteria at room temperature, and indeed become quite dangerous in a picnic or buffet setting.

So even though caution should still be exercised when serving mayonnaise-based salads on a buffet table at a picnic or indoor party, when the food must sit at room temperature for long periods of time, the mayonnaise itself is not the culprit; in fact, because of the acid and salt it contains, it may help the salads to stay safe for a little longer time.

Homemade mayonnaise will last in the refrigerator for about a week. The longer it stays in the refrigerator the thinner it will get; the cold seems to congeal the oil and break down the thick emulsion. Julia Child recommends not stirring refrigerated homemade mayonnaise until it has come back to room temperature.

HOW TO JUDGE MAYONNAISE

Tasting Media

Mayonnaise samples should be spooned into clear glass bowls and tasted with plastic spoons.

Color/Eye Appeal

Since no coloring is allowed in commercial mayonnaise, all brands are similar in color: a slightly off-white or eggshell color. Some have more of a waxy sheen than others, a signal that they may have been made with strong emulsifiers in addition to egg yolk.

Taste/Aroma

The great twentieth-century chef Louis Diat once wrote that the appeal of mayonnaise "lies in its smooth delicacy rather than in any pronounced flavor." Even though he was talking about the homemade variety, the same thing holds true for commercial mayonnaise; the best brands taste smooth and mellow with very few identifiable flavors.

Some defects, however, are evident in many brands of mayonnaise. These include excessive sweetness, from the addition of sugar; sourness; too much acidity; and no acid flavor at all (the lemon or vinegar is not apparent). In addition, some mayonnaises taste unpleasantly "eggy" from the use of powdered egg yolk in the mix.

Consistency

A proper commercial mayonnaise should be thick enough to mound on a spoon, without being "plastic" and dense. Inferior mayonnaise is oily rather than rich-tasting.

Aftertaste

Some brands of mayonnaise have an inferior metallic aftertaste, which comes from the type of vinegar used.

CONCLUSIONS AND SUGGESTIONS

Mayonnaise, as many cookbooks counsel, *always* tastes infinitely better when made by hand. They go on to say that since it takes only a minute to make a homemade mayonnaise in a blender, why not whip it up whenever you need some?

As a born-and-bred-American who grew up with mayonnaise in all the right places, I have to admit that there are some dishes that just have to be made with commercial bottled mayonnaise. They may taste *better* if made with a fresh mayonnaise, but they don't taste right. A tuna fish salad sandwich, for example, is just not the same one my mother made for me without that dollop of mayo from a jar.

On the other hand, I've had an outstanding egg salad sandwich at the Moondance Diner in New York City, made with warm freshly boiled eggs, roughly chopped and mixed with delicious tangy homemade mayo, and piled high on toasted challah bread; it was one of the best I've ever had.

I guess the point is that homemade mayonnaise and mayo from a jar can live side by side in the same kitchen. Nine times out of ten I will spend the 60 seconds to make up a batch of homemade, but that tenth time (maybe at midnight after a rough day) I will reach for the jar.

Of the commercial brands of mayonnaise I have sampled, the three best sellers are *very* close in taste: Kraft, Best Foods, and Hellmann's. The Kraft won out because it is much less salty than all of the rest of mayonnaises. Of reduced calorie mayonnaise, Kraft Light is my favorite.

MAKING YOUR OWN MAYONNAISE

Making your own mayonnaise by hand *is* tricky, no matter what many Pollyannish cookbooks try to tell you. Making it in a machine, however—blender or food processor—is not difficult at all. The texture of machine-made mayonnaise is different from handmade: the kind you whip by hand (at the risk of a sore arm the next day) is much thicker and richer than machine-made, more like commercial bottled mayonnaise. Machine-made mayonnaise is really very good, though, and so easy that I don't believe it is worth it to make it by hand, unless Queen Elizabeth II is coming to dinner.

Keep these few things in mind before tackling your own homemade mayonnaise:

• All of the ingredients must be at room temperature. Imagine trying to incorporate stiff cold oil into firm cold egg yolks, and you can see why it's more difficult that way.

• Add the vinegar and lemon juice to the egg yolks halfway through the making of the mayonnaise: the acidity will help prevent the egg yolks from "cooking" with the heat of the beating.

• Add the oil a little at a time in the beginning. Since the purpose of the emulsion is to break the oil into tiny droplets, it is easier at first if you work with only a little bit of oil at a time, incorporating that and then adding more. After about half of the oil has been added, the oil already in the emulsion helps to emulsify the oil you add afterward.

• Traditionally, mayonnaise is made only with egg yolks. But when you make mayonnaise in a blender or food processor, the whole egg is used because the protein in the egg white acts as a stabilizer, to prevent the high speed of the machine's blades from breaking up the emulsion.

• If the mayonnaise you are making never goes beyond the thickness of heavy cream, or the oil refuses to combine with the egg yolk properly, you can rescue it by pouring out all of the "broken" mayonnaise into a glass measuring cup, adding another egg yolk and a teaspoon of dried mustard powder to the blender or food processor, and pouring the first batch of mayonnaise onto the egg yolk, with the machine running, just as you dribbled the oil onto the eggs in the first place. This will almost always rescue a failed mayonnaise.

Some cooks believe that it is impossible to make a successful mayonnaise just before or during a thunderstorm; although scientific tests refute that belief, home cooks prove it time and again.

RECIPE

Homemade Mayonnaise Made in a Machine

If you are at all worried about salmonella you should not try this recipe, since it contains raw eggs. (Makes about 1½ cups)

- **1 whole large egg**
- **1 large egg yolk**
- **1 teaspoon Dijon mustard**
- **¼ teaspoon salt**
- **5 grinds of fresh pepper**
- **1 cup vegetable or olive oil, depending on your preference, and how you will use your mayonnaise (olive oil might be appropriate for vegetable salads and vegetable oil for fruit salads, to name one example)**
- **1 tablespoon vinegar (adjust according to how piquant you like your mayonnaise)**

1. Place the whole egg, egg yolk, mustard, salt, and pepper into the bowl of a food processor or a blender and process for a few seconds.

2. Leaving the machine on, begin to pour in the oil in a very thin stream. When about half of the oil has been added, add the vinegar to the machine (it should still be running throughout this step), and then continue adding the oil mixture in a thin stream until it is all used. Turn the machine off. Taste for seasoning and adjust if necessary.

NOTES: For a delicious mayonnaise sauce to use on fruit salad, add ½ cup fresh whipped cream and a tablespoon of sugar.

If you are going to use the mayonnaise for a salad or a dish that has to stay in the refrigerator for more than a few hours before serving it, add 2 teaspoons powdered unflavored gelatin that you have melted in ¼ cup water over very low heat; cool slightly and stir into the mayonnaise.

MUSTARD

Ounce for ounce, more mustard seed is sold around the world than any other spice, even pepper.

In this country, 69 percent of all households use mustard, and the volume of consumption is increasing. Americans eat 26.5 million gallons annually. Today the average American consumes about half a pound each year, whereas our grandparents used only about 2 tablespoons of mustard per person per year. Sixty-seven percent of the mustard sold in this country is the bright yellow ballpark mustard (French's alone has 33 percent of the market), which largely accompanies the 9 billion hot dogs eaten annually. Another 13 percent consumed is spicy brown mustard (Gulden's type), 13 percent is Dijon, and all other mustards make up 5 percent of the market.

The average Frenchman goes through 2 pounds of mustard in a year, but his mustard is not yellow, nor is it slathered on hot dogs, but rather it is used as a condiment for *charcuterie* or in vinaigrette salad dressings. Of late, Americans are changing their habits somewhat to conform with the French, and are learning to appreciate the complex flavors and the wide variety of sophisticated mustards that are increasingly available in the fancy food marketplace.

The market for ordinary mustards (French's, etc.) has increased by only 2 percent since 1977, but the market for specialty mustards has increased by 24 percent. More and more families are keeping two jars of mustard in the refrigerator—one jar of yellow mustard for the kids and one jar of specialty mustard for the adults. Users of specialty mustards have higher income levels and larger households than the average American.

In 1982, 2.9 million pounds of prepared mustard were imported into the United States, which represented a 16 percent increase over 1981; by far, the majority of these imports came from France, followed by England and Germany. Americans bought $189 million worth of mustard in 1985.

Citizens of New Orleans, Louisiana, and Mobile, Alabama, eat more mustard per capita than any other cities in the country. The Southeast is the region of the country that consumes the most mustard, followed by the Southwest. The Central and Southern United States eat more specialty mustard than other regions.

The United States gets most of its mustard seed from Canada, buying half of Canada's total production. American mustard seed is grown in Montana, North Dakota, California, Oregon, and Washington.

A DASH OF HISTORY

Archaeological investigations and radiocarbon dating have established that mustard was gathered and used as a seasoning from the earliest history of civilized man. As early as 10,000 years ago, it appears, the seeds were chewed with meat to give it extra flavor.

The ancient Greeks and Romans added mustard seed to their stews, and both used the same word for the spice: *sinapis.* One of the most basic sauces of the Romans, *muria,* was made of the brine of fish mixed with mustard powder, and it was used in the way we might use Worcestershire sauce. A similar sauce was used in ancient Gaul, which later became France, and was made with honey, Spanish oil, strong white vinegar, and mustard.

The pre-Christian Romans felt so strongly about mustard that military legions were instructed to plant the seeds in all conquered lands. The word "mustard" can be traced to the Latin *mustum ardens,* which means "burning must," referring to the Roman practice of making a condiment by mixing ground mustard seeds with the leftovers from wine pressing (must).

The roots of modern-day mustard in the West can be traced to an ancient Roman colonial town called Divio, which is today's Dijon in France, where mustard seed took root not only in the soil of the region, but in its soul. This refrain was written in the fourteenth century in Jean Millot's *Proverbes:*

There is no city but Dijon;
there is no mustard but Dijon.

In the Middle Ages, prepared mustard added some interest to the bland and monotonous winter diet of salted meats; by the thirteenth century in England, every self-respecting English town had a "mustarder" who ground seeds to order. Many households of that time had mustard grinders on their tables and used them as we use pepper grinders today.

In 1634, the 23 mustard manufacturers of Dijon received from the government the exclusive right to make prepared mustard for sale within the town. In addition to regulating the quality of the mustard, the new laws stipulated that the manufacturers wear clean and modest clothing. They could also own only one shop in a town, so that if there were complaints as to the quality of the mustard there would be no question as to the source of the bad mustard seed.

In 1713 a mustard-maker named Jean Naigeon came up with the idea that was to make Dijon mustard different from others. The standard formula for prepared mustard had included vinegar. Naigeon replaced the vinegar with *verjus,* unfermented green grape juice; a fitting innovation, since Dijon is also in the heart of one of the important wine districts of France. Naigeon's firm was the ancestor of today's Amora, the largest mustard manufacturer in Dijon.

Also in the eighteenth century, Spanish priests on the west coast of the American continent marked the path of their missionary travels by scattering mustard seeds, which took root readily. This Mission Trail still exists in parts of California and can be identified by the ubiquitous mustard plants.

In 1814 in England, Jeremiah Colman began milling the mustard that has since become world-famous. Perhaps Queen Victoria helped the firm's progress, since Colman's mustard was said to be her favorite. Colman's has long had international ties; in fact, in 1926 it absorbed R. T. French Company of Rochester, New York, where this country's favorite hot dog mustard was—at one time—produced on One Mustard Street.

Mustard's importance as an all-American condiment began in 1904 when Francis French cabled to his brother, "Eureka!" upon discovering that a French's plant supervisor had perfected a mustard that was to be labeled "French's Cream Salad Brand"; the name was chosen because the addition of a little cream turned the mustard into a salad dressing, especially good on potatoes. Today French's sells 5.8 million 16-ounce units each year of what the experts call "ballpark mustard." Fifty-nine percent of Americans prefer French's over all other mustards.

Gulden's, on the other hand, outsells any other mustard on the market in New York City.

VARIETIES OF SEEDS USED IN MUSTARDS

Brown (Brassica juncea)

This type of mustard seed, native to the northern Himalayas, is variously known as Oriental, Asian, Indian, or Brown mustard. There are two types of *Brassica juncea* seeds—brown and yellow. Although the two are not identical, they share the same chemical makeup. In the last few decades, this variety of mustard seed has almost entirely replaced black mustard seeds because it is less expensive. This is the type of mustard used in the piercing Chinese mustards as well as in English mustards.

Yellow (Brassica hirta)

Also known as *Sinapis alba,* yellow or white mustard, this variety is indigenous to southern Europe and the Mediterreanean region. It has a sharp, burning taste without aromatic pungency. Its heat is delayed—released when swallowed and in the throat, making it a good seed to use in flavored mustards because the flavoring prevails in the mouth, while the mustard's spiciness comes as an aftereffect. Almost all American mustards are made from white seeds, which is why they are not as pungent and complex as Dijon and other imported mustards.

This is the type of pale whole mustard seed found in pickling mixtures. It is valuable both for flavoring and for its properties as a preservative because mustard seeds can inhibit the growth of some yeasts, bacteria, and molds.

Black (Brassica nigra)

This seed, also native to Europe and the Mediterranean region, is known as black or brown mustard. This is the most aromatic and pungent of the three mustard varieties. Its heat is felt in the mouth. In bottled mustards, this seed retains its strength and is slower to fade. Unfortunately, because the high-quality seed is so difficult and expensive to harvest, very little of it is being used commercially anymore.

HOW MUSTARD IS MADE

Trying to decipher the differences among mustards by reading labels is of little use. The same four ingredients appear again and again, revealing no clues to their variety: mustard seeds, vinegar (or wine), salt, and spices. Despite the constancy of these ingredients, a vast range in quality and taste among mustards exists. This range results from the several variables among the basic ingredients: the character of the seeds used, the type of vinegar or other liquid that is added, and the spices that are chosen for flavoring. Sugar is also added to some mustards. Formulas vary from producer to producer and are usually highly guarded secrets. Depending on the particular formula employed and on the origin of the mustard seeds, prepared mustard can be sunny and mild, brown and spicy, or superhot.

The Chemistry of Mustard

When mustard seeds are whole, they are odorless and mild. However, when they are ground and mixed with any liquid, a chemical reaction takes place between an enzyme and a glucoside in the mustard, producing a spicy oil.

In the case of black seeds, the enzyme is *myrosin* and it acts on *sinigrin,* the glucoside, yielding *allyl isothiocyanate,* a pungent, irritating oil, which is the same substance that gives bite to radishes and watercress.

In yellow mustard seeds, this enzyme reaction takes place between *myrosin* and the glucoside *sinalbin,* producing *sinalbin mustard oil.* There is little odor in this oil, and it has a less pungent taste than in the black seeds.

The chemical reaction in mustards is weakened by heat and by acids, such as vinegar and wine. The amount of acid in a recipe makes a milder mustard and, along with salt, helps preserve the flavor of the condiment for a longer time. Sugar is another preservative used in mustard.

Mustard seeds are composed of an *outer shell* plus an inner heart that includes the *bran* and the *endosperm,* like a grain of wheat. The bran gives mustard its thickening power, and the endosperm gives mustard its flavor. The endosperm, when ground, is called *mustard flour* or *dry mustard,* the kind found in the spice sections of supermarkets.

If a prepared mustard is made only with mustard flour, it will have a loose consistency. Many American mustards are made with mustard flour, together with thickeners, such as flour, starch, or eggs; manufacturers employ this procedure to save money, the bran being more expensive than fillers.

Manufacturing Mustard

Stricter governmental controls exist for the manufacture of mustard in France than in the United States. For example, the mustard of Dijon must be made only from mustard seeds, white wine and/or wine vinegar, and spices. Manufacturers must not add fillers (such as flour or sugar), amplifiers (such as mustard oil), chemical preservatives, or coloring.

In mustards prepared from whole seeds, the seeds are first dried slightly to encourage a naturally thick compound. The hulls of the mustard seeds are then cracked, and the cracked seeds are soaked in water or in an acid solution (wine, wine vinegar, distilled vinegar, salt, etc.). The mixture is then run through a mill (some manufacturers feel a stone mill is best). If, however, only mustard flour has been used without the seed hulls, a thickener must be added at this point.

After the seeds are milled or thickened, a manufacturer must decide whether to make smooth or grainy mustard. Coarse-grained mustards retain the skins of the seeds, while smooth mustards are strained in order to remove the grainy skins. The mustard is then aerated and homogenized to prevent oxidation and spoilage.

At this point, many mustards are aged in wooden casks; the kind of wood used and the length of time spent in the barrel will affect the flavor of the condiment, in the same way that aging in wood improves a fine wine.

After some American mustards are bottled, they are allowed to mellow during a two-week storage period before being shipped to stores. Because many American mustards are made with yellow mustard seeds, this mellowing period is necessary to tone down the sharpness of the mustard.

VARIETIES OF MUSTARD

English

English, English-style, and Chinese mustards are made with mustard flour (from yellow seeds) and water. (Some companies add fillers and spices.) They are powerful and guaranteed to clear your sinuses. Colman's is an example of a brand of English mustard.

Dijon

Dijon and Dijon-style mustards are smooth, suave, and complex. Traditionally, they are made with wine or vinegar and black or brown seeds. These mustards can range in strength; they are generally richly flavored. Grey Poupon is a Dijon-style mustard, although it is no longer made in the city of Dijon but in Oxnard, California, by Del Monte.

Coarse-Grained

Coarse-grained mustard is also called *à l'ancienne,* farmhouse, or old-fashioned mustard. It has the same consistency as mustard made before the advent of smooth mustard in 1720, with coarsely ground mustard seeds left in the mixture. The flavor of this mustard is usually (but not always) mild, sweet, and musty. It is cheaper to make this kind of mustard than the smooth variety, but, ironically, it usually costs more at the retail level. A widely available brand of coarse-grained mustard is Pommery Meaux.

German

German and German-style mustard is usually very mild and often sweet; not surprisingly, being German, it is excellent with cold meats, wursts, and sausages. This mustard is usually made from mustard flour (again from yellow seeds) and vinegar, with the addition of spices and sweeteners. The two styles of German mustard are Bavarian, which is sweet and dark, and Düsseldorf, which is more spicy. Hengstenberg is a brand of German mustard.

Flavored

Flavored mustard is any kind of mustard to which a significant amount of outside flavoring is added, such as herbs, spices, onions, etc. Many brands of flavored mustards crowd the shelves of gourmet stores; among them is Maille.

Ballpark

The so-called ballpark mustard is the prototypical American condiment; examples are French's and Heinz. It is made with yellow mustard seeds, which are not very pungent, a great deal of vinegar, and turmeric for a strong Day-Glo yellow color.

HANDLING AND STORAGE

A good mustard never goes bad, it just fades away. Because of its high amount of acidity, a mustard will not spoil or turn rancid, but will simply become weaker and lose heat, gradually becoming a shadow of its former self. As mustard gets older, its liquid is forced out of it by a gas that has formed. The liquid gradually oxidizes and forms a dark crust at the lid opening.

A general rule of thumb for mustard's shelf life is 6 months, even if it has not been opened. Unfortunately, much of the mustard imported into the United States has spent almost that much time getting here from its country of origin, not to mention the time it spends subsequently on the American grocer's shelf.

Because mustard is such an inexpensive and showy way of filling a gourmet shop, many store owners order much more than they can sell quickly. Turnover is in the range of four times a year, on average. Therefore, one should be on the lookout for dust on the jars to spot a stale, old mustard.

To keep mustard in top shape, it must be refrigerated after opening. If you have a large family that loves the stuff, buy mustard in big jars, but if you consume it slowly, buy a small amount at a time.

To help keep a jar of mustard fresh after it is opened, cut a thin slice of lemon and place it over the mustard before replacing the lid, or pour a thin layer of oil over the mustard to keep out the air and prevent oxidation.

HOW TO JUDGE MUSTARD

Tasting Media

Each manufacturer has a preference for foods to accompany a mustard tasting. Various examples are salt-free pretzels, bland and unsalted crackers, Jarlsberg cheese, bland meats (such as unspicy ham), celery, and hot dog sections (guess which company prefers the last one?). I have found, however, that in many cases food accompaniments seemed to interfere with the flavor of the mustards.

Color/Eye Appeal

Dryness around the top of a mustard jar when it is opened indicates oxidation from age.

A mustard that is naturally gray (made with yellow seeds without added coloring) or too vibrant (bright yellow/orange from the addition of too much turmeric) can be unappetizing.

Taste/Aroma

Mustards should not taste as strong as pepper, but should be rich and satisfying and should have a flavor that is a combination of good, wholesome ingredients. Mustard should taste good all by itself; it should not be overpowering.

A mustard should not taste of the individual ingredients, such as salt or vinegar. It should have a clean flavor, neither too sweet nor too tart, and should not smell "eggy" when opened.

Consistency

The ratio of liquid to mustard seed will determine a mustard's thickness or thinness. The thinner the mustard, the cheaper. On the other hand, a mustard without emulsifiers has a chance of separating and might need stirring when the jar is opened. Separation is not a sign of a bad mustard, as you might expect, but often an indication that it is less commercially emulsified and more like homemade. A mustard that is perfectly homogenized probably contains emulsifiers.

If a mustard is meant to be smooth, it should be smooth throughout. If it is meant to be rough, it should be consistently and evenly so.

Aftertaste

A slow burn at the back of the throat as an aftertaste is an indication that the mustard is not of top quality. Obviously, chemical or bitter aftertaste is not acceptable.

THE BALLPARK MUSTARDS

I tasted the two biggies, French's and Gulden's, against each other and feel that French's tastes better than Gulden's, which tends to be a little bitter. Heinz' ballpark mustard is sour, bitter, and decidedly inferior.

CONCLUSIONS AND SUGGESTIONS

The majority of the mustards on the market today are of low quality. I feel that I would use very few of them, even if they were given to me for free—the surest test of any food product.

Overall, flavored mustards are the most disappointing. They are often gimmicky and expensive at best, and bizarre and unpalatable at worst. The flavored mustards made in Dijon are exported for the most part, as the French prefer their mustard straight and strong. Rather than buying a flavored mustard, it might be wiser, from a culinary point of view, to add one's own flavorings to mustard to control the strength and quality, not to mention the freshness of the mustard.

Simply add 2 tablespoons of a particular flavoring, such as minced fresh herbs, finely chopped orange or lemon peel, chopped shallots, to 8 ounces (1 cup) of the best Dijon mustard, to create a flavored mustard better than any manufactured variety.

I was happy to discover that the mustards I prefer often offer value as well: some of the best Dijon mustards are also the cheapest, always a pleasant discovery. Recorbet and Old Monk are two examples.

COOKING WITH MUSTARDS

If you like your mustard as strong as possible, use dry powder and mix it with cool water (hot water will make it bitter) to make a paste just before serving. Allow about 15 minutes for the flavor to develop completely; then add flavorings, such as tomato paste or salt.

Mustard, dry or wet, has the useful property of stabilizing an emulsion, such as mayonnaise. A little bit of mustard in the egg yolks when making mayonnaise, for example, will help to prevent them from separating from the oil.

If you're cooking with mustard, add it toward the end of the cooking time if you want to keep its pungency. If you'd like the flavor of mustard, but not the sharpness, add it when beginning a dish.

RECIPES

Dijon-Style Mustard

(Makes about 1 cup)

- **1 1/2 cups dry white wine**
- **1 1/3 cups white-wine vinegar**
- **1/2 cup chopped onion**
- **1/2 cup chopped shallots**
- **1 tablespoon minced garlic**
- **1 bay leaf**
- **8 whole allspice**
- **2 teaspoons salt**
- **2 teaspoons sugar**
- **1 teaspoon dried tarragon**
- **1/2 cup cold water**
- **1 cup dry mustard powder**

1. In a noncorrosive saucepan, combine the white wine, white-wine vinegar, onion, shallots, garlic, bay leaf, allspice, salt, sugar, and tarragon. Boil, uncovered, until reduced by half, about 15 minutes. If you like your mustard hotter, reduce by a little more.

2. While wine mixture is boiling, stir together the water and mustard powder in a glass bowl. Let stand for 10 minutes.

3. After the wine mixture has reduced, pour it through a wire strainer into the reserved mustard paste. Pour mixture back into the saucepan and cook over very low heat, stirring often, for about 20 minutes, until almost as thick as sour cream. Cool, cover, and chill. Mustard will get even thicker as it cools.

NOTE: To make an herb mustard, stir in about 2 tablespoons minced fresh herbs, such as tarragon, basil, parsley, or thyme, as mustard comes off the heat.

Coarse-Grained Mustard

(Makes about 1 cup)

- **1/2 cup cold water**
- **1/2 cup whole yellow mustard seeds**
- **1 tablespoon dry mustard powder**
- **1/2 cup white-wine vinegar**
- **1/2 cup dry white wine**
- **1/2 cup chopped onion**
- **1 teaspoon minced garlic**
- **1 teaspoon salt**
- **1 teaspoon sugar**
- **1 bay leaf**
- **1/2 teaspoon powdered allspice**

1. Mix together in a glass bowl the water, mustard seeds, and mustard powder. Set aside for at least 3 hours.

2. In a noncorrosive saucepan, combine the vinegar, wine, onion, garlic, salt, sugar, bay leaf, and allspice. Simmer, uncovered, over moderate heat until mixture is reduced by half, about 10 minutes.

3. Pour the reduced mixture through a wire strainer onto the mustard-seed mixture. Mix it in a blender or a food processor until it is coarsely ground.

4. Pour the mustard back into the saucepan and cook it over very low heat, stirring, until it is thick, about 10 more minutes. Cool, cover, and chill.

TWO EASY MUSTARD DISHES

Fish with Mustard Coating

Mix together mayonnaise and your favorite mustard in equal proportions. Spread this mixture onto fillets of a white-fleshed fish and put the fillets under the broiler for just a few minutes, until the fish is cooked through and the top is golden brown. The mustard and mayonnaise mixture becomes almost souffléed and makes a delicious topping for the fish.

Simple Deviled Chicken

Spread a flattened boneless chicken breast with a thin coat of mustard, sprinkle with fresh bread crumbs, and broil for 1 or 2 minutes, until golden brown.

OLIVE OIL

Waverley Root, the eminent food authority, observed that the food of a region is shaped by the fat it is cooked in more than by any other ingredient. Some of the most delicious food in the world comes from places where olive oil is traditionally used for cooking: Provence in France, Italy, the Catalan section of Spain, and the Middle East.

Until about 20 years ago, Americans had to be content with eating authentic versions of dishes from these regions only in their native countries, largely because the outstanding olive oils with which they were made were not available here. Fortunately, the situation changed for the better in America. The new gastronomic era brought to our shores some delicious olive oils. Importers sought oils made by small, local producers in Spain, France, and Italy, and these are now available in shops all across the United States. Ironically, many cooks in countries that have traditionally used olive oil have switched to blander, cheaper vegetable oils that are mass-produced and widely advertised. In Italy, for example, the per capita consumption of vegetable oil was 5.5 kilograms in 1964, and almost double (10.4 kilograms) in 1980, while the consumption of olive oil remained almost exactly the same throughout those years.

The majority of the olive oil imported into this country (88.1 percent) comes from Italy and Spain. Total figures for olive oil imports from these two countries in 1994 were 244 thousand pounds of oil. Overall, Spain is the largest producer of olive oil in the world.

In 1983, Americans consumed almost 9 million gallons of olive oil, both imported and domestic, which represents a 30 percent increase over consumption in 1980, just three years earlier. In the early 1980s, per capita yearly consumption in the United States was about 5 ounces (a little more than half a cup), which was minimal compared to French per capita annual consumption of 1½ gallons, 3 gallons for Spain, and 5 gallons for Greece. Since that time, American olive oil consumption has ballooned to ½ liter (about two cups) per person, and European consumption has grown by about 1 percent per year.

California produces 99 percent of the olives grown in America, thus all of its olive oil. Total California olive-oil production accounts for less than 5 percent of the olive oil we use in this country.

Two thirds of all the olive oil used in the United States is refined in much the same way as vegetable and corn oils; much of it is made by one of four companies: Berio, Bertolli, Progresso, and Pompeian. Extra virgin is the second best-selling category with about 17 percent of the volume, followed by "light" with 15 percent.

A DASH OF HISTORY

The olive tree was first cultivated more than 5,000 years ago in Syria, Lebanon, and Israel. In those times, sesame oil was the primary cooking fat and olive oil was used as a cosmetic and an unguent. Athletes and wealthy people were massaged with it, others used it to anoint hair and bodies for warmth and cleansing. Still today, the Roman Catholic church uses olive oil to anoint bishops, to baptize babies, and during Extreme Unction to bless sick people. Queen Elizabeth II was anointed with olive oil during her coronation.

In the early days, olive oil was also thought to have medicinal qualities. In recent times, modern science has substantiated this belief by proving that olive oil contains salicylic acid, which is the main ingredient in aspirin.

From ancient Syria, the cultivation of the olive tree spread to the rest of the Mediterranean basin. Around the sixth century B.C., the Greeks exported the knowledge of making olive oil to areas that are now parts of Italy and southern France. At around the same time, the Phoenicians took olive oil to Spain and northern Africa. After that time, while olive oil was made in many of the lands around the Mediterranean, it was also still imported to many of those lands from Crete.

Once olive oil began to be used as a food, it became a vital substance in the countries where it remains a significant cooking ingredient today. The writings of many ancient Romans tell us that olive oil was extracted from olives then in almost exactly the same way as it is done today. The working classes of the time, as well as the rich, counted olive oil as a prominent part of the diet.

In the Middle Ages, olive oil lost favor when lard began to be used as a cooking fat. Spain, however, was occupied by the Moors, who didn't eat pork products, and so olive oil remained in common use there.

Eventually, the tide turned back to olive oil. John Evelyn, an English writer of the seventeenth century, felt olive oil was "an ingredient so indispensably and highly necessary be very clean, not high colour'd, not yellow, but with an eye rather of a pallid olive green, smooth, light, and pleasant on the tongue . . . fit to allay the tartness of vinegar and other acids."

A century later, America's Thomas Jefferson so esteemed olive oil that he tried, without success, to cultivate the olive tree at Monticello. He loved olive oil "because there is such an infinitude of vegetables which it renders a proper and comfortable nourishment."

At the same time, around the turn of the nineteenth century, olives were introduced to a part of America with a more suitable climate than Jefferson's Virginia. Franciscan monks planted the mission variety of olive trees in California, and some of these original trees are still alive today, mostly in Butte, Calaveras, and Stanislaus counties.

Right after World War II, over 70 olive-oil factories existed in California. Foreign olive oils, whose production was and still is subsidized by foreign governments, began to come into the American market in great quantities, and American companies could not compete with their low prices. Today only about nine of these olive oil companies remain in California, and they bottle olive oil under several different labels. Lately, though, several new producers of California olive oil have emerged.

During his lifetime (in the twentieth century), the controversial American author Henry Miller said that the four cornerstones of good health are garlic, yogurt, honey, and olive oil. Considering that Miller lived an active life to the very old age of 88, perhaps he was right!

In January 1985 the worst freeze of the century struck the area of Tuscany in northern Italy, where many of the world's excellent olive oils are made and one of the northernmost places in the world where olives are grown. By summer of

1985, the Italian government reported that 90 percent of Tuscany's olive trees had been destroyed by the freeze. The area recovered from the devastation, and new trees are now producing.

HOW OLIVE OIL IS MADE

It is vital to the understanding of olive oil to know that it is the only oil that is extracted from a fruit rather than a grain, seed, or nut. Darrell Corti, one of the most knowledgeable olive-oil importers in the United States, feels that olive oil should be regarded as "wine made from olives," rather than an oil to be grouped with seed oils. This helps to understand the complicated production of olive oil and how it should be handled.

The most important olive-oil-producing countries in the world are Algeria, E.E.C. countries, Egypt, France, Greece, Italy, Libya, Morocco, Portugal, Spain, Tunisia, and Turkey. All of these countries are members of the International Olive Oil Council (I.O.O.C.), an active government-sponsored agency which sets regulations.

About 60 types of olive trees exist, but flavors and characteristics of olives are much more varied because of the variation in climate and soil around the world. In this respect, and in many others, olives and their cultivation share another commonality with grapes and viticulture. A saying in Italy attests to this: "Where there's good wine, there's good oil," which refers to the fact that both grapes and olives grow well in a similar climate. In fact, many Italian Chianti vineyards grow olive trees in among the vines and produce some of the best olive oil in the world, notably Badia a Coltibuono and Frescobaldi.

The olive tree is a hardy tree, which requires a lot of sunlight and heat but not much rain. Every other year the tree produces a small crop; this is because the fruit appears only on the new wood that has grown in the previous year. Pruning imparts a regular and consistent annual rather than the olive's biennial natural tendency.

One of the complications in the production of olive oil is in the harvesting. In Tuscany, as in other parts of the world, old-fashioned olive trees, some of them hundreds of years old, are grown for oil. In the southern part of Italy, however, a hybrid olive shrub that grows low to the ground has been developed to make harvesting easier. Harvesting machines (sometimes nut-harvesting machines imported from California) are used on these new shrubs, and the yield is very high, but the oil is not of top quality.

The olives for the best oil must be picked by hand as they ripen. Pickers use special plastic harvesting rakes to pull the olives off the trees so they fall onto nets that have been spread on the ground. Another device that is commonly used is a harvesting glove that allows the pickers to comb the trees to pull the olives off the branches, like combing burrs out of a horse's tail. Olives for good oil are sometimes stripped by hand from the branches and put into canvas or wicker baskets that harvesters wear around their waists.

Poor-quality oil is made from olives that have been allowed to overripen and fall to the ground. In the Apulia province of Italy, which produces the largest amount of olive oil in Italy, harvesters beat the trees until the olives fall to the ground. Oil made from these bruised olives contains a great deal of acidity and becomes rancid more quickly than oil made from olives harvested by hand. Therefore, very often these fallen olives are used to make oil that is later refined to remove the off-flavors. (One expert Italian oil maker comments: "When an olive falls it is dead. Obviously.") It is easier to make olive oil from olives that have fallen to the ground, but the best olive oil is made from olives that are picked.

Almost all good olive oils are a blend of not only varieties of olives, but also of olives at various stages of ripeness. The harvest takes place over a period of weeks, sometimes months, beginning in the fall. It takes 1,300 to 2,000 olives to make 1 quart of olive oil.

Olive oil made from olives that are just beginning to ripen by turning from green to purple is bright green in color and strong and peppery in flavor. Its flavor can be grassy-tasting and quite strong. It is very difficult to harvest green olives, as they are not easy to see against the green leaves until they begin to ripen and turn darker.

When olives ripen, they turn purple-black. Overripe olives are black. The oil from ripe olives is less piquant, more subtle, than that from the green olives. Oil from ripe and overripe olives also tastes more oily than oil from underripe olives.

Olive oil can be pressed on the farm where the olives are grown; some producers have their own presses, called *frantoio* in Italian. Alternatively, an olive grower can take his olives to a small local co-operative for pressing; Poggio al Sole oil is made in this way. A third procedure, used by large commercial processors like Berio and Bertolli, is to gather olives from many sources and press them in huge mechanized plants.

Producers of cheap oils will store their olives for long periods so that pressing can be stretched out over time. Since these oils are invariably refined, the off-flavors that develop in storage are eventually processed out.

If the olives are to be pressed on-site, they are first washed in water and then ground, pits and flesh together, into a paste by stainless-steel rollers revolving at little more than 40 rpm. After crushing, the olives are stirred to make a paste, and sometimes, if the weather is very cold (as the pressing usually takes place in December), the paste is heated in some way.

Heat is a natural enemy to good olive oil. Sometimes the room in which olive oil is being pressed is heated in order to make sure the olive paste is not stiff with cold. For the same reason, sometimes hot water is added to the olives while they are being pressed, or the paste itself is heated. The best oil comes from olive paste that has not been allowed to heat to over 25°C. (75°F.). Some olives are pressed at 30°C. (86°F.), which produces a good, if not great, olive oil. Some olives are pressed at temperatures as high as 80°C. (176°F.) in order to extract a higher percentage of oil from the olives, and the resulting oil is of inferior quality, with very little olive flavor. This oil is almost always later chemically refined.

The olive paste is spread out on round hemp mats that are stacked on top of each other with metal discs between them. Then, this stack of mats is pressed to release the oil.

The hemp mats that are used in pressing are used more than once and must be cleaned thoroughly before being used again, as olives will pick up any off-flavor or smell that lingers nearby. For example, if someone smokes a cigarette or if a gasoline-powered motor is being used in the vicinity of the olive press, the oil may be flavored by the extraneous odors. In the North of Italy and in France, cleanliness is religiously practiced during the pressing process; in some places, however, producers are not as rigorous about cleanliness and their oil is not always of top quality.

In factories, the olives are stored for a time (short or long, depending on the factory), then washed. The olives are then crushed between two stone or metal crushers. The olive paste is put into pressing bags that are hydraulically pressed under 300 to 400 tons of pressure.

No matter where or how the olives are pressed, if the olives are pressed for the first time, the process is called *first-pressed*. The liquid that results from the pressing is olive oil and water mixed together. To separate the two, the liquid is placed in a centrifuge; pure oil comes out one side and water and other waste comes out the other.

First-pressed oil is actually quite cloudy just after pressing, because it contains infinitesimal particles of skin, pulp, and pit and water (called *mosto oleoso* in Italian) suspended in the liquid. Sometimes this oil is bottled immediately and sold (but not necessarily marked) as "unfiltered and undecanted." Many experts feel this oil is the best: fresh, fruity, and robust, yet others believe filtering contributes to a fresher, cleaner taste. Some first-pressed oil is poured into large terra-cotta urns, called *orci* in Italian, so that the particles can settle to the bottom during the winter months before bottling. This is "decanted but unfiltered" oil and is clearer and lighter in flavor than that which is undecanted.

Most of the first-pressed oil is filtered through cotton cheesecloth or synthetic paper canvas to remove the vegetable particles. Filtering through cotton cheesecloth, the most widely used method, produces a better-tasting oil than filtering through synthetic paper canvas. Olive-oil producers say that an oil has "lost its nerve" if it has been filtered through synthetic materials, meaning that it no longer has a balanced, rounded flavor. Any oil that has been filtered looks clearer, is more light-bodied, and has an extended shelf life.

Sixteen to 22 percent of an olive is made up of oil, depending on the olive variety, its degree of ripeness, and the year in which it is harvested. Only about 30 percent of the oil extracted by the first pressing can be used as is after the pressing, and bottled as unrefined oil. The remainder is refined. The pulp that remains from this refining process is called *sansa* in Italy and Spain. Heat and water are applied during a second (and possibly third) pressing to remove the rest of the oil, and oil made from *sansa* is always refined.

When olive oil is refined, it is handled in the same way as vegetable oil, to render it neutral and tasteless. It is first treated with sodium hydroxide to bring the acidity level to 0 percent, then it is heated and filtered through charcoal or through an earth filter to remove the color. It is sometimes distilled, or treated with acetone and methanol to neutralize the flavor completely. After this complicated refining process, the chemicals that have been used must be eliminated from the oil by the use of filters or a centrifuge, which spins the chemicals out of the oil. Since the resulting oil is completely colorless, odorless, and tasteless and contains 0 percent acidity, very often this refined oil is mixed with a little bit of nonrefined oil (first-pressed oil) to give it some olive flavor and a little bit of acidity, in much the same way vanilla is added to a custard to flavor it.

Label Language

After an oil is made in an I.O.O.C. member country, it must undergo two tests of quality. The objective test determines the acidity level of the oil. If the oil qualifies as having a minimum amount of acidity to remain unrefined (see "Label Designations" chart, page 81), then it is submitted to a further, subjective taste test to assure that it has "impeccable odor and flavor." Only if an oil has passed these two tests can it legally be labeled "extra virgin," or "virgin." ("Virgin" olive oil is not exported to the United States. Thirty-four percent of all of the olive oil imported into the U.S. is extra virgin.) All of the oil that does not qualify to be labeled "extra virgin," etc., according to I.O.O.C. regulations, is then sent to be refined.

Some olive oil contains too much natural acidity to qualify as "extra virgin" or "virgin" (see chart, page 81), so to render it edible, it must be refined in the same way as vegetable oil is refined, which makes it completely tasteless. (Think of the flavor or lack of flavor of corn oil or vegetable oil available in the supermarket.) Then, in some cases, a small amount of nonrefined virgin or extra virgin oil is added to give the refined oil a bit of olive oil flavor. These oils are labeled "olive oil" or olive pomace oil (or the foreign equivalents). They contain neutral refined oil, often pressed from the pits and pulp of low-grade olives, mixed with from 5 to 25 percent virgin oil; by law, the final product cannot contain more than 1.6 percent acidity. These refined oils account for 64 percent of the oil imported into this country. Some of the companies that mass-produce these refined oils, such as Bertolli and Berio, are capitalizing on America's awareness of extra virgin olive oil by marketing extra virgin versions of their oils.

Deliberate obfuscation also exists, as in the case of manufacturers who place meaningless phrases such as "extra first" and "extra #1" and "cold pressed" on their labels. Eugenio Pozzolini of Dean & DeLuca Imports warns of olive oils simply labeled "imported," and of oils labeled "packed in Italy" rather than "product of Italy"; they could be low-quality Spanish or Tunisian oils which are refined and repacked under Italian labels.

United States labeling regulations for olive oil made in this country do not concern the acidity level of the product. They require that a product labeled "virgin olive oil" must be from the first pressing of the olives without further processing. Any oil that is a blend of refined and virgin oil may be labeled "olive oil" but not "virgin."

The United States government has no specifications for extra virgin oil, but many American oils labeled "virgin" qualify as extra virgin with respect to acidity.

When trying to find a good olive oil among a forest of bottles with confusing labels, look for one that has the grower's name on it, or the district from which it comes; and the date on which the olives were harvested; the more specific the better, just as with wine. Even a listing of a place of origin on a bottle of olive oil can be misleading, since it may designate where the oil was pressed, rather than where the olives were grown. However, when a small farm is listed, where they press their own oil and no facilities for any but a first pressing are likely to be available, you are reasonably assured of the real thing.

The important words to look for on a bottle of olive oil are "bottled in the country of origin" (or words to that effect). These words, in addition to "extra virgin" if the oil is imported and "virgin" if the oil is made in the United States, are your indication that the olive oil has a low amount of acidity and a chance of tasting like the olives from which it was made.

You can check to see if an oil has been refined by refrigerating a small amount. Refined oil will remain clear and liquid as if it were at room temperature, while nonrefined oil will become opaque and cloudy, and form light green gobules; it will become clear again when brought to room temperature.

The region of Tuscany in Italy produces some of the best olive oils in the world. The olives often come from trees planted in among the renowned vineyards. In 1989, a group was formed in Chianti to regulate the quality of locally-produced olive oil. It is called Laudemio and 51 different estates are members. Only a few of these olive oils are available in the American market, notably Laudemio Frescobaldi and Laudemio Antinori. Any oils that are part of this consortium will bear the Laudemio name prominently on the label. By the same token, if you see the words *denominacio d'origen* on a bottle of olive oil from Spain, as on the Siurana brand, it has come from the Catalan

LABEL DESIGNATIONS FOR IMPORTED OLIVE OIL

	ITALY	FRANCE	SPAIN	ENGLISH (translation*)
Unrefined Olive Oil:				
Up to 1% acidity	*extra vergine (or vierge extra)*	*extra vierge*	*verge extra*	*extra virgin*
Up to 3.3% acidity	*vergine*	*vierge*	*verge*	*virgin*
Refined, Neutral-flavored Olive Oil:				
Possibly with the addition of 5 to 25% virgin oil for flavor; up to 1% acidity	*olio di oliva*	*huile d'olive*	*aceite de oliva*	*olive oil*
	sansa e olio di oliva		*sansa y aceite de oliva*	*olive pamace oil*

* These are the words that might appear on a label of *imported* olive oil as translations of the foreign words; they do not apply to American-made olive oil, for which there are different labeling regulations not pertaining to acidity.

section and has less than 0.5 percent acidity (less than the maximum 1.0 percent for regular extra virgin).

Light or extra-light olive oil is so-called because it has almost no olive flavor whatsoever; it is designed for the American consumer who wants to cook with olive oil but doesn't like the taste of it. Generally, it is refined olive oil to which a very small amount of extra virgin has been added.

HANDLING AND STORAGE

Once you get a wonderful bottle of olive oil into your own kitchen, it's important to know how to keep it fresh and delicious. You can save money by buying in large quantities, but the oil will turn rancid quickly if it is exposed to heat, air, and light, especially if it is the unrefined variety. To avoid this, decant olive oil into smaller, preferably opaque containers and use one, keeping the others in a cool, dark place. The practice of many cooks of keeping a bottle of olive oil handy next to the stove is bound to cause the oil to become rancid very quickly.

Experts caution against refrigerating olive oil; the condensation that results from the cold in the refrigerator causes water droplets to form on the inside of the bottle and drop into the oil, hastening randicity. Continual cooling and reheating of the oil also has an effect on general quality. The best place to keep olive oil is in a wine cellar, or in the same dark, cool spot as you would store potatoes.

When selecting an oil, keep in mind that oils packed in screw-top bottles will last longer than those closed with a cork or a plastic stopper. If unopened, you can expect that an oil in a screw-top bottle will remain fresh and safe to use for 2 years; otherwise, count on about a year, if unopened. If an oil has been opened, it will stay fresh for about 2 months, a month or two longer if in a screw-top bottle.

Vintage dating of olive oils is useful so that you won't buy an oil that is more than a year old, although vintage dating does not necessarily connote high quality, as is sometimes the case with wine.

If your olive oil has gone off, it will smell and taste rancid—sharp, bitter, and stinging. Before rancidity sets in, however, the oil will become stale and will taste flat.

Often olive oil fresh from the presses will taste strong and sharp, sometimes with a piquant bite which hits you in the back of your throat, especially if it has been made with a large percentage of unripe olives. Aficionados of rustic, earthy oils love this piquancy. After a few months, however, the strength of an oil fades and it becomes more mellow.

Sometimes olive oil has a cloudy layer at the bottom of a bottle if it has been sitting on a shelf for a long time. This is caused by crystals of saturated fatty acids, which settle to the bottom. This does not affect the flavor of the oil and it is still perfectly safe to use.

HOW TO JUDGE OLIVE OIL

Tasting Media

A professional olive-oil buyer tastes oil raw, but some use chunks of bread to taste olive oil, although cold boiled potatoes are sometimes used. Those buyers who go to olive groves to test the oil just as it comes out of the press often pour a little of the oil into their palms and rub their hands together to generate heat, then they bring their cupped hands to the nose to smell the oil.

To taste at home, you can use chunks of bread, celery sticks, and spoons made of plastic, so that metal doesn't interfere with the taste of the oils.

Color/Eye Appeal

Depending on the state of ripeness of the olives when they were pressed, and the type of olives used, the color of an olive oil ranges from deep bottle green to almost clear white. Oil pressed from unripe olives has a green, and sometimes deep green, color. Ripe olives produce a straw-colored oil. On the other hand, oil that is *too* pale and almost white will most likely taste too bland. Oil that is freshly pressed will be darker in color than oil that was pressed months earlier and has faded.

The depth of color of the oil is not necessarily an indication of its strength of flavor, although it can be a rough guideline. Color can be misleading, however. For example, some manufacturers press the leaves along with the olives to extract a deep green color from the chlorophyll. The chlorophyll also acts as an antioxidant, making the oil last a little longer before becoming rancid.

An oil that is crystal clear has been filtered; one that is not clear is probably an unfiltered oil which still has tiny particles of fruit suspended throughout. Rather than being a defect, many experts feel that this kind of oil is superior to filtered oil. The better the oil, the longer it takes to settle and become clear because the particles are so tightly bound.

Taste/Aroma

The mechanics of an olive-oil tasting are much the same as with wine. First the oil is swirled around the glass and the color and body are checked. Then the taster smells the oil in the glass. The olive oil is then either sipped and swished around on the tongue, or tasted from a piece of bread, or both.

Some general defects exist in the taste of bad olive oil: rancidity, oxidation, greasy (or fatty), leaving an unpleasant coating in the mouth; bitter; sour; bland (a common problem with the pure oils).

Consistency

Some olive oils are very thin and runny, especially those that are refined. Some are so thick that their texture is unpleasant. A good olive oil should have a certain amount of body, thicker than a refined vegetable oil. The best olive oils have a rich texture that is not viscous or fatty.

Aftertaste

The piquancy of a freshly pressed olive oil that lingers after the oil is swallowed, called *pizzica* in Italian, is considered desirable. For some, however, especially those new to the genre, it can overpower the flavor of the oil. It is an acquired taste.

CONCLUSIONS AND SUGGESTIONS

The proper flavor of an olive oil is a highly subjective judgment. If you like your food to be robust, bold, and pronounced in flavor, if you can't get enough moussaka or chili, for example, there are olive oils for you. If, however, your palate is happier with subtly flavored dishes, such as poached salmon, there are gentle and fine olive oils you might prefer. Both heavy and light olive oils are a matter of style, often one of national character.

Although there are glaring exceptions to these general classifications, imported olive oils can be described thusly:

Italian

Italian oils, notably those from the center and north, are the finest oils in the world. They are more sophisticated than oil from other countries, but also more difficult to get used to if you are just beginning to learn about first-pressed olive oils. Northern Italian oils are generally heavy, robust, often with a peppery flavor, while southern Italian oils are strongly flavored with an oily consistency, instant taste recognition, and very little aftertaste. Colavita is a reliable brand.

Spanish

Olive oil from Spain comes in many different styles; some taste "green" or herby, some are fruity with the peppery afterbite characteristic of Tuscan oils, some taste nutty. Siurana is an extra-virgin standout; Pompeiian is also good, the best of the supermarket oils.

French

Because French olive oils are usually pressed from ripe olives, they are golden in color and have a light body; they taste fruity, sometimes with nutty overtones. French oils are not nearly as thick and viscous as oils from other countries, and also not as complex in flavor. French oil is good for homemade mayonnaise, and a good oil to use if you like subtle food and/or you are just beginning to use first-pressed olive oils. Old Monk is a good brand of French oil.

Some French oils imported into the United States carry designations of *douce* (sweet) and *fruité* (fruity). These are voluntary label words that indicate whether the oil was pressed from ripe or unripe olives. *Fruité* olive oil has been pressed from unripe olives and will be stronger in color and taste than oil labeled *douce.*

Greek

The Greek oils we get in this country are generally not of the extra virgin, first-pressed variety, but some of the humbler Greek oils can be of a higher quality than the lesser grade oils of other countries. They are strongly redolent of olives, full of character, and very hearty, as well as thick in consistency.

The Greek label language for raw oil—"agourelaio"—denotes oil that has been pressed from green olives; it is dark green in color and strongly redolent of olives. An example of a superb extra-virgin oil of this type is Peloponnese.

California

I don't think California oils come up to the level of quality of imported oils, with the exception of Sciabica, a company that bottles under its own label and for others as well.

COOKING AND USING OLIVE OIL

A top-quality first-pressed olive oil is used in Europe almost as a condiment, and we have learned to do the same here. Italian food expert Franco Tommaso Marchi, referring to the way Italians use olive oil, wrote, "Olive oil? It's like parsley!" It is placed on the dinner table and poured over cooked vegetables, pasta, salads, even good crusty bread, in order to appreciate its flavor, its aroma, its almost winelike communal effect, rather than simply used as a lubricant or a cooking fat.

Many experts feel that the traditional French way of making a vinaigrette salad dressing—with vinegar, mustard, salt, and pepper—kills the taste of a top-quality extra virgin olive oil. Because a good olive oil has such integrity of flavor on its own, the Italians often dress a lettuce salad with olive oil and a little salt, nothing more; if they add vinegar at all, they only add a few drops, but certainly no other distracting flavors.

The smoking point of olive oil, the temperature at which the oil gives the first trace of smoke when it is heated, is almost as high as peanut oil, which smokes at 420°F. So you can panfry or deep-fry foods in olive oil without fear of burning, as was previously believed, as long as the temperature is carefully monitored and is kept below 400°F. Use an electric frying pan or an electric deep-fryer with a thermostat for the sake of convenience. Whole small fish and batter-dipped vegetables are particularly delicious fried in olive oil.

RECIPE

Eggplant Spread

Many countries have a similar dish, and it is often called "Poor Man's Caviar." It is stylish and delicious when served as an hors d'oeuvre with all of the traditional caviar garnishes: minced onion, minced parsley, chopped hard-cooked egg white and egg yolk, sour cream, lemon wedges, and toast points. It can also be served as a canapé on slices of cucumber, or used as a dip for raw vegetable "spatulas," or simply with wedges of pita bread. (Makes 3 cups)

2 **medium-size eggplants, about 2 pounds**
5 **large or 6 medium-size garlic cloves, or 2 elephant garlic cloves**
3/4 **cup full-bodied extra virgin olive oil**
juice of 1 lemon, or to taste
salt and freshly ground pepper

1. Put the eggplants and garlic cloves, both unpeeled, on one or two baking pans; cake pans or pie tins work nicely. Pour a little of the $^3/_4$ cup olive oil over the garlic. Put the baking pan(s) into a 325°F. oven for approximately 1 hour, or until eggplants have become wrinkled and collapse when pressed. Baste the garlic cloves with the oil in the pan a couple of times during the cooking time. If garlic begins to brown too much, remove it from the oven and continue to cook eggplant. When cooked, garlic should be soft but no browner than golden brown. Let eggplant and garlic stand until cool enough to handle. Reserve the basting oil in the pan.

2. Cut eggplants into halves, scoop out soft flesh including seeds, and put into a large mixing bowl. Squeeze garlic pulp out of the skins onto the eggplant. Add lemon juice and salt and pepper to taste. Begin to mash ingredients together with a fork. While stirring, drizzle in the olive oil to make a purée. Also add the reserved olive oil from the baking pan. Adjust seasoning to taste.

HOT SAUCE

The baton has passed from *nouvelle cuisine* (small portions, exotic ingredients, artful arrangements) to *down-home cooking,* American style. That means heaps of homemade mashed potatoes, red-eye gravy, pot roast, barbecued chicken and ribs, Tex-Mex, chili con carne, jambalaya. A staple ingredient that has profited from this trend is hot sauce, the ubiquitous red American sauce seen next to the salt and pepper on many southern and southwestern dining tables, a product technically known as Louisiana-style hot sauce.

The term is apt, because this sauce originated in Louisiana over 125 years ago. Some say it was the Mexicans coming over the border who introduced the gringos to the fiery condiment. It is distinguished from other hot sauces in that it has only three main components—hot chile peppers, vinegar, and salt. The "heat" and flavor vary from brand to brand.

As befits such a volatile condiment, controversy rages over which of these Louisiana hot sauces is the best. They are often called *Tabasco,* in much the same way that tissues are often called *Kleenex;* both terms refer to specific brand names and not the entire genre, which gives work to batteries of lawyers to keep the distinction clear in the minds of typical consumers when they go to the supermarket.

In Louisiana, and all over Texas, Southern California, Georgia, and other parts of the South, especially in those states where barbecue is popular, bottles of this sauce sit on every home and restaurant table. They are used to flavor "everything except dessert," an expression I've heard from more than one Southerner. One Louisiana native even demonstrated to me the technique of casually shaking a bottle over an already dressed salad while having a lengthy conversation with one's neighbor.

The popularity of hot sauce is not confined to the South. Hot sauce is also a favorite condiment in other areas where there is a significant Spanish-speaking and/or Black population: Miami, Chicago, Cleveland, New York. Buffalo, New York, uses phenomenal amounts of Louisiana hot sauce, for its most famous regional dish, Buffalo Chicken Wings (page 90). The north central states consume the least amount of hot sauce.

The Japanese are the biggest foreign consumers of Louisiana hot sauce (perhaps they use it on Western-style spaghetti, postulates Japanese food expert Elizabeth Andoh), followed by the West Germans, who even have designed elegant silver hot-sauce holders for the table service. Arabs buy Louisiana hot sauce by the shipload.

It is not uncommon for an Arab to use a 3-ounce bottle of hot sauce on a single portion of beans, sopping up the remains with bread.

Louisiana-style hot sauce can be found in over half of all American homes. Its use has increased significantly over the past 10 years, partly because of the resurgence of interest in hearty foods; Americans seem to be able to stand the "heat" more than they used to. The McIlhenny company, which makes Tabasco, reports that it receives complaints that its sauce isn't as "hot" as it used to be. In fact, the sauce is as strong, but apparently consumers' tolerance is greater.

The biggest months for hot sauce consumption are November and December, chitlin season. May and June are also big, probably because of barbecuing.

A technical and very appealing explanation for the popularity of hot sauce in general may lie in the fact that Capsicum peppers are from a psychotropic plant, which means that, according to the book *Hot Peppers* by Richard Schweid (Madrona Press, 1980), "they heighten the awareness of a given moment by disrupting normal thought patterns and attention spans. Mundane, temporal consciousness is superseded by the sharp, intense rush of the sensation, and attention is focused on the mouth, on the 'heat' and food." Other psychotropic plants in the same family are nutmeg, poppies, and psilocybin mushrooms.

The physical jolt from the capsaicin in hot peppers also has an effect on the digestive system: it helps in the secretion of saliva and gastric juices. Perhaps because of this fact, hot peppers are known to counteract the negative effect of alcohol (commonly known as a hangover), which may explain why a Bloody Mary is often prescribed as a morning-after medication drink.

A DASH OF HISTORY

Louisiana hot sauce began with McIlhenny's Tabasco, first sold commercially in 1868. That was an eventful year in the history of American food: the Libby company was founded, Fleischmann began to produce compressed yeast, White Rock Spring first bottled its water, and the first regularly scheduled dining car went into service.

Edmund McIlhenny and his family returned to their homestead on Avery Island in southern Louisiana after the Civil War. Their land was in disarray; only a few things survived the Yankee invasion, including the pepper plants in the kitchen garden, descendants of seeds given to McIlhenny by a friend returning from the Mexican-American War of 1846–47.

The outlook during the days of the Restoration of the South was bleak; food was scarce, and the financial structure of the South had been destroyed. In a search for income-generating activity, McIlhenny began to bottle and sell hot sauce made from the Mexican-origin peppers. He named the sauce Tabasco, which means "damp earth" in Spanish.

Tabasco's success was meteoric. In 1870, McIlhenny patented his process for making the pepper sauce and in 1872 opened a London office to accommodate the flood of foreign business. Today Tabasco is sold in almost 100 countries. The McIlhenny firm, which is still family-run, can make as many as 180,000 bottles of Tabasco a day.

The second biggest-selling sauce is Frank's Redhot!, first made by Jacob Frank during World War I in Louisiana. In 1977, Frank Foods was bought by Durkee Foods. Although it's tough to find the name Frank's on the label because the print is so small, the sauce is still affectionately known as "Frank's" to devotees, notably Buffalonians, who swear by it for their chicken wings. Frank's sauce uses cayenne peppers, also known as Louisiana Sunlongs.

HOW HOT SAUCE IS MADE

Far more than half the Louisiana-style hot sauce sold in America today is made by the McIlhenny company; they sell over 100 million bottles annually in the United States. Since this kind of hot sauce was invented by McIlhenny, what follows is an explanation of their methods. Almost all of the other Louisiana-style hot sauces are also made in Louisiana, many in New Iberia, just a few miles from McIlhenny's Avery Island. Other brands use similar techniques for manufacture, with a few minor variations.

To begin, peppers are picked in the early fall. Only the red ripe peppers are used so that the final hot sauce will have an authentic red color. Some of the peppers are grown in Louisiana; many are grown in South and Central America. The picking is an arduous business, done by hand by stoop labor, pickers whose hands are accustomed to the burning sensation of the fiery peppers.

After picking, the peppers are then crushed and put into white oak barrels with salt equal to 8 percent of the weight of the peppers; this mixture is called a *mash.* A wooden cover into which five small holes have been drilled is put on top of each barrel. A layer of salt is spread on the cover of each barrel and the mash is left to ferment. Fermentation slows during cool weather, when the salt dries and it becomes a seal for the barrel.

This fermentation, which is much like the curing of sauerkraut, takes place over a period of 1 to 3 years, depending on the brand of sauce. McIlhenny Tabasco cures its sauce for 3 years, Frank's for 2 to 3 years, Cajun Chef for 1 year.

After fermentation, the mash is mixed with distilled vinegar, twice as strong as the regular, home-style vinegar, in a ratio of 1 gallon of vinegar to 2 pounds of mash. The vinegar acts as a liquid base for the "heat" of the peppers and helps to preserve the sauce.

After 4 weeks of stirring the vinegar and the fermented mash together, the skins and seeds of the peppers are strained off and the sauce is bottled. The skins and seeds that have been removed are sold to manufacturers of muscle-rubbing compounds and red-hot candy manufacturers.

At the time of bottling, Tabasco sauce is about 2 percent salt, 23 percent pepper mash, and 75 percent vinegar. Some other hot sauces also contain a vegetable gum thickener used to emulsify and stabilize it.

Tabasco sauce is never cooked. Frank's, on the other hand, is an example of a cooked sauce: the skins and seeds are removed after the fermentation process, vinegar and garlic are added to the pulp, and the sauce is simmered slowly for about half an hour. Then comes the bottling.

The Scoville Organoleptic Test is used to measure the "hotness" of hot peppers. This was devised in 1912 by Wilbur Scoville, a pharmacist who was frustrated at the unpredictability of "heat" of hot peppers, even within the same type. An ordinary green bell pepper rates 0 Scoville units, since it isn't hot at all, a spicy jalapeño is about 4,000 units and a Tabasco pepper rates about 40,000 units. Pure capsaicin tops the chart at 16 million Scoville units.

Thus, all hot sauces have a Scoville rating that can be used to compare their heat levels. Trappey's is 2,400 units; Frank's is 3,200, and Tabasco's Scoville rating is a whopping 9,500 units.

This test, by the way, which is based on oral evaluations, is giving way to a modern machine called a High Pressure Liquid Chromatograph, which tests the heat of peppers electronically and is thought by some to be more accurate.

HANDLING AND STORAGE

In the bottle, Louisiana hot sauce will last up to about 5 years, although some manufacturers recommend only 12 months. If it is exposed to heat or light, the color will fade to a dull, watery unappetizing brown. The vinegar flavor of the sauce will predominate as the sauce gets older, and the "heat" may fade slightly. If you don't go through a bottle too quickly, keep it in the back of your cupboard, away from the light, with the top tightly screwed on.

HOW TO JUDGE HOT SAUCE

Tasting Media

Sample the hot sauce from shallow glass bowls, diluted in the proportion of 10 parts water to 1 part hot sauce. Tasters sip icy cold water between tastes to clear their palates.

In addition to the above method, professional hot sauce manufacturers sprinkle undiluted sauce onto unsalted crackers to taste. Tasters wait 10 minutes between tastes of different hot sauces. Palates can also be cleared with milk, which is a logical choice, since cold milk is also used to soothe hands burned from picking hot peppers.

Color/Eye Appeal

The best hot sauce is red, with a cast ranging from orange to brown. Pale sauce may be old, watered down, or weak.

Taste/Aroma

Saltiness and sweetness should be well balanced in a good hot sauce, and the vegetable flavor should also come through the "heat." Sourness, bitterness, or an excessive vinegar flavor indicate defects.

Consistency

Hot sauce should be on the thin side, but enough pulp should be present to give it a little bit of body.

Aftertaste

A chemical or metallic aftertaste takes away from the quality of a hot sauce.

CONCLUSIONS AND SUGGESTIONS

I like Trappey's the best because I can taste the peppers from which it is made as well as their fire. Tabasco, the world's best-selling hot sauce, is a superhot vinegar, much, much hotter than the other sauces without much pepper flavor.

Hot sauces have different "heat" values, and Tabasco is proud of the fact that their sauce is the hottest—by far! But it's what happens after the "heat" that matters. Other hot sauces have more pepper flavor than Tabasco, or any flavor other than hot.

Tabasco is the most consistent sauce, year in, year out, of all of the Louisiana hot sauces, a point in its favor.

The hot sauce you choose depends on whether you are trying to give your food flavor or "heat" or both. It takes much less Tabasco, compared to other sauces, to make a dish hot. If it's only "heat" you're after, then the concentrated properties of Tabasco are fine and, in fact, may be desirable in some dishes.

On the other hand, I'd prefer less "heat" and a little more flavor. If it takes twice or three times as much of a better-tasting hot sauce to provide "heat," so be it. At 2 to 3 drops of Tabasco per portion you're not talking about very much more of another sauce to give a desirable pepper flavor.

When using a less hot sauce, you can vary the flavor of the dish you're making from piquant to superhot by adding a little bit or a lot. With a sauce as hot as Tabasco, the range of piquancy is limited because of its extreme "heat."

COOKING WITH HOT SAUCE

When cooking with Louisiana hot sauce, keep in mind the "heat" value of the brand you've chosen. Tabasco, as mentioned above, is much hotter than others. The McIlhenny company recommends 2 to 3 drops per portion, for a Bloody Mary, an omelet, or salad dressing.

They also make the following cooking suggestions for their hot sauce, and these could be followed when using any Louisiana hot sauce:

• Add hot sauce at the end of a recipe. If it's added at the beginning, the "heat" will cook away.

• When using it to marinate meat, allow the meat to rest in the marinade overnight; the flavor of the sauce will remain, but the "heat" will disappear.

• The "heat" will dissipate more readily in oily foods, such as butter, oil, or mayonnaise. You can add enough hot sauce to turn a mayonnaise pink before the "heat" becomes overpowering.

• For a simple and tasty fish supper, soak fish fillets in a combination of milk or water and hot sauce, then dust with seasoned flour. Sauté the fillets in butter until crisp and golden brown on both sides.

RECIPE

Authentic Buffalo Chicken Wings

This dish, Buffalo, New York's answer to the American regional food craze, was born in 1964, on a wintery Friday night (is there any other kind in Buffalo?) when Teressa Belissimo served it up to the barflies of her establishment, the Anchor Bar. It is now served in bars and casual restaurants around the nation, a great finger food, delicious washed down with pitchers of beer. (Makes snacks for 4 to 6 people)

5 pounds fresh chicken wings
about 3 quarts vegetable oil for deep-frying
12 ounces ($1\frac{1}{2}$ cups) Frank's or other Louisiana-style hot sauce (if you are using Tabasco, make sure you cut down the quantity to 2 ounces, which is 4 tablespoons)
4 ounces butter, melted
1 batch Blue Cheese Dressing (recipe follows)
25 celery sticks

1. Cut each chicken wing into 3 pieces, discarding the tips or saving them to use in soup or stock. Dry the chicken pieces carefully.
2. Heat the oil to 375°F. Fry the wings for 6 to 8 minutes, or until they are completely cooked.
3. In a large bowl, mix together the hot sauce and the melted butter. Add the cooked wings and toss thoroughly to coat the chicken. If the wings are too hot, add some more melted butter; if they are not hot enough, add more hot sauce ("Nobody up here measures," says Janice Okun, the food editor of the *Buffalo Evening News* and chicken wing expert.).
4. Serve with the blue cheese dressing and the celery sticks on the side. Save leftovers for breakfast.

BLUE CHEESE DRESSING

(Makes 2 cups)

1 cup mayonnaise
2 tablespoons finely chopped onion
1 teaspoon finely minced garlic
$\frac{1}{4}$ cup finely chopped parsley
$\frac{1}{2}$ cup sour cream
1 tablespoon lemon juice
1 tablespoon white vinegar
$\frac{1}{4}$ cup crumbled blue cheese
salt and freshly ground black pepper
cayenne pepper

Combine all ingredients, adding seasoning to taste. Chill.

SOY SAUCE

To say "soy sauce" to an Asian is the same as saying "wine": the words only open the door to myriad styles and varieties, rather than describing one particular kind of liquid. Just as a serious wine drinker would not simply ask for "wine" without specifying red, or white, or sparkling, a soy sauce aficionado would not settle for just the generic "soy sauce"; he would specify Japanese or Chinese, light or dark. By the same token, as with wine, no one "best" soy sauce exists, but several "best of class" soy sauces, each one suitable for a separate cooking task.

Those who search for good soy sauce have had an easier time lately. Since the American love affair with Asian foods bloomed a few years ago, more and more brands have been imported from the Far East, and now a wider variety of soy sauces is sold in ethnic and gourmet stores. The sales of poor-quality, domestic soy sauces, the kind that used to be served in a shaker bottle next to the chop suey in any local Chinese restaurant, have fallen off as a result. Nevertheless, all domestic soy sauces are not poor; in fact, one of the best available in the United States is made in Wisconsin (see "How to Judge Soy Sauce," page 93).

A DASH OF HISTORY

Soy sauce originated in China. The soybean plant, which produces the same beans eaten as sprouts, tofu, and all other soy products, was first cultivated in China 4,000 years ago.

The first soy sauce was probably produced by an accident, the result of bacteria working on a batch of fermenting soybeans. Soy sauce was first introduced into Japan by Buddhist priests in the sixth century A.D., and in the eighth and ninth centuries, the Chinese exported to Japan advanced techniques for manufacturing soy sauce. By the fifteenth century, the Japanese were making their own kind of soy sauce commerically, lighter in flavor and more subtle than the sort they had inherited from the Chinese.

Soy sauce traveled to the West in the seventeenth century, probably with Dutch sailors returning from Nagasaki. It was served as a secret seasoning at the table of Louis XIV of France and soon became popular in Britain. In fact, soy sauce is still one of the main ingredients in Worcestershire sauce, the quintessential English condiment. Soy sauce was first seen in the United States in the late nineteenth century, having emigrated along with the Chinese and Japanese workers to the West Coast.

HOW SOY SAUCE IS MADE

The first step in making "naturally brewed" (words always seen on the label of the better-quality brands) soy sauce is to boil the soybeans in order to soften them. As the soybeans brew, wheat or barley is roasted and cracked and then mixed with *Aspergillus oryzae* and *Aspergillus soyae,* two types of microorganisms that start the fermentation process.

The proportion of wheat to soybeans depends on the type of soy sauce being made: Chinese use an average of 4 parts soybeans to 1 part wheat; Japanese use about half and half. This difference accounts for the fact that Japanese soy sauce is much lighter in flavor than Chinese. The Japanese developed these proportions in order to make a soy sauce that is more subtle than Chinese soy sauce and does not interfere with the delicate flavors of their foods.

The inoculated wheat and the mashed soybeans are then mixed together and set aside in a warm room for a couple of days; during this time the fermentation process gets under way, turning the starch in the wheat to sugar and the proteins in the soybeans into amino acids. Then, a strong salt-water solution is combined with the soybean/wheat paste, and the resulting liquid is inoculated again with *Lactobacillus,* the same strain of bacteria used to culture milk into yogurt.

A long, quiet aging process begins at this point, the length of which depends on the manufacturer. Generally, good soy sauce is aged anywhere from 6 to 24 months, during which time the flavor and characteristic color of the soy sauce develops. After aging is complete, the giant vats of liquid are strained to obtain light soy sauce; the solids that remain in the vat are pressed to extract a thick black liquid that will become dark soy sauce.

Artificial soy sauce—and into this category fall most of the soy sauces made in America—is made from "hydrolized soy protein," or a soybean/wheat mixture treated with hydrochloric acid, reducing the "fermentation" to just a few days. Caramel and corn syrup are then added for color and flavor.

VARIETIES OF SOY SAUCE

In general, Chinese soy sauces are thicker and much saltier than Japanese; in fact, they are almost too salty for Western palates. Because Japanese soy sauce is made with equal amounts of wheat and soybeans, it has a brighter, lighter, less salty taste than Chinese soy sauce. It is also generally more translucent than most Chinese soy sauces.

Japanese

• *Light* Light Japanese soy sauce is thinner and clearer than dark Japanese soy sauce, but it is also more salty than dark soy. It should be used when you wish to add a small amount of liquid as well as a seasoning to a food, without darkening the color.

This kind of soy sauce is used—together with fish stock, sweet rice wine, and grated radish—to make the traditional dipping sauce for tempura.

• *Dark (also called Regular)* Darker and richer than light soy sauce, this sauce is also not as salty so it can be used more liberally without fear of oversalting a dish. It also gives a nice brown color to foods to which it is added. This kind of soy sauce is commonly served with sushi and sukiyaki.

Chinese

• *Light (also called Thin, Pale, Regular, or Superior)* This is the thinnest of the Chinese soy sauces; it is very light brown, almost translucent, delicate in flavor, and not very salty in comparison with dark soy sauce. It is used to preserve the flavor of subtle foods, for example, for sauces to accompany whole fish.

• *Dark (also called Thick)* This is a dark, thick soy sauce to which caramel has been added for sweetness. It is used to give a good color, as well as strong and salty flavor, to a dish. It is the only kind of soy sauce to use in "red-cooked" Chinese dishes, which are braised slowly and develop a reddish-brown color when cooked.

• *Black (also called Double Black or Heavy)* This is the darkest of all Chinese soy sauces because molasses is added to black soy for texture and flavor. It is also by far the saltiest type and is best used in foods where the *flavor* of soy sauce is needed, but little additional liquid is required to preserve the consistency of the dish, such as in cold sesame noodles.

American

• *Tamari* This is a type of soy sauce that seems to be popular in the United States, although it may have originated in Japan as a runoff from the production of bean paste (Japanese *miso*). It is now sold mostly in health-food stores in this country. Tamari is made the same way as ordinary soy sauce, only without the wheat (or with very little wheat), therefore, it has a much stronger and saltier flavor. Because it is so strong, it is often cut with water before bottling. It is usually used as a dipping condiment or for marinades.

HANDLING AND STORAGE

If soy sauce will be used infrequently, buy it in small bottles. Despite some advice, soy sauce does go bad, albeit slowly. In time it darkens, becomes more concentrated and salty, and loses its lively, fresh flavor. Soy sauce should last about 2 months after opening, if it is kept in the refrigerator; soy sauce lasts about 6 months if it has not been opened.

Canned soy sauce should be decanted into glass bottles after opening so that it does not pick up a metallic flavor once it has been exposed to the air.

HOW TO JUDGE SOY SAUCE

Tasting Media

Taste each sauce from a clear glass bowl, with plastic spoons or fingers.

Color/Eye Appeal

A good soy sauce should not look muddy, but should be translucent or opaque, depending on the variety. The colors of soy sauces vary from tan and brown for the "light" types, to deep thick black for "heavy" types.

Taste/Aroma

A complex aroma is desirable in a good soy sauce; it should remind you of the soybeans and wheat from which it was made, and should have acquired a fragrant bouquet from long aging. The taste of a good soy sauce should be equally complex. Some positive flavors detected in good soy sauces include: meaty, nutty, and winy. Drawbacks to a soy sauce are a heavy concentration of salt (especially in the types where it is not expected), and bitter and medicinal flavors.

Consistency

Depending on what type of sauce is being tasted, it will be almost as thin as water, or thick and viscous from the added molasses. The consistency of the sauce should be true to its type.

Aftertaste

A bitter, overly salty aftertaste takes away from the quality of a soy sauce. Some soy sauces have a pleasant, sweet afternote.

CONCLUSIONS AND SUGGESTIONS

The understanding of Japanese and especially Chinese foods is so complicated for a born-and-raised American that it is difficult to appreciate a flavor as basic to Asians as soy sauce. On the other hand, more and more cooks are learning about Chinese food, the most sophisticated food in the world, and how to prepare it at home, and thus have had to learn about the panoply of soy sauces. As many as 40 varieties are sold in markets in China, and Chinese cooks use several kinds, often blending together many brands to get a particular taste. One sticking point, however, is that many of the heavier Chinese and Japanese soy sauces are simply too strong for American tastes. Americans have gravitated toward the lighter, less salty soy sauces, which give our Chinese-American and Japanese-American dishes a less intense, and less authentic, flavor.

This could be the reason that a surprisingly large number of renowned cookbook authors recommend Kikkoman soy sauce to their readers, and this includes authors of books on Chinese cooking as well as those who've written about Japanese food. For example, Shizuo Tsuji's *Japanese Cooking: A Simple Art* and Elizabeth Andoh's *At Home with Japanese Cooking* both mention Kikkoman. Barbara Tropp, in her acclaimed *The Modern Art of Chinese Cooking,* also recommends Kikkoman, even in cases where a Chinese soy sauce might make the dish taste more authentic.

These points were evident in the conclusion of my tastings, that the Japanese soy sauces are more attractive overall, the lighter the sauce the better. (Although this is not the conclusion in every case; the reduced-salt sauces didn't automatically get a high rating.)

The Kikkoman soy sauce that got the highest marks in my Japanese tasting was the one imported from Japan, not the one made in Wisconsin. It is technically a "light" soy sauce (see "Varieties of Soy Sauce," page 92), meaning it is a little more salty than the dark sauce made in America, but it has the most complex, pleasing flavor. All of the Kikkoman made in Wisconsin, as Tsuji pointed out in his book, is dark soy sauce.

For my cooking purposes (both Asian and Occidental), I use the imported Kikkoman as an all-purpose condiment and seasoning. I prefer the lighter Japanese flavor, even in Chinese-style dishes. Because I don't do a great deal of Japanese or Chinese cooking, I find that one soy sauce is enough variety for me, and the light one fits my overall needs.

When it comes to assessing quality among the light or dark soy sauces, the naturally brewed sauces are far superior to the artificial brands. This comparison parallels the difference between Champagne made by the *méthode champenoise* in France (fermented in the bottle) and American cold duck (made in stainless-steel vats with added carbonation.) The words "naturally brewed" often appear on the label of a top-quality soy sauce, but if in doubt, shake the bottle to see if a "head" forms, a clue that the sauce was brewed in the proper manner.

RECIPE

Braised Beef with Soy Sauce

(Makes 6 servings)

1 cup soy sauce
1 cup sliced onion
3/4 cup dark brown sugar
3 garlic cloves, minced
1 tablespoon minced fresh ginger
2 pounds beef shin meat
cilantro (fresh coriander) for garnish

1. Put all ingredients except meat and cilantro in a heavy saucepan with 4 cups water. Bring to a boil and simmer for 5 minutes, stirring once.

2. Add shin meat to saucepan. Simmer for 45 minutes, or until meat is tender. Remove meat from saucepan and slice.

3. Boil juices in the saucepan until slightly thickened and pour over meat slices. Garnish with sprigs of cilantro.

WINE VINEGAR

Throughout the millennia, vinegar has been used for all sorts of practical and gastronomic purposes. It has long been indispensable for preserving many fruits and vegetables, for example. Today its most popular use in America is for salad dressings; after that we use it most often as a cooking ingredient, and then for pickling. Then, of course, there's nothing better for shining patent leather shoes, cleaning windows, or opening a clogged drain.

Because of its versatility, vinegar can be found in 98 percent of American homes, with its consumption rising dramatically during the spring and summer months when it is used for spring cleaning and home canning, two of its most common uses.

Despite its long and universal acceptance, vinegar has recently been the subject of an even greater burst of popularity. In the past few years, sales of vinegar have risen 10 percent, a large jump for a market that had been static for years.

This new interest in vinegar has nothing to do with cider vinegar or clear white distilled vinegar, the kinds most suited to household chores. Instead, we have gone back to vinegar's beginnings to rediscover that the tastiest and mildest vinegar is made from wine in a process as careful as wine making itself. Its very name explains these origins: *vin* and *aigre* are the French root words meaning "sour wine." With the enormous worldwide trend toward strongly flavored foods, we have begun seriously to appreciate its flavor, which can be piquant, complex, and subtle, all at the same time.

A DASH OF HISTORY

Vinegar is one of the oldest foods known to man. Its discovery was concurrent with the discovery of wine more than 10,000 years ago when, no doubt accidentally, someone left wine exposed to the air; it gathered yeasts and fermented naturally, creating vinegar.

Sour foods made with vinegar were very important to the ancient Greeks and Romans; meats, for example, were often cooked in a sweet/sour mixture of honey and vinegar. *Oxybaphon* and *acetabulum,* bowls containing vinegar that were placed on the dining table, were commonly used by the Romans to dip their bread into throughout the meal. These bowls contained not only vinegar made from wine, but also vinegar made from dates and figs and other fruits as well. Vinegar was also used often for preserving fruits and vegetables by both the Romans and Greeks.

Vinegar is mentioned in the Bible almost as many times as wine. The Book of Ruth alludes to the practice of using vinegar for flavoring bread: "And Boaz said unto her, 'At mealtime come thou hither, and eat of the bread, and dip thy morsel in the vinegar.' "

Practicality and gastronomy came together in the case of Roman soldiers, who carried vinegar with them to dilute with water for drinking; the undiluted vinegar took up much less room than wine and provided an invigorating beverage.

Egyptian vinegar was highly prized among Greeks and Romans. Cleopatra made Egyptian vinegar infamous. According to Pliny: "To gain a wager that she would consume at a single meal the value of a million sisterces, she dissolved pearls in vinegar which she drank."

Street vendors sold vinegar as early as the thirteenth century in Paris, offering a large selection of flavored vinegars, such as clove, chicory, fennel, ginger, truffle, raspberry, mustard, and garlic vinegars. These vinegars (not unlike lemon juice in later centuries) were often used to flavor sauces and to sprinkle on foods to disguise spoilage. Pepper vinegar became very popular in the Middle Ages because at that time wine that contained pepper was not taxed when imported into Paris.

Throughout the ages, vinegar was thought to have medicinal properties. Hippocrates used it on his patients as early as 400 B.C. During the Middle Ages, when the town of Marseilles was ravaged by plague, a gang of thieves robbed the houses of victims and used vinegar to protect themselves from infection. In America, during the Civil War, vinegar was used successfully to combat scurvy.

During the seventeenth and eighteenth centuries, when open sewers and exposed garbage created vile smells on the streets of large cities, well-bred people carried little silver boxes called *vinaigrettes* containing sponges soaked in vinegar, which they held to their noses to ward off foul odors.

The use of vinegar as a beverage was rediscovered in eighteenth- and nineteenth-century America. One of the many household tasks women were expected to perform was to make a variety of flavored vinegars using raspberries and other fruits. These vinegars were used as flavorings exactly as lemons are used in lemonade. Mild fruit vinegars mixed with carbonated water and a touch of sugar are still refreshing summer drinks today.

HOW VINEGAR IS MADE

Making wine vinegar is twice as difficult as making wine because it requires two steps; first you have to make the wine, then the vinegar. Fine wine vinegars are the result of a double fermentation. The first fermentation turns the natural sugar of the grapes into alcohol, then the alcohol is turned into acetic acid, the major component of vinegar. This process must be carefully controlled to achieve a refined taste.

Many vinegar manufacturers buy juice from the second pressing of the grapes used to make wine, or they buy wine directly from the vintner. Because vinegar making is so closely related to wine making, many vinegar producers are located in areas where wine also is produced.

Just because vinegar is made with wine, however, is no guarantee that a vinegar is good or well made. The cook's adage that one should never cook with a wine that is not fit to drink is also applicable to the making of vinegar. Vinegar made from a wine not fit to drink will be inferior because all of the defects of the wine will be evident in the vinegar.

The method used in manufacturing a vinegar is as important as the quality of the wine from which it is made. The best method is the *Orléans process,* the oldest commercial method, named after the city in France where the method originated in the seventeenth century. The *Orléans process* is also called the *slow process.* In this method, 3 parts wine and 2 parts unpasteurized vinegar are placed in wooden barrels or vats with a "mother of vinegar," which is a starter of vinegar bacteria *(Mycoderma aceti),* used on the same principle as a yeast starter is used for making bread. Fermentation begins and continues over a period of 4 to 12 weeks. When the liquid reaches the right stage of acidity (usually between 4 and 7 percent), it is drawn off and bottled.

The acidity (or acetic acid) level of the vinegar is often expressed on the label as, for example, 6° or 6% or 60 grain, all of which mean the same thing. This rating can be compared to the rating of the alcohol level of a wine, but in this case it indicated how acidic the vinegar will taste. For example, a 5° vinegar is milder than a 6° vinegar, which is milder than a 7° vinegar. However, exceptions to this rule occur because many of the flavorings used in vinegars can heighten or mask its acidity. A commercial vinegar is required by law to have at least 4 percent acidity. The cheaper, less-quality vinegars have a lower acidity level than those made by more expensive processes.

Acetic acid, the acidic element in vinegar, is developed during the fermentation process when bacteria in the "mother," or starter, attack the alcohol in the wine and begin to oxidize it. These bacteria need oxygen, so they grow on the surface of the wine, penetrating the liquid more and more, coalescing into a thick, sticky skin, which is the new "mother." Once this bacterial process is finished, no alcohol from the wine remains.

The Orléans process is considered the best for making vinegar because it is slow (4 to 12 weeks compared to just a few days) and takes place without heat, preserving the flavor of the wine from which the vinegar was made. It is also expensive, and vinegar made this way costs more than other vinegars. Louis Pasteur himself lectured at Orléans, explaining his new pasteurization process, and is quoted as saying that the Orléans process for making vinegar was the best.

A less-expensive and more efficient way to make vinegar is by the "quick process." Wine is slowly trickled into a tank that is loosely filled with wood shavings, charcoal, or corncobs. The bacteria in the wood or other materials act on the wine, while at the same time air is blown in through the bottom of the tank to provide oxygen. In about a week, the vinegar is ready. During the fermentation process, the tank is kept at a temperature of about 100°F., and this heat drives off many of the more delicate flavors of the wine. Sometimes this vinegar is aged for several weeks in wooden barrels, to mellow its flavor.

A third process for making vinegar, called the *continuous* or *submerged fermentation* process, is used to make the least expensive kinds of vinegar. The "acetator" forces air up through wine, which has been placed in a stainless-steel tank at a constant temperature under pressure. Vinegar is made within 24 hours. This vinegar is also sometimes aged in wooden casks to mellow its flavor.

If vinegar is made by either of these quick processes, it is often necessary to dilute it to bring down the acidity level to between 4 and 7 percent. All vinegar is almost always clarified through filtration and then pasteurized in order to kill bacteria to stabilize it and prevent it from growing a "mother" after bottling.

A special kind of wine vinegar that has come to prominence in the United States in the last few years is the Italian *aceto balsamico,* or "healthful vinegar," so-called because of the medicinal properties it was thought, in the past, to possess.

Aceto balsamico has been made for 800 years in the region around Modena, Italy, from grapes high in sugar content, which are cooked down and subjected to carefully controlled alcoholic fermentation. The juice is moved through a succession of wooden barrels made of oak, chestnut, cherry, locust, ash, mulberry, and juniper. The aging can take as long as 50 years or more. What comes out is a mellow, rich amber-colored viscous liquid that is suited to sipping from a tiny liqueur glass, which is exactly what the folk of Modena do after dinner.

These days, 2 types of *aceto balsamico* exist: *Tradizionale,* which is made from boiled-down grape juice in the traditional way. It is thick and syrupy, and aged for a minimum of 12 years, with nothing added to it except that which comes from the natural maturity. *Di Modena* begins its life as vinegar and is manufactured by a quick process: Grape juice is caramelized to make it extra-sweet, then it is added to the vinegar, poured over wood chips, and given a dash of oak extract. The result is an interesting and tasty vinegar, but quite different from the *aceto balsamico tradizionale.*

Although this vinegar has a high acidity level, the sweetness masks the tartness, making it more mellow than the usual wine vinegars. Excellent for salad dressing, *aceto balsamico* is also tasty as a condiment, much like Worcestershire sauce. Italians often sprinkle it on fresh strawberries for dessert.

Only 4 producers of *aceto balsamico di Modena* ship their products to the United States, but these 4 producers pack under many different labels. You can determine which company has made your vinegar by looking under the plastic seal on the cap, which sometimes bears the name of the producer, or by reading the fine print on the label.

"There is not enough *aceto balsamico tradizionale* in all of Modena to supply the Modenese with their own," discloses Darrell Corti, an importer and one of the foremost vinegar experts in this country. "The true *aceto balsamico tradizionale* should cost about $95 per liter and up (as much as a first-class Italian wine), because of the long aging process." Some of these exorbitantly expensive vinegars can be found in American gourmet stores, notably Dean & DeLuca in New York City and Corti Brothers in Sacramento, which import their own (see "Mail-Order Sources" for ordering information).

HANDLING AND STORAGE

Almost all commercial vinegars (except for a few kinds, notably those found in health-food stores) are pasteurized, so if a bottle of vinegar is unopened, it will last indefinitely in a cool, dark place. Once opened, a bottle of vinegar will last for about 3 months, if it is tightly capped to prevent the flavor from dissipating. If you have to keep a vinegar for several weeks after it has been opened, add some fresh vinegar or wine to it from time to time to preserve its flavor. If a vinegar has thrown off sediment, it can be strained and used, but if a mold has developed on it, the vinegar should be thrown away.

HOW TO JUDGE VINEGAR

Tasting Media

Tasting vinegar is a tricky process, but not nearly as awful as it sounds. A vinegar tasting is much like a wine tasting, except for one important factor: the high acid content forces the taste buds to become numb so that detecting the flavor of one vinegar after another is impossible. To neutralize the acidity of the vinegar in order to "fool" the taste buds into staying open, vinegar is tasted from sugar cubes, so that the flavor can be perceived, and the taster can move from one vinegar to another without losing his sense of taste.

Use slow-dissolving sugar cubes, which are rectangular. Dip a cube into the vinegar and gently suck it in order to get a true taste. A hint of sweetness comes with the flavor of the vinegar from the sugar cube, but it is easily discounted, especially after a little practice.

Color/Eye Appeal

A top-quality vinegar must have a clean, clear look; it should never appear cloudy or murky, which results from poor grapes, imperfect filtration, or bacterial action due to insufficient pasteurization. Murkiness may also indicate old vinegar. A white-wine vinegar should be brilliant and clear; if it has a brown tinge, it has oxidized. Red-wine vinegar would be a rosé color, or a shade or two lighter than the red wine from which it was made.

Taste/Aroma

Detecting the aroma of a vinegar requires a little care; sticking your nose into a vinegar as is done with wine will result in an assault on your nasal passages. Instead, the vinegar is swirled in the glass and gently sniffed, a few inches away from the rim of the glass, to detect the quality of the bouquet.

The vinegar is then tasted from sugar cubes, as described. As with wine, vinegars can have a panoply of flavors: weedy, berrylike, brambly, bell peppery, complex, grapy, woody, well-balanced, corky, delicate, earthy, penetrating, flowery, fruity, nutty, subtle. Tarragon vinegars can sometimes have a licorice flavor; if it is not overwhelming, a hint of licorice can be pleasant.

Consistency

Except for *aceto balsamico,* all wine vinegars are of a similar consistency, very close to that of water. Because they are made up mostly of water, this is not surprising. The *aceto balsamico* vinegars are expected to have a little more body than ordinary wine vinegars.

Aftertaste

A sharp, biting, pungent aftertaste is a drawback in a good wine vinegar, which should be subtle and not terribly strong.

CONCLUSIONS AND SUGGESTIONS

I have conducted tastings of red-wine vinegars, tarragon vinegars, and *aceto balsamico.* As with wine, red wine vinegars are the most sophisticated and versatile of wine vinegars; tarragon vinegars are a good example of the quality of manufacturers' herb vinegars, and *aceto balsamico* is in a class all its own.

All in all, red-wine vinegars are the most satisfying. The quality of tarragon vinegars is more variable. *Aceto balsamico* is a personal favorite of mine, partly because I like sweet flavors. Extremely expensive, *aceto balsamico tradizionale* is awesome because of its age (up to 50 years old) and costliness; it is smooth, mellow, and delicious, like a good red wine. However, *aceto balsamico di Modena,* the price of which is closer to ordinary wine vinegars, is also quite pleasing. I use *aceto balsamico* often as a replacement for all or part of the vinegar in an ordinary vinaigrette salad dressing. I also use it to marinate cooked vegetables, such as sliced baked beets, potatoes, baked onions, and roasted peppers. The vinegar is so mild that it almost acts as a dressing all by itself, without the addition of oil.

The same situation holds true for vinegars as for mustards: I would rather add my own herbs and flavorings than buy mixtures ready made. The large array of flavored vinegars in gourmet stores today is part of a marketing strategy to increase sales through variety. Flavored vinegars are delicious, but only if made with first-class wine vinegar and fresh, high-quality flavoring ingredients, such as a mixture of fresh herbs, hot or dried peppers, garlic, onions, fresh ginger, and so on. If it is made well with a subtle flavor and low acidity, flavored vinegar can be used as a condiment, put onto the table in a decorative shaker bottle, preferably clear so you can see the herbs or vegetables inside.

One of my favorite flavored vinegars is made with chile peppers. It is simple to make: a month before you are planning to use it, push about 20 dried or fresh hot chile peppers (the tinier the peppers the hotter they are) into the mouth of a glass liqueur decanter or an empty liquor bottle. If you are using fresh peppers, cut them in half first. Pour a good red-wine vinegar into the decanter to cover the peppers. Cap the decanter and let the peppers steep until the vinegar is as hot as you like it, at least 1 month.

The same method can be used to make vinegar with fresh or dried herbs, or any other flavoring ingredient. Simply steep the vinegar until the flavor is as strong as you like it, then use it for cooking or at the table. If you are not using it right away, strain the vinegar through a cheesecloth into another bottle, to remove the flavoring agent.

COOKING WITH VINEGAR

Salad dressing in France and Italy is much different from that in the United States, mainly because of the difference in the way vinegar is used. Many French chefs dilute their vinegar with water when making a salad dressing, because they feel that a salad should not taste too acidic. In Italy, partly because of the flavorful olive oil they use, chefs often add only a teaspoon or two of vinegar for every cup of oil. The result in both countries is a salad that tastes of the greens and vegetables rather than of dressing.

A standard French vinaigrette salad dressing recipe calls for 1 part vinegar to 4 (or even 5) parts oil, and coarse salt and freshly ground pepper to taste. An optional addition is a teaspoon or two of plain Dijon-style mustard.

Many two- and three-star restaurants in France today feature dishes made with vinegar-based sauces, a refreshing change from standard heavy classical cuisine. An example of the simplest way to use vinegar in cooking is this procedure for sautéed calf's liver: Deglaze the pan with red-wine after sautéing the liver, scraping up the browned bits stuck to the bottom of the pan. Add a few tablespoons of broth and boil the liquid for a minute or two until it is syrupy; pour over the meat and serve.

RECIPE

Vinegar Pie

This is reminiscent of the nineteenth-century American pioneer pie recipes, where vinegar was used in a pie filling when fresh fruit wasn't available. Surprisingly, there is only a hint of vinegar in this filling, and the pie is delicious. (Makes one 9-inch pie)

PIE DOUGH

- 1¼ **cups all-purpose flour**
- **pinch of salt**
- 6 **tablespoons very cold unsalted butter, cut into 6 pieces**
- 2 **tablespoons lard**
- 3 **tablespoons ice cold water**

PIE FILLING

- 4 **large eggs**
- 1¼ **cups sugar**
- 4 **tablespoons unsalted butter, melted and cooled**
- 1 **tablespoon plus 1½ teaspoons vinegar**
- 1 **teaspoon vanilla extract**
- 1 **cup heavy cream, whipped to stiff peaks**
- ¼ **cup chopped pecans or walnuts, for garnish**

1. Put the flour and the pinch of salt in the bowl of a food processor fitted with the metal chopping blade. Whirl for a few seconds to mix.
2. Sprinkle the 6 tablespoons cold butter and the lard on top of the flour. Process with pulsing action for about 10 seconds, until mixture resembles coarse oatmeal.
3. Sprinkle water over mixture. Process with pulsing action for about 10 seconds, until dough just begins to stick together, but before a ball forms. Shape dough into a ball and chill for 1 hour.
4. Roll dough out between 2 sheets of lightly floured wax paper and set it into a 9-inch pie pan. Trim edges and crimp to form a decorative edge. Chill for 1 hour.
5. Preheat oven to 450°F. Set a square of wax paper inside the pie shell and fill with raw beans, rice, or pie weights. Bake for 10 to 12 minutes, until dough looks set. Remove beans and wax paper.
6. Prick dough with a fork, then continue baking for 10 minutes longer, until baked through. Remove pie shell from oven. Reduce oven temperature to 350°F.
7. In a large bowl, beat eggs. Beat in sugar, 4 tablespoons melted butter, vinegar, and vanilla and mix well. Pour into baked pie shell.
8. Bake for 35 minutes, until filling is firm and a knife inserted in center comes out clean. Remove and cool completely on a wire rack.
9. Spread whipped cream over pie, then sprinkle with chopped nuts. Refrigerate until ready to serve.

CANNED FOODS

BROTH

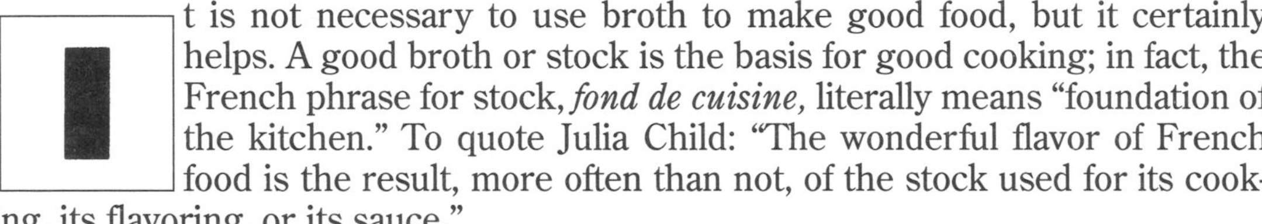

It is not necessary to use broth to make good food, but it certainly helps. A good broth or stock is the basis for good cooking; in fact, the French phrase for stock, *fond de cuisine,* literally means "foundation of the kitchen." To quote Julia Child: "The wonderful flavor of French food is the result, more often than not, of the stock used for its cooking, its flavoring, or its sauce."

Even ordinary, everyday food becomes rich and satisfying with the addition of a well-flavored broth; a rice pilaf cooked with broth is much tastier than one cooked with water, and a dumpling poached in broth is more delicious than one poached in water.

Technically speaking, the difference between stock and broth is that a stock is made from bones and a broth is made from meat—beef, chicken, or even lamb or pork. "Bouillon" is the French term for stock or broth, and "consommé" is the term for a broth clarified with egg whites. For practical purposes, however, the terms broth and stock are often used interchangeably, especially (curiously) on the labels of commercial products.

Cooking with a good stock is one procedure all fine restaurants have in common. A silent competition rages among chef/instructors at the Culinary Institute of America, my alma mater, concerning which instructor makes the best stock. The students whisper to each other, "I think Chef Smith makes the best stock in the school," and "But have you tasted Chef Jones's consommé? I'd like to know how he makes his stock!" The ability to make an outstanding stock is an accomplishment of which any cook can be proud.

Although most of us who cook at home know how to make a good stock or broth from scratch, we don't always have the time and so we rely on canned broth or bouillon cubes. Cooks who wouldn't dream of using any other processed foods often buy canned broth by the caseload. As a matter of fact, the good ones can be a reliable substitute for the real thing.

Statistics show that in the last few years, the sales of canned broth and bouillon cubes have increased by almost 10 percent in the United States, with sales highest in the Northeast and the West. Marketing experts surmise that these regional variations exist because of the high Jewish population in the Northeast, which uses broth to make a lot of chicken soup, and the large number of Asians in the West, who often use broth in stir-fried and simmered dishes. More broth is sold during the cooler months, particularly around Thanksgiving and Christmas, when it is used to make gravy and stuffing for the holiday turkey. Sales of broth and bouillon go up during economic recessions, showing that for a relatively small amount of money the flavor of meat can substitute for the meat itself.

All in all, 31 percent of American households purchase at least 6 cans of broth per year. Two thirds of the canned broth sold in the United States is used as a recipe ingredient. Americans buy slightly more chicken broth than beef, not realizing, perhaps, that canned chicken broth has twice as many calories as beef. The typical broth user is a middle-aged female in a high income bracket.

A DASH OF HISTORY

To give a history of broth means giving a history of cooking throughout the millennia. Suffice it to say that around 7000 B.C., when vessels were invented that were both heatproof and waterproof, peasants and village people placed meat, vegetables, and water in a pot and made soup, from which broth resulted.

The canning of broth in America began around the turn of this century (Campbell's began business in 1869), and canned broth became widely popular as a soup in the early twenties. Bouillon cubes were first made in the United States in 1910 by Herb-Ox, which remains the only company devoted exclusively to the production of bouillon and broth products.

HOW BROTH IS MADE

Canned Chicken Broth

The chickens used to make canned chicken broth are subsequently canned as chicken à la king or canned boned chicken. The broth is sometimes fortified by boiling chicken skins and bones in a small amount of water in a pressure cooker, the resulting extract being added to the broth in the tanks where the chickens have been cooked. The liquid is then strained through a filter to remove small bone fragments and bone marrow. Seasonings are added, according to the manufacturer's own recipe.

Canned Beef Broth

None of the major or minor manufacturers of beef broth would tell us how they make their product. In my investigation, I discovered that the three major manufacturers of broth—Campbell's, College Inn, and Swanson—hold a patent on the formula, so the federal government allows the manufacturing information to be withheld from the public, so that no one else can use the recipe.

Bouillon Cubes

Bouillon cubes start with a real broth made from chicken parts or beef bones. The broth is concentrated and dehydrated until it contains only 15 percent moisture and has the consistency of a paste. This paste is mixed with spices and salt, and further dehydrated until it contains a 3 percent moisture content. This mixture is ground into a powder, which goes into large machines to form cubes.

Base (Bouillon in Powder Form)

Beef base is made by cooking beef broth until it is concentrated into a thick, rich, caramellike substance. This concentrate is poured into trays and vacuum-dried until it contains only 6 percent moisture. It is then ground up and put into jars or packets.

Chicken base is made the same way, except that it starts with a mixture of freeze-dried chicken meat and spices that have not been cooked. The fat content in powdered bouillon keeps the powder from caking.

HANDLING AND STORAGE

Canned broth will keep safely for up to 5 years if the can is kept in a cool, dry place. To store a partially used can of broth, transfer the broth to be stored to a nonmetal container before refrigerating so the broth doesn't pick up a metallic taste.

Extra broth can also be stored in a spare ice-cube tray and frozen into convenient small cubes. After a week or two, transfer the frozen broth cubes to a sealed plastic bag in the freezer, so that they don't pick up freezer smells. Each cube holds about 2 tablespoons of broth, so whenever broth is called for, simply use as many cubes as needed.

Powdered and cubed bouillon will keep almost indefinitely, provided it is kept in a cool, dry place. The reason bouillon cubes don't spoil or become moldy is that their water content is so low that bacteria will not grow. It is possible, however, that the flavor of the herbs in the bouillon will dissipate after a year or two. Fats in bouillon cubes or powder may turn rancid over a long period of time (a couple of years or more), so some manufacturers also recommend refrigeration.

If bouillon powder has caked from exposure to dampness, simply dissolve it in hot water.

HOW TO JUDGE BROTH

Tasting Media

Those broths that require diluting are mixed with the specified amount of water. Canned broth should be tasted from clear glass bowls with plastic spoons.

Powdered broth and bouillon should be dissolved according to package directions and tasted at room temperature from clear glass bowls with plastic spoons.

Color/Eye Appeal

A good chicken broth should have a clear, deep golden color; a good beef broth should be auburn-brown. Many of the broths I tasted have off-putting unnatural colors, which range from green to bright yellow to orange. Also, many of the powdered and cubed bouillons, after diluting, have an herb and fat fuzzy scum across the top of them that is unappetizing.

Taste/Aroma

A good, basic broth should taste like the chicken or beef from which it was made. In so many, another flavor predominates: salt, onions, vegetables, sugar. Since the majority of the broths bought in this country are made to be used as an ingredient in a recipe, the flavor should be straightforward and meaty; an imbalance will detract from the dish.

Consistency

All broths should have a standard consistency: the liquid should have a bit more body than plain water.

Aftertaste

Broth should not have an artificial aftertaste, which can come from the metal can in which it was packed, or from the addition of artificial ingredients. These faults are easily identifiable, and most unpleasant.

CONCLUSIONS AND SUGGESTIONS

I was pleasantly surprised at the results of my tasting. I tasted bouillon cubes and powder in a separate category from canned broth due to my assumption that the quality of the broth in the cans would be far superior to the cubes. It turned out that I was partly wrong.

The best canned broth *is* better than the best powdered bouillon, to be sure, but the taste of quite a few canned broths is unacceptable, and what's more, they sell at high prices. Moreover, the very best powdered bouillons are quite good, and certainly would be adequate for use when no homemade or canned stock is available. The best canned chicken broth is made by Swanson, hands down. This comes as a surprise, since many home and professional cooks have touted the superiority of College Inn for decades. These days, I always use the reduced-sodium version of Swanson chicken broth, and thus I can control the saltiness of my dishes myself.

The best chicken bouillon is Knorr-Swiss Instant, and the best beef bouillon is Wagner's Beef Soup Base.

The major drawback to most of the unacceptable powdered and cubed bouillon is saltiness. Saltiness is less of a problem in the canned broths, but still a concern. If a broth contains a lot of salt to begin with, then it will become unbearably salty if it's cooked down in a recipe. To avoid the saltiness, mix broth half and half with water if it is to be used in a recipe that calls for reduction or evaporation, such as a risotto or a long-cooking sauce.

Although I often use canned broth when I'm cooking, I find it relatively easy to make homemade stock, even if it is made in an unorthodox way. Since it usually takes about 30 minutes to get to the point in a recipe where the broth is called for, I begin the whole cooking process by casually combining in a pot a few chicken bones (which I keep in the freezer), an onion, a carrot, and a piece of celery, and whatever other vegetable trimmings I have at hand. I cover these ingredients with water and simmer until I need to use the stock in the recipe, at which point I strain it through a mesh strainer right into a heat proof measuring cup. Half an hour is enough time to develop a good chicken flavor, and the yield is at least 1 cup of stock. Obviously, I agree with the famous New Orleans chef, Paul Prudhomme, who says that cooking a stock for half an hour is better than having no homemade stock at all.

MAKING STOCK AT HOME

The same rule applies to broth as to wine in cooking: any broth unfit to drink is unfit to cook with. Of course, the best broth for cooking is homemade, partly because the cook can vary the ingredients according to his or her needs and taste. What follows is a method for making a homemade stock. To increase the yield, simply double or triple the ingredients.

Homemade Stock

- **1 pound meat or bones; you can use all meat or all bones or some of each; beef and chicken are best, or a combination of the two; a fowl (and older chicken) gives excellent flavor; veal shank bones give excellent flavor and make the stock gelatinous when cold**
- **1 medium-size carrot, roughly chopped**
- **1 large onion, roughly chopped**
- **1 large celery rib, roughly chopped**
- **optional: any other cleaned vegetable trimmings, except for strongly flavored varieties, such as cabbage and turnips**
- **10 sprigs of parsley, or 20 parsley stems**
- **1 bay leaf**
- **5 black peppercorns, roughly crushed (use the bottom of a heavy skillet)**

Put all of the ingredients in a heavy stockpot, cover with water and simmer, uncovered, for about $1^{1}/_{2}$ hours for a stock made with only chicken meat and/or bones, 3 hours if the stock contains beef or veal.

2. Put the stockpot into the refrigerator, if it fits. After it has cooled completely, remove the fat that has congealed on the top of the stock and strain the stock through cheesecloth. If the stockpot

doesn't fit in the refrigerator, carefully strain the stock before storing in a nonmetal container.

3. If you are keeping the stock for more than about 10 days, freeze it in an airtight, nonmetal container. If you are keeping it in the refrigerator, bring it to a boil every 4 or 5 days and put it back into the refrigerator, so that it doesn't spoil. Store it in an airtight container so it doesn't absorb refrigerator odors.

Additional Tips for Cooking Homemade Stock

• The best stock comes from bones that have not been frozen, but stock from frozen bones, as in the case of my unorthodox chicken stock, is still better than no homemade stock at all.

• Avoid using starchy vegetables, such as potatoes, in stock; they will cloud it.

• An electric slow-cooker is handy for making stock. Simply put in all of the ingredients, turn it on, and go away for the day. A little unorthodox, but a boon for busy people.

Another method for those who won't be home all day is to stop the simmering at any time during the cooking process, refrigerate the stock in its pot, and continue the simmering when you return.

• After cooking, never cover a stockpot airtight until the ingredients have cooled completely; the stock may turn sour.

• Never add salt to a stock. It is easier to season a dish without having to take into consideration the salt in the stock. Also, if the stock reduces, the salt will become too concentrated.

• When straining a stock, wet the cheesecloth so that you don't lose any stock in the cloth.

• Stock can be made out of lamb or pork bones, but lamb stock should be used only in lamb dishes, pork stock only in pork dishes. Chinese restaurants make stock out of bones of all meats in one pot, which makes a strong and tasty stock. Experiment with various meats and bones to make a "signature" stock of your own.

• To make the flavor of a finished stock stronger, boil it down to evaporate some of its water content. If a meat stock is boiled down completely until it is thick, dark brown, and syrupy, it becomes a *glace de viande,* or meat glaze, which is very concentrated. Meat glaze freezes well in plastic containers and can be easily spooned out to amplify a sauce.

• Save the fat skimmed off the top of the stock and use it instead of oil or butter when sautéing.

• Use canned chicken broth for part of the liquid when making a homemade stock, especially if simmering time is short.

• Add a few whole cloves to stock to create a haunting, spicy flavor.

TOMATO PRODUCTS

The type of tomato product Americans automatically buy depends a great deal on ethnic heritage. Tomato paste is usually bought by people of Mediterranean descent, perhaps due to the memory of a great-great grandmother who dried her garden tomatoes in the strong summer sun to make a homemade concentrate for use throughout the winter. Italian-Americans, or those following authentic Italian recipes, often buy whole canned tomatoes. Tomato purée is favored in Hispanic neighborhoods. Stewed tomatoes are an old-fashioned American treat, many times eaten cold from the refrigerator right out of the can!

Most canned tomato products are "first generation" foods, which means they contain only one major ingredient: tomatoes. Because of this, the price of tomato products closely reflects the current price of the raw tomatoes with which they are made. Besides being one of the oldest canned foods, tomatoes are the largest canning crop in the United States, far surpassing such other popular canned foods as corn, green beans, and peas.

Restaurants use 40 percent of the nation's supply of tomato products, compared to only about 22 percent 20 years ago. This figure seems perplexing until the dramatic growth of fast-food places is factored in: consider the amount of ketchup used on hamburgers, tomato sauce used on pizzas, and spicy tomato *salsa* lumped on tacos.

In spite of the increased use of tomatoes in the restaurant trade, per-capita consumption of all tomato products fell by 3.3 pounds—to 73 pounds per person—in 1994.

A DASH OF HISTORY

The importance of the tomato in Italian cuisine might lead one to believe that tomatoes have grown in Western Europe since cooking began. In fact, tomatoes were first introduced to the Old World from the New World in the sixteenth century. Spanish explorers carried the exotic fruit from Peru to Naples, which was then under Spanish rule. The tomato was called *pomo d'oro* or "apple of gold" in Italy because the fruits were small and yellow at the time; Italian horticulturists developed the large red tomato later in the sixteenth century. It took two centuries for Italian cooks to figure out what to do with the tomato; as a result, printed recipes for tomatoes didn't exist before the nineteenth century.

By the eighteenth century, the tomato had also gained recognition in France where it was called the *pomme d'amour,* or "love apple," perhaps because it was thought to be an aphrodisiac. The tomato's popularity increased slowly, and it wasn't until around the turn of the twentieth century that the French public accepted it widely.

Americans were slow in learning to like tomatoes; fearing at first their close botanical relationship to poisonous plants of the Solanaceae family, such as deadly nightshade. Although Thomas Jefferson planted one of the first "tomata" crops in America in 1781, it was thought to be an ornamental plant rather than an edible fruit until a few decades later. Cautious experts in the early nineteenth century still advised cooks to boil their tomatoes for three hours to turn them into a purée. It wasn't until the turn of the twentieth century that tomatoes were eaten raw in this country. Tomatoes began to be grown commercially in the middle of the 1800s, and around the time of World War I tomatoes became the important commercial canned crop they remain today.

Tomatoes were one of the first foods to be canned in the late nineteenth century, when canning methods were perfected. Tomato paste was first made in Italy long before commercial canning. Even today, housewives set cooked tomato sauce out in the sun to concentrate it further. According to Waverley Root, the ultimate result is "loaves the color of dark mahogany, of the consistency of stucco, cylindrical in form, well oiled, and wrapped in oiled paper." This homemade paste is used in the winter, when fresh tomato flavoring isn't available.

HOW CANNED TOMATO PRODUCTS ARE MADE

The breed of tomato grown today in America for canning was developed in the early 1960s by the University of California at Davis. Unlike its foreign relatives, it ripens uniformly and can withstand mechanical picking. These tomatoes are grown anywhere from 3 to 250 miles away from the canning plants.

The canning process begins when the tomatoes are harvested by automatic pickers that pick up the vines and shake them into gondolas. They are then taken into the plant where they are put onto sorting belts. Next, they are crushed in giant stainless-steel vats where the temperature is raised to 198°F. to set the natural pectin in the tomatoes.

Next the tomatoes are cooked, usually in a type of a large pressure cooker, or sometimes in a steamer. The length of time the tomatoes are cooked depends on how they will eventually be canned (as purée, paste, etc.). After cooking, salt and spices, if they are called for, are added to the tomatoes, and then the product is sent through pulpers and finishers, which take out skins, seeds, and cores. Finally, the products are canned.

When whole tomatoes or stewed tomatoes are processed, they are first steamed, then an abrasive device rubs off the peels. They are then sorted; the best-looking make up cans of whole tomatoes, and the next best are canned as stewed tomatoes. After the cans are filled, juice, purée, or paste is added (as well as spices in the case of stewed tomatoes).

VARIETIES OF CANNED TOMATO PRODUCTS

Tomatoes

These are simply tomatoes that may be whole, diced, sliced, or cut into wedges; if the tomatoes are not peeled, the label will say "unpeeled." *Solid pack* means the can does not contain any added liquid or packing medium. If liquid is added, it will be tomato juice, purée, or paste, and the label will state which one has been used.

According to the Food and Drug Administration, a can of tomatoes can contain a calcium salt, which keeps the fruit firm; acidifying ingredients (the modern strain of tomatoes has been bred to be low in acid); sugars to neutralize the acids; salt; spices and flavorings; and other vegetables, such as onion, green pepper, and celery. If a significant amount of these vegetable ingredients is added to the can, the product is considered *stewed tomatoes.*

Tomato Purée

This form of canned tomatoes has the consistency of a thick homemade sauce, but without added flavoring ingredients. Purée is a concentrated form of tomato liquid, which may come from whole tomatoes, or from the peels, cores, and other residues of the canning or juicing process. The label must say that the purée comes from residual materials, if that is the case. In effect, purée is tomatoes that have been liquefied and then cooked down to a thick consistency; the government specifies that purée must contain between 8 and 24 percent tomato solids. The label will state if salt has been added.

Tomato Sauce

Tomato sauce is the same as tomato purée, with salt, sweet peppers, herbs, and spices added for flavoring. The degree of these flavoring ingredients is sufficiently mild so as to make sauce and purée practically interchangeable.

Tomato Paste

Paste is the most concentrated form of tomato product. It is cooked down to a consistency so thick that it must be spooned out of the can. Government regulations specify that paste must contain at least 24 percent tomato solids. If the product contains salt or spices, the label will contain this information.

HANDLING AND STORAGE

An unopened can of tomato product will last for about 2 years, as long as the can is not subjected to wide swings in temperature.

Once opened, any kind of tomato product will last in the refrigerator for about 10 days. To make sure the acid in the tomatoes doesn't interact with the metal in the can and give the tomatoes an off-flavor, transfer the contents of the opened can to a glass container and secure with a tight lid before storing.

To store an opened can of paste, pour a 1/4-inch layer of oil on the top of the unused portion of the paste (to prevent oxygen from getting to the tomatoes and causing mold to grow) and refrigerate.

Store tomato paste that comes in tubes in the refrigerator.

Tomato products can be frozen successfully, but first they should be taken out of their original cans and packed in airtight containers.

Tomato paste freezes especially conveniently if it is dropped by level tablespoons into an ice-cube tray, frozen for at least 3 hours, or until the pieces are solidly frozen, and then transferred to a tightly closed plastic bag. An icy piece will melt quickly when added to a hot dish on the stove.

HOW TO JUDGE CANNED TOMATO PRODUCTS

Tasting Media

Transfer tomato paste from the can (or tube) to clear glass bowls and sample them with plastic spoons. Next to the bowls with the straight tomato paste place clear glass bowls with a solution of 1 part paste and 1 part water, so that each tomato paste can also be sampled in less intense form, a common practice for tasting tomato paste in the industry.

The entire contents of each can of whole tomatoes should be poured into clear glass bowls, where tasters can see the shape of the tomatoes and the consistency of the accompanying liquid. Another can of each brand of whole tomatoes should be puréed in a blender and cooked over moderate heat for 20 minutes, in order to approximate the texture of a cooked (unseasoned) sauce, and to evaluate the cooking properties of each of the brands.

Panelists taste tomato sauce and purée by pouring them into clear glass bowls and sampling them with plastic spoons.

Color/Eye Appeal

In any tomato product, the color should remind the viewer of fresh tomatoes; paleness or uneven color are drawbacks. In whole tomatoes, appearance can indicate whether the tomatoes were picked when ripe or unripe; this is especially evident when looking at the stem end of the tomatoes; a green or pale color indicates the tomato was picked too early.

Whole tomatoes should be in one piece, and of an even color and consistent size. Blemishes and rotten spots on the tomatoes are unattractive and detract from the taste.

Taste/Aroma

The most desirable canned tomato products taste like *ripe* tomatoes, with a rich, full flavor that will stand up to robust seasoning or on its own in a simple sauce.

Too much acid or sweetness in a tomato product is undesirable. Bitter, metallic, overripe, or underripe flavors are characteristic of badly canned tomatoes.

Consistency

Unripe tomatoes will turn mealy when canned; overripe tomatoes will disintegrate. Badly canned tomato paste can be grainy or oily.

Aftertaste

Many poor tomato products taste metallic, as a result of bad canning practices.

CONCLUSIONS AND SUGGESTIONS

For years, prominent cookbook authors have been advising readers to buy only whole plum tomatoes canned in Italy, assuring them that the taste of Italian tomatoes is better than California-produced tomatoes. Some even went so far as to specify a region in Italy known for canning the best tomatoes in that country: San Marzano, near Naples. This region has such a reputation that many Italian and American canners specify San Marzano-*quality* tomatoes on their labels, as if the words were enough to assure a pedigree. Sad to say, only one of the *genuine* San Marzano tomatoes that I have tasted (Guido) is acceptable. Many are bland, thin in flavor, and disintegrated. It's possible that it takes so long to ship the tomatoes from Italy to the United States that the tomatoes suffer in the process, or perhaps the metal used in the canning process is of an inferior grade to that used in the American brands.

In fact, although the clear winner in the canned whole tomato competition is an Italian brand, Francesco Rinaldi, most of the Italian tomatoes we tasted, even those not from San Marzano, were of poor quality and were inferior to the American brands.

The real news of this tasting is that American tomatoes are delicious and do very nicely for cooking. The great James Beard specified Redpack tomatoes for his recipes, and this brand rated very high in my tasting. The most obvious difference between Italian-packed and American-packed whole tomatoes is that the American brands are saltier, because of the addition of salt to the cans, and markedly sweeter, due to the variety of tomatoes used.

Another important point is that since tomatoes used for canning are allowed to ripen on the vine, they are much tastier than most fresh tomatoes, especially those that are picked green and allowed to ripen on the way to market. Unless you grow your own tomatoes, or live in an area that produces terrific local tomatoes in season (like the outstanding New Jersey beefsteak tomatoes), use canned tomatoes; they will almost always be the superior choice for a tomato sauce or stew.

Canned tomatoes are priced so consistently that only one brand differs substantially in price from all the others. The exception, Elvea, not only costs five times more, but also doesn't taste very good.

COOKING WITH TOMATO PRODUCTS

The technical term "product" in the title of this chapter comes from professional kitchens, where recipes and chefs call for "tomato product," meaning anything from paste to ketchup, depending on what's on hand in the storeroom. That's because chefs know something that home cooks are just discovering: all kinds of tomatoes put up in cans or jars are essentially the same product in different forms. Here are a few common sense hints for substitution.

In general, when cooking with canned tomato products, the most common problem is too much acid flavor. The easiest and safest way to avoid this is to cook the tomato product for a long time over *very* low heat. I put one of my gas burner grates on top of another, so that the pot is raised above the low flame and the sauce cooks that much more slowly.

Old wives also advise adding a pinch of sugar or baking soda to a tomato sauce or soup that has turned too acidic. Although these methods work, I prefer to cook the sauce slowly to achieve a natural sweetness.

Tomato paste is particularly acidic and should be used sparingly—a teaspoon or a tablespoon to a sauce or a soup to give color and a bit of tomato flavor. Many of the Italian tomato pastes are labeled "doppio concentrato," or double concentrated, and should be used even more sparingly than domestic brands. These imported double-concentrated versions usually come in toothpaste-like tubes.

RECIPES

Tomato Biscuits with Cumin Seeds

I developed these southwestern-type biscuits, best eaten steaming hot right out of the oven. You can make the dough an hour or two ahead of time and bake the biscuits just before serving, if you like. They are also delicious as a dumpling topping for a hearty American beef or chicken stew: Make this recipe through step one and drop the dough by tablespoons onto the top of the stew about 20 minutes before it is finished cooking. Place a tight cover on the casserole or Dutch oven and finish cooking the stew on the top of the range or in the oven. (Makes about 20 biscuits)

WHEN A RECIPE CALLS FOR:	YOU CAN USE:
1 pound fresh tomatoes	*1 cup (8 ounces) whole tomatoes* or *1 cup (8-ounce can) tomato purée* or *1 cup (8-ounce can) tomato sauce*
1 cup tomato purée	*1 cup (8-ounce can) tomato sauce* or *3 ounces tomato paste (6 tablespoons or 1/2 can) plus 1/2 cup water*
2 cups whole tomatoes	*1 cup tomato sauce or purée plus 1 cup water*
1 can condensed tomato soup	*1 cup (8-ounce can) tomato sauce plus 1/4 cup water*
1 cup tomato juice	*1/4 cup tomato sauce plus 1/2 cup water*

2 cups all-purpose flour
1 tablespoon baking powder
1 teaspoon salt
3 tablespoons cold unsalted butter
1/4 cup grated Parmesan or dry Monterey Jack cheese
3/4 cup tomato purée or tomato sauce
1/4 cup heavy cream
1 tablespoon butter, melted
2 tablespoons whole cumin seeds

1. Into a large mixing bowl, sift together the flour, baking powder, and salt. Cut the cold butter into the dry ingredients with a pastry blender or a fork, until the mixture resembles coarse cornmeal. (You can also do this with your hands, quickly rubbing the flour and butter between your palms until the mixture is like coarse cornmeal.) Add the grated cheese, tomato purée and heavy cream and mix with a fork or your hands until a dough is formed.

(If you have a food processor, substitute the following directions for step 1: Into the bowl of a food processor, sift together the flour, baking powder, and salt. Add the cold butter, cut up into pieces, and the grated cheese. Process for about 15 seconds, until the mixture resembles coarse cornmeal.

Add the tomato purée and heavy cream to the mixture in the processor and process just until all ingredients are blended, about 10 seconds.)

2. Drop heaping tablespoons of the mixture onto a greased or nonstick cookie sheet. Using a pastry brush, dab some of the melted butter onto the top of each biscuit, and then sprinkle a few cuminseeds onto the top of each biscuit. Bake at 450°F for 15 to 18 minutes, or until biscuits are very lightly browned and dry inside.

Easy Basic Tomato Sauce

Tomato sauce is best when it is uncomplicated and straightforward. This one couldn't be simpler; it is delicious whether served over pasta or meat loaf or in a casserole. It also freezes well, so you can make up a batch and put it away for those times when nothing can be found in the cupboard except a box of spaghetti. (Makes approximately 5 cups)

8 tablespoons (1 stick) sweet butter, or 1/2 cup olive oil or 4 ounces (8 tablespoons) lard
1 large onion, chopped (about 1 1/4 cups)
4 garlic cloves, chopped
2 large cans (either 28-ounce or 35-ounce) whole tomatoes
1/4 cup chopped fresh parsley or fresh basil, or a combination of the two
salt and freshly ground pepper

1. In a heavy saucepan, melt the butter (or olive oil or lard) and add the chopped onion and garlic. Sauté over moderate-low heat until onion is light golden, about 10 minutes.

2. Add the entire contents of the 2 cans of tomatoes and roughly break up the whole tomatoes with a wooden spoon or kitchen fork. Simmer over the lowest heat for 20 minutes.

3. Put the contents of the saucepan through the large disc of a food mill (or roughly chop in a food processor or a blender, if you don't have a food mill).

4. Put puréed sauce back into the saucepan and add herbs and salt and pepper to taste. Simmer over the lowest heat for 30 minutes or so, stirring occasionally. If you would like your sauce to be thicker, simmer further until reduced to desired consistency.

OPTIONS: You can add 2 cups of cooked ground beef or sausage, shellfish, sautéed mushrooms, or any other food that will flavor and amplify this sauce. You can also add hot pepper flakes or hot sauce to make the sauce spicy.

SARDINES

s Americans have traveled more and have become familiar with the habits and foods of other countries, we have observed that they value a food that is considered in this country a rather lowly item—the sardine. Instead of a midnight snack, eaten straight out of the can, as sardines have long been "served" in the United States, canned sardines are considered a highly sophisticated food in other countries of the world—a delightful staple on the menus of Parisian brasseries, an elegant addition to an English canapé tray, and an integral part of elaborate Scandinavian smorgasboards.

The most popular sardines sold in the United States are the expensive Norwegian variety, which are usually packed with skin and bones intact. Regionally, consumers in the Northeast prefer skinless and boneless sardines, while people in the upper Midwest (many of whom are of Scandinavian descent) like their sardines with skin and bones.

All in all, Americans eat fewer sardines today then in years past, perhaps because in the nineteenth century sardines were one of the few foods packed in cans, while today many more varieties of foods come canned, including tuna, salmon, and oysters, so the competition for ready-to-eat foods is much stiffer.

A DASH OF HISTORY

By the turn of the nineteenth century, fishermen in Brittany had developed a method of preserving sardines that was the predecessor to industrial canning: they sautéed fresh sardines in butter or olive oil and then packed them in clay jars called *oules.* In 1824, a Frenchman named Joseph Colin began to put up sardines in tins in the city of Nantes, using the Brittany tradition as an example. Sardines were first canned in 1834 on the island of Sardinia.

By the 1880s, sardine canning had spread to various other European countries, such as Spain and Portugal, which developed their own canning industries. Norway's sardine-canning history began with Norwegian sailors who, in 1890, started to can the small fish for their own consumption. Today, sardine packing is an important European industry in Portugal, France, Norway, Italy, Spain, and Yugoslavia.

In the United States, in the first part of the twentieth century, sardine canning became an important support for the West Coast fishing industry and was immortalized by John Steinbeck in his books *Cannery Row* and *Sweet Thursday.* (The Sardine Factory in Monterey, California, is one of the most prominent restaurants in the country; its name reflects the region's past.)

In the 1930s, so many sardine-type fish were taken from Pacific waters that most of the supply was used up. Soon after the Pacific sardines disappeared, the same species of fish (a large variety of pilchard) appeared in South Africa, where they were fished for 15 years. The fish never returned to Pacific waters, however, and now most of the sardines canned in America come from

Maine, where the American industry started in 1874.

oil that comes naturally from the fish). The cans are sealed and sterilized in pressure cookers.

HOW SARDINES ARE MADE

The term "sardine" has come to mean any small, oily fish with weak bones that can be canned efficiently. The true sardine, however, is the *Sardina pilchardus,* a young version of the pilchard fish, and it was these fish that were originally canned as sardines in the nineteenth century. These days, the type of fish used for sardines depends upon the country in which it is canned. Twenty-five types of fish exist world-wide that are canned as sardines, including pilchard, brisling (or sprat), alewife, and herring. Since these fish also vary among themselves according to species (a brisling from one country may not resemble a brisling from another), the native species of fish affect the flavor of the various kinds of canned sardines. Moreover, in some countries, several kinds of fish are packed together and sold as sardines. The *Codex Alimentarius Commission of the Food and Agriculture Organization of the United Nations* requires that any canned fish other than a true sardine must be named on the label, along with the name of the country in which it was packed.

Generally, the procedure for canning sardines goes as follows: regardless of the fish used, they are first caught in nets and hauled onto the fishing boats, where they are descaled. They are chilled on the boat and taken to the canning factory. In the factory, the fish are held in refrigerated brine tanks until they are ready to be processed further.

The fish are then trimmed (sometimes the skin and bones are removed, sometimes just the heads) and packed into little cans by hand. In some cases, the sardines are lightly smoked or fried before being put into the cans. After the fish are put into cans, the cans are steamed to cook the fish, then cooled and dried. Then oil, water, or a sauce (such as mustard or tomato) is added to the cans. The oil used may be olive, peanut, cottonwood, soybean, or sild sardine oil (the type of

VARIETIES OF SARDINES

Here are some guidelines for what to expect of cans of sardines available in the United States, grouped according to country of origin.

U.S. (Maine)

Herring are the fish canned in Maine, and only the young, small fish are used as sardines. They are packed four or five to a can in one layer and are generally chubby and slightly dry; they are canned with skin and bones intact, as well as with skin and bones removed.

Sardines from the Pacific are no longer canned in the United States, as they were in the early part of the twentieth century before overfishing ruined supplies.

Canada

Since they come from the same waters, Canadian sardines are almost identical to Maine sardines.

Norway

Brisling (also known as sprats) are what the Norwegians market as sardines. Brisling are tiny, oily, flaky fish canned in two tight layers. Most of the time Norwegian sardines are lightly smoked over wood chips. A small percentage of sardines from Norway are young herring, a larger fish than brisling, packed in one layer with the skin and bones removed.

France, Portugal, Spain

Young pilchards are packed by the French, Portuguese, and Spanish as sardines. Pilchards are chubby, oily fish and take up one layer in a can. They are packed with and without skins and bones; often the fish are fried before being packed.

Italy

Young herring from the Mediterranean Sea are packed in Italy as sardines, and five or six fish, each about 4 inches long, take up one layer in a typical can. Italian sardines are usually packed in olive oil; the fish are often fried before packing.

England

Sardines bearing an English label are actually almost always from Norway, canned in Scotland in the Norwegian style.

HANDLING AND STORAGE

The French, who take sardines somewhat more seriously than anyone else (they eat 200 million cans per year), actually can vintage sardines that are meant to be eaten years after being canned.

Aficionados have long felt that at least 1 year's aging in the can improves the flavor of sardines, and 2 years is ideal, partly because the oil in which they are packed has a chance to penetrate the fish more thoroughly, giving them a more mellow flavor.

Sardines packed in oil can be "aged" at home (inadvertently or on purpose) simply by leaving an unopened can on a cool pantry shelf for up to 2 years. The can should be turned over every 2 months or so to redistribute the oil.

Manufacturers suggest that a can of sardines packed in oil will keep for 2 to 3 years safely. Sardines packed in water or sauce will keep for a shorter time, about 1 year. An opened can of sardines will last for about 5 days, if kept in an airtight container in the refrigerator.

HOW TO JUDGE SARDINES

Tasting Media

Group the sardines according to type: lightly smoked, packed in oil, skinless and boneless, low sodium, and packed in salt. Open each of the cans and turn the contents into a shallow white saucer, so that the amount of liquid is visible.

When manufacturers test their products, they strain the contents of a can into a clear beaker so that they can measure the amount of oil and water in the can.

Color/Eye Appeal

The fish should be clean, shiny, and bright. There should be no evidence of dirt, scales, brown spots, or detached fins. Fish over 5 inches or under 2 inches long are undesirable, and every fish in the can should be of the same size and length. The sardines should be tightly and evenly layered, and the flesh firm and unbroken. The skins should be silvery and the backbones white. The liquid surrounding the fish should be clear.

Taste/Aroma

A good sardine tastes lightly salty, with a good, clean fish taste, and a rich, smooth flavor.

Manufacturers taste a sardine by taking a piece from the top of the back of the fish; they chew it and suck the juices from it without swallowing.

Consistency

Sardines should be neither too dry nor too mushy; they should not fall apart too easily, and the bones should not be obtrusive.

The professional way to check the texture of a sardine is to lift a fish with your thumb, middle finger, and ring finger, with the thumb on the bottom. The feel of the fish should be firm, and it should not fall apart when lifted.

Aftertaste

Sardines should not have a metallic, bitter aftertaste, nor a strong fishy aftertaste.

CONCLUSIONS AND SUGGESTIONS

Another food myth evaporated after my sardine tasting: sardines packed in olive oil are not necessarily better than those packed in other (less expensive) oils. Beach Cliff sardines from Maine, which were packed in soy oil, prove overall to be the tastiest. They are also the cheapest. Thus, I concluded that sardines packed in mediocre olive oil are not as good as those packed in *good* soy oil. Moreover, simply because sardines are packed in *good* olive oil is no guarantee of quality: the Gravier Ainé & Co. brand from France, packed in extra-virgin olive oil, has an impeccable pedigree as well as a high price (and a long name!), and yet they taste merely good, not great.

After all of the hullabaloo made by food snobs about vintage sardines, I was surprised to find that the one example in my tasting (Maxim's) did not fare better than a fair ranking. Although they were tasty, they had an unmistakable flavor of the tin. Could the tinny flavor have come from being cooped up in a can for 4 years? They are definitely not worth $1 per fish, which is approximately what they cost in high-priced gourmet stores.

Another surprise is the vast difference in quality between the skinless and boneless sardines and those packed with skins and bones. The skinless and boneless variety are rather like boneless chicken breasts: a polite, bland, characterless food. Most of the ones I have tasted are also rubbery and dry (often a problem with chicken breasts, by the way).

Sardines packed with skins and bones have a deeper, more interesting flavor, and do not actually "taste" of the bones and skins.

My personal favorite of all the categories are those that are lightly smoked. For my pantry, I would never buy sardines packed in water; to me they are worse than having no sardines at all. If I were worried about calories, I would simply rinse them in water gently to remove as much oil as possible.

COOKING WITH SARDINES

For me, sardines are a soothing food, satisfying and delicious, particularly when simply dressed with fresh lemon juice and accompanied by crisp unsalted crackers. My husband recently convinced me, however, that there may be another way to eat sardines: he mashes equal amounts of sardines and soft sweet butter, flavors the mixture with a couple of drops of both fresh lemon juice and hot sauce, and spreads the rough paste on thin crisp toast. It's delicious enough to serve as an elegant canapé.

Sardines packed in salt can be used for cooking in the same way as salted anchovies are used. Before adding them to a dish, rinse them under cold, running water and take out the backbones, which come up easily with your fingers. Salt-packed sardines are a little firmer than the sardines packed in oil, and thus perhaps are more appropriate for any cooked recipe.

A dish with canned sardines I have had many times in Venice is called *bigoli,* an unusual pasta specialty of the Veneto region. It is made with whole-wheat spaghetti, tossed with a sauce made of onions slowly sautéed in good olive oil and sardines added at the last minute together with a generous amount of freshly ground pepper. As with many pasta dishes in Italy containing fish, no cheese should be added. In spite of its simple preparation, it makes a highly original last-minute dish, suitable for company or a dinner for one.

RECIPE

Pasta with Sardines

Herewith another, somewhat more elaborate, sardine and pasta dish. This is a traditional Sicilian recipe, usually made with fresh sardines, which are plentiful there. (Makes 4 to 6 servings)

3 tablespoons raisins
5 dried tomatoes (optional)
2 pinches of saffron
1 bulb of fresh fennel
1 cup chopped onion
1/2 cup olive oil
4 anchovy fillets
2 tablespoons pine nuts
1 tablespoon tomato paste
salt and freshly ground pepper

- **1 pound pasta (penne, small ziti, or macaroni)**
- **$1/2$ cup freshly grated Parmesan cheese (optional)**
- **2 cans (approximately $4^1/2$ ounces each) sardines packed in oil, drained**

1. Soak the raisins and dried tomatoes in $3/4$ cup boiling water for 15 minutes. Drain, discard water, and chop raisins and tomatoes roughly; reserve for step 3. Cover the saffron with 1 tablespoon warm water from the tap and soak until ready to use in step 3.

2. Bring about 8 quarts of salted water to a boil. In the meantime, cut off the feathery tops of the fennel and discard, cut the fennel bulb into the thinnest possible strips (julienne) by cutting across the width of the bulb. Boil the cut fennel strips in the water for 5 minutes. Take out fennel with a slotted spoon and reserve the water to cook the pasta in step 4.

3. Sauté the chopped onion in the olive oil in a medium-size frying pan over moderate heat until onion has wilted, about 5 minutes. Add the reserved parboiled fennel, chopped raisins and tomatoes, saffron along with its soaking water, anchovies, pine nuts, tomato paste, and salt and pepper to taste. Cook stirring, over very low heat until the pasta is ready, about 10 minutes.

4. Boil the pasta in the water in which you cooked the fennel until *al dente.* Drain pasta and mix with the cheese. Place the sardines on top of the pasta and pour the warm fennel mixture from the frying pan onto the top of the sardines. Stir all together very gently, so the sardines don't break up too much. Serve immediately.

TUNA

"You might say that it is neither meat nor fish," wrote Alexander Dumas, neatly describing tuna, while at the same time probably pinpointing why it has become one of the staples of modern America.

Tuna is one of the more well-known foods in this country, and yet maybe it is *too* well known. How many times do shoppers absentmindedly head for the tuna aisle in the supermarket, stocking up on the brand they've always bought, not even seeing the words anymore, but buying the shape and color of label with which they are most familiar? Americans *eat* tuna in much the same way, cavalierly opening yet another can, mashing it with mayonnaise and celery (or minced onions or, heaven forbid, pickle relish), and slapping it onto a piece of bread. No doubt everyone makes his tuna salad exactly the same way as his mother did.

On the average, each American gets through 3.5 pounds of tuna per year that way, mostly in tuna sandwiches, closely followed by tuna salads and then by tuna casseroles (with noodles? topped with potato chips?). Tuna is a family food, especially popular with children. Over 80 percent of the households in the United States have an average of 2 to 3 cans of tuna on their pantry shelves at all times. Americans consume 2.39 billion cans of tuna every year, making it an $1.2-billion-per-year industry, representing more than 78 percent of all canned fish eaten in the United States.

The sales figures on tuna are up from 20 years ago, when each American ate 3.1 pounds per year.

A DASH OF HISTORY

Little did our nineteenth-century forebears know, as they were feeding the local tuna to their chickens (they wouldn't *think* of eating it themselves), that future generations of American children would grow up on the stuff. By contrast, salmon didn't suffer from the same scorn, and by the end of the nineteenth century canned salmon was very popular and available cheap all over the United States.

In 1903, a sardine canner in East San Pedro, California, named Alfred P. Halfhill was at a loss about what to do when the sardine catch fell short. He decided to put up albacore, one species of tuna. He turned out 700 cases of it, and the new item was a hit.

Ten years later, in 1913, 9 tuna canneries in California packed and sold a total of 115,000 cases. When World War I came along, America needed a cheap and ready source of protein, and so by 1917, the tuna industry had expanded to include 36 canneries on the West Coast, which sold a total of about 500,000 cases that year. The tuna business got another shot in the arm during World War II, when Americans again needed low-cost protein foods, made on home turf.

Up until just before World War II, the tuna industry was based solely in California, but in 1938 tuna was discovered swimming off the northern Pacific Coast, so many northwest salmon canners began to pack tuna as well. In 1948, tuna from the Atlantic Ocean was first caught and canned. Since then, American tuna canning has expanded to Hawaii, Puerto Rico, and American Samoa.

The fledgling industry was threatened soon after it began by the economic hardships of the Depression and by canned tuna imported from European countries. In 1932 the California Fish Canners Association (later to become the Tuna Research Foundation) was formed to lobby for domestic tuna by Americans and against imports. They were successful then, and again in 1950 when Japanese tuna imports posed similar threats to the American canners. The TRF is still a strong representative for the tuna industry; its five member companies—Bumble Bee, Neptune Packing, Star-Kist, Van Camp, and Mitsubishi—comprise 97 percent of all the tuna packed in the United States. In 1993, packers in the United States canned 618.7 million pounds of tuna and imported 224.4 million pounds, mostly from Thailand.

The 1982 tuna recall was just another in a long line of public relations disasters for the tuna industry in recent years, beginning in the 1970s when environmentalists boycotted to protest the canning of porpoise meat along with tuna. In 1959, purse seine nets (which operate on the principle of drawstring bags) were introduced, and often porpoises were caught along with the tuna. The boycott ended when tuna skippers devised ways to separate the yellowfin tuna and the porpoise, which swim together. The most commonly used method today is a panel in the nets through which only porpoise can pass, leaving the tuna captured within.

HOW TUNA IS MADE

After the tuna is caught, it is frozen on board the ships. When the clipper docks, the frozen tuna is put directly onto a conveyor belt going into the cannery.

The first stop for the tuna in the cannery is the giant thawing tanks. After it is thawed, the tuna is inspected and sorted by size. The fish are then loaded onto racks and taken into huge steam cookers where they are cooked for anywhere from 2½ hours for a 10-pound fish, to 10 hours for a 100-pound fish. The cooked fish is then taken into a huge processing room where it is skinned and boned. A 20-pound fish provides about 9 pounds of canned tuna, which is enough to fill 22 average-size (6½-ounce) cans.

The tuna is then packed into cans, and the cans are sent along conveyers where tiny spigots add oil, vegetable broth, water, and/or salt. The liquid that is added moistens the fish as well as acts as a buffer between the hot cans and the tuna.

Sodium acid pyrophosphate, often listed as pyrophosphate, is often added to canned tuna to inhibit the formation of struvite, harmless crystals that look like fragments of glass.

After the liquid is added, cans of tuna are vacuum-sealed and put into huge pressure cookers, or retort ovens, at 240°F. for from 40 minutes to 4 hours, depending on the size of the can. The most common size of can for tuna used to be 7 ounces, but in recent years manufacturers have been changing that can size to 6½ ounces; the prices have stayed the same.

VARIETIES OF TUNA

Solid Pack or Fancy

This is tuna packed with large pieces of meat, with no more than 18 percent flakes or fragments. It is usually the most desirable, thus the most expensive.

Chunk or Standard Pack

Chunk tuna must consist of at least 50 percent ½-inch pieces; the remainder of the weight is made up of flakes.

Flaked or Grated

Flaked or grated tuna is made entirely of small crumbs of tuna (often remaining from the packing of the first two grades), packed down into a solid cylinder. The meat for all three grades will be of the same quality, so for making a salad, croquettes, or any recipe where the shape of the tuna doesn't matter, the cheaper grades are the wisest choice.

White Meat Tuna

Only tuna that comes from the albacore species, a fish that weighs 8 to 12 pounds on average, can be called *white meat tuna.* Americans prefer it over all others, and pay a premium for it; it has the mildest flavor, the least amount of fishy taste, of all canned tuna. Overfishing has caused a decline in the catch of albacore tuna throughout the world.

Light Meat Tuna

Light meat tuna can be made primarily from yellowfin, but bluefin or skipjack tuna may also be included in a can. Even though it's called "light," this tuna has a slightly darker, sometimes much darker, color than white meat tuna. It tends to be more strong-flavored than albacore.

Yellowfin tuna average 12 to 24 pounds, although 80-pounders are not uncommon, and they can get as big as 150 pounds. Bluefin tuna weigh up to 1,000 pounds, but on average they weigh 80 pounds. The flesh of the bluefin is the darkest of all tuna and is the type of tuna preferred by the Japanese for *sushi.* Skipjack is the smallest species of tuna, weighing from 4 to 24 pounds.

Tuna Fillets

These are whole, small fingers of tuna packed in cans that resemble sardine cans. They are ideal for summer salads, such as Salade Niçoise, for example, when the whole pieces are desirable. All tuna fillets are imported from Spain and are packed in olive oil.

Ventresca

This is the part of the tuna that is highly prized by the Japanese as *toro,* or tuna belly, and is also considered a delicacy in Europe. *Ventresca* is from the stomach area of the fish; it contains more fat than the other parts of tuna.

Italian Tuna

Italian tuna, labeled "tonno" on labels of imported tuna, is skipjack tuna packed in olive oil; it has a darker meat than we are used to seeing in domestic tuna.

Select Prime Catch

This is a new product on the tuna market, a sort of "designer tuna" for the upscale consumer, made by StarKist. It is all yellowfin, lighter, milder and firmer than regular albacore.

Packed in Water

The vogue for tuna packed in water these days stems from the fact that you save substantial calories over tuna packed in oil. Water-packed tuna, drained, has 36 calories per ounce; oil-packed tuna, drained, has 56 calories per ounce.

Packed in Oil

When a tuna label reads "packed in oil," the oil is almost always soybean oil, which is relatively tasteless. If the product is packed in olive oil, it will be specified on the label.

Diet

Diet tuna can be either white or light tuna. It is processed with spring or distilled water and no salt is added.

Federally Inspected

The presence of a federal inspection stamp on a can of tuna is not necessarily an indication of high quality but simply a statement that the tuna is acceptable to the U.S. government. Canned tuna does not require inspection by law.

HANDLING AND STORAGE

An unopened can of tuna will stay in good condition for at least a year, probably up to 3 years, if it is stored under 65°F. Before opening, tuna in a can does not need to be refrigerated. If a can of tuna has gone bad, it bulges, and dents or rust appear on the can, so avoid old or damaged-looking products. If the tuna has gone off, it will smell like spoiled fish and will also taste extremely peppery.

After opening, a can of tuna should be transferred to a nonmetal container for storage. It will last in a tightly sealed container in the refrigerator for 3 days.

HOW TO JUDGE TUNA

Tasting Media

Pour the contents of the cans of tuna into shallow white bowls, undrained, so that the amount of liquid packed with the fish is evident. Taste the tuna with plastic forks, to minimize interference of the metallic taste of silverware.

Color/Eye Appeal

If a can of tuna is labeled "solid pack," it should contain solid chunks of tuna, without flakes or small pieces. If it is labeled "chunk tuna," a few flakes are acceptable. Flaked tuna can be made of compressed flakes. Rate tuna on its adherence to its type, as well as consistency of color; in other words, if some of the tuna in a can is pink and some is white, the tuna is of inferior quality.

Taste/Aroma

A good canned tuna should taste fresh and clean; a fishy aroma is a clue that the tuna is not freshly canned. The oil should not taste strong or rancid. Iodine flavor is a drawback. If tuna is packed in olive oil, a clean, olive-oil flavor should be present, but not so much so that it overwhelms the taste of the tuna. The salt level should be consistent and not too strong.

Consistency

Tuna should be tender. Tuna with poor consistency will look and taste dry and/or rubbery, as opposed to being tender.

Aftertaste

Tuna packed in old or off-tasting oil leaves a bitter and strong taste in the mouth, which is unacceptable.

CONCLUSIONS AND SUGGESTIONS

In any discussion of canned tuna, the subject of fresh tuna must come up. There are those who don't like fresh tuna and feel, as James Beard did, that it is often dry. On the other hand, there are those who find fresh tuna vastly superior to the ubiquitous canned variety.

Whatever your preference, fresh tuna bears very little resemblance to canned tuna. The bluefin tuna is the variety most often sold fresh, and in its raw state it looks very much like raw beef. In fact, sashimi lovers say it even tastes very much like raw beef. Fresh tuna is denser and richer than most fish. The fat content of tuna varies from one catch to the next, but, in general, tuna is a fatty fish.

The general consensus from my tasting is that tuna packed in water is much more dry and rubbery than tuna packed in oil. Although you save calories using water-packed tuna, you sacrifice flavor.

I tasted the tuna packed in vegetable oil and olive oil separately, because the olive oil gives a strong flavor to tuna and makes it into a somewhat different food. Surprisingly, I did not find that the tuna packed in olive oil is substantially better tasting than the tuna packed in vegetable (soybean) oil, a common perception. In fact, the best tunas packed in vegetable oil (Atun Blanco Bonito del Norte and Star-Kist Chunk Light) are much better tasting than most, though not all, of the tunas packed in olive oil.

Because tuna in olive oil costs much more than tuna in vegetable oil, I have switched to the latter, even in recipes where I would like the taste of olive oil, such as Vitello Tonnato, an Italian summer dish of sliced veal covered with a tuna and mayonnaise sauce. I simply discard the vegetable oil from the can of tuna (actually, I give it to my cats) and add a good olive oil to the recipe in its place. My favorite brand of tuna is Bumble Bee.

COOKING WITH TUNA

All of the most widely sold brands of tuna add salt; many also include vegetable broth as a seasoning, which also contains salt. If you are worried about sodium in your diet, it is a good idea to drain tuna well before using it to remove much of the sodium. The American Dietetic Association also reports that, in addition to draining, rinsing canned tuna with water for 1 minute will remove 76 to 79 percent of the sodium. A 3-minute rinse will remove an additional 5 percent of the sodium, leaving 65 milligrams of sodium in a 6½-ounce can, compared to 1,472 milligrams in the same amount of unrinsed tuna.

In addition to the tried-and-true recipes for canned tuna, you might like to consider some of the following ideas:

- Make your usual tuna salad with a garlicky-mayonnaise and put it into tacos with shredded cheese, jalapeño peppers, grated onion, and Monterey Jack cheese.
- Mix large chunks of tuna with nice wedges of fresh grapefruit and oranges. Top with thin-sliced Bermuda onion and a vinaigrette with fresh herbs (chives, tarragon, basil).
- Make a tabbouleh with tuna and serve in small Boston lettuce cups with a pesto dip.

RECIPES

Five-Minute Tuna Sauce for Pasta

Sicilian fishermen catch most of the tuna in Italy. This sauce is a variation of a very simple Italian sauce. Italians almost never add cheese to a sauce made with fish, but add some grated mozzarella, if you wish. This is also good for a last-minute dinner, as you can keep almost all of the ingredients on your pantry shelf. (Makes 4 servings)

1 cup minced onion
1 teaspoon minced garlic
½ cup olive oil
1 can (1 pound) whole peeled tomatoes
2 tablespoons chopped fresh basil or parsley
salt and freshly ground pepper
1 can (7 ounces) tuna packed in olive oil or vegetable oil (reserve the oil)

1. In a medium-size saucepan, sauté the onion and garlic in the ½ cup olive oil and the oil you have drained from the can of tuna. Cook stirring, over moderate heat until the onion is very light brown, about 10 minutes.

2. Place the contents of the can of tomatoes in a blender or food processor and process until smooth. Add to the onion and garlic and cook over moderate heat, stirring, until the sauce has reduced by about a third and is thick.

3. Add the basil or parsley and salt and pepper to taste. Add the tuna, breaking it up lightly with the back of the spoon. Heat through and serve on 1 pound of pasta, cooked.

Tuna and Pistachio Terrine

This recipe is from the late Helen McCully, whose personality was as no-nonsense as her recipes. Serve this pretty and delicious terrine as an hors d'oeuvre. (Makes 6 to 8 servings)

1 can (7 ounces) tuna packed in oil (reserve the oil)
2–3 tablespoons Cognac
2 hard-cooked eggs
6 ounces cream cheese, at room temperature
white pepper, freshly ground if possible

3 tablespoons shelled pistachio nuts, coarsely chopped
canned consommé, refrigerated until almost jelled

1. Break the tuna into small pieces. In the container of an electric blender or a food processor, purée a small amount at a time, with the tuna oil and Cognac; add the eggs. Add the softened cream cheese and white pepper to taste. Blend again at high speed until you have a very smooth mixture.

2. Place mixture in a bowl. Taste for seasoning. It may (doubtfully) need salt. Stir in the pistachio nuts. Spoon into a 1½- to 2-cup mold that can go to the table. Smooth the surface with a spatula.

3. Cover top of terrine with consommé that is just beginning to jell, and refrigerate until firm. Serve straight from the terrine with plain, unflavored crackers or French bread.

HERBS AND SPICES

HERBS AND SPICES

Good food can never be *great* food without the use of herbs and spices; they serve the same function as perfume for a woman, enhancing her natural attributes. Simply by charting the enormous increase in the use of herbs and spices in the United States, it becomes obvious that American food has gotten much better of late.

Alain Dutournier, chef of the Au Trou Gascon restaurant in Paris, could have been speaking for many illustrious French chefs when he said in *The Journal of Gastronomy,* "I use a lot of spices because I hate food with no taste . . . I like food with pronounced flavors. I've tasted wine since I was 13, marking down all the subtle flavors I detected. But I maintain that you really have to make an effort when you eat a cube of raw tuna as the Japanese do and say you find a wonderful taste. I'm not a cat. I don't find the taste so wonderful."

A spice is the dried flower, seeds, leaves, bark, or roots of various aromatic plants, usually from the Tropics. Cinnamon, nutmeg, and pepper are examples of spices. An herb comes from nonwoody plants that are generally grown each year from newly planted seeds; it is usually taken from the leaf of the plant. Examples of herbs are basil, dill, orégano, mint, and rosemary. However, rather than making a distinction between the two, the American Spice Trade Association calls both of these substances spices, and treats herbs as a leafy subcategory of spices.

In 1984, consumption of herbs and spices in the United States reached a high of 622,393,000 pounds, which represents a whopping 33 percent increase over 10 years earlier. Put another way, the 1984 per capita consumption of herbs and spices in the United States was 42 ounces, 10 ounces more than in 1974. In 1994, that consumption increased to 730 million pounds, or 45½ ounces per person.

In the past 20 years, the consumption of "hot" spices, including chile peppers, white and black peppers, mustard and ginger, increased by more than 73 percent. Red pepper—the hottest of the "hots"—has shown by far the largest spurt. As a yardstick for measuring these gains, consider that a single ounce of black pepper is sufficient to season 1,230 boneless chicken breasts with generous sprinklings. And red pepper will go a lot farther than that, no matter how hot you like your food. The "hots" now represent 41 percent of U.S. spice consumption.

The 5 most popular spices throughout the United States are dehydrated onion and garlic, mustard seed, red pepper, sesame seed and black pepper. Many regional variations exist, however, in the list of the most popular spices in the country; residents of Los Angeles and Miami, for example, use a lot of cumin for their Hispanic dishes.

In the Mid-Atlantic states, the list of the most popular herbs in order of preference is dill, basil, orégano, parsley, bay leaves, tarragon, thyme, rosemary, chives, and marjoram. In Southern California and Arizona: basil, dill, leaf orégano, tarragon, bay leaves, parsley, rosemary, thyme, marjoram, and ground orégano. In the South: basil, orégano, dill, parsley, bay leaves, chives, tarragon, rosemary, thyme, and sage. In New England: tarragon, basil, bay leaves, orégano, parsley, dill, thyme, chives, rosemary, and sage. In the Midwest: dill, basil, orégano, tarragon, parsley, rosemary, thyme, chives, and sage. In the Southwest: basil, orégano, bay leaves, chives, dill, parsley, tarragon, rosemary, thyme, and sage. In Northern California and Nevada: basil, dill, orégano, bay leaves, tarragon, rosemary, parsley, thyme, marjoram, and chives. In the Northwest: basil, dill, orégano, bay leaves, tarragon, parsley, chives, thyme, rosemary, and sage.

People who call themselves "light users" of herbs and spices are likely to have on hand cinnamon, orégano, paprika, nutmeg, chili powder, bay leaves, and dried parsley flakes. People who call themselves "heavy users" will also have basil, cloves, and sage in their spice cabinets.

Eighty-two percent of the households in the United States have used herbs or spices in the last 6 months and have a substantial inventory of at least 15 jars in their spice cabinets. Generally, herbs and spices are used mostly at dinnertime.

Two of the reasons for the increase in use of herbs and spices are some consumers' reduced salt and sugar consumption. Instead of adding sugar to a tomato sauce, for example, parsley and basil are used to enhance the flavor; and mustard powder or sage may disguise the fact that a dish is made without salt. Another reason for the increase is the recent popularity of pizza, barbecue, and Italian food, which account for interest in orégano, chili powder, and basil. Until just at the beginning of World War II, when pizza became popular, annual sales of orégano were so small in the United States that they weren't even recorded in consumption figures for herbs. Basil wasn't listed separately in government import figures until 1964.

The fact that Americans have traveled around the world more in recent decades also accounts for interest in what used to be considered "exotic" herbs and spices.

Forty percent of the herb and spice market in the United States is held by Schilling/McCormick (same company—the Schilling brand is sold west of the Mississippi and McCormick in the East); the next-largest producer is Burns Philp Food, Inc., which produces Durkee and Spice Islands.

A DASH OF HISTORY

Since ancient Roman times, trade in spices has been a profitable activity in the Middle East. At least as far back as A.D. 300, the probable date of the oldest known cookbook, written by the Roman Apicius, the best food was highly spiced. The Romans brought spices to their empire from China and India by way of expensive, cumbersome, and dangerous caravan journeys, which made spices scarce and out of the reach of all but wealthy citizens.

After the fall of Rome, Arab spice traders gained total control of the market, and they never divulged the source of their supplies, thus discouraging European competition. In the thirteenth century, the writings of Marco Polo told of the spices he'd seen in the Orient, which inspired many Europeans to think of finding a direct supply by themselves. Soon afterward, some adventurous men set out in search of viable routes to obtain spices for Europe, and in the process stumbled on many new lands, including ours.

In 1492, Christopher Columbus started his journey across the Atlantic to find a westward passage to India and found America instead. His trip wasn't a total loss for those interested in spices, however, since Oriental spices, including ginger, were later planted successfully in the Caribbean.

Vasco de Gama, a Portuguese sailor, rounded the southern tip of Africa in 1498 and forged a path for future journeys to India and China. One immediate result of his discovery was that the price of pepper in Europe fell dramatically; beforehand, it was so expensive that it was sold by the individual peppercorn.

Spaniard Ferdinand Magellan's around-the-world expedition that began in 1519 discovered what were to be called the Spice Islands; today these islands are part of Indonesia, called the Moluccas.

A colonial American, Elihu Yale, was one of the first natives of the New World to become a part of the spice trade. In 1672, he reached India and started a spice business that eventually yielded a fortune, with which he founded Yale University. During the latter part of the eighteenth century, America was active in world spice trade, but dropped out in the latter part of the nineteenth century because of the unavoidable devastation of piracy on the high seas.

HOW HERBS AND SPICES ARE MADE

Most of the herbs and spices used in the United States are imported, but some (about 37 percent of total consumption) are grown in this country, primarily in California. Although California produces paprika, chile peppers, basil, tarragon, mint, parsley, sage, marjoram, mustard seed, dill, and fennel, most of the domestic poundage is made up of dehydrated (and some freeze-dried) vegetable products, such as onions, garlic, chives, shallots, bell peppers, and mixed vegetable flakes.

The second largest provider of spices to the United States is Canada, which mostly exports mustard seed, used largely by mustard producers and meat-packers. Third place goes to Mexico, which supplies Americans with sesame seeds, chile peppers, and orégano. Indonesia is America's fourth-largest supplier, followed by India.

Many of the countries to which herbs and spices are native have been politically unstable for generations, and so the source of supply of a particular substance often changes every few years. For example, the United States used to import a great deal of top-quality cinnamon from Vietnam, but during the embargo on products from that country, Americans got much of their cinnamon from Sri Lanka. Fewer and fewer herbs and spices are imported to the United States because, although India produces just as many as before, many Indian products are now being traded with Russia in exchange for heavy equipment.

Many of these countries from which herbs and spices are imported are also climatically unstable, causing fluctuations in market prices. For example, before 1957, half of the nutmeg imported came from Grenada. When a hurricane wiped out most of Grenada's production, the United States turned to Indonesia to fill 80 percent of the required nutmeg supply.

The herbs and spices that are imported into this country are generally hand-harvested, while those in California are harvested by machine. Hand-harvesting is labor-intensive, but labor in countries where herbs and spices are grown is generally inexpensive. Harvesting is also time-consuming: a careful selection must be made of what will be picked, then it must be separated from the tree or plant by hand, sometimes accompanied by hulling, shredding, sifting, and so on, and then, in some cases, the substance must be dried or ripened before being packed and shipped. Many countries rely on the hot tropical sun to dry herbs and spices.

Imported herbs and spices enter the country from both coasts, with the vast majority coming in through New York. They generally arrive dried in whole form, in burlap bags, laminated paper bags, rattan baskets, or wooden crates. This system allows American spice companies to clean the raw materials according to their own specifications. Only paprika comes to this country already ground.

It takes about three weeks by ship for herbs and spices to arrive in this country after being harvested, but some whole spices that don't lose aroma or flavor when stored, such as whole peppercorns and whole cinnamon, may take years to get here. Farmers in the countries where these spices are grown sometimes stockpile their wares and wait to sell them at a time when they need the money, for example, when a daughter is getting married and the farmer needs to provide her with a dowry, when he needs a new piece of machinery, or when the prices rise.

After arrival in the United States, imported herbs and spices are shipped to grinding plants where they are cleaned, ground (or processed, according to the spice variety), and packaged.

Several types of mills are used to grind spices because of the wide variety of materials that must be processed—bark, seeds, flowers, leaves, and so on.

VARIETIES OF HERBS AND SPICES

Basil

Basil is an herb that is native to India, where it originated more than 4,000 years ago. The ancient Greeks and Romans used basil in much of their cooking. The name basil comes from the Greek *basileus,* which means king. Basil was planted in the American colonies and was offered for sale in the *Virginia Gazette* in 1775.

The modern city most associated with basil is Genoa in northern Italy, where the specialty is *pesto,* a basil, garlic, and olive-oil purée used in everything from soup to pasta.

Although different varieties of basil exist, the most common is *sweet basil,* which, when fresh, has a spicy, minty flavor, not surprising, since basil is a member of the mint family. The sweet basil plant is an annual and grows to a height of about 1½ feet. The leaves look like large mint leaves—oval with pointed ends, about 2 inches long. Dried sweet basil has a different flavor from fresh basil; it tastes almost like licorice.

After being dried, during processing basil leaves naturally break up into bits of different sizes, sold as "leaf basil." Imported dried leaf basil is sold as a mixture of these different-size bits, but California basil is available dried in three different sizes: *coarse,* ¼-inch bits; *medium,* ⅛-inch bits; and *fine,* 1/16-inch bits. Basil is also sold in powdered form.

Imported basil comes from France and Egypt. Experts consider the flavor of French basil superior to all others. However, California basil commands a higher price because it has better color, uniformity, and cleanliness.

More than 60 different types of basil grow all over the world, and most are cultivated for use in perfumes. Other types of basil that are available fresh in this country, usually in potted plants and sometimes in fresh bunches in specialty food stores, are *dark opal basil* (also called *purple basil*), which has purple-black leaves and a pungent flavor; *bush basil,* which has tiny leaves and a mild flavor; *lemon basil,* which is a hybrid plant with a lemony-basil flavor.

Basil is often paired with tomatoes and tomato-based dishes; its minty flavor seems to complement the acidic flavor of tomatoes very well. A delicious summer beverage (a variation on May wine) can be made by steeping a handful of basil in some German wine at room temperature for a day or so. Strain the wine and chill it before serving.

Bay Leaves

Bay leaves played an important part in Greek and Roman mythology: the beautiful nymph Daphne, fleeing from Apollo, was turned into a laurel tree, and forever after its leaves have symbolized victory, honor, and scholarship. The ancient Greeks crowned their poets and heroes with wreaths of bay leaves, which is where our modern term "laureate" comes from.

The laurel tree, which can grow to a height of 60 feet, is native to the Mediterranean. Although its leaves are most often called *bay leaves,* they are also sometimes called *laurel leaves* in the trade. Bay leaves can be as long as 3 inches, with pointed ends. They are most often sold dried in whole form, but sometimes are packaged as powdered bay leaves. Bay leaves have a flowery, sweet aroma and a perfumed, peppery, aromatic flavor with a slightly bitter aftertaste; they are usually used whole in cooking and removed before a dish is served.

Bay leaves are imported into the United States from Turkey, Greece, Portugal, and Yugoslavia; California bay leaves are also available. Mediterranean bay leaves are slightly serrated on the edges, greenish-brown in color, and have a medium strength; California bay leaves are much bigger and smoother, brighter green, oilier, and three times as strong as Mediterranean bay leaves, with a slightly medicinal taste. Overall, Turkish bay leaves are considered superior to all others.

In Victorian England, bay leaves were used to flavor custards and can be used the same way today in sweet milk-based dishes, such as rice pudding, for a haunting, spicy flavor.

Chili Powder

Chili powder, a truly American spice mixture, was first made in 1835, when English settlers in Texas devised a blend of spices that would facilitate the making of Mexican-style dishes. Chili powder was first made commercially in 1910 in California.

Chili powder is not one spice, but a combination of several. Depending on the brand, it is usually made of ground chile peppers (mild, not hot), orégano, cumin, garlic, and salt. Some brands may contain cloves, allspice, anise, and coriander. It is meant to be used in chili con carne, barbecue sauce, on potato chips, and in Tex-Mex-style foods, such as tacos.

The chiles used in chili powder are largely grown in California, although some come from New Mexico and Mexico. Large manufacturers usually mix several different types of mild chiles in order to get a standard flavor and heat level from batch to batch.

I sampled a dozen brands of packaged chili powder (in tins, bottles, paper, and foil packets), including supermarket and "gourmet store" brands. The very best was the Durkee brand packed in a glass jar (not Durkee in a tin), which was both sweet and hot at the same time. Second best was Spice Islands, which had an interesting citrusy flavor, and third in order of preference was Dean & DeLuca's own brand (see "Sources," page 237, for ordering information), which was flavorful albeit mild.

I have also found some fabulous varietal chili powders from a company called Chile Today Hot Tamale. If you can't find that brand in your local store, check for mail order information in "Sources," page 237.

Cinnamon

The Chinese mentioned cinnamon in their earliest herbals, written thousands of years ago. The ancient Romans felt the scent of cinnamon was sacred and so Nero burned an entire year of Rome's supply of it at the funeral of his wife, Poppaea. Cinnamon was one of the major spices sought by the oceanic expeditions of the fifteenth and sixteenth centuries. Today, cinnamon is one of the most popular spices in America.

The term "cinnamon" actually refers to the bark of two different evergreen trees in the same botanical family, relatives of the laurel tree. Almost all of what we call *cinnamon* in this country is actually *cassia,* which is different from *cinnamon,* also called Ceylon cinnamon. Cassia is reddish-brown in color with a characteristically strong aroma and flavor. True cinnamon is a light tan color, with an exceptionally mild aroma and flavor. Most of the cinnamon imported into the United States is in turn re-exported to Mexico, where its mild flavor is preferred for native sweets. In this country, both cassia and cinnamon can legally be called *cinnamon.*

Cassia is imported into the United States from Indonesia, mainland China, India, Taiwan, and—at one time (before the end of the Vietnam War)—from Saigon, where the highest-quality cassia grows. The best cassia today comes from Sumatra. True Ceylon cinnamon, usually used in cinnamon blends, is imported from the Seychelles Islands in the Indian Ocean, mainland China, and Madagascar.

The trees when cultivated are about 6 feet in height; wild cinnamon trees can grow as high as 50 feet.

Cinnamon is harvested during the rainy season, when the inner bark of the trees is easiest to handle; the bark is stripped from the tree trunk and branches. When dried, the bark curls up tightly into shapes known in the trade as *quills* and by consumers as *cinnamon sticks.* The cinnamon imported into the United States usually comes in the form of these quills, which can be up to $2^1/_2$ feet in length, several nesting together in big bunches. Like pepper, cinnamon will retain its aroma and flavor in this whole form for an indefinite amount of time.

Cinnamon quills are cut into smaller lengths and sold as cinnamon sticks, or they are ground fine and packaged. Stick cinnamon is too hard to grind into a fine powder with any kind of home machine. Many brands of ground cinnamon on the retail market today are actually blends of cinnamon of different strengths from different sources, in order to ensure a consistent flavor from jar to jar. Cinnamon packaged for sale to food processors is labeled according to strength of flavor.

In the United States, cinnamon is most often used in baked goods, such as breads, cookies, and pies. It is also an ingredient in mixed pickling spices; it adds a delicious flavor to stewed fruits.

Around the world, cinnamon is used in many savory as well as sweet dishes. Greeks add a cinnamon stick to beef stews, and the Pennsylvania Dutch sprinkle cinnamon-sugar over tomato slices. Mexicans use cinnamon in coffee and chocolate drinks. A stick of cinnamon is also a good addition to the ingredients for a rice pilaf.

Curry Powder

When Indians make a traditional curry (which is a dish with scores of variations), they begin by mixing up to 25 different spices together in order to get the right balance of flavors; the Indian word for a personal spice mixture of this type is "masala." Curry in India can be mild, sweet, sour, spicy, hot, or any combination of these characteristics, depending on whether the main ingredient in the dish is meat, fish, poultry, or vegetables, and on the preference of the cook.

Some of the spices used in these homemade curry mixes are black pepper, cardamom, cumin, coriander, fennel, turmeric, fenugreek, mustard, cayenne, cinnamon, ginger, cloves, caraway, allspice, nutmeg, poppy seeds, and saffron. When these spices are blended together properly, the diner should not be able to pick out any one ingredient, but should perceive an indefinable "curry" flavor.

Interestingly, these homemade curry mixtures often contain an herb little known in the West called *curry leaf.* According to Julie Sahni, author of *Classic Indian Vegetarian and Grain Cooking,* "It is almost impossible to create the authentic character" of certain dishes without using fresh curry leaf, which is difficult to obtain in this country. Nevertheless, Americans have become used to bottled curry powder without the taste of curry leaf (even in the brands imported from India), and so have developed a kind of inauthentic national taste.

Commercially blended curry powders generally use 6 to 8 ingredients, with the choice of spices and proportion varying according to the brand; heat levels vary greatly from brand to brand as well. These blends are almost always made in the United States, although a few curry powder blends are imported from India.

Curry powder must never be added dry to a dish but must first be cooked in a little butter or oil (olive oil or vegetable oil) to take away its raw taste. Many instructions call for the curry powder to be sautéed along with the onions and/or garlic in the first step of a recipe, in much the same way that flour is sautéed with fat to make a *roux,* which is also an appropriate way to cook out the raw flavor of curry powder.

Because of its association with colonial India, curry is a flavor found in many English dishes, such as mulligatawny soup. *Cassell's Dictionary of Cookery,* published in England in the nineteenth century, lists a recipe for essence of curry liquid, which is really a simple curry vinegar, used for flavoring anything from sauces to salads to relishes. The recipe recommends stirring 3 ounces of curry powder into a quart of vinegar (white-wine vinegar or cider vinegar would be good choices), and letting this mixture steep for 2 weeks. Strain and store in a tightly closed jar.

I sampled 16 brands of curry powder available on the American market, both supermarket and "gourmet store" brands. The best was the Sun Brand Madras, which was exceptionally spicy; second best was Spice Market, which was mild; and third in order of preference was Sharwood's Mild.

Marjoram

Like many other herbs, marjoram also plays a part in Greek mythology: It was created by Venus to poultice a wound caused by one of Cupid's darts. Because of this legend, marjoram has always been associated with romantic love.

A native of western Asia and the Mediterranean, marjoram is the cultivated version of orégano. It has a slight taste of camphor, with warm, aromatic overtones. Sometimes called *sweet marjoram* to distinguish it from orégano, it is another herb that is a member of the mint family, like basil.

Marjoram grows in a small, compact bush about 12 inches high; it is a perennial herb where winters are not too cold. It is imported into America from France, Egypt, Chile, and Peru; Egyptian marjoram is superior. It is usually available dried in leaf form, and the grayish-green leaves generally break up into bits as they are processed and packaged. Some marjoram is sold in ground form. Marjoram is one of the few herbs whose flavor increases when it is dried.

Nutmeg

Nutmeg is the seed of a tree native to the Spice Islands in Indonesia. In the eighteenth century the Dutch held total control of this area and a monopoly on all the valuable nutmeg imported into Europe. To keep their monopoly, Dutch merchants coated with lime all of the nutmeg shipped out of Indonesia, thinking this would make the seeds infertile. As was bound to happen, someone smuggled some seedlings out of the Spice Islands and nutmeg became an important crop of other tropical locations as well, including the island of Grenada in the West Indies.

Today the nutmeg tree is still cultivated in Indonesia as well as in Malaysia and in the Caribbean. East Indian nutmeg is stronger and more aromatic in flavor than nutmeg from the West Indies (primarily in Grenada and Trinidad).

The nutmeg tree is an evergreen which can grow to a height of 40 feet. The spices nutmeg and mace both come from the same tree. The fruit that contains both nutmeg and mace looks something like an apricot. The outer shell is the husk, not used for commercial purposes, covering a reddish, leathery membrane, which is mace, in turn covering the nutmeg, which is the seed of the tree. The fruits are harvested by hand in some countries, and in others they are allowed to fall to the ground when ripe. The mace and nutmegs are removed from the fruits and allowed to dry separately. Nutmeg is exposed to the sun for several days (in some places it is dried over charcoal fires instead), and when it has dried enough, the seed rattles inside its shell; the shell is removed by hand or by simple mechanical means.

The flavor of nutmeg is warm, sweet, aromatic, and slightly bitter. It is sold whole or ground; whole nutmeg will keep its aroma and flavor indefinitely, like other whole spices. Whole nutmeg is shaped something like a football with rounded ends, an inch or so long and 3/4 inch in diameter. It is brown with wrinkled striations on its surface. Although nutmeg graters are sold for the purpose of grating whole nutmeg, the smallest holes of a four-sided kitchen grater work just as well.

Nutmeg is used in many baked goods, such as cookies and doughnuts. It is also traditionally sprinkled on eggnog. In Victorian times it was mixed with rosewater to add to sweets. Professional chefs add a sprinkling of freshly grated nutmeg to many potato dishes to take away the "earth" flavor that some potatoes have; nutmeg is sometimes added to spinach dishes for the same reason. In both cases, however, it's important to add just enough so that the flavor of nutmeg is not identifiable.

Orégano

Orégano is the wild version of marjoram, also native to the western Mediterranean. It was brought by Spanish explorers to Central America, and so a type of orégano became important in Mexican cooking as well as Mediterranean cooking. Today, orégano grows wild in Mexico as well as in its native countries—Turkey, Greece, Italy, and Spain.

The orégano plant is another herb related to mint. The United States imports roughly equal amounts of orégano from Mediterranean countries and from Mexico. Mediterranean orégano, which comes primarily from Turkey and Greece, has a small, light green leaf and a mild, sweet flavor. Mexican orégano has larger, darker leaves, and its flavor is much stronger than the Mediterranean herb, and is sometimes slightly medicinal. Orégano from both places is sold in ground form and in leaf form, which is actually broken bits of dried leaves.

Because of its long history in the soil of that country, Mexican orégano has developed into quite a different herb from Mediterranean orégano, and so Mexican orégano is best used in Mexican dishes; its extra-strong flavor stands up well to spicy foods, such as chili and barbecue. Mediterranean orégano is best suited to all other foods, including pizza, for which it is used most often in this country.

Paprika

It is difficult to think of Hungarian cooking without paprika, but paprika is actually native to the New World and not to Middle Europe. Columbus identified fiery hot peppers on his journeys to America and took some back to Spain, where natives cultivated them and incorporated them in their cooking. From Spain, peppers moved to Italy and then to the Ottoman Empire, of which Bulgaria was a part. The Bulgarians learned how to cultivate the peppers, and took the knowledge with them to Hungary in the sixteenth century. Peppers and paprika, the ground spice made from dried peppers, were always spicy hot until the middle of the nineteenth century, when paprika millers in Hungary invented a technique of removing the veins and seeds of the peppers (where all of the "heat" is isolated), and sweet ground paprika was born. Eight different "heat" levels of ground paprika are available in Hungary, from sweet to very hot, but only three versions are sent to the United States: sweet (labeled "Noble Rose"), medium-hot, and hot. Sweet paprika is also sometimes labeled "capsaicin-free," meaning the seeds and membranes were not ground along with the pepper. The best towns in Hungary that produce paprika are Kalocsa and Szeged; these words should appear on a label of the best paprika.

Hungarians (and Romanians, Yugoslavians, and Bulgarians) don't sprinkle a tiny bit of paprika on top of food to color it, as many novice cooks in this country do. In Middle Europe, paprika is used by the tablespoon as a primary flavoring, a cross between a flour thickener and a dried vegetable powder, which becomes a purée when combined with liquid. Characteristic dishes using paprika include paprika chicken and fish stew. The flavor of the best paprika is rich and pungent; it should smell and taste like fresh peppers; the texture should be almost as fine as face powder.

Most of the paprika used in the United States does not come from Hungary, however, but from Spain, and the second most important supplier is California. Paprika from Spain and California is always of the sweet type, and is sold commercially in a range of colors, from light orange to deep red. America also imports small amounts of paprika from Yugoslavia, Morocco, Bulgaria, Czechoslovakia, Chile, Romania, Turkey, Greece, and Portugal.

The most flavorful paprika, however, comes from Hungary; that is the only type suited to use as an ingredient rather than a coloring agent. When cooking with paprika, according to the native Hungarian Paul Kovi, who is the author of *Transylvanian Cuisine,* it should be noted that it contains a lot of natural sugar and so it will caramelize and burn easily if not handled with care. It should be cooked over low heat, allowed to cool, and then heated again to prevent the burned taste that is characteristic of dishes from the Hungarian equivalent of our "greasy spoons."

Rosemary

From ancient times, rosemary has been a symbol of remembrance and fidelity, which is why brides have carried it at their weddings. The name of rosemary comes from the Latin *ros marinum,* which means "dew of the sea."

Rosemary comes from an evergreen shrub, also in the mint family, that can grow as high as 15 feet tall. It grows wild in several countries around the Mediterranean. It is imported into the United States from France, Spain, Portugal, and Yugoslavia; California also supplies the United States with rosemary. French rosemary is considered superior to all others.

Rosemary leaves look like little pine needles, about 1/2 inch to 1 inch in length. The taste of rosemary is green and pungent. It is available dried in whole leaves or ground.

Although it is used most often with fish, pork, and poultry in its home countries (particularly France and Italy), rosemary's fresh flavor also goes well with fresh fruit and fruit compotes.

Sage

An old superstition about sage predicts that anyone who keeps a sage plant will be well as long as the plant is well, and the plant will droop when the owner is doomed. Even the name of sage comes from the Latin *salvere,* which means to cure. Sage was the most important herb in colonial American gardens. Although it has lost some of its importance, America uses sage today more than any other country in the world.

The sage plant is a small perennial shrub, also in the mint family, with elongated, fuzzy gray-green leaves about 2 inches long. Sage is native to the Mediterranean region and grows prolifically along the Adriatic coast in Yugoslavia. The United States imports sage from Yugoslavia, Albania, Turkey, Greece, and Italy. The characteristic flavor of sage is minty and spicy with camphor overtones. Dalmatian sage from Yugoslavia is considered superior, more mellow in flavor, to sage from other countries. Albanian sage is from the country right next door to Yugoslavia, but it has a harsher flavor than Dalmatian sage.

In this country, sage is sold in whole leaf form, chopped (for which the leaves are chopped into 1/8-inch pieces), "rubbed," and finely ground. Rubbed sage is ground minimally and put through a coarse sieve. Because the texture of fresh sage leaves is fuzzy, ground sage becomes fluffy, with a cottony texture. Finely ground sage is completely pulverized and has a powdery texture.

Traditionally, sage is used in poultry stuffing. It is used by many meat processors as a flavoring for sausage. It is especially well suited to flavoring pork and other fatty meats.

Tarragon

Tarragon is related to the sunflower; it is a perennial plant about 4 feet high, which is a native of Siberia. It was used extensively in cooking in Europe beginning in the sixteenth century, although already in the thirteenth century the Arabs incorporated it in their cooking. In the nineteenth century tarragon was introduced to the United States, and it is now cultivated in California. The United States also imports tarragon from France and Yugoslavia. French tarragon is considered superior because it is much sweeter than other tarragon.

French cuisine makes use of the sweet, faintly aniselike flavor of tarragon in a number of classical dishes, such as *sauce béarnaise* and in *fines herbes* preparations. The leaves of tarragon are slender, pointed, and dark green. It is sold in dried form as whole leaves or ground. Tarragon vinegar, which is sold commercially as a way of preserving the herb and flavoring the vinegar, can be easily made by putting fresh or dried sprigs of tarragon into a bottle, boiling good red- or white-wine vinegar, pouring the boiled vinegar into the bottle, and allowing it to steep for at least a week to develop flavor.

Thyme

Thyme, yet another member of the mint family, is native to the Mediterranean. In ancient Greece, thyme was thought to be a symbol of elegance. One of the most complimentary things one Greek could say to another was, "You smell of thyme." Thyme was also said to be in the hay of the manger on which the baby Jesus lay.

The thyme plant grows only about 12 inches high, and the leaves are very tiny, seldom more than 1/4 inch in length, and gray-green in color. In addition to the ordinary *French thyme,* which is the most commonly seen and has a warm, strong green taste, citrus-flavored *lemon thyme* also exists and can be sometimes found fresh in specialty food shops. French thyme is available dried as whole leaves or in ground form. Dried thyme tastes earthy and pungent.

Although thyme is grown commercially in California, the best dried thyme comes from France, specifically from the Provence region. It is an indispensable part of *herbes de Provence,* a dried herb mixture characteristic of that area.

Spaniards and Italians used to graze sheep on thyme for the flavor it gave the meat. In the United States, thyme is traditionally used in clam chowder, as well as in poultry stuffings and processed meats. Thyme is also an important flavoring agent for Benedictine liqueur.

HANDLING AND STORAGE

Whole spices, such as peppercorns, cinnamon sticks, cloves, nutmeg, and allspice, will keep their flavor indefinitely as long as they are kept in tightly closed containers away from heat and light. Herbs in leaf form will keep longer than herbs in ground form. Ground spices and herbs will keep their flavor for up to a year after purchase (whether opened or unopened), as long as they were fresh when purchased and are kept in tightly closed containers in a cool place, ideally in the refrigerator. (The best place to keep herbs and spices is in the freezer. However, if you take the jars out of the freezer and put them back in again and again, condensation could possibly cause humidity to ruin the herbs and spices stored there.) If kept at room temperature, in a pantry, for example, herbs and spices will keep for only 6 months. Herbs and spices should never be kept in a warm spot; many cooks keep them handy next to or above the stove, which will shorten their life considerably. Dampness is also an enemy of herbs and spices, as it will cake them. To tell if an herb or a spice has lost its flavor, smell it; if it has no aroma, it should be discarded.

Screw-top jars protect the flavor of spices and herbs best. To assure freshness at the time of purchase, it is a good idea to buy spices from stores that have large turnover; dusty jars should be avoided.

Many herb and spice companies do not specify the country of origin on their products, which is a disadvantage for customers who want to know they are buying the highest quality. As with wine, the more information on a label, the better for the buyer, who can use the specific details to make an informed decision.

HOW TO JUDGE HERBS AND SPICES

Tasting Media

I chose to taste orégano and cinnamon, because they are among the 10 most popular herbs and spices used in the United States. Orégano is an example of the quality of herbs a company produces, and cinnamon a good example of spices.

The best way to perceive the flavor of herbs and spices is to mix them with a bland food. Professionals in the industry often use instant mashed potatoes as a vehicle for carrying the flavor of herbs for tasting purposes, in a proportion of 1/4 teaspoon dried herb to 1 cup of mashed potatoes. I used this method to taste orégano, first crumbling the 1/4 teaspoon orégano into the proper amount of boiling water (following the instructions on the box of potatoes), which was then used to reconstitute the dried potato flakes; the hot water begins to develop the flavor of, or slightly "cook," the herb.

To taste cinnamon, I made cinnamon toast with very thin slices of white bread, unsalted butter, and equal parts of sugar and cinnamon.

I also tasted examples of two blended products: The chili powders in my tasting were assessed in sour cream; I mixed 1/2 teaspoon chili powder into 1/2 cup sour cream and then sampled the sour cream mixtures with plastic spoons. (Find results under "Chili Powder," above.)

To taste curry powder, I first sautéed 1 tablespoon of each brand in 2 tablespoons of vegetable oil for 3 minutes; then I combined half of this sautéed mixture with 1 cup of instant mashed potatoes. (Find results under "Curry Powder," above.)

Color/Eye Appeal

Herbs and spices sometimes contain extraneous materials, such as stems, twigs, and bits of dirt or dust, and a visual examination will determine their purity. Herbs and spices should be bright-colored, not faded, and consistent throughout each jar—for example, herbs such as orégano should have clear, bright green colors; sage should be evenly gray-green; cinnamon should be evenly brown or rust-colored, depending on the type of cinnamon bought. Brown bay leaves have faded from age and should be avoided. Paprika should always be bright red in color; if it is any paler, it has aged and will not be flavorful.

Taste/Aroma

Leaf herbs should be rubbed in your palm before smelling so the aroma is released. Any herb or spice with no aroma or with a very faint aroma is probably old and will also have a faded taste. Whole spices, such as cinnamon stick and cloves, can be chewed to assess their flavor. Since spices and herbs are used in such small quantities, they should taste strong, intense, and fresh, characteristic of their variety. (The flavors of specific herbs and spices are described under "Varieties of Herbs and Spices," page 129).

Consistency

Bay leaves should not be brittle, but flexible enough to bend before they snap in half. In the case of leaf herbs, the size of the leaves (or the pieces of leaves, depending on the herb) should be consistent throughout the package. Any spices with a high oil content, such as poppy seeds or caraway seeds, should not be clumped together, which results from improper storage in high humidity.

Aftertaste

Many spices and herbs have a medicinal aftertaste that can be most unpleasant. Stale spices and herbs have a bitter or musty aftertaste that overwhelms their natural flavor.

CONCLUSIONS AND SUGGESTIONS

Many of the herbs produced in countries outside of the United States are wild, not cultivated as they are in California, which might account for the fact that many California herbs are considered more beautiful to look at, but not as flavorful as their wild foreign counterparts—think of the flavor of cultivated white button mushrooms versus that of wild mushrooms; large, attractive California bay leaves versus small but tastier Turkish bay leaves is but one herbal example. Sadly, however, consumers often have no way of knowing where their herbs come from because labels do not specify country of origin. Because of increased interest in cooking and good-quality raw ingredients, some new herb and spice companies have begun to offer products that are top of the line—expensive, but worth it. I would compare these companies to boutique vineyards in northern California.

The owners are dedicated to a high-quality product, better than has ever been available before in this country, and are almost evangelical about educating people about their work. One example from our tasting is Select Origins, which is run by a young husband-and-wife team formerly in the financial world in New York City. Their herbs and spices are among the best I tasted, much, much better than supermarket competitors.

Next to dull knives, the most common abomination in the typical American kitchen is ancient herbs and spices. Unfortunately, however, if someone pays over a dollar for a bottle and uses only one quarter of the contents, it is easy to understand a reluctance to throw it away even though it may be years old. If one compares bottled herbs and spices to fresh vegetables, however, it becomes easier to accept the waste: you wouldn't eat a head of lettuce that is over three weeks old, nor should you use a jar of basil that you bought in the last decade.

When buying herbs and spices in the supermarket, it can be confusing to see, for example, sweet basil packed by the same manufacturer in three types of containers: glass jars, tins, and plastic jars. According to a spokesperson for Durkee, all herbs and spices are available in all three types of containers, but the glass jars contain the "top of the line," a higher quality product, as well as some more exotic offerings, such as crystallized ginger and whole coriander. Plastic jars and tins contain "commercial" or lesser quality grades of herbs and spices. The same grade product is packed in both plastic jars and tins, but some herbs and spices are more appropriate for one type of container than another—for example, plastic jars are best suited to hold powdered herbs and spices.

COOKING WITH HERBS AND SPICES

Fresh herbs, in addition to their characteristic flavors, have a fresh, green taste that is rarely found in dried varieties. Rather than being poor substitutes for fresh, however, dried herbs often become very different entities, with personalities that bear little resemblance to their fresh counterparts. The difference between fresh and dried basil is but one example; dried basil is a lighter, less perfumed cousin to fresh, but nonetheless pleasant in itself.

Nevertheless, on occasions when fresh is not available, dried herbs can be fine substitutes; they will make a dish different and not necessarily worse than if it were made with fresh. Dried herbs are stronger in flavor than fresh; therefore, when adding dried leaf herbs to a recipe that calls for fresh herbs, substitute one third the amount called for in the ingredients; for example, if 1 tablespoon of chopped fresh mint is required, add 1 teaspoon dried as a substitute.

Ground herbs are also stronger in flavor than leaf herbs, and so should be used more sparingly. If you find yourself with leaf herbs on hand and you need to use powdered, crush leaves very finely in the palm of your hand or powder them in a mortar with a pestle.

In any recipe, leaf herbs should always be crushed between your fingers or in the palm of your hand before adding them to a dish; this releases their essential oils, which contain the flavor. Alternatively, you can accomplish the same thing by soaking the herb for 10 minutes in a liquid that will be incorporated in a dish, such as stock, wine, oil, or water.

When adding whole spices to a recipe that calls for ground spices, use 1½ times as much as the recipe calls for; for example, use 1½ tablespoons of whole allspice if the recipe calls for 1 tablespoon of ground allspice.

When doubling a recipe, do not double the herbs and spices, but increase them by 1½ times; then taste, adding more if necessary.

If you are cooking without a recipe, gauge ¼ teaspoon of a dried herb or a spice for every pound of meat or pint of sauce or soup. Taste and add more if necessary.

When cooking with fresh herbs, such as basil, thyme, and parsley, I often find that one bunch is more than I need for one dish. In that case, I usually chop or mince the entire bunch, use the amount called for in the recipe, put the rest on a dinner plate, and leave it, uncovered, on my kitchen counter for a day or so until it is completely dried. I put the dried minced herb in a screw-top container and use it in the next recipe calling for parsley or whatever; it's much fresher than the dried herbs I buy in the supermarket.

The American Spice Trade Association reports that a cook needs to flavor microwave dishes differently from food cooked in a conventional oven. Because of the short exposure to heat in a microwave, their testing shows that you need to add as much as double the amount of flavoring called for in an ordinary recipe.

In hot dishes, fresh herbs should be added toward the end of cooking time to preserve their delicate flavor, while spices can be added at the beginning. In cold foods, such as dressings or dips, herbs should be added several hours in advance (if possible) to the dish to allow the flavors to mellow with the other ingredients in the dish.

A coffee grinder or a strong electric blender can be used to grind whole spices, which will ensure a fresher flavor from preground spices. However, home-ground spices will rarely have as fine a consistency as those bought in jars.

RECIPES

Herbes de Provence

One of the characteristic flavors of the food in Provençal France is this mixture of herbs native to the region along with some spices, used in many dishes from grilled fish to fresh vegetable stews. You can buy fetching little cloth bags or terra-cotta jars of the mixture in Provence or in fancy shops in the United States, but it is more fun and interesting to blend your own, using proportions of herbs that please you. This recipe is from The Wonderful Food of Provence *by Jean-Noël Escudier and Peta J. Fuller.*

4 tablespoons powdered bay leaves
3 tablespoons dried basil leaves
3 tablespoons freshly grated nutmeg
3 tablespoons dried thyme leaves
3 tablespoons dried rosemary leaves
2 tablespoons powdered cloves
2 tablespoons dried savory leaves
2 tablespoons freshly ground white pepper
1 tablespoon powdered coriander
1 teaspoon dried lavender leaves

Mix all ingredients together and store in a screw-top container.

Simca's Herbes de Provence

The book Herbs *by Emelie Tolley and Chris Mead discloses the personal Provençal herb mixture of the famous French cook and author, Simone Beck (called Simca). It is much simpler than the previous one, and quite different, as it contains no spices.*

2 parts dried thyme leaves
1 part dried marjoram leaves
1 part dried orégano leaves
1 part dried savory leaves

Powder all ingredients together in a blender or food processor (or in a mortar with a pestle) and push powder through a strainer. Store in a screw-top container.

Shaker Herb Soup

This classic Shaker recipe come from The American Table *by Ronald Johnson. Any combination of fresh herbs can be used, although these make a particularly happy flavor. (Makes 4 servings)*

2 tablespoons unsalted butter
1 cup minced inner celery ribs with leaves
2 tablespoons minced fresh chives
2 tablespoons minced fresh chervil
2 tablespoons minced fresh sorrel or 1/4 cup minced watercress leaves
1/2 teaspoon minced fresh tarragon

4 cups chicken stock
salt and freshly ground pepper
pinch of sugar
few drops of fresh lemon juice
4 slices of trimmed white bread, toasted
freshly grated nutmeg
3/4 cup grated Cheddar cheese

1. Melt the butter in a saucepan and when it has stopped sizzling, add the celery and chives. Cook over low heat for 5 minutes, or until the celery is soft. Add herbs, stock, salt and pepper to taste, and a pinch of sugar.

2. Cover the pan and let simmer for 20 minutes. Taste for seasoning and add a few drops of lemon juice; soup should be fairly tart. To serve, place a slice of toast in the bottom of each soup plate, ladle the soup over, grate a little nutmeg over, then sprinkle the cheese on top.

PEPPER

lack pepper has been the world's most popular spice ever since it was first tried by man over 3,000 years ago. Although it is not necessary to our diet, which makes it different from salt, our most common seasoning, the flavor of pepper is so enticing that large parts of the old and new world were discovered in search of it.

Today, pepper accounts for about 25 percent of the world's total production of spices. In the United States, average annual consumption is about 5 ounces, the equivalent of more than a cup of whole peppercorns or about 2,000 black peppercorns. Per capita consumption of pepper in the United States has increased by 60 percent since 1975, and by 156 percent since 1950. In fact, we are the world's largest consumer of pepper, followed by India, Russia, West Germany, France, and Britain.

A DASH OF HISTORY

Pepper, botanically named *Piper nigrum,* is a native of the southwestern part of India, where Sanskrit references to it were made as long as 3,000 years ago. The ancient Romans and Greeks loved pepper in their food, and valued it as a form of currency not only because it was worth a lot of money, but also because it was much easier to transport than gold.

After the Roman Empire fell and the trade routes to India were closed, pepper became much more scarce, and thus even more valuable. At the time of the Crusades, pepper was rediscovered by the warriors who traveled to the Holy Land, and it was sought after once again. "He hath no pepper" was a phrase used then to describe someone of no consequence, as once more pepper became a form of currency. A legacy of this era is the fact that to this day many churches and public lands are rented for what is called a "peppercorn rent," in other words, for nothing more than a symbolic token. The Ritz Hotel in London, for example, rents its garden from the Queen, who owns the land, for a yearly fee of 1 peppercorn.

Vasco da Gama, a Portuguese explorer, is credited with changing the course of history when, in 1498, he was the first to discover a way to Calcutta and back again to Europe with his ship's hold full of pepper. This reduced the price of pepper considerably, as well as shifting the balance of power in the world from Venice and Genoa (former ports for spice trading) to Portugal, then Holland, followed by England and, in the nineteenth century, to Salem, Massachusetts, as more and more explorers set out in search of pepper and other spices.

Today, most of the pepper in the world comes from Indonesia, India, Malaysia, and Brazil.

HOW PEPPER IS MADE

Pepper grows on a vine that thrives in tropical climates, such as India and Indonesia, clinging to stakes and trained to grow up to 15 feet high. Each vine produces hundreds of flower spikes, and each one of these eventually bears a cluster of 50 berries or peppercorns.

For black pepper, these berries are picked before they have a chance to ripen, when they are still green. To harvest the tiny fruit, the spikes are beaten or rubbed by hand until the peppercorns are separated from their stalks. The berries are soaked in water for 7 to 10 days, then spread on mats to dry in the sun for 3 or 4 days. Large manufacturers dry their peppercorns in machines rather than in the sun. This process constitutes the beginning of fermentation, which brings out pepper's pungency and blackens the skin of the berries, causing them to become dry, wrinkled, and spicy. The fermentation process is completed after the peppercorns are shipped to their final destination, where they are cleaned by running them through a conveyor device that blows air over them to remove vines and twigs.

White pepper is made from the same plant, but the berries are allowed to ripen fully on the vine, to turn from green to yellow to red; the peppercorns are white underneath this red skin. They are soaked in water for a few days to soften the skin. The softened berries are rubbed to remove the skin; in some countries they are first trampled to begin this process. After the skin is removed, the peppercorns are dried in the sun for a day or two. White pepper can be produced more cheaply by mechanically rubbing the dry skins of black peppercorns, producing what is called *decorticated white pepper.* This pepper is mostly used by manufacturers to add to light-colored foods like bottled mayonnaise and salad dressings.

VARIETIES OF PEPPER

Choosing pepper is like choosing coffee beans: the range is large and varied. It is fascinating to experiment with a few to find those that suit your tastes and cooking style. Although the botanical species of pepper is the same the world over, the climate and growing conditions and the way the pepper is treated account for the different flavors, much like a single variety of wine grape, which makes different wine depending on where it is grown.

Black Peppercorns

• *Lampong* From the Lampong district of the Indonesian island of Sumatra, these peppercorns are small and thin-shelled with a very bold, pungent, and aromatic flavor.

• *Malabar* Grown on the southwest coast of India, these peppercorns have a full-bodied, strong aromatic flavor, but not as strong as Lampong. The peppercorns are small and irregular in shape. They are a favorite of renowned cook and food writer, Elizabeth David.

• *Tellicherry* Also from the Malabar coast of India, these peppercorns are large and even-size, mildly pungent, and fruity, with a toasted flavor. They are used often in Italian sausages and hard salamis. These are considered the best of all peppercorns by many aficionados and thus are usually the highest priced.

• *Sarawak* These peppercorns come from the northern coast of Borneo in Malaysia, a former British colony, which explains why this variety is so popular in Britain. They have a mild, mellow flavor and fruity bouquet. The peppercorns are brownish-black, small, and produce light-colored pepper.

• *Brazilian* From the relatively new pepper plantations of Brazil, started by the Japanese after World War II, these peppercorns have a very mild flavor.

• *Ponape* This variety of peppercorn is grown on the Micronesian island of Ponape. These are mild, with a distinctive aroma, and are sold packed in bamboo jars.

White Peppercorns

• *Muntok* Grown on an island off the coast of Sumatra, this variety is cultivated expressly to make white pepper. These have a slightly musty aroma and a refined, hot flavor.

• *Brazilian* From Brazil, these peppercorns are lighter in color and less pungent than Muntok.

• *Sarawak* From Malaysia, Sarawak peppercorns are usually used in blends.

Green Peppercorns

Green peppercorns, having appeared on the European and American markets only about 30 years ago, are a relative newcomer in the pepper field. They are also made from the same plant as white and black pepper (usually from Brazilian plantations), but are most often sold fresh rather than dried, although they are sometimes freeze-dried. The peppercorn is picked while green and unripe and immediately packed in brine, vinegar, or water to preserve it. It has the soft consistency and appearance, but not the flavor, of capers. The flavor is mildly sour, but not piquant.

Pink Peppercorns

A few years ago there was a rage for pink peppercorns, which are not related to *Piper nigrum* at all, but come from an unrelated weed sometimes called *Florida holly.* The berries are rosy pink and about the size of black peppercorns. They are known to cause severe allergic reactions in some people.

Szechuan Peppercorns

These are also not related to the *Piper nigrum* family, but are rust-colored and about the size of black peppercorns. They are native to China and have a spicy, menthol flavor, without the characteristic fire of other hot peppers.

Cayenne Pepper

Cayenne pepper is finely ground dried red-Capsicum pepper, made from a variety of extremely hot peppers grown in Africa, India, Mexico, Mainland China, Japan, and Louisiana. Oddly enough, the peppers are no longer exported from Cayenne in French Guiana, where they originally got their name. Some manufacturers label their ground hot pepper simply "red pepper" rather than "cayenne pepper"; many brands of cayenne pepper contain salt.

Cayenne is used in many native Louisiana recipes.

HANDLING AND STORAGE

Whole peppercorns have an indefinite shelf life as long as they are kept away from heat and humidity. If stored in a cool, dry environment for 100 years, peppercorns will lose no flavor and only a small amount of their weight.

Preground pepper is sometimes compared to sawdust, because once the oils inside the peppercorns are exposed to the air the flavor and bite fall off quickly. The longer ground pepper sits, the drier it gets and the more you have to use to get the pepper flavor you seek; 6 months is the maximum shelf life for ground pepper. Also, if peppercorns or ground pepper are exposed to light they will eventually turn gray, so they should be stored in an opaque container; if the pepper's original container is made of clear glass, transfer it to a jar or tin that does not let the light through.

The two best hand pepper grinders on the market are Bounds and Peugeot, both available at gourmet and cookware shops, or by mail order from Zabar's, 2245 Broadway, New York, NY 10024.

Green peppercorns will stay in good condition for 1 year, if unopened. Once opened, they will last in the refrigerator for about a week. They can be successfully frozen for about 6 months. Always rinse them before using to remove the briny taste. Freeze-dried green peppercorns will last in a cool, dry pantry for 6 months.

Szechuan peppercorns will keep in a cool, dark place for 6 months if stored in their original container.

HOW TO JUDGE PEPPER

The flavor and freshness of peppercorns is evident in their aroma; the smell of peppercorns that have been freshly cracked will provide a good indication of how they will taste. If they smell sharp or even musty, they have not been well handled in manufacturing or transporting and will not taste good. Good-quality peppercorns will smell aromatic and interestingly complex.

The best way to taste pepper is to grind different peppers over pieces of slightly warm French bread spread with unsalted butter or cream cheese. The taste of good pepper, like its smell, should be complex and aromatic.

COOKING WITH PEPPER

The articulate and renowned twentieth-century French chef Louis Diat wrote that pepper is one of the few seasonings that is used three times in almost all savory food: first, when the dish is being prepared, second, when the seasoning is corrected before the dish is sent to the dining table, and third, at the table when the diner adds pepper to the dish himself. It is also economical, since an ounce of peppercorns will season over 1,000 eggs.

The difference between white and black peppercorns is subtle, but important for those who care about nuances of flavor: white pepper is hot and biting like black pepper, but without the bouquet and aroma that is also characteristic of black pepper. In both cases, the sting of pepper is provided by an alkaloid called piperine, which aids digestion and stimulates the gastric juices. All in all, white pepper is less strong-tasting than black pepper. Generally, it is almost always used in dishes where specks of black pepper would be visually objectionable, such as mayonnaise, hollandaise, and other light-colored sauces. Some chefs, especially those from New Orleans, recommend using white and black pepper together (sometimes along with cayenne pepper), to get heat, spice, and pepper flavor all in the same dish.

Since the best pepper must be freshly ground to achieve its maximum flavor, many chefs recommend keeping two peppermills handy next to the stove, one for white pepper and one for black pepper. I keep these two for cooking, as well as one other small peppermill that grinds pepper fine to use at the table. Some chefs keep yet another peppermill with a blend of peppercorns, such as Muntok, Szechuan, Sarawak, Tellicherry, or any other blend that pleases them, to use in particular dishes.

Pepper will burn and taste bitter if exposed to heat; therefore, many professional chefs never put pepper on meat before it is broiled, but only after it is cooked.

RECIPE

Salmon Gravlax with Mustard-Dill Sauce from the Café des Artistes Restaurant

The best way to judge pepper is in a recipe that relies almost exclusively on it for flavor, as in this Scandinavian dish, which is a speciality of my husband's restaurant in Manhattan. After choosing the pepper, or the combination of peppers, that pleases you, try it with gravlax to appreciate its flavor fully.

For best results, use only very fresh salmon. As an extra garnish, slice salmon skin into thin shreds and fry it until crisp in a mixture of vegetable oil and butter; sprinkle on the gravlax at serving time. The same recipe can be applied to whitefish, king mackerel, salmon trout, or any other oily fish suitable for marination. (Makes 10 servings)

2 pounds fresh center-cut salmon, bones removed and skin left on, cut crosswise into halves
2 tablespoons aquavit
1/3 cup Kosher salt
1/3 cup sugar

2 tablespoons freshly crushed (not ground) black peppercorns (you can use the bottom of a heavy frying pan to crush the peppercorns roughly against your kitchen counter)
1/4 pound fresh dill

MUSTARD-DILL SAUCE

1 1/2 tablespoons white-wine vinegar
1 3/4 tablespoons granulated sugar
1/2 cup olive oil
5–6 tablespoons Dijon mustard
1 tablespoon chopped fresh dill
1 heaping tablespoon freshly ground white pepper

GARNISH

10 sprigs of dill
5 lemons, cut crosswise into halves

1. Wipe salmon fillet dry with paper towels. Place one half of salmon fillet on top of the other, and trim so that they are even in length. Sprinkle each half of fillet with 1 tablespoon of aquavit.

2. Combine salt, sugar, and crushed pepper, and rub some of this mixture into each side of the fillet without skin.

3. Put half of the fillet, skin side down, in a baking dish. Evenly distribute the 1/4 pound dill over the fillet. Cover with the other fillet half, skin side up. Sprinkle remaining salt mixture over the top. Cover with foil.

4. Place a large platter or chopping board over the fillets and weight with a brick or a couple of soup cans. Put in the refrigerator and let marinate for at least 24 to 36 hours, turning the salmon fillets over together every 12 hours.

5. While the salmon is marinating, prepare mustard-dill sauce by whisking vinegar and sugar together in a small mixing bowl until sugar is dissolved. Slowly add olive oil, whisking well until all of the oil is incorporated. Blend in mustard and chopped dill, and season with white pepper. Cover and refrigerate until needed.

6. After salmon has finished marinating, remove foil and dill. Using a stiff pastry brush, remove all of the seasoning mixture.

7. When ready to serve, slice the salmon very thin on the bias. Put 4 or 5 slices on each serving plate. Ladle a small portion of mustard-dill sauce alongside and garnish with a sprig of dill. With each plate serve a lemon half.

SALT

Salt is one of the most enigmatic ingredients found in our food. As one of the four basic tastes—sweet, sour, bitter, and salty—ideally, it must be added to almost every savory dish we cook, and yet many sweet dishes and baked goods also benefit from the addition of a small amount of salt. Even though it is not technically an herb or a spice but a mineral, I have included it in this section because salt and spices are grouped together in the kitchen.

Our human taste buds can detect a salty taste in a solution of 1 part salt to 400 parts liquid, yet we cannot smell "saltiness." Food cooked on a bed of pounds and pounds of salt will not taste salty, and yet an extra teaspoon in a sauce or a soup will spoil the taste of the dish altogether. No amount of old wives' remedies will really correct the mistake, but we add a pinch of sugar or a quartered potato in desperation anyway.

A DASH OF HISTORY

Without salt, an essential mineral for all mammals, history would have been different. The early Greeks revered salt as much as they worshiped the sun. The Via Salaria, or "salt road," is one of the oldest roads in Rome and was used to transport salt in ancient days. Many wars throughout the ages were won or lost because one side captured the all-important salt cache of the other. Military experts, for example, feel that if the South had been able to protect its salt factories in Virginia and Louisiana, the Confederacy could have held out much longer. In nineteenth-century America, the Erie Canal was called "the ditch that salt built," because it was made partly to transport salt more easily and cheaply from Syracuse to Chicago.

Even some of our language has been formed by the importance of salt: the word "salary" comes from the Latin *salarium argentum,* or "salt money," which was paid to Roman soldiers. Another example is the phrase "he's not worth his salt," which originated in ancient Greece where salt was used to buy slaves.

HOW SALT IS MADE

Over 20 billion tons of salt are produced every year in America, but only 5 percent of it is used in food; the rest goes for industrial and chemical purposes. Three basic methods are used to "harvest" salt in the United States, which is the biggest producer of salt in the world: mining, solar evaporation, and vacuum pan.

Mining

Salt is mined, in much the same way coal is mined, from underground salt beds. After the salt is brought to the surface, it is crushed and screened to reduce it to its commercial size. In the United States, the most important salt deposits are in Louisiana, Texas, Michigan, New York, Ohio, Pennsylvania, Kansas, and Oklahoma. All rock salt and salt used for industrial purposes is harvested this way.

Solar Evaporation

This method of harvesting salt has been used for thousands of years. It is employed in areas where rainfall is scarce and sunshine and favorable winds are plentiful, such as in San Diego and San Francisco in California and the Great Salt Lake in Utah. Salty sea or lake water is captured in shallow ponds where the hot sun and wind evaporate most of the water. The remaining salt is then washed, dried, screened, and ground. Leslie Salt, a brand available in the western United States, is made this way.

Vacuum Pan

This is the most modern method of salt production. Water is pumped into an underground salt deposit. The salt-saturated water is then recovered and treated in a device that works on somewhat the same principle as a double boiler. As the brine is vigorously boiled and agitated, it produces salt in the shape of small cubes that look like the dice used in gambling. All Morton brand table salt is made this way.

Regardless of how salt is obtained, the naturally occurring other minerals, which make up about one fourth of its total composition, are removed so what remains is almost completely pure sodium chloride. In addition, virtually all commercial salt produced in the United States is treated with about 2 percent sodium silicoaluminate or magnesium carbonate, minerals that coat every grain of salt and keep it from absorbing too much moisture, therefore keeping it always free-flowing. Without these additives, salt would naturally clump in environments where humidity reaches more than 75 percent, or on humid or rainy days.

Potassium iodide is another additive manufacturers can choose to use. In areas of the United States where iodine does not occur naturally in the soil in sufficient amounts (most notably the North Central and Rocky Mountain states), a high incidence of a disfiguring disease known as goiter, the enlarging of thyroid glands in the throat, used to be prevalent. Health authorities discovered that when iodine was added to the diet, goiter did not occur; thus, in 1924 salt manufacturers began to add potassium iodide to their product, creating iodized salt. Once iodized salt came on the market, incidence of goiter was almost eliminated in this country, until about 20 years ago when succeeding generations grew careless in their selection of salt, not realizing the reason for the added iodine. A great deal of processed food is made with noniodized salt; purified sea salt, popular with some cooks, also does not contain iodine. After goiter began to reappear, a law was passed (in 1973) requiring manufacturers to state on the labels of noniodized salt: "This salt does not supply iodide, a necessary nutrient." The reverse statement appears on iodized salt.

Those who eat a lot of seafood and food grown in iodine-rich soil (commonly associated with coastal areas), or drink water that has acquired the mineral from such soil, do not have to be as concerned about using iodized salt as others.

Salt that contains potassium iodide, in the amount of .001 percent, also contains dextrose, a form of sugar, to stabilize the iodine and prevent it from giving a medicinal odor to the salt. There are 2 milligrams of dextrose in a teaspoon of iodized salt.

LABEL LANGUAGE

As of July 1986, by law all food manufacturers must follow standardized label language if they choose to refer to the sodium (or salt) content of their products, which is designed to help consumers who must watch their sodium intake because of high blood pressure and other medical reasons. It is not mandatory for labels of food products to refer to the salt or sodium contained within, but if they do, the required phrases are:

- *Sodium Free* Each serving contains 5 mg sodium or less.

- *Very Low Sodium* Each serving contains 3 mg sodium or less.

• *Low Sodium* Each serving contains 140 mg sodium or less.

• *Reduced Sodium* Usual level of sodium reduced by 75 percent.

• *Unsalted* Processed without salt when salt is ordinarily used.

VARIETIES OF SALT

Table Salt

This is the salt most familiar to Americans. The only brand distributed nationally is Morton; that and all regional brands, such as Sterling, Leslie and Carey, contain 99.9 percent sodium chloride (NaCl), and the remaining 0.1 percent is made up of the additives, such as potassium iodide and magnesium carbonate.

Granular table salt is necessary for recipes where a fine-grained salt must dissolve quickly or dissipate well in a mixture, such as in bread or pasta dough or in batters. The two types of ordinary table salt are:

• *Flaked* Flaked salt is manufactured by the Diamond Crystal company and is available in the eastern half of the United States. The grains of this salt are "crystals" or snowflake-shaped flakes, a much finer consistency than ordinary or granular table salt, which is made up of miniature cubes. It dissolves in liquids more easily and gives a more immediate, intense salt flavor, without the satisfying texture of granular salt.

• *Granular* Granular is the most common form of table salt; the grains are shaped into miniature cubes. When using salt in a liquid, such as a soup or a sauce, granular and flaked salt are interchangeable; for use at the table, however, it takes more granular salt to achieve a salty taste.

Sea Salt

Sea salt is sometimes called *bay salt.* Because all salt at one time or another comes from the sea, the term and snob appeal of "sea salt" is largely the product of gourmet merchandising. Technically, sea salt should be salt that is evaporated naturally from sea water. The naturally occurring minerals are almost always removed from sea salt in the same way as from table salt. Most sea salt has magnesium carbonate added, the same as table salt, to keep it free-flowing.

Sea salt can be stronger tasting or milder tasting than table salt, depending on where it is made; it is sold in the same granular form as table salt, as well as in coarse crystals. To my palate, the basic taste of sea salt is very similar to ordinary table salt.

In some gourmet shops you can find unprocessed sea salt, called *sel gris* if it is imported from France. It has not been washed or purified in any way, nor does it contain additives to keep it free-flowing. It has a gray color and has a slightly different flavor from ordinary table salt but not, to my mind, a flavor so fine that it is worth the extra money it costs—about 80 times as much as ordinary table salt!

Kosher Salt

Also called *coarse salt* or sometimes *dairy salt,* Kosher salt comes in large, irregularly shaped grains; it is produced under conditions approved by the Orthodox Jewish faith. The large crystal shapes make them well suited for drawing blood from meat, a necessary practice for "koshering" food.

Decades ago, salt was cut with pork fat to allow it to flow easily, thus Kosher salt required a designation in order to specify salt to which pork fat was not added.

Kosher salt has no additives (which means it is not iodized), and measure for measure, it is less salty than ordinary table salt, because of the size of the crystals. It takes about 2 teaspoons of Kosher salt to equal the "saltiness" of 1 teaspoon of table salt.

Some professional chefs belief that Kosher salt will not become as concentrated as table salt after long cooking. I believe this is a dangerous presumption, which could lead to oversalting of food. In my experience, Kosher salt does indeed become as concentrated as table salt after long cooking. Nevertheless, when adding salt to a dish that will not cook down for a long period of time, I do add a little more Kosher salt than I would if I were using table salt; the large crystals seem to be a little less salty than ordinary salt.

I prefer to use Kosher salt in my cooking because I agree with Julia Child that it is easier to pick it up with my fingers to add it to a pot. I use Kosher salt at the table, served in salt cellars or tiny egg cups, because I like the satisfying crunch of the large crystals. I should say, however, that I live near the sea and my source of iodine is in the fish I eat, and so I don't need to use iodized salt.

Rock Salt

This chunky, unrefined salt is marketed in both edible and inedible versions. Sometimes called *ice-cream salt,* it can be used in salt grinders or as a bed on which to cook oysters or clams, or even to salt the water in which you are going to boil pasta or vegetables. The flavor depends on the impurities, naturally occurring minerals, it contains.

Rock salt that is freshly ground in a salt mill does have a slightly fresher taste than granulated table or sea salt. The grinding process also produces irregular crystals, which have a satisfying crunch, especially in salads.

Pickling Salt

This is a superfine, fast-dissolving salt that contains no additives to cloud the brine in a pickling recipe.

Sour Salt

Also called *citric salt,* this is a crystallized substance extracted from lemons and limes, used to give a citric flavor to Jewish-style food, such as borscht or stuffed cabbage.

Maldon Salt

This is a salt from Essex, England, that is a large, clear flaky sea salt. It is expensive in this country and has an intense flavor.

HOW TO JUDGE SALT

Food authority and cookbook author Paula Wolfert has devised a method to teach her students about the taste of salt, so they can choose the variety that appeals to them.

Wolfert recommends taking about 2 tablespoons each of Kosher salt, Maldon salt, French sea salt, and Morton's table salt. She grinds each to a fine powder using a mortar and pestle. Then she directs her students to wet their fingers and pick up a small amount of each salt, tasting for differences.

The Maldon salt is invariably the "saltiest," the most intense. Although the flavors of the four salts are slightly different, they are close enough so that a wise consumer might choose his or her salt according to price and texture, rather than by taste.

HANDLING AND STORAGE

Salt will last indefinitely if kept in a cool, dry place. In very humid areas, where the sodium silicoaluminate or magnesium carbonate is not enough to prevent the salt from caking, a few rice grains in the salt shaker will act as a dessicant and keep the salt free-flowing.

COOKING WITH SALT

"Salt to taste" can be a frustrating directive for an exacting cook, but it is a necessary one, because everyone's perception of saltiness is different, depending on the sensitivity of his palate (whether or not he smokes!), and his long-standing habits. Those who habitually "salt to sight" at the table have developed a low threshold for the taste of salt. Those who have weaned themselves away from salt for health reasons can perceive a salty flavor in foods with very little salt added.

The salt in room-temperature foods is more easily perceived than in foods that are cold or hot. So if you are cooking a dish that is to be eaten at room temperature, go easy on the salt. If a dish is to be eaten boiling hot, such as soup, you will need to add more salt.

RECIPE

Homemade Sauerkraut

Sauerkraut made at home has little in common with the supermarket variety. It is much fresher tasting and more flavorful, definitely worth the time it takes to ferment. This is so good it should be used in a special dish, such as Alsatian choucroute garni, a hearty stew of sauerkraut, sausages, smoked pork, and white wine. Homemade sauerkraut would also dress up a good knackwurst. (Makes about 3½ quarts)

10 pounds firm white cabbage
6 tablespoons Kosher salt

1. Remove the tough outer leaves from the heads of cabbage; cut heads into quarters and remove the cores. Using a sharp knife or a food processor, slice cabbage as thin as possible.

2. Using your hands, mix sliced cabbage thoroughly with the salt. If it's easier, mix half the cabbage with half the salt, repeat with the second half of cabbage and salt, then mix the two batches together. Allow the salted cabbage to rest for about 15 minutes so the wilting process can begin.

3. Pack the salted cabbage firmly and evenly into a large clean ceramic crock or glass jar, large enough to hold all the cabbage. (You can often find large glazed jars in flea markets.) Using your hands, press down firmly on the cabbage until the juice rises and covers the surface of the cabbage.

4. Half-fill a sturdy plastic bag with water and close the bag tightly. (If you don't feel the plastic bag is strong enough, use 2 plastic bags and put one inside the other.) Place the bag on top of the cabbage so that the entire surface of the cabbage is protected from the air. The bag filled with water also acts as a weight on the cabbage to help bring out its juices. Add enough water to the bag so that the brine exuding from the cabbage just covers the surface.

5. Cabbage ferments best at a temperature of 68° to 72°F.; therefore, it should not be kept in a refrigerator but in a cool cellar, pantry, or back porch (depending on the season). At that temperature, the fermentation should be completed in 5 to 6 weeks. Taste it after about 5 weeks; if it is too crispy, let it ferment for another few days. If you're not using it all right after it has finished fermenting, put up the remaining sauerkraut and process in a water bath. (See any basic cookbook for canning instructions.)

BEVERAGES

BOTTLED WATER

ottled water came out of nowhere about 20 years ago and made a meteoric rise to the top of the shopping lists of hip and health-minded consumers. Perhaps an apt analogy might be to compare bottled water with crude oil—it comes out of the ground and has made a lot of people rich.

In America, the term "bottled water" means two different things, depending on where you live. One third of the residents of California, and smaller percentages elsewhere, get their everyday drinking water delivered in 5-gallon containers, and this bottled water is called *bulk* or *commodity* water. When the rest of the nation refers to "bottled water," it means quart- or liter-size bottles (or "splits" of about 6 or 8 ounces often served in restaurants) of upscale carbonated mineral water with eye-catching labels. Bulk waters are alternatives to tap water; for most people, bottled mineral waters are drunk *in addition to* tap water. Whereas the bulk, noncarbonated waters are a necessary part of everyday life, especially in those regions with tainted public drinking water, the "bottled waters," or recreational waters, are a luxury.

Because it was the first of the ubiquitous bottled mineral water genre, and so well publicized, many of us ask for "Perrier" when we order bottled water, in the unthinking way we say "Kleenex" when we need a paper tissue. More often than not, our Perrier comes poured over ice with a wedge of lime. Today a whole generation of people drinks mineral waters in social situations where ten years ago they might have drunk wine, hard liquor, soda, or coffee.

Since 1975, when Perrier began its campaign to make the American public aware of imported mineral waters, many other brands have braved the market. Now about 700 brands of imported water are sold in this country. Nevertheless, Perrier still controls about 60 percent of the imported sparkling water market.

Bottled water is the fastest-growing segment of the beverage industry. After an impressive jump when sales of bottled waters doubled from 1977 to 1978, the growth rate has been strong and steady—between 1984 and 1994 sales tripled.

Per capita consumption of bottled water in this country is 10.5 gallons. We spend approximately $3 billion annually on bottled waters, and only a little more than half of that figure is for bulk waters; the rest goes for all kinds of mineral waters (see "Varieties of Bottled Water"). Residents of California, Texas, and Florida consume the most bottled water (Californians consume about 32 percent of the bottled water in America), and New York and Pennsylvania are close behind.

A DASH OF HISTORY

It is interesting to contemplate that the same glass of water you drink today could have also been drunk by Marie Antoinette or Cleopatra or Julius Caesar. In fact, no new water has been created since the beginning of time; 72 percent of the earth's surface has always been covered by water, and it is continually recycling itself through evaporation, condensation, and precipitation.

The health value of drinking certain waters was discovered in ancient times when it was observed that people who drank water from some sources during an epidemic kept illness at bay. Even before bacteria had been identified, the therapeutic nature of some noncontaminated mineral waters became obvious. In the eighteenth and nineteenth centuries, many resorts developed around these naturally occurring springs in Europe and America, where people went to "take the waters," both internally and externally, for drinking and for bathing. In Europe, some of the spas that became famous are Baden-Baden, Vichy, Bad Gastein, and Bad Ischl. (You can still take water cures in about 500 health spas in Europe.) In America, these water spas are mostly a thing of the past, but two that were famous in the nineteenth century are Mountain Valley at Hot Springs, Arkansas, and Saratoga Springs, New York.

Beginning in the eighteenth century, canny resort operators surmised that if they bottled the water that bubbled up out of the earth, they could sell it to people who couldn't travel to their spas. Myths and fantasy abounded concerning these waters and their supposed curative powers. Then came the era of traveling salesmen selling bottled water, "guaranteed to cure what ails you."

Europeans have continued an unbroken tradition of drinking bottled waters as a matter of course. They have also continued the tradition of making therapeutic claims for their bottled waters, most of which are unsubstantiated. It took Americans a lot longer to come to the conclusion that bottled mineral water is an important addition to a civilized table and a good-tasting alternative to poor tap water. Given the geometrically increasing sales figures, however, it seems as if we are making up for lost time.

VARIETIES OF BOTTLED WATER AND HOW THEY ARE MADE

The range of bottled waters is vast, and confusing, because no standardization of label language with regard to waters exists in this country. (A federal law is now under consideration that will standardize label language nationwide.) Roughly speaking, however, the following list represents the main categories of bottled waters (excluding bulk waters, described above).

Mineral Water

It would make sense that mineral water should be distinguished from other bottled waters by its mineral content, but the truth is that *all* water is mineral water, because all water, even tap water, contains some minerals. Without minerals, water would have no taste. Distilled water has no taste for that very reason: all the minerals have been removed so they don't clog up your iron or other machinery.

No legal definition exists for mineral water in the United States, except in California, where to be called mineral water a bottled water must contain at least 500 ppm (parts per million, which number can be roughly calculated to equal milligrams per liter) total dissolved solids (industry acronym is TDS). Common mineral waters range up to a TDS content of about 4,000 ppm. The most common minerals contained in mineral waters are calcium, magnesium, potassium, sodium, and iron. The proportion and the amounts of these minerals vary with the source of water. These natural "recipes" are what distinguish the flavor of one water from another.

In addition to the law governing California mineral waters, the International Bottled Water Association, to which 85 percent of the companies that produce bottled water in this country belong, has further specified that mineral waters are those "that are derived from a natural, underground source, usually a spring, whose mineral content is specific and constant, whose source is protected and whose water is safe and free of contamination."

When the word "natural" appears on a bottle of mineral water, it usually means the minerals in the water are those that occur naturally in the spring from which the water came. Water picks up these minerals from the rocks as it travels to the surface of the earth. Without the word "natural," it is likely that minerals were added or taken away from the water, and that it falls into the "processed water" category, despite its claims.

Beware of label language such as "springlike" or "spring pure," which are deceptive terms that indicate the water is not natural but processed.

Throughout the countries of Western Europe, a legal definition of mineral water exists. It must flow freely from its source; in other words, it may not be pumped or forced from the ground. It must come from one source only, which must be listed on the label. It must be bottled at the source, in a maximum size of 2 liters and it may not be stored before bottling. (There is no specification for TDS in European mineral waters.)

The carbonation in mineral water can occur naturally, in which case you will probably see the words "naturally sparkling" on the label; natural carbonation contains trace minerals not found in artificial carbonation. But these words can also signify water to which natural carbonation is added *after* the water comes out of the spring. That is the case with Perrier, which, in order to ensure a consistent amount of carbonation, removes the carbon dioxide from the earth before the water bubbles up from the ground, and puts it back into the water at the time of bottling, or at least that is their explanation. It is also possible, however, that there isn't enough natural carbonation in the water as it emerges from the source, thus this process. Poland Spring also injects into its water natural carbon dioxide, which is shipped from Colorado to the bottling plant in Maine.

If the word "sparkling" is on a label of mineral water, then chances are good that it has had artificial carbonation added.

Processed Water

Eighty percent of bottled waters come under the heading of "processed water." This is water from any source that is treated before bottling. Into this category fall tap water, bulk water, and, in the recreational water subgroup, club soda and seltzer.

• *Club Soda* This is usually city water, taken from the tap in the locality where the club soda is made, from which impurities are removed by one of three methods. The first is *ozonation*, which is done by using two electrodes with dry compressed air to change oxygen in the water to ozone. The water becomes more oxidized and the natural bacteria content is reduced; it is then run through carbon and sand filters to take out any dirt particles.

Water is also filtered through *deionization* and *reverse osmosis.* When water is deionized it is passed through resins, which remove most of the minerals. Reverse osmosis forces water under pressure through membranes that remove almost all minerals.

After this purification to take out unwanted minerals and undesirable elements, minerals are added to the water and it is carbonated by running it over a number of plates through which carbon dioxide is injected under pressure.

The reason the carbonation is not visible in a sealed bottle of water is that, under pressure, the carbon dioxide is in the form of liquid carbonic acid. When the cap of the bottle is removed, the pressure is released and the carbonic acid changes into water and carbon dioxide.

The two largest-selling club sodas, Canada Dry and Schweppes, are bottled regionally. The parent companies send their own special blend of minerals to the regional bottlers, who add them to the purified local tap water. Most major brands of club soda have between 40 and 50 milligrams of sodium in an 8-ounce glass.

It's called *club soda,* by the way, because after Prohibition, bottlers wanted to strike an association with elegant private clubs and the water they served.

• *Seltzer* Seltzer goes through the same purification and carbonation procedure as club soda, but no minerals are added.

The term "seltzer" is a derivation of *Selterser Wasser,* a mineral water bottled in the German town of Nieder Selters.

HANDLING AND STORAGE

Since carbonation lowers the pH of the water, the chances for bacteria to grow are reduced tremendously. If the seal is not broken, carbonated water will last indefinitely. If tightly sealed again after opening, the bubbles should stay in the bottled water for at least a few days.

HOW TO JUDGE BOTTLED WATER

Tasting Media

Taste water at an approximate temperature of 40°F. (normal refrigerator temperature), from small plastic cups.

Color/Eye Appeal

A good bottled water should be clear and clean-looking, not cloudy or murky.

Taste/Aroma

This is very much a matter of personal preference, but a good standard mineral water should taste clean, crisp, and refreshing. Any off-odors or tastes, such as bitterness or sweetness, are undesirable.

One of the most important characteristics of a good water is that no one obvious flavor predominates. If any of the mineral flavors, such as sulfur or saltiness, is evident, then the water is flawed.

Many of defective waters taste soapy, which is an indication that they are extremely alkaline. Some taste faintly of plastic, as a result of the water's container.

Consistency

In carbonated waters, the consistency comes from the size and frequency of the bubbles. Those that are made with natural carbonation have smaller and longer-lasting bubbles, and generally are more refreshing than waters carbonated with manufactured carbon dioxide. Artificially carbonated waters often attack your mouth and nose with aggressive bubbles, a most unpleasant sensation. To counteract this sensation, mix the artificially carbonated water half and half with still water to cut the bubbles.

Aftertaste

Poor waters leave a heavy taste in the mouth. Strong mineral waters often leave a long-lasting mineral residue in the mouth that can be unpleasant. The best waters have a lilting, light aftertaste.

CONCLUSIONS AND SUGGESTIONS

Ideally, one would stock an array of waters, to use for different purposes, in the same way that one drinks all sorts of wine on different occasions—champagne for celebrations, white wine for light meals and apéritifs, red wine for stronger-tasting foods, chilled Beaujolais for picnics, and so on.

One would need a mild-tasting, lightly effervescent water to go with everyday foods, and club soda or seltzer (depending on how salty you like your water) to mix with wines and liquors. Then a strong-tasting mineral water to sip throughout the workday as an alternative to soft drinks and caffeinated beverages. One needs a bulk still water, of course, for cooking, and perhaps a still mineral water for setting your hair (Farrah Fawcett uses Evian, she says), then maybe a mineral water in an aerosol can to cool yourself while sunning, *ad absurdum.*

The reality of it, however, is that most of us find one water and stick with it. We buy it at the supermarket, or have it delivered by the case, out of habit. Most of our lives are too complicated to think about having several different types of water on hand. In that case, one should find a mineral water or a seltzer that is all-purpose, one that can mix well with either white wine and Scotch without clashing, taste good over ice, chilled plain, and even at room temperature. In other words, one wants a pleasant-tasting innocuous, all-around water. I like Voslau and San Pellegrino equally, because they are clean, light, with long-lasting small bubbles; both are refreshing to drink alone and both mix well.

COOKING WITH BOTTLED WATER

To cook with carbonated bottled water is a waste of money, except in a few instances: Substitute club soda or seltzer for the water in any recipe for matzoh balls and you will have the lightest, fluffiest matzoh balls you have ever seen or tasted.

The following recipe is a traditional French preparation of carrots, and the Vichy water really adds a special flavor and cuts the natural sweetness of the vegetable.

RECIPE

Carrots Vichy

(Makes 4 servings)

1 pound carrots
5 tablespoons unsalted butter, melted
1/4 cup Vichy water
1 tablespoon freshly squeezed lemon juice
salt and freshly ground pepper
3 tablespoons minced parsley

1. Peel the carrots and cut them into paper-thin slices.

2. Place the sliced carrots in a pan with the butter, Vichy water, lemon juice, and salt and pepper to taste. Cover and cook slowly over low heat until carrots are tender but still slightly crunchy, about 10 to 20 minutes, depending on the age of the carrots.

3. Stir in the parsley and serve immediately.

COFFEE

ine gives rise to dreams, coffee to thoughts." So goes an old Anglo-Saxon proverb, prompting one to be thankful for both beverages. Nevertheless, one of the thoughts coffee is inspiring within the industry these days is a negative one: far fewer people are drinking coffee today than a generation ago. According to the National Coffee Association, coffee consumption has dropped by 50 percent in the last 33 years.

There are several reasons for this enormous decline. First among them is the fault of the coffee manufacturers themselves. I was told by industry experts (who, of course, do not want to be named) that about 35 years ago manufacturers surmised that consumers couldn't detect minor changes in standard coffee blends and began to reduce the quality slightly, bit by bit. Just like the old story of the farmer who decides to save money by each day feeding his horse a tiny bit less, until one day, to the farmer's surprise, the horse drops dead from starvation, coffee manufacturers today find themselves scrambling for the lost business resulting from inferior products.

Another reason for the turn away from coffee drinking is that until very recently, homemade coffee was prepared so poorly. Most coffee brewed in American homes was boiled in an electric percolator, usually made of aluminum, a procedure guaranteed to make poor coffee. Percolators circulate *boiling* water through the coffee grounds, which removes some aroma and flavor components and results in a bitter or woody taste. The water should be at a temperature slightly less than boiling to get the best flavor. Percolators also make poor coffee because they continually recirculate brewed coffee through the grounds, making for a high percent of extraction and dark, bitter coffee. For properly made coffee, 19 percent of the weight of the grounds must be extracted into the brew.

In the early 1970s, Joe DiMaggio popularized the superior drip method of coffee making by selling the "Mr. Coffee" machine on television. In 1970, 80 percent of the coffeemakers sold in the United States were percolators, versus 15 percent drip-type machines; just 4 years later, in 1974, only 20 percent of the coffeemakers sold were percolators, while 70 percent were drip machines; the remaining 10 percent were so-called specialty coffee makers, such as Melior and espresso machines. The gourmet food boom of the 1970s also inspired consumers to turn away from inferior commercial brands of coffee and search for better coffee, turning coffee making at home into a serious ritual. Thus while fewer people are drinking coffee overall these days, many of those who drink it are partaking of a superior brew. Many, however, still buy inferior supermarket coffee for their new coffee machines.

About 35 years ago, three quarters of the population of the United States drank coffee and one third drank soft drinks. During the subsequent three decades, the youth revolution swept through the country, inspiring rebellion against "adult" habits, including drinking coffee. The "Pepsi generation" preferred cold drinks rather than hot ones and the swing was disastrous for the coffee industry. Today, only a little more than half of all Americans drink coffee, and about the same number of people drink soft drinks. Since many of these soft drinks contain sugar and/or caffeine, the reason for drinking soft drinks today instead of coffee may be the same as in the past—for a stimulating "lift."

Perhaps most important among the main reasons for a decline in coffee consumption is the concern about health. Information about deleterious effects of coffee, such as cancer of the pancreas and breast, and decreased fertility in men, alarmed consumers. The fact that some of this data was unsubstantiated or later disproven did not reinstate coffee drinkers; they had moved on to other beverages.

A silver lining exists within this dark cloud, however. Even though Americans have been turning away from commercial (supermarket) coffees, setting off an overall decline from 3.12 cups per person per day (among those over the age of 10) in 1962 to 1.56 cups per person per day in 1994, the country has turned toward so-called specialty coffees, whole bean coffees, in increasing numbers. Specialty coffee now accounts for $300 million of the $5-billion-per year coffee industry, and the percentage is increasing geometrically. Included in the ever-expanding specialty coffee figures are flavored coffees, those that are mixed with such things as chocolate, cinnamon, coconut, or mint. As we've gotten more diet-conscious, we drink more and more of these low-calorie flavored coffees as after-dinner or between-meal treats. Since they lack the characteristic bitterness of regular coffee and are usually sweet, they are easier to like, and so flavored coffees also appeal to the regular soft-drink drinker.

Americans are also drinking much more decaffeinated coffee today. Twenty-one percent of the coffee-drinking public drinks decaffeinated, a figure that has tripled in 10 years.

The age breakdown of coffee-drinking today is interesting: those between the ages of 50 and 59 drink the most coffee (3.27 cups per person per day), followed by those in their 40s, then the 60s, 30s, over age 70, ages 25 to 29, and 15 to 19.

Almost half of the coffee-drinking public drinks it at breakfast; a third drinks it between meals. Three-quarters of coffee drinkers take it in mugs rather than in cups with saucers. Throughout the decline in coffee drinking in general, regional preferences have stayed pretty much the same: the northwestern, north central, and southwestern parts of the country drink weak coffee; those in the New York

City area, in New Orleans, and in the southernmost tip of Florida drink strong coffee, while the rest of the nation drinks a medium-strength coffee. No matter how they like it, Northeasterners drink more coffee per capita than those in other parts of the country.

The custom for making coffee in the United States calls for an average of about 90 cups per pound of coffee. Since those in the western part of the country drink weaker coffee, they expect more cups per pound; Easterners drink stronger coffee, and they expect fewer cups per pound. Europeans drink their coffee even stronger and, on the average, are accustomed to making 40 cups out of a pound of coffee.

Those in the eastern part of the United States generally like their coffee with cream, while those in the West drink black coffee. Some coffee historians have theorized that this is a throwback to the pioneer days, when travelers in covered wagons were lucky to get coffee at all, and had to make do without the cream.

The most encouraging point within all of these negative and positive coffee trends is that more people are drinking better coffee now than ever before. Probably more than any other food, coffee symbolizes Americans' newfound concern with good food, well prepared.

A DASH OF HISTORY

The exact origins of coffee are obscure, but the most educated guesses pinpoint its discovery over 1,300 years ago in Ethiopia, where the *Coffea arabica* tree still grows wild today. Soon after it was discovered, beans were taken to Arabia and there the coffee tree began to be cultivated. By the sixteenth century coffee had become an important part of Middle Eastern society. It was known as "the wine of Islam," partly because the word for coffee, *kahwah,* was the same as the Arabic word used for wine, which is forbidden to Moslems by the Koran.

The first time coffee appeared outside Arabia was early in the seventeenth century in Venice, which was an important port and the gateway to the Orient and the Middle East. The first coffee tree to grow outside of Arabia was transplanted to Holland in 1616. The Dutch East India Company established cuttings in colonial Java about 80 years later.

A French army officer took a coffee plant to Martinique in the early eighteenth century, and from this plant all of the arabica coffee now grown in the Western Hemisphere descended.

After the introduction of coffee to Europe, its popularity spread, followed logically by the establishment of coffeehouses. Wherever a coffeehouse existed, it became important not only as a place to drink coffee, but also as a center for discussing literature, the arts, and political ideas, often seditious ones. By the end of the eighteenth century, about 2,000 coffeehouses had been established in London alone, where they were known as penny universities because of the one-cent admission charge and their intellectual atmosphere. In the same century, Vienna came (occasionally) to be known as the mother of cafés, and it was there that the practice of coffeehouse-visiting was raised to an art that is still practiced in the Austrian capital.

The elegant Parisian Café Procope, which opened in 1686 in a spot opposite where the Comédie Française was soon to be built, was a favorite meeting place of such literary luminaries as Racine and Voltaire, who spent 2 hours there every day drinking *choca,* a mixture of coffee, chocolate, and milk. (Café Procope was also the place where ice cream was introduced to Paris; see "Ice Cream," page 49.)

Being a British colony, America at first followed the English practice of drinking tea as a daily beverage. But after the Boston Tea Party of 1776, drinking tea became unpatriotic, and the populous en masse turned to coffee. Coffee emerged as a symbol of patriotism and one Boston coffeehouse, The Green Dragon, was described by Daniel Webster as "the headquarters of the Revolution."

In the nineteenth century in America, a typical housewife bought green (unroasted) coffee beans, then roasted and ground them at home as she needed them. It was also a common practice to buy a few different types of beans and blend them at home according to personal taste, a precursor to today's experimentation. If the housewife lived after 1865, she could have made her coffee in a percolator, which was invented in that year by James H. Nason of Franklin, Massachusetts.

Decaffeinated coffee was discovered by accident in 1903 in Germany. A coffee importer, Ludwig Roselius, received a shipload of beans that had been soaked in seawater by a storm. When the beans were turned over to researchers, it was found that most of the caffeine had been stripped away by the water. Roselius developed a similar process to strip caffeine from the beans deliberately, and named the new coffee Sanka, a contraction of the French words *sans caffeine* (without caffeine).

Instant coffee (called *soluble* by the trade) was first perfected in 1938, when beans were dehydrated with hot air. Freeze-drying, a method of freezing, grinding, and evaporating concentrated coffee, was invented in the 1960s.

HOW COFFEE IS MADE

Growing the Beans

Coffee beans grow in tropical climates on trees that are pruned back to a height of about 6 feet to make the fruit easier to pick. When the fruit (called *berries* or *cherries*) ripens it turns a cranberry-red color. One tree produces about 2,000 coffee berries in a year, or enough to fill a 1-pound bag of coffee. When the berries ripen, they must be picked by hand, regardless of how they are going to be processed. If they are going to be processed by the *dry method,* all the ripe and unripe berries are stripped from the trees at the same time; for the *wet method* of processing, only the ripe berries are picked.

Processing the Beans

The dry, or natural, method of processing is the simplest and oldest means of processing coffee beans. The whole berry is allowed to dry on the tree or is picked and spread out on cement patios and allowed to dry in the sun. After 2 to 3 weeks, the coffee beans, which are green, are removed from the dry hulls by grinding them between stones or in modern milling machines.

Sixty percent of the world's coffee is processed by the wet method. For the wet method, the berries are brought to a central pulping station within a day after being picked. There the berries are put into receiving tanks filled with water; any fruit that floats to the top (indicating that it is empty or unripe) and extraneous materials (stones, twigs, leaves) are removed. The fruit is put into a pulping machine, which extracts the beans from the hulls. At this point, the product, called *parchment coffee* (which is the beans with papery skins), is taken in channels to separators, which segregate the beans according to size.

The next stop is the fermentation period, which ideally takes place right after separation to prevent the growth of bacteria. Fermentation consists of holding the wet parchment coffee in tanks or troughs for 24 to 48 hours to let the enzymes in the beans dissolve. When fermentation is complete, the coffee is rinsed in clear water in large channels where long paddles push it back and forth.

The next step is drying, which takes place on cement patios under the sun for 24 to 48 hours and then in giant rotary hot-air dryers for 8 hours or more, until the coffee's moisture content is reduced to 12.5 percent.

Now the coffee is cured to conserve its quality. Dry-processed coffee goes into a kind of milling machine to remove the dried skin and parchment. Wet-processed coffee goes into either a huller or a peeler, a machine used specifically for parchment removal. The hulled coffee then goes through a blower or screening machine to winnow out sand or pebbles. The final step is polishing, which is done by machines that remove the delicate layer of silverskin remaining.

The result of these preliminary procedures is *green coffee,* or unroasted coffee, the form in which coffee is exported from its country of origin to the country where it will be roasted and sold. Before exporting, however, the green coffee is graded by size. Size has nothing to do with quality; segregating beans by size is important only to ensure that each batch roasts uniformly, which ultimately affects the taste of coffee.

The United States imports more coffee from around the world than any other country. Almost 100 percent of the coffee imported into the country is green coffee. The main reason for importing it green is that once coffee is roasted, it will begin to go stale after about 3 weeks. Green coffee, on the other hand, has an almost indefinite storage life. Until it is roasted, coffee has no flavor or aroma.

Blending the Beans

Blending of coffee beans usually takes place before roasting. The coffees that are destined to go into vacuum-packed cans are almost always blended from quite a few different varieties of beans to ensure a consistent taste in the same brand from year to year, despite the vagaries of the agricultural market.

Decaffeinated Coffee

Coffee that is to be decaffeinated is treated before the roasting process. In the *chemical method* of decaffeination, the green beans are softened by steam and water and then put into a rotating drum where they are exposed to steam and a solvent. This process is repeated up to 24 times, until only 3 percent caffeine remains in the beans.

Until the mid-1970s, the solvents used were benzene, chloroform, acetone, ethyl alcohol, and ethyl ether, among others, but these were found to cause cancer in laboratory animals and have since been banned. Today, the solvent used is either methylene chloride or ethyl acetate, both of which are approved by the Food and Drug Administration but nevertheless have also been proven to cause cancer in laboratory animals.

Another method used to decaffeinate green coffee beans is practiced only in Europe, not in the United States, and is called the *water method.* In this method, the green beans are soaked in hot water, leaching out oils and caffeine, and then a secret process using activated charcoal absorbs the caffeine. This process was developed by the Swiss and Germans, and details about how it works are closely guarded. The machinery for water-decaf coffee is very expensive, which is why the coffee costs so much on the retail level, but it is highly prized because many consumers feel it is safer to drink than chemically decaffeinated coffee. The controversy over water-decaffeinated vs. chemically decaffeinated coffee has more to do with the use of chemicals than flavor. In fact, many people feel decaf coffee made by the chemical method tastes better than water-decaffeinated coffee.

Most of the water-processed decaf coffee comes from Belgium (Rombouts brand) and Switzerland (Coffex brand). The Rombouts company ships only roasted beans to the United States, but Coffex ships green beans, so coffee companies in this country can roast to their own specifications. Some smaller European companies are experimenting with water-decaffeinated coffee beans, and some American companies are experimenting with other methods of decaffeination, such as a carbon-dioxide/low-heat method, but experts feel the Belgian and Swiss products are best.

Different coffees have different natural levels of caffeine; robusta coffees have twice as much caffeine as arabica coffees (see "Varieties of Coffee," page 220), for example. So, contrary to popular belief, all decaffeinated coffees are not equally decaffeinated. Since the decaffeinating process removes some of coffee's oils, which give flavor, the structure of the bean is altered and the beans develop differently when roasted, and so should be roasted darker than untreated beans for full flavor development.

Roasting the Coffee

Two methods exist for roasting green coffee:

• *Batch Roasting* The roasters, made of steel, range in capacity from 1 to 4 "bags"; each bag equals 132 pounds of coffee. A 1-bag roaster is about 4$^1/_2$ feet in diameter and 6 feet deep.

The equipment most often used to roast coffee beans by the batch method is the Burns Thermalo, named after Jabez Burns who invented it in 1935, which blows hot air through the roasting cylinder. It usually takes about 16 minutes at 500°F. to roast a batch of beans, but some modern roasting machines can do the job in 7 minutes by blowing more heat (although not at a higher temperature) through the beans. A relatively new machine, the Jet Roast, can roast beans in 1$^1/_2$ minutes, but some experts feel this machine results in inferior coffee.

• *Continuous Roasting* In the continuous roasting method, the green beans are put onto a conveyor belt, which moves through a roasting chamber and allows very large quantities to be roasted, a little at a time. Each section of beans is roasted at 500°F for about 5 minutes. It takes less time to roast a few pounds of beans on a conveyor belt than a few hundred pounds at a time, which is the capacity of most batch roasters.

Some roasting plants use a combination of batch and continuous roasting methods. Specialty coffee roasters only use the batch method, while large coffee manufacturers, such as Maxwell House, use only the continuous method, which is best for high-volume roasting.

Specialty coffee roasting is done by large distributors, such as First Colony, or by retail stores, such as Gillies. These stores generally use a 1-bag roaster, roasting 100 pounds of beans at a time, which yields 86 pounds of roasted coffee. It's easy to tell if your coffee purveyor roasts his own, which means his beans are likely to be fresher, because the smell will pervade the store. You can also ask him to show you his roaster, if you're in doubt.

It takes a highly trained person to determine if coffee beans have roasted to the proper degree. Beans are judged by surface color, uniformity of the roast, and, except in completely automated roasting plants, the comparative standard of the beans. Different types of beans show different colors when roasted, depending on their country of origin and processing. The expert hears the beans popping as they expand in the roaster and smells them for good aroma. After tasting a couple of beans, if full development has occurred, he turns the heat off and removes the beans from the roaster, allowing them to cool naturally. Sometimes, in large continuous roasters a spray of water is used to cool the beans quickly.

Several companies have recently begun to make coffee roasters for home use. Some resemble small toaster ovens (toaster ovens would also work to roast green coffee); some look like old-fashioned chestnut-roasting pans. The best machine is made by Melitta; it is available by mail-order (along with green coffee beans) by writing to Melitta, Inc., Customer Service Department, 1401 Berlin Road, P.O. Box 900, Cherry Hill, NJ 08003. Telephone: (609) 428-7202.

After roasting, some coffee is sold to the consumer in the roasted, whole-bean form, as specialty coffee. The vast majority of coffee, however, is ground and vacuum-packed and sold in cans on supermarket shelves. Supermarket coffees are produced to be sold at a relatively low retail price, and every step of the processing is undertaken with this in mind.

After coffee beans have been roasted, they must go through a degassing stage during which the carbon dioxide created in the roasting process and trapped in the bean must be released. Degassing must take place before packing; otherwise the bag in which the beans are packed would explode. This degassing takes at least 18 hours, during which time the coffee begins to oxidize and go stale.

The increased awareness of coffee quality has brought with it an encouraging new packaging development which gets around this problem; it is called the *valve pack.* This new technology was developed in Italy, and it is slowly replacing most other forms of coffee packaging.

In using this state-of-the-art packaging, the beans are vacuum-packed immediately after roasting. When the carbon dioxide is released, the bag puffs up gradually; when it reaches a certain size a one-way plastic valve releases some of the gas. No oxygen can seep in to begin oxidation, and the package won't explode.

Whole coffee beans packaged in the old way had at best a 3-month shelf life and at worst a 2-week shelf life after roasting. Beans packed in the new valve pack are guaranteed to stay fresh for 6 months to a year, if the package is unopened. Once the package is opened, the beans will go stale just as quickly as conventionally packed beans.

This has changed the profile of the American coffee industry, allowing shippers that had been regional companies to send their goods around the nation without fear of their coffee turning stale. This also means that buyers of specialty coffee no longer have to buy coffee as close to the roasting source as possible. Ask your retailer if his bulk coffee is shipped to him this way; valve packs are also used to ship large quantities of beans to stores.

VARIETIES OF COFFEE

The best way to get to know quality coffee is to taste it unblended in the bean form, in other words, as specialty coffee. Once you find a bean you like, you can create your own blends or better understand the blends sold in your retail coffee store. However, with so much confusing labeling and deliberate obfuscation in the industry, it's difficult to know what the names of different coffees mean. Are you buying an unblended variety of coffee, or was the name made up by a wholesaler or retailer as a fanciful dodge? The name under which coffee beans are sold does not always mean that it is pure, unblended coffee from that particular region. For example, a coffee labeled "Kona Style" may not contain any Kona beans at all.

Like learning about wine, the only way to become really knowledgeable about coffee is to get to know the terminology, then set about tasting many different varieties.

Species of Coffee

Although others are cultivated, the two main species of coffee used today are arabica and robusta:

• *Arabica* Arabica trees produce the highest-quality coffee, much more complex and subtle than robusta. Industry practice dictates that only arabica beans be used for anything that is called *specialty coffee.* However, some "sneaky companies" (in the words of Don Schoenholt, former president of the Specialty Coffee Association) do adulterate their coffee with robusta beans.

Arabica coffee trees can be, and often are, grown at higher elevations than other species, and the resulting slower growth assures a better coffee. When arabica coffee is grown at high elevations it produces some of the best coffee in the world.

• *Robusta* This is the hardier and cheaper of the two main species of coffee bean. It can be grown at lower altitudes than arabica, and it is more resistant to disease. Robusta coffee also contains more caffeine than arabica coffee. Virtually all of the vacuum-packed coffees are made up mostly of this species, although most do contain some arabica beans. Instant coffee, however, is usually 100 percent robusta because it holds up better than arabica during the manufacturing process.

Robusta beans are smaller and rounder than arabica beans. The flavor is harsh (feels raw in the throat) or totally neutral. Roasted robusta beans have a distinctive cereal-like aroma, like toasted barley, that is detectable even in the bean form.

Types of Coffee Beans

Although this is just a sampling, these types represent some of the hundreds of *arabica* beans you are likely to find in a specialty coffee store.

• *Bourbon Santos* This is one of the best coffees grown in Brazil; it has a medium body and a sweet, nutty flavor. It is often used in blends.

• *Celebes Kalossi* A rare Indonesian coffee, which is spicy, with a rounded flavor and rich aroma.

• *Colombian* Beans from Colombia make a rich, full-bodied cup of coffee; they are often used in blends and for flavored coffees. A strong government program has standardized production and marketing, giving Colombian coffee a reputation for a middle-of-the-road consistency.

Two grades of Colombian coffee exist: *excelso,* which is the standard grade, rich and mellow; and *supremo,* a superior grade, smooth and light-bodied.

• *Costa Rican* These beans make a strong, robust cup of coffee with a pungent aftertaste, often compared in character to a dry Burgundy wine. Costa Rican coffee is favored by Europeans.

• *Ethiopian Harrar* This bean makes a highly acidic and heavy-bodied coffee often described as winey.

• *Guatemala Antigua* A spicy, mild coffee, Antigua is grown at high elevations and is particularly sought after by American consumers.

• *Haitian* Coffee from Haiti can be rich and mildly sweet, but its quality varies greatly.

• *India Mysore* From the southwestern part of India, Mysore makes a full-bodied and spicy coffee.

• *Jamaican Blue Mountain* The flavor of the true Jamaican Blue Mountain coffee has been compared to a delicate broth, aromatic and mellow.

Only small amounts of this coffee are produced (about 1 million pounds annually), partly because the plant takes a very long time to mature and produces a low yield. Eighty percent of it is sent to Japan, where it commands a very high price indeed. The tiny amount that comes into the United States (some from Japan, by the way), sells for four times as much as regular specialty coffee.

Because it is so sought after, Jamaican Blue Mountain coffee has sparked a great deal of competition among brokers and many false claims about who does and who does not have the real thing. As a result, the Jamaican government has put tighter controls on its exports. For example, much of the Jamaican Blue Mountain coffee now comes into the United States already roasted.

A coffee that is a true Jamaican Blue Mountain must have a seal that reads, "Certified by the Coffee Industry Board of Jamaica." If the coffee is sold in bulk, the retailer should be able to show you the same certificate of authenticity that comes from the importer.

• *Java* Java is an Indonesian coffee which, when at its best, is full-bodied and spicy with low acidity. Arabica Java is rare, so beware of robusta imitations.

• *Kenya AA* This full-bodied, acidic, rich, and smooth coffee is the highest grade of Kenya coffee.

• *Kona* Kona beans are from Hawaii and the only coffee grown in the territorial United States. It is rare to find the real thing, but when you do, it is sweet, smooth, and acidic, and highly prized by gourmets.

• *Maracaibo Venezuela* Maracaibo is the main port for Venezuelan coffee. Coffee thus labeled can exhibit a range of flavors.

• *Mexico Altura Coatepec* "Altura" means the coffee was grown at a high altitude. This bean makes a full-bodied coffee.

• *Mexico Pluma Oaxaca* This bean was developed from the Mocha plant and has a heavy body and strong acidity.

• *Mocha* Real mocha coffee is very hard to find. The name is so well known among the coffee-buying public that many imitations are sold, usually made of Ethiopian beans. True Mocha comes from Yemen and is bittersweet, smooth, and full-bodied. Mocha coffee has nothing to do with chocolate, by the way, but pastries containing coffee and chocolate often have mocha as part of their names.

• *Sumatra Boengie* This Indonesian coffee has an unusually concentrated flavor, heavy full body, and slightly herbal aroma.

• *Sumatra Mandheling* Real Sumatra Mandheling is rare. It is spicy, full-bodied, and almost syrupy; its strong flavor is not for beginners.

• *Tanzania Kilimanjaro* This coffee comes from an African bean that is smooth and low in acid.

Typical Store Blends

Blended coffees likely to be found in a local coffee specialty store are limited only by imagination. Theoretically, any purveyor can put together two or more types of coffee beans and attach a made-up name to the resulting blend. The following blends are the ones most commonly found, and no real consistency of flavor exists from store to store for blends of the same names.

• *Breakfast* This is usually a mixture of Bourbon Santos and coffee beans from Africa.

• *House* Although this is bound to be aimed at the broadest possible range of taste, it is also the signature coffee of a specialty foods store. One of the most highly regarded retailers of coffee in New York, Joel Schapira, recommends that when gauging a purveyor, you should try his house blend first. If it doesn't suit you, then you probably won't like the rest of his coffees either.

• *Mocha-Java* Originally this was blended from pure Arabian Mocha and Java Arabica, but now, since both of these coffees come from very small areas, they are extremely rare, and the blend is usually "created" by blending other coffees together. This style should be an acidic, full-bodied coffee.

Your Own Blend

It is fun and educational to create your own personal blend by experimenting with various beans. Joel Schapira, the aforementioned well-known specialty coffee expert, favors one of three ways to put together a "signature" blend of coffee:

• Make a combination of light and dark roasts.

• Use a well-balanced coffee as the base and add another coffee for sharpness and sweetness, such as one third Java, one third Celebes Kalossi, and one third Mocha.

• Mix one of the world's greatest coffees (Columbian, Costa Rican, Kenya AA) with a coffee from Haiti or Ethiopia for flavoring.

• To make an authentic New Orleans-style coffee blend, add 20 percent chicory to 80 percent coffee. Chicory is the root of the same bitter green sometimes used in salads. It was originally used to stretch out coffee to save money, but now the taste of it is favored in New Orleans. Chicory makes coffee look darker and taste more bitter and heavy.

The following list, which first appeared in the *Coffee Connoisseur* newsletter (a lively publication, unfortunately now defunct), will help you to combine beans in interesting combinations, by choosing among the characteristics you prefer.

• *Richness and Body*

Sumatra Mandheling
Java
Costa Rican
Tanzania Kilimanjaro

• *Flavor and Aroma*

Kona
Jamaican Blue Mountain
Celebes Kalossi
Colombian Supremo
Mocha

• *Strong Acidity*

Mexican
Ethiopian Harrar
Kenya AA

• *Sweetness*

Haitian
Vintage Colombian
Venezuelan Maracaibo
Indian Mysore

• *Mellowness*

Brazilian Bourbon Santos

Types of Roasts

One of the myths about coffee is the darker the roast, the stronger the taste. Certainly a particular roasted flavor typifies a dark-roasted coffee, but strength in coffee comes from its concentration with water, not the relative degree of roasting of the beans. Roasting brings the oils to the surface of coffee beans, making them shiny, and develops some flavors while dissipating others, as well as reducing the natural level of caffeine in the beans. Manufacturers often dark-roast low-quality coffee because the roasted flavor masks defects.

The more a coffee is roasted, the more moisture is evaporated from it and the less it weighs. Therefore, a pound of dark-roasted beans is bulkier than a pound of light-roasted beans, making dark-roasted coffee more expensive for a purveyor to produce than light-roasted coffee.

Commercial vacuum-packed coffees are always very light roasted. Specialty coffees are sold in a range of roasting styles, with a range of terminology.

The following lists the grades of roasts, starting with the lightest roast and ending with the darkest. All the various regional names for each roast are listed.

• *Light City/Cinnamon/Light* This type of roast is popular in the western United States; it enhances acidity in coffee and produces a thin-flavored brew.

• *Medium High* Medium High coffee is not quite as light as Cinnamon coffee, but not as dark as City roast.

• *City/American/Regular* This is the most popular roasting style in the country. It makes coffee richer than Light Roast, but the taste of coffee roasted this way may be slightly flat.

• *Full City/Dutch* Coffee roasted this way is slightly darker than City Roast coffee, which makes it slightly less acidic; it results in a deep, hearty brew. It is the most popular roast in New York City and other large urban areas in the country.

• *Brazilian* This roast is a bit darker than Full City, with a hint of characteristic dark-roasted flavor.

• *Vienna/Viennese/Continental* This type of coffee is roasted midway between Full City and French; it is rich, spicy, and full-bodied.

• *French/New Orleans/Dark* This kind of roast makes a slightly oily bean and has a burnt umber color; its flavor is sweet and smooth.

• *Spanish/Cuban/French-Italian* Coffee roasted this way is darker than French, with a taste approaching Espresso, but no bite.

• *Italian/Espresso* Espresso-roasted coffee has black, very oily beans, with a bitter, carbonized taste.

• *Turkish* Turkish coffee is the darkest; it has a burnt taste and almost no acidity.

HANDLING AND STORAGE

Coffee can go stale two ways: the oils oxidize and the volatile compounds evaporate. Freezing coffee slows these processes somewhat, but does not stop them. The safest way to store coffee to keep it fresh is to put it in an airtight container—a glass jar with a tight-fitting lid is ideal—and keep it in the freezer, where whole beans will last for up to 3 months and ground coffee will last for

1 month. The paper bag that many coffees are packed in will not keep coffee fresh in the freezer, but if the paper bag is wrapped in a tightly closed plastic bag it will stay relatively fresh.

Joel Schapira recommends not disturbing the coffee you have stored in the freezer, but to store up to 1 pound of coffee in the refrigerator, preferably in a tightly closed glass jar, taking out the container for your daily supply. If you take your daily coffee out of the freezer batch, too much air gets into it and the moisture condenses, giving the coffee an off-flavor. Refrigerated whole-bean coffee will last for about 2 weeks; ground coffee will last for about 1 week.

Vacuum-packed coffee in a can, unopened, will keep up to only 6 months. If it is opened, it will keep for just 2 to 4 weeks. Peter Quimme, in his book *The Signet Book of Coffee and Tea,* remarked that "customers who wonder why canned coffee always smells wonderful the moment the lid is pierced but rarely so good afterward will probably be somewhat disenchanted to hear that the aromatic *pfffft* sniffed on opening most likely contained a good deal of the aroma the coffee had."

The very best coffee in the world can be spoiled by a retailer who doesn't know or doesn't pay attention to his business. You should befriend your local merchant, and then ask him how often he receives his beans from his supplier; once a week is ideal. If he sells his beans from open containers, such as burlap bags, there is a much greater chance that they will be stale, unless he sells several sacks of beans every day. Plexiglas containers, or any containers with lids, will keep beans fresher longer.

Coffee sold in *valve packs* will stay fresh much longer than coffee in old-fashioned packages; see "Roasting the Coffee," above, for an explanation of this revolutionary new packaging method.

Check on your local coffee store by taking a close look at the dark roasted beans it sells. If they seem to be losing their shine, or if they have no shine at all, those beans may be truly ancient, and you should reconsider your purchase.

HOW TO JUDGE COFFEE

Tasting Media

Brew whole bean coffee using the "drip" method, which is most accepted by the coffee industry (see "How to Make the Best Coffee from Beans," page 229). Supermarket canned coffees should be brewed in a Mr. Coffee automatic drip coffee maker, according to each of the coffee manufacturer's directions. All coffees should be freshly brewed and served one by one, so that each can be tasted hot, lukewarm, and cool, the way it is done in all professional "cuppings" or coffee tastings. The coffees should be served in wide-mouthed white china cups.

It should be pointed out that a professional cupping has a different goal from amateur tastings. Professional tasters use the procedure to discover any defects in coffee rather than trying to determine which coffees are better than others. In a cupping, the ground coffee is put directly into the coffee cup and 190° to 200°F. water is poured into the cup. The wet grounds form a crust at the top of the cup. The taster breaks the crust with his spoon, then he smells and tastes the coffee, in a similar manner to the one professional wine tasters use. The liquid is noisily sucked into the mouth along with a bit of air (slurped) so that all of the taste buds are exposed to the coffee.

Color/Eye Appeal

A good coffee should have the color of a deep claret; it should not be brown or black. You should be able to read large print through it.

Taste/Aroma

Smell is a very important part of our taste perception of coffee; almost all coffee tastes the same if you hold your nose while you drink it. The aroma of good coffee should be pleasing, rich, and complex.

Acidity in coffee is considered a positive attribute, and it should be equivalent to the percentage of acidity generated by the carbon dioxide in club soda. If a cup of coffee has too little acidity, then its pleasing effect seems to be lessened. The proper amount of acidity will make a coffee lively and pleasantly sharp.

By the same token, if a coffee has no astringency, then it has no character; good coffee astringency tastes sharp and somewhat lemony, as Kenya coffee does. However, if coffee has too much astringency, the pucker can be most unpleasant.

Another word used to describe the flavor of coffee is *fermented,* which can come from the berries or the green coffee having been exposed to dampness too long at some point during the production and shipping process. It takes only a few fermented beans in a 5-pound batch of coffee to make it taste "off." The word "rioy" refers to a heavy and harsh flavor, reminiscent of coffees grown in the Rio district of Brazil. *Mild* flavor is the opposite of rioy. *Caramel* comes from the roasting, during which the beans are caramelized and become sweet-tasting; this flavor is desirable only in certain coffees, such as Kona and Colombian. *Harsh* is a flavor that tastes like raw weeds. *Musty* flavor comes from coffee that has been improperly dried.

Consistency

If the consistency of coffee is close to that of water, the taste will disappear shortly after it is swallowed, which is a defect. Underroasted coffees and certain varieties contain gum extractives which give a thicker liquid, making a better-tasting cup of coffee.

Body in coffee is the sensation of weight and texture in the mouth. Different coffees should be light-, full-, or heavy-bodied, depending on their style.

Aftertaste

Coffee should have a distinctive and pleasing aftertaste. Today in the Middle East, coffee is freshly brewed for each visitor, and it is set out with a glass of water which is sometimes scented with rose water, to be drunk before, not after, so that the taste of the coffee lingers in the mouth.

CONCLUSIONS AND SUGGESTIONS

The two top-selling types of specialty coffee are House Blend (although it may go by another name, such as Special Blend) and Colombian. Since these represent a blended and a non-blended type of coffee, I decided to test these two types.

I also tasted vacuum-packed canned coffee, the kind found in the supermarket. In this group, there is a type of coffee on the market called *High Yield* or *Flaked* coffee. This is the result of new technology which exposes more of the surface of the beans to puff them during processing. Because of this, 13 ounces of coffee, the contents of the new cans, has the same volume as 16 ounces. The manufacturers call for the same amount of this coffee per cup as they did with the old coffee, but a weaker brew results. Considering the fact that manufacturers' instructions for their coffee make a pretty weak brew to begin with, this coffee is a sacrifice.

The vast majority of the specialty coffee retailers in America buy their coffee from just a handful of wholesale suppliers. If you can find out from your coffee purveyor where he buys his whole beans, you can judge the quality of his wholesale product that way. Some of these distributors sell coffee beans in retail packages with their label on display, and so it is even easier to determine the source of the beans.

One of the most consistently good coffees, both wholesale and retail, is Starbucks.

I was also told by the experts in my tasting that many of these large wholesale suppliers sell green coffee to smaller distributors, who in turn sell to the same specialty coffee stores. Therefore, many retail coffee purveyors are unwittingly buying coffee from the same ultimate importer without really knowing it. Even such an august and experienced store as Dean & DeLuca, for example, at the time of my tasting was buying their whole bean coffee from three sources, two of which bought green coffee from the third.

The same sort of cartel exists among supermarket coffees. Seventy-five percent of the supermarket coffee consumed in the United States is made by three firms: Maxwell House, which makes Yuban and Sanka, among other brands; Folgers; and Nestlé, which makes Hills Brothers, among others.

The key to understanding why supermarket coffee is so poor is to realize that it is a high-volume, competitive, price-conscious business. Whereas a specialty coffee roaster will create a blend and then come up with a price, commercial companies work backwards; they target a price point and then work out a blend that can be made for that price.

Consumers used to be loyal to particular brands because their mothers bought them, but now people buy coffee that's on sale and no wonder—most supermarket coffee is of a uniform, mediocre quality. ("It is a beverage tasting something like a very weak broth, but not really coffee," stated one of our tasters.) In an effort to get a standard flavor, manufacturers of supermarket coffee blend up to 20 different types of beans so that if one bean isn't available due to bad weather in that growing region or other market conditions, they can substitute something else and the flavor of the brand will remain the same.

Other techniques manufacturers use to make their coffee cheaply are roasting beans less to get less shrinkage, cooling beans with large amounts of water to add weight, and grinding chaff with the beans to add volume.

The best supermarket canned coffee is Master Blend.

HOW TO MAKE THE BEST (AND THE EASIEST) COFFEE FROM BEANS

When it comes to discussing how consumers make coffee, specialty coffee suppliers often roll their eyes with exasperation. Nothing can ruin the best intentions of a conscientious retailer more than an inept coffee maker. The following system is absolutely foolproof and couldn't be easier. No expensive gizmos to worry about; all the tools you need are a small electric coffee grinder (even an electric blender will do), paper filters and a cone, a set of measuring spoons, and a measuring cup. The "recipe" makes very strong coffee, so if you like it weaker, simply use a bit more water.

1. Grind the beans just before you are going to use them. For this method they should be ground medium-fine, the texture of granulated sugar.

2. For each cup of coffee you are going to make, measure out 2 tablespoons of coffee into the paper filter, resting in a cone over a coffeepot. If you have one of those official coffee measuring spoons, you can use one of those for each cup of coffee instead.

3. Measure 6 ounces of cold water for each cup of coffee you are making and bring all of the water to a boil. Remove the kettle from the heat and wait until the boiling stops. Wet the coffee grounds in the filter with a bit of the hot water, then slowly pour in the rest of the water. Serve immediately, and try not to let it sit for more than half an hour.

NOTES: For a hint of spicy flavor, Elizabeth Schneider Colchie and Helen Witty, in their book *Better Than Store-Bought,* recommended grinding "a tiny scrap of cinnamon, an allspice berry, a clove or a few cardamon seeds with your coffee beans."

Diana Kennedy, in her book *The Cuisines of Mexico,* recommends sweetening coffee with brown sugar and adding a cinnamon stick to resemble a Mexican coffee called *café de olla.*

RECIPES

Ham with Redeye Gravy

In case you've ever been stuck with leftover coffee and you've discovered that the cat won't touch it, here's an old-fashioned American technique for using it up.

1. Sauté a thick slice of uncooked fatty ham in a skillet until nicely browned on both sides.

2. Put ham on a warm plate and deglaze the skillet with black coffee. Stir and scrape up the browned particles in the pan and reduce the liquid by half. Pour the gravy over the ham and serve.

Your Own Flavored Instant Coffee

Those flavored coffees on the market aren't really very good, but they are convenient. Here is one that you can make yourself and keep on hand for cold winter mornings or evenings when you don't feel like brewing up a whole pot of coffee. (Makes about 40 cups of coffee)

- **1 cup instant coffee powder**
- **1/2 cup powdered cream substitute**
- **4 teaspoons grated lemon rind**
- **4 teaspoons ground cinnamon**
- **1 teaspoon ground cloves**

1. Mix together all ingredients and store in a tightly closed jar.

2. For each cup of coffee, use 2 teaspoons of this mixture to 3/4 cup boiling water; sweeten to taste.

Coffee Truffles

This recipe is from my husband's book The Cuisine of Hungary, *where it is called Coffee Mignon, or Kávécsemege in Hungarian. These little candies were served to him at zsúr (from the French word jour), which were afternoon teenage parties in Hungary when he was growing up. (Makes 24 truffles)*

- **3/4 cup plus 2 tablespoons sugar**
- **1/3 cup prepared strong espresso coffee**
- **1 cup ground walnuts**
- **2 tablespoons roasted coffee beans, ground fine**

1. Combine the 3/4 cup sugar and the liquid coffee, and simmer, stirring occasionally, until the mixture becomes quite syrupy, about 10 minutes over moderate heat.

2. Add walnuts, stir, and remove pan from heat. Refrigerate mixture until cool enough to handle, at least 1 hour but preferably overnight.

3. Make little balls of the mixture, about 1/2 inch in diameter. Mix the ground coffee with the 2 tablespoons sugar and roll the balls in it to coat the outsides.

4. Place coated balls in fluted paper truffle cups and store in the refrigerator until ready to serve.

Espresso Ice Cream Made Without a Machine

This recipe comes from Italian Country Cooking *by Judy Gethers, who recommends taking the ice cream out of the freezer and putting it into the refrigerator for 1 hour before serving, to soften it. (Makes 2 quarts)*

- **4 eggs, separated**
- **1/3 cup sugar**
- **2–3 tablespoons powdered instant espresso coffee**
- **2 cups heavy cream, whipped**

1. Using a wire whisk or rotary beater, whip egg yolks and sugar until mixture is pale yellow and ribbons form when whisk is lifted from bowl.

2. Stir in instant espresso to taste. Fold in whipped cream.

3. In a clean bowl, using a whisk or rotary beater, beat egg whites until soft peaks form. Stir one quarter of the egg whites into the batter, then quickly but gently fold in remaining whites.

4. Pour into a glass bowl, cover tightly, and place in the freezer for 2 hours. Whip again and return to freezer.

5. To serve, scoop out ice cream into individual bowls.

Mocha Cheesecake

Makes one 8-inch cheesecake

- **3/4 cup graham-cracker crumbs**
- **1 cup plus 1 1/2 tablespoons sugar**

4 tablespoons unsalted butter, slightly softened
6 ounces semisweet chocolate chips
2 tablespoons heavy cream
1½ pounds cream cheese
2 eggs
1 cup sour cream
½ cup prepared strong espresso coffee
1½ teaspoons vanilla extract

1. In mixer or a food processor, blend the graham-cracker crumbs with the 1½ tablespoons sugar and the butter and press this mixture onto the bottom of an 8-inch springform pan. Place prepared pan into the refrigerator to chill while preparing cake batter.

2. Melt the chocolate chips with the heavy cream over low heat; cool slightly.

3. Place the cream cheese in the bowl of an electric mixer; add 1 cup sugar and eggs and beat until smooth, creamy, and well blended. Add melted chocolate, sour cream, espresso, and vanilla and continue to mix until well blended.

4. Pour batter into the prepared pan and bake in a preheated 350°F. oven for 45 minutes. Cool on a wire rack; cake will become firm as it cools.

TEA

The tea industry in the United States is in the process of being redefined.

Although colonial ladies and gentlemen loved tea, it took stubborn Americans about 200 years to get over the Boston Tea Party and appreciate once again this drink for which the rest of the world thirsts.

In the 1960's and '70's, tea consumption rose dramatically, perhaps due to several factors: Coffee declined in consumption during that period, as well as becoming much more expensive. The soldiers in the youth revolution took naturally to tea as a logical accompaniment to Eastern philosophy and reflective attitudes, and drinking tea was also one more way to rebel against parents' habits.

Health concern is another reason for tea's rise in popularity. As more and more alarming disclosures were made about the strong caffeine in coffee, health-conscious consumers looked for an alternative. Interestingly, brewed tea has only about half as much caffeine as coffee, depending, of course, on how long the tea is brewed. Moreover, the tannin in tea slows the release of its caffeine and makes it less of an immediate shock to the nervous system than the caffeine in coffee, while also prolonging the stimulating effect.

None of these elements would have been enough to push tea consumption into the stratosphere as has happened in the last few years, were it not for the exploitation of the ready-to-drink tea market. Tea in various packaging—bottles, cans, aseptic boxes, plastic containers, cartons—has tapped into the soft-drink market. Tea is now convenient and available, and sales of close to $1.5 billion per year for ready-to-drink tea reflects the new era. Compare that figure to $300 million for the same category in 1991, and you can see the dramatic change.

The tea industry altogether chalks up almost $4 billion in sales annually. The average American now drinks 7 gallons of tea per year, compared with 5.5 gallons about 25 years ago. At the same time, this American drinks almost 50 gallons of soft drinks per year, 26 gallons of coffee and 23 gallons of beer.

A DASH OF HISTORY

The discovery of tea has been placed by Chinese legend in the year 2737 B.C. As is the case with many other good things, tea started out in the West as a very expensive luxury. It was brought to England from Japan by the Dutch during the seventeenth century. (The name of tea comes from the ancient Chinese *t'e.*) By the end of the eighteenth century, tea had become the national drink of England, partly because of the high tax placed on gin, which had been a very popular beverage among the poor.

At one time beer had been made at home and was the all-day drink of the typical Englishman. Tea, when it became cheap enough, took beer's place. The words "mashing" and "brewing," used to describe the preparation of beer, were applied to the making of tea, and we still use the terminology today. It is interesting that the use of tea as an everyday drink is strongest in those countries where wine culture is weakest—the countries of northern Europe, the Middle East, China, and Japan.

The first iced tea appeared in the United States around the end of the nineteenth century. It was called *iced tea à la Russe* or *Russian iced tea,* referring to the fact that it was served in a glass. Russians, then and now, drink tea from glasses instead of cups.

In Salem, Massachusetts, around the turn of the eighteenth century, it was written that dried tea leaves were boiled until the brew turned bitter, and the tea was drunk without milk or sugar. The leaves were then salted and eaten with butter. This curious Puritanical custom fortunately didn't last long. Later in the eighteenth century, English customs and manners became fashionable in the Colonies and elegant (and far less stoical) tea parties for the ladies were the order of the day.

In the first half of the twentieth century in the United States, tea drinking fell off by two thirds, but then rose again after World War II.

HOW TEA IS MADE

The three main components of tea are caffeine, tannin, and essential oils. The tannin in tea gives it body and provides astringency. The essential oils, which are released during fermentation, supply flavor and aroma. Tea also contains small quantities of three important B vitamins: riboflavin, pantothenic acid, and niacin. When milk is added to tea, the protein in the milk reacts with the tannin in the tea and prevents the body from absorbing the tannin. In addition, the calcium in the milk neutralizes the acidity in the tea.

(In England, where tea is traditionally taken with milk, the rate of cancer of the esophagus is much lower than in Japan, where tea is also the national drink, but milk is not usually added. No hard evidence exists that tea without milk causes cancer, but these statistics are interesting.)

The major tea-producing countries are Sri Lanka, India, Africa, Indonesia, Japan, Pakistan, China, and Formosa.

Immediately after they are picked, tea leaves are processed in factories on the plantations where they are grown. They are then put into foil-lined tea chests and shipped to an auction port either in the country where they were grown or to London, a major auction center. After being bought at auction, a batch of tea goes to an entry port; in the United States the primary ports are New York City and New Orleans. From there, the tea goes to factories for packaging as either loose tea or in tea bags.

When tea leaves are first picked (3,200 tea shoots yield 1 pound of tea), they are green and shiny. Only the top two leaves and the bud are picked form each bush to ensure the most tender leaves. Great care is taken not to crush the leaves during the picking, otherwise the fermentation process will begin too quickly.

The expertise of the tea maker in his factory while processing, fermenting, and drying the tea leaves determines the quality of the final product. The first step in the processing of the freshly picked tea leaves is called *withering:* The leaves are spread out on racks where for 24 to 48 hours currents of warm, dry air are circulated to evaporate some of their natural moisture. Another method of withering is to put the leaves in drum dryers for just a few hours. The leaves are fed into a circular brass table from an open-bottomed round box which rotates under pressure, crushing the tea against the top of the box and the sides and surface of the table. Oxidation begins, heat is generated, and the juices remaining on the leaf start to develop the essential oils in the tea, which are important for aroma and taste. The twist of the leaf that results from the rotating determines the rate at which the tea will infuse when brewed.

The tea leaves are then put into a fermentation room while they are still green. The leaves are placed in piles about $1^1/_2$ inches thick on long tables in a humid environment at about 80°F. This is the beginning of the process called *fermentation,* a misleading name for a process that actually has nothing to do with bacterial growth, but instead refers to an inherent enzyme called *polyphenol oxidase* that works on the tea leaves. This is the same enzyme that causes fruit (apples or pears) to turn brown after it's been cut. In tea, this enzyme brings out the tannin as well as changes in the color of the tea leaves to yellow, then orange-red, and finally brown.

It is the intuition of the experienced tea maker that tells him the optimum moment at which to stop the fermentation process. The fermentation process lasts from as long as 3 hours for black tea to a few minutes for oolong tea; see "Varieties of Tea," below. In order to stop it, he puts the leaves into a 212°F. drying oven which gives off hot blasts of air. The tea must be fired in this way until the leaves contain 3 to 5 percent moisture so that they will not molder in the aluminum-lined plywood chests in which they will be packed for shipping. In some cases the tea is brought out of the drying ovens too quickly and must be re-fired. When the tea is fired twice, it has a telltale burned and sour taste.

In 1926, a new method for processing tea was invented called the *CTC method,* for Cut, Tear, Curl. This method speeds up the withering, fermentation, and drying process considerably by shredding the green leaves and pushing them over rollers. The result is broken leaves rather than whole leaves, and these broken leaves make a strong and brisk tea, with a quick, high color. It is an inferior tea and is used most often in tea bags. Sometimes a manufacturer will pack his better tea loose and his CTC tea in bags.

An endless variety of scented and flavored teas is on the market today. This alteration of the basic tea is done by drying flowers or leaves, pulverizing them, and mixing them with tea after fermentation; this kind of flavored tea is called *spiced* tea and can also contain such flavorings as bits of lemon peel and cinnamon. Finished teas can also be sprayed with authentic or artificial essences to vary the flavor and aroma; these resemble black teas with no visible flavoring agents and are called *scented* teas.

VARIETIES OF TEA

Tea is as varied and interesting a beverage as wine. All teas, like all grapes, come from the same type of plant, a member of the Camellia genus, but as with wine, regions, soil, microclimates, and traditional growing methods all influence the production and quality of tea. Over 3,000 varieties of tea are available in the world. Once grown, however, tea leaves are not tea in the same way that grapes are not wine; the distinction and fine-tuning comes in the processing of both beverages.

Tea Categories According to Fermentation

Three general categories of tea exist, based on the length of time they are fermented:

• *Black* Black tea is completely fermented. It is by far the most popular in the United States, accounting for 97 percent of all the tea sold. The lifting of the embargo on tea from mainland China a few years ago greatly enhanced the available quantity, variety, and quality of black teas in the United States.

Black tea is first partially dried to remove some of the moisture; then it is fermented for about 3 hours. The tea is completely dried and packaged. The leaves turn black after the tea is dried.

As a result of the longer fermentation time, black tea has the highest concentration of oil and, therefore, the least resemblance to the natural leaf. The more oil, the more caffeine released during fermentation, so that black teas contain the most caffeine of any category of tea.

• *Oolong* Oolong is the classic Chinese restaurant tea. This tea undergoes the same fermentation process as black tea, except that it is fermented for less time. Formosa oolong tea is almost as fermented as black tea, while Cantonese oolong tea is very lightly fermented.

Oolong, being half-fermented, possesses qualities of both green and black teas and is somewhere in the middle in the caffeine it contains.

• *Green* Green tea, which is unfermented, is the preferred tea in Japan. It was more popular in the United States before World War II, but supplies were cut off by the war; it never regained its popularity when it became available again. Nowadays green tea is combined with other teas in the manufacture of instant tea.

When green tea is picked, the leaves are steamed or heat-dried to stop the action of the natural enzyme, so that the leaves remain green. The green leaves are then dried and packaged. Green teas are nearly caffeine-free.

Tea Categories According to Leaf Grades

Tea leaves are also identified according to grades, and since grading terms appear on packaging, they deserve some explanation.

After black tea is fermented and dried, it is graded, or separated according to the size of the leaves. Although size has nothing to do with quality, a distinction should be made between *leaf* grades and *broken* grades. Leaf grades are the larger of the two grades; in descending order of size they are *souchong; orange pekoe* (in India this grade is called *flowery orange pekoe* or f.o.p. for short); and *pekoe.* In descending order of size, the broken grades are *broken pekoe souchong; broken pekoe,* shortened to b.p.; *broken orange pekoe,* shorted to b.o.p.; *fannings;* and *dust.* The last two grades are used only in making tea bags because they infuse tea into water so quickly, giving a high color in just a few seconds.

Orange Pekoe, which is pronounced "peck-o" not "peek-o," was originally a Chinese term used thousands of years ago for tea with a tinge of white, which was sometimes flavored with orange blossoms. Today the term only refers to the size of the tea leaf and does not reflect the quality or flavor. The old boast of a commercial American tea company that uses a "special" kind of Orange Pekoe leaves is more than a little misleading.

Green teas are graded by leaf age and style rather than size. *Gunpowder* has leaves shaped like pellets and a gray-green gunpowder color. *Young Hyson* leaves are longer and thinner, and so on down to *Dust,* which are the smallest siftings resulting from the sieving process, used in commercial blends for high color and a quick brew.

Tea Categories According to Names of Tea

Names of teas can be just as confusing as the names of wines, and for the same reasons. Some teas (and wines) have fanciful names, referring to blends made by producers; for example: Earl Grey (tea) and Emerald Dry (wine). Other names refer to districts, such as Darjeeling, at the foot of the Himalayas (tea), and Bordeaux, in southwestern France (wine). Still other names refer to the processing, such as Oolong (tea) and Auslese (a type of German wine).

Many familiar brands of tea are blends of two or more of the basic categories or grades of tea. There is nothing especially wonderful about the professionally flavored and blended teas. By buying unblended tea in bulk and experimenting on your own, you can come up with very pleasant and personal combinations to suit your own taste and mood. To blend your own tea, you might like to start with a strong, full-bodied black tea as a base and mix it with some lighter teas, such as Jasmine or Gunpowder.

The following is a list with descriptions of some of the major and more popular tea varieties and blends:

Black Tea Varieties

• *Darjeeling* The favorite tea of most connoisseurs is from the Darjeeling region of India where Himalayan winds impart a special flavor to the leaves. It is sometimes called the Champagne of teas. The best Darjeelings (special vintages can fetch as much as $100 per pound at the retail level) leave a characteristically fresh aftertaste; some are reminiscent of muscatel.

Different quality levels of Darjeeling exist; the best is First Flush, which is the first tea picked in the season, in March or April; it is highly prized and easily the world's most expensive tea with a typical wholesale price of $27 per pound at auction. Darjeelings labeled f.o.p. (flowery orange pekoe) and g.f.o.p (golden flowery orange pekoe) are made of the tip of the plant.

The Second Flush is a product of the next growth and is a lesser-quality tea. After the Second Flush come the rains and the Darjeeling tea bush grows so much that the quality deteriorates. Later in the season comes the autumnal growth, which can also be of high quality, depending on the growing conditions of the particular year.

Because Darjeeling is such an expensive tea, much of what is on the United States market is not 100 percent Darjeeling but a blend of Darjeeling and other teas. The Tea Board of India has begun a worldwide campaign to guarantee a minimum standard of quality for teas labeled "Darjeeling," and it has created a symbol, a picture of a woman's profile with a basket of tea, which appears on the labels of packages that contain 100 percent Darjeeling. If a Darjeeling tea does not have this symbol, it does not mean that it is not pure, but the presence of the symbol *is* a guarantee of quality.

- *Assam* Assam is a robust, strong tea from India. It should have big leaves.

- *Ceylon* The best Ceylon teas are from the high districts: Uva, Nuwara, Eljii. They have intense flavor and often smell of flowers.

- *Keemun* Keemun is the best of the Chinese black teas: heady, superb bouquet, excellent served with food. It is popular for use in English blends, because milk brings out its flavor.

- *Lapsang Souchong* Lapsang Souchong is a distinctive Chinese tea with a smoky flavor; often used as a part of a blend.

- *Nilgiri* Nilgiri tea is from a mountainous area in southern India. It is mild, mellow, and brisk.

- *Kenya* Kenya tea is from Africa. The plants are high-grown and the taste is similar to that of teas from Sri Lanka and India, probably because the original plants came from India. Much of it is used in blends now, although several companies are selling it unblended. It has a strong, sweet flavor and aroma.

- *Yunnan* Yunnan tea is from southwest China. It is similar to Sri Lankan tea, but it has a lighter and more aromatic flavor. Some tea experts say it tastes peppery.

- *Ti Kuan Yin* From Fukien in south China, Ti Kuan Yin tea has good body and a lively taste.

- *Ching Wo* Ching Wo is a south China congou (black) tea from the Fukien province. It makes a bright reddish brew that tastes aromatic and delicate.

Oolong Tea Varieties

- *Black Dragon* Black Dragon is the English translation of the word "oolong." It is applied to any semifermented tea that has been hand-rolled and heated to dryness over a charcoal fire. It looks and tastes like half black and half green tea; it has an elegant flavor.

- *Pouchong* Pouchong is often scented with jasmine and gardenia. It has a brownish color and a nutty taste. Most of it is used in the Far East; very little makes it to the United States.

- *Jasmine* Jasmine is a scented tea, usually a Pouchong (see above), flavored before the final firing with jasmine blossoms.

Green Tea Varieties

• *Gunpowder* Gunpowder has a bitter flavor and yellow-green color; it should be steeped for only 1 or 2 minutes.

• *Bancha* Bancha is an inexpensive Japanese tea with a mild flavor.

Blends

• *English Breakfast* This name was originally applied in the United States and Canada to China congou (black) teas, which at one time were considered among the best teas in the world. Later the term was used only for Keemun, which is a variety of congou tea. Now, although it no longer identifies these superior teas, the term identifies blends of black teas in which the China character predominates.

• *Earl Grey* Until recently, Earl Grey was not a very popular tea, but the basic formula was changed to conform to current tastes, thus it is now the best-selling tea not only in the United States but also throughout the world. It is generally made by blending Darjeeling, Ceylon, and China black teas, and flavored with oil of bergamot, a Turkish pear-shaped orange. It is named after Earl Grey, who was Prime Minister of Britain in 1830. The recipe is supposed to have been given to an emissary of Earl Grey's by a grateful Mandarin.

• *Russian Caravan* Russian Caravan was highly prized at one time because it took 16 months to transport from China to Russia. Today this term refers to blends made in the Russian style, which is very strong. The strength of this tea may account for the Russian custom of sipping tea through sugar cubes.

• *Irish Breakfast* Irish Breakfast is a strong blend of black teas, good mixed with milk.

• *Prince of Wales* The Prince of Wales blend is exclusive to Twinings. It is a congou tea from Anhwei province in northern China. Twinings describes it as the "Burgundy of China teas."

• *Lady Londonderry* A strong-tasting blend of black teas from India, Formosa, and Sri Lanka, Lady Londonderry tea was originally custom-blended by Jackson's of Picadilly for a well-known English hostess of the early twentieth century. Now the blend is sold to the public by Jackson's.

HANDLING AND STORAGE

The enemies of tea are light, air, heat, and humidity. Tea bought in bulk from big chests dries out more slowly than tea sold in small tins, because the surface area of the leaves exposed to the air is small in chests in comparison with the volume of tea. In tins, many teas are past their peak of flavor after a year on the shelf, and since many of the teas we buy have been stored for more than a year before we ever see them, staleness is common among these kinds of teas.

Tea in tea bags will keep for only a few months; it becomes stale most quickly in this form.

Different varieties of teas become stale at different rates. Keemuns and Darjeelings keep especially well, green teas lose their quality very quickly, and oolongs fade at a rate somewhere in the middle. In general, top-quality teas lose quality the quickest; they have more to lose. Black tea packaged in an airtight container will keep its full flavor for about 2 years, green and oolong for about half that time. Scented teas are best used within 6 months after opening. The scenting can dissipate, and the flavor will not stay as sweet. Over a period of time the flavor of the tea will overpower the flavor of the scent.

Different teas and blends are best stored separately. Tea is so susceptible to odors that it will pick up the flavors of other teas and other foods stored nearby. Lapsang Souchong, for example, can easily lend its smoky flavor to other teas with which it is packed.

Try this test to learn to detect staleness: Take some tea out of a tin, put it on a saucer, and leave it exposed to the air for a few weeks. Then make 2 cups of tea; one from the tea in the tin and one from the tea in the saucer. The tea from the saucer will make a very stale cup, tasting papery and dull.

Most retailers are not qualified to judge the quality of the tea they buy. They must rely on the product and the reputations of the suppliers they use. Standards for tea imported into this country are set by the United States Board of Tea Experts, a part of the Food and Drug Administration. The standards are very high, in fact higher than in any other country. The experts meet every year in Brooklyn, New York, for organoleptic testing (relating to the taste, feel, and smell of the tea) in which they deliver their impressions of various teas and set the standards for imports.

HOW TO JUDGE TEA

Tasting Media

Tea is tasted in just the same way as wine, only with the tea the process is called "cupping." The color is analyzed, the tea is drawn into the mouth along with air (actually "slurped") to reduce the liquid to a spray in order to come in contact with all the tastebuds, and the tea is not swallowed but is spit into buckets.

Steep 1 teaspoon of loose tea (or 1 tea bag, if the tea is not available loose) in 8 ounces of boiling water for 3 minutes, and then strain into a wide white china cup. This method is taken from the British technique for tea tasting; American professional tasters sample the tea with the leaves still in the cup. The tea should be first smelled and tasted hot, then lukewarm, and then allowed to come to room temperature before tasting again, which is the way it is done professionally.

Professionals often use slices of apple to remove the "fuzzy tongue" they get from the tannin after tasting many teas, but the apples are not kept in the same room as the tea samples, in order to prevent the odor of the fruit from tainting the tea.

Color/Eye Appeal

Black and oolong tea should have good clarity and depth and a bright appearance. The best tea is a rich, lively, ruby red color. If it is dull or dark brown, the tea has not been stored properly or is of a poor quality.

Greenish teas should have a sparkling greenish-gold color; a dull, brownish-yellow color signifies old or poor-quality green tea.

Professional tasters examine brewed tea leaves after the tea has been poured off. The leaves should look bright, not dead. Leaves that are too dark, almost black, indicate a moldiness or a mustiness.

Taste/Aroma

Tea should have body and strength from the tannins, but not so much that it makes you pucker from the astringency. Americans do not like their tea to be very astringent, although professional tea tasters feel that the more astringent the tea the better. In professional language, "brisk" means astringent.

A cooked (or "bakey") taste indicates that the tea was overfired or burnt. The tea should taste bright and lively, not dull or flat, which might mean that it is stale or old. A chesty (resinous) aroma or taste indicates that the tea was packed in a tea chest of uncured wood. Some teas that are shipped from their country of origin in polyethylene-lined burlap bags will smell and taste like plastic if they are allowed to get too hot during shipping. The flavor of fermented fruit in a tea is a clue that it has been allowed to molder.

A "malty" flavor is considered desirable in black teas, reminiscent of the flavor and aroma of malt—a cooked, sweet, caramelized flavor.

The best teas are complex, with a sophisticated mingling of a variety of flavors.

Consistency

The viscosity, or body, of a tea will be full, or light and thin, or anything in between. The best teas will have a full body, with just the right amount of weight on the tongue.

Aftertaste

The aftertaste of a good tea must not be too pungent, biting, or sour, nor should it fall off too quickly.

CONCLUSIONS AND SUGGESTIONS

The three top-selling teas in the United States are Earl Grey, English Breakfast, and Darjeeling. Both Earl Grey and English Breakfast are blends. The formula varies with the manufacturer and each one is a closely guarded secret.

In general, Earl Gray teas are of a poorer quality than the Darjeelings; the most common fault among the Earl Greys is that the citrus flavor overpowers the flavor of the tea, which might be acceptable in an iced tea, but not for hot tea.

The British humorist George Mikes once wrote a very funny piece about the English cult of tea. Experts were sent to the far reaches of the world to search out and cultivate the best-quality tea they could find, for which the British paid a great deal of money. Then, when he got the tea back home, the average Englishman carefully brewed it, according to centuries-old tradition, and served it in the finest, costliest bone china cups. Then, to top it all off, he dumped milk and sugar into the tea and couldn't taste a thing!

The finest Darjeeling I have tasted, McNulty's, is really quite delicious and should be savored, but not with milk or—heaven forbid—lemon. If that's how you drink your tea, then any supermarket brand will do. For me, McNulty's also makes the best Earl Grey tea. See page 237 for mail-order information.

HOW TO MAKE THE PERFECT CUP OF TEA

Fill a kettle with freshly drawn cold water and bring it to a boil. While the water is coming to a boil, warm the teapot by filling it with hot tap water. The pot can be earthenware, porcelain, stainless steel, silver, or heatproof glass. (There are pros and cons to the use of each type of pot, but aluminum is not recommended.) Empty the pot, add 1 teaspoon of loose tea (or 1 tea bag) per person and one for the pot, then fill with boiling water. Stir and steep for 3 to 5 minutes. To weaken the tea, add hot water; never try to strengthen it by adding more tea.

To make iced tea, proceed as above, but add twice as much tea to counter the melting ice. Or, fill a 2-quart pitcher with cold water, add 8 to 10 tea bags, cover, and let stand at room temperature overnight.

RECIPES

Tea Eggs

As every well-bred Victorian lady knew, tea will give a lovely sepia color to anything allowed to steep in it, from tired white lace blouses to porcelain cups. The following recipe is yet another example, borrowed from the Chinese. The eggs have a delicate salty-spicy flavor and make delightful snacks or appetizers. The steeping gives the eggs a beautiful marbleized appearance. (Makes 12 eggs)

12 large eggs, at room temperature
6 tea bags
2 tablespoons salt
2 tablespoons soy sauce
about 6 inches cinnamon stick
1/2 teaspoon whole aniseed

1. Hard-cook eggs in boiling water for 12 minutes. Drain. Fill pan with cold water and allow eggs to sit in the cold water for 5 minutes.

2. Tap each egg on countertop until shells are cracked evenly all over; do not peel. Reserve for step 3.

3. Pour 2 quarts water into a medium-size saucepan; add remaining ingredients and bring to a boil. Add cracked eggs and reduce heat to low. Simmer for 1 hour, adding more water as needed to keep eggs just covered. Remove from heat. Store eggs in cooking liquid in refrigerator

overnight, or for several days. To serve, drain eggs and peel.

Tea Cream

This recipe comes from the section on Portugal in Jane Grigson's European Cookery *(Atheneum, 1983). She recommends using a good Indian tea, such as a Darjeeling. (Makes 10 to 12 servings)*

scant 2 cups strained prepared tea
1 rounded tablespoon flour
1 whole egg, plus 2 egg yolks
2 cups sugar

1. Use a little of the tea to mix the flour to a smooth paste in a large bowl. Add the rest of the tea gradually, and beat in the eggs thoroughly. Set the oven to 325°F.

2. Make a thick syrup: Boil 3 tablespoons of the sugar with a little water until it is transparent. Swirl the thick syrup around a 5-cup ring mold.

3. Beat the rest of the sugar into the tea mixture and pour it into the mold. Stand it on a low rack in a roasting pan filled with enough boiling water to come halfway up the sides of the mold. Cook in the preheated oven for 1 hour. If it is still liquid and not thick enough, give it another 15 to 30 minutes. Take the mold out of the roasting pan and let the cream cool. Chill. Turn out no more than 1 hour before serving.

NOTE: To make the cream in individual custard cups, reduce the recipe by 1 egg yolk, mix the ingredients as directed, and pour the cream into the cups.

BAKING GOODS AND SWEETS

BAKING POWDER AND BAKING SODA

aking powder and baking soda are essentially the same thing, which may account for frequent confusion between them. Both are kitchen chemicals that give off carbon dioxide gas to provide leavening in a dough or a batter.

A DASH OF HISTORY

Both baking powder and baking soda are relative newcomers to cooking. Before the turn of the nineteenth century, all leavening in baking was done with yeast; with alcoholic spirits, such as beer and wine, which expanded into a gaseous state when heated; or by manually beating air into the dough or batter. Many recipes called for "beating for an hour or two."

The breakthrough in leavening came in 1790 when it was discovered in America that pearl ash, a refined form of wood ash, could make cakes rise. By 1792, 8,000 tons of it were exported to Europe. The use of this leavening was restricted to highly spiced cakes, such as gingerbread, however, because of a soapy taste, which required masking.

In the nineteenth century, it was discovered that bicarbonate of soda, another name for baking soda, could be used as a leavener. However, many people believed bicarbonate of soda to be responsible for dyspepsia, a common complaint at the time. Unlike our modern refined versions, bicarbonate of soda was coarse and had to be dissolved in a little water before being added to dough. Until 1979, because of a legal requirement pertaining to the ownership of the recipe, the original recipe for Toll House Cookies called for 1/2 teaspoon of water to be added to the dough, a holdover from the time when baking soda had to be dissolved.

By the mid-nineteenth century baking powder was introduced. It was a mixture of bicarbonate of soda and a mild acid, either cream of tartar or tartaric acid (obtained by scraping down the insides of wine vats after grape juice had fermented and been removed), plus rice flour, added as a filler and to absorb moisture. This became known as "single-acting" baking powder, which is no longer available in commercial form. The widespread use of baking powder in the United States in the nineteenth century fostered the development of a large variety of "quick breads" and other wholly American sweets, such as banana bread and applesauce bread, as well as baking powder biscuits and strawberry shortcake.

When single-acting baking powder was in common use, cakes had to be mixed quickly and popped straight into the oven, as the leavening gases were released as soon as the baking powder came into contact with the moisture in the batter. If the batter was allowed to sit before baking, the carbon dioxide would dissipate and the cake would not rise during baking. This made baking a much trickier business than it is today. However, some modern bakers contend we have sacrificed a supremely fine grain in our baked products with the switch to "double-acting" baking powder.

HOW BAKING POWDER AND BAKING SODA ARE MADE

The more familiar double-acting baking powder in our modern kitchens still contains bicarbonate of soda as its alkaline ingredient plus a combination of acids to provide a *double action.* Leavening gases are released first on contact with moisture, and then a second time during baking.

Substances that neutralize acids and combine with them to form salts are known in chemistry as bases; alkalis are bases that are soluble in water. Bicarbonate of soda, or baking soda, is an alkali that does not have the caustic qualities of other alkalis, such as washing soda or lye. In fact, the flavor of baking soda is even desirable in such foods as soda bread, scones, and old-fashioned brick-oven bread.

Modern baking powder combines an alkali (baking soda) and an acid: calcium acid phosphate, sodium pyrophosphate, or sodium aluminum sulphate. The sodium in these ingredients can be a problem for those with high blood pressure or those on low-sodium diets. In double-acting baking powder, only a small amount of the carbon dioxide is released when it is moistened; most of the gas is released during heating, or when the dough or batter is baking. Therefore, when single-acting baking powder went out of use, so did tiptoeing past the oven on baking day to prevent the cakes from falling.

MAKING YOUR OWN BAKING POWDER

For those who would like to hearken back to old-fashioned baking practices, which may have been more tenuous than today's, but gave results far preferable (for perfectionists) to those we get with double-acting baking powder, you can make your own. One who feels this way is Edna Lewis, author of *The Taste of Country Cooking* (Knopf, 1976). "For my tastes," she writes, "double-acting baking powder—the only kind you'll be able to buy now—contains so many chemicals that it gives a bitter aftertaste to baked goods, and even more so if the product is held over a day or so."

To make your own chemical-free baking powder, combine 2 teaspoons cream of tartar with 1 teaspoon baking soda; add 1 teaspoon cornstarch if you plan on storing your supply.

This recipe is useful if you are caught in the middle of a baking spree with no baking powder in the house. But remember: you've just made single-acting baking powder, so it must be used more carefully than the double-acting kind. Work quickly and bake your mixture just after adding the baking powder, especially with a thin batter, where the carbon dioxide gas spreads more quickly.

HANDLING AND STORAGE

Making your own is a good solution if you've suddenly discovered that your supply of baking powder has gone inactive. All types of baking powder lose potency on standing, so it's best to buy in small quantities and store tightly covered. If you suspect your tin might be too old, test by mixing 1 teaspoon baking powder with 1/3 cup warm water; if it fizzes, the powder is still good.

COOKING WITH BAKING POWDER AND BAKING SODA

Baking powder is used in doughs or batters that require a vertical leavening action. In other words, when you would like a baked item to rise up rather than spread out, use baking powder; when you want a baked product to spread out, rather than rise up, use baking soda.

However, bear in mind this important exception: when you're making something that incorporates an acid among the ingredients, such as buttermilk, lemon juice, vinegar, or molasses, and in which you desire vertical leavening, use baking soda rather than baking powder to get a more refined taste. When the baking soda reacts with the acid in the dough the leavening action will be the same as with baking powder, but the taste will be better.

Nevertheless, relying on chocolate in a recipe to provide the acid for a chemical reaction with baking soda, as some chefs recommend, is not advisable, because the acid content of chocolate varies from brand to brand, depending on how the chocolate was processed. Therefore, use baking powder when cooking with chocolate.

The reason baking soda is used in chocolate chip cookies is that Americans prefer a flatter, more spready cookie, rather than a cakelike cookie that rises higher. Both baking powder and baking soda would work well in a chocolate chip cookie recipe, depending on what kind of cookie you prefer.

RECIPE

Shortcake for Fresh Fruit

(Makes 6 servings)

2 cups sifted flour
1/2 cup sugar
1 tablespoon baking powder
1/2 teaspoon salt
1/2 cup (1 stick) cold unsalted butter
3/4 cup milk
1 1/2 cups heavy cream, whipped to soft peaks with 1/4 cup sugar
2 pints fresh strawberries (cut into halves or quarters, if they are large), or raspberries, or blueberries, washed and drained

1. Stir together the flour, 1/2 cup sugar, the baking powder, and salt. Cut the cold butter into small pieces and add to the bowl with the flour mixture. Using a pastry blender, or working quickly with your hands, rub together the butter and flour mixture until it resembles coarse cornmeal.

2. Add milk to the dough and mix quickly with your hands or a wooden spoon until a soft dough is formed. Divide dough into 2 equal pieces and pat each piece into a greased 8-inch cake pan; bake in a 425°F. oven for 15 to 20 minutes, or until lightly browned. Cool on a wire rack.

If you wish, you can bake the dough into individual shortcakes by rolling it out to 1/4-inch thickness and cutting 12 rounds or squares. Bake on a greased cookie sheet at 425°F. for 10 to 15 minutes, or until light brown, and cool on a wire rack.

3. To serve: If you are making one big shortcake, place one of the rounds on a serving platter and top with half of the berries, then half of the whipped cream. Cover with the second shortcake round and top that with the other half of the berries and the other half of the whipped cream. Cut into wedges to serve.

If you are making individual shortcakes, follow the same procedure, using 2 small shortcake pieces for each serving.

SUGAR AND OTHER SWEETENERS

Sugar, in some form, accounts for 11 percent of the calories consumed each day by the average American. This does not include the amount of sugar from natural sources such as fruits, vegetables, and milk products. Some sugar is added by manufacturers to processed foods and some is added by consumers themselves. In fact, the typical American eats "as much sugar as his combined intake of eggs, all fruits, all vegetables and whole-grain cereals," according to Dr. Amanuel Cheraskin of the University of Alabama.

The overall average intake of "caloric sweeteners" (the industry term for cane and beet sugar as well as corn sweeteners) is 145 pounds per person per year. Our total per capita intake of sweeteners is not decreasing significantly, but we are eating less beet and cane sugar and more corn sugar. The reason is that in recent years there has been a rise in the price of beet and cane sugar and food manufacturers are switching to less-expensive corn sweeteners to save money. Corn sweeteners now account for 55 percent of the entire sweetener market, compared to about 4 percent in 1975.

When you account for waste and other uses for sugar, actual consumption of sugar is 43 pounds per person per year, or 11 percent of total calories.

About two-thirds of the sugar we eat is added by food manufacturers; the rest is added by consumers themselves.

Possibly because of the expense of shipping it, no national brand of sugar exists, but many small regional companies, such as C & H in California and Hawaii, Spreckels in the western United States, Supreme in Louisiana, and Dixie Crystals in the Southeast. The largest sugar-refining corporation in the country is The Domino Sugar Corp., which produces the Domino brand. Private-label sugars (such as the little packets of sugar in restaurants), made by the manufacturers of larger packages of sugar, make up 50 percent of the sugar market.

A DASH OF HISTORY

Sugar is a native of New Guinea in the South Pacific. Thousands of years ago its use spread north from there to India—our word "sugar" comes from the Sanskrit—and then to Persia. The first sugar refineries were built in the Middle East in the seventh century A.D.; it was the Arabs who first developed efficient ways of manufacturing sugar. In the twelfth century, during the Crusades, sugar was discovered in the Middle East by Europeans, and they carried the taste for it to their own countries. Before that time, the predominant sweetener in Europe was honey. Thereafter, Venice became an important shipping point for cane sugar, which was brought to Europe from the Middle East at great expense.

Brillat-Savarin noted that "sugar entered the world by way of the apothecary's laboratory," commenting on the fact that sugar was first used in Europe to take away the bitter taste of medicines. Even after it was widely used for candy and confectionery, sugar remained prohibitively expensive for all but the very wealthy. After the seventeenth century, with the introduction of tea, coffee, and chocolate drink, sugar was consumed more and more by the masses to sweeten these beverages.

It was Christopher Columbus who had the bright idea to take sugar cane to the newly discovered Caribbean islands, where it grew exceptionally fast. By the eighteenth century the West Indies supplied most of the world with sugar, and workers were imported from Africa to help with its production. The enormous prosperity that had come to West Indian planters, slave traders, and shipping companies began to diminish when, in the middle of the nineteenth century, the process of extracting sugar from beets rather than cane was perfected. In order to free France from reliance on English colonies, Napoleon sponsored the search for an alternative to cane sugar. As a result, it became possible for many countries to grow beets and make their own sugar rather than rely on imports from the West Indies. It was also at this time that Brillat-Savarin wrote that sugar had become a prime necessity, "for there is scarcely a woman, especially a woman of means, who does not spend more on sugar than on bread."

In this century, the consumption of sugar has increased much more than in any other time: The world production of sugar in 1964 was seven times greater than at the turn of the century.

HOW SUGAR IS MADE

The white crystallized sugar that is most familiar to us as table sugar is sucrose, a disaccharide, made up of two monosaccharides (simple sugars) called *fructose* and *dextrose*. Forty percent of the world's supply of table sugar is made from sugar beets, and 60 percent is made from sugar cane, and they taste identical; no one, not even experts, when tasting sucrose can tell from which plant it was made.

The process of making both beet and cane sugar is somewhat similar: First cane is washed and crushed to extract the juice, which is green. In the case of beets, the vegetable is shredded instead of crushed to extract the juice. In both cases, then heat and lime are used to clarify the raw juice and remove impurities. The juice is strained through a carbon filter to take out all of the color and make the juice clear. The juice is boiled down to evaporate much of the water content, then filtered again by a sedimentation process: Natural gravity forces sediment to the bottom of the tanks, where it is pumped out continuously for 2 hours. The resulting clear syrup is subjected to pressure that causes crystallization.

At this point the wet crystals are put through a centrifuge and dry white crystallized sugar is produced. The syrupy by-product of this step is called *first molasses;* which in turn is boiled down, crystallized, and centrifuged to obtain more dry white crystallized sugar. The syrupy by-product of this step is *second molasses;* which is boiled down once more to produce still more dry white crystallized sugar. The last and thickest of all the syrupy by-products is *final molasses;* or black-strap molasses, the darkest and most concentrated of all types of molasses.

VARIETIES OF SUGAR

Granulated

This is commonly known as "white sugar," or ordinary, white crystallized table sugar; it is 99.8 percent sucrose, made from cane or beets; the remaining 0.2 percent is made up of trace minerals.

Superfine

Superfine is also called *extra fine* sugar, and *castor* or *caster* sugar in England. This is ordinary granulated sugar that is more finely ground than table sugar, the smallest granulated particles that remain when liquid sugar is crystallized, dried, screened, and sorted. Because of its fineness, superfine sugar dissolves more quickly in liquids, and for this reason is recommended by some bakers as an all-purpose sugar.

Confectioners'

Confectioners' sugar is also called *powdered* sugar and *icing* sugar, and is an even finer version of granulated sugar, actually ground into a powder. After granulated sugar is made, it is pulverized in machines to create confectioners' sugar. 10X, written on many labels of confectioners' sugar, refers to the number of times the sugar is sifted; most commercial bakers use a less fine version, 3X to 8X, which is less expensive than 10X. Confectioners' sugar is most often called for in recipes where granulated sugar would cause graininess, generally in uncooked foods, such as cake frosting. It is not ideal for cold drinks because it tends to lump in liquid mixtures if it is not heated. Confectioners' sugar will also cloud a clear liquid. Since most manufacturers add cornstarch to confectioners' sugar as an anticaking agent (check the label to be sure), it should not be used to sweeten whipped cream because it will make the cream gummy; superfine sugar should be used instead.

Brown

Nowadays, there are three ways to make brown sugar:

The *old-fashioned* or traditional method accounts for over 50 percent of the brown sugar production in the United States. This type of brown sugar is a less-refined version of white table sugar, removed from the manufacturing process while the molasses is still intact to color and flavor the sugar. This type of authentic brown sugar is made by the Amstar, C & H, and Imperial companies.

The resulting "light" brown sugar is made up of about 8 percent molasses with about 92 percent granulated white sugar; the moisture from the molasses makes the sugar moist and lumpy. The higher the molasses content of the sugar, the darker the sugar becomes. "Dark" brown sugar is more strongly flavored than "light" brown sugar; the molasses flavor in it is more pronounced. Dark brown sugar tends to burn more easily than light brown sugar when used for baked goods, such as cookies, because it has a higher invert sugar content, which makes for caramelization at a lower temperature. Dark brown sugar is also slightly acidic, so it is likely to curdle milk or cream if a recipe requires heating the two together, whereas light brown sugar does not cause milk or cream to curdle. Otherwise, light or dark brown sugar can be substituted, cup for cup, for white sugar in a recipe.

In the *constructed* method, brown sugar is a mechanical mixture of cane syrup (a type of molasses) and white granulated sugar.

Although it is not labeled as such, *synthetic* brown sugar is white granulated sugar mixed with caramel coloring rather than true molasses.

Brownulated sugar is a Domino brown sugar product that is granulated and dry rather than moist and lumpy. It is white sugar to which molasses is added to make brown sugar; then it is crystallized in such a way that each grain is evenly coated with molasses, making it pourable. It is easier to use than ordinary brown sugar because it pours readily. Many professional chefs use Brownulated sugar to sprinkle over the top of *crème brûlée,* for example, rather than going through the extra step of sifting ordinary brown sugar. It can be used cup for cup in place of light brown sugar.

Cube

Also known as *lump* sugar, cube sugar is refined and crystallized sugar that has been moistened and compressed into little blocks. It is used at the table to sweeten hot drinks, and in baking to rub on the skins of citrus fruits to extract the flavorful oils. Both brown and white sugars are made into cubes. White sugar cubes come in two forms: rectangular cubes (one brand manufactured by Domino called *Hostess Tablets*), which are more firmly compressed and dissolve more slowly, and square cubes, which are called *Dots* by the same company.

Turbinado

Turbinado sugar is partially refined, removed from the manufacturing process before all of the molasses has been separated from the sucrose. About 15 percent of turbinado sugar is molasses, as opposed to 8 percent for brown sugar. Turbinado sugar is very similar in color to brown sugar, but is usually more coarsely crystallized.

Demerara

Demerara is partially refined sugar, very similar to turbinado sugar except that it has larger crystals; it also seems less sweet than turbinado sugar, because turbinado sugar dissolves faster. It is most often served today in fine restaurants to sweeten coffee. Originally it was named after the Demerara district in Guyana.

Raw

Raw sugar contains dirt, bacteria, and insect parts and is not legal for human consumption in the United States unless it has been purified and refined.

OTHER SWEETENERS

Molasses

Molasses, the brown syrup that remains after the dry white sugar crystals have been extracted, is the primary by-product of the sugar manufacturing process. Although molasses results from both beet and cane refining, only cane molasses is palatable.

Technically, molasses contains all of the impurities that are removed from the pristine sucrose, and these impurities include ash, minerals, a small amount of B vitamins, and potassium. Lighter-colored molasses is extracted early on in the manufacturing process, and darker molasses comes from the succeeding extractions. Blackstrap molasses, which is so bitter that it is almost unpalatable except in tiny amounts, is from the final extraction. About half of the darkest, blackstrap molasses is made up of sugar, and the other half is ash, minerals, and water.

In some brands, sugar is extracted from cane using sulfur dioxide, which gives the taste of sulfur to the molasses; that's why so many recipes specify "unsulfured molasses" in their ingredients.

Most of the molasses sold today is made from molasses blended with clarified cane syrup in order to produce a standard product, which is of medium strength with medium sweetness. However, sometimes two different varieties of molasses are packaged, to give consumers a choice: *Barbados* is the lightest and sweetest variety of molasses, and *blackstrap* is the strongest, least sweet, and most bitter molasses. Blackstrap contains about 10 percent ash, and barbados contains from 3 to 5 percent; it's the ash in the molasses that makes it bitter. Most supermarket molasses, simply labeled "molasses," falls between the two extremes in flavor and sweetness.

When used in baking, any kind of molasses adds flavor, color, and softness to pastries and breads. Molasses can be substituted for up to half of the white or brown sugar in a recipe. For every cup of molasses added in place of sugar, add 1/2 teaspoon baking soda and omit 1/2 teaspoon baking powder, and reduce the liquid content by one third.

Sorghum Molasses

Not a true molasses, sorghum is a dark syrup made from a grass. The first sorghum seeds were brought to this country from France in 1854, and shortly afterward syrup production began when it was determined that sorghum's high starch content made it unsuitable for making granulated sugar. Sorghum syrup has been popular with rural people in the South ever since that time, partly because they can grow it themselves and thus remain self-sufficient on remote farms. It was also the only sweetener slaves were allowed to have. During World War II it became popular again because of the unavailability of cane sugar. Now it is sometimes sold in healthfood stores, although it is often badly processed and quite bitter. Sorghum is grown today mostly in Kentucky and Tennessee.

Corn Syrup

Manufactured from cornstarch and diluted with water, corn syrup is made up primarily of *dextrose* (also known as glucose), which is a simple sugar and one of the two components of sucrose. The other is *fructose* (see below). All corn syrup is made of a combination of pure corn syrup and high fructose corn syrup, making it lighter and thinner than pure corn syrup, which is usually very viscous.

Light corn syrup is translucent, mildly flavored with a bit of vanilla, but mostly tastes sweet. Dark corn syrup contains *refiner's sugar,* which is similar to molasses and lends a stronger flavor to the syrup. It also has caramel color and caramel flavoring added to it.

Many people use corn syrup as a pancake syrup, or as a way of stretching the more expensive maple syrup. Corn syrup is one of the primary ingredients in southern pecan pie; it is added for all or part of the sweetener in many recipes because it does not crystallize like white sugar. It is also about 75 percent as sweet as white sugar and gives a chewy texture to foods that contain it. Light and dark corn syrups can be used interchangeably in recipes.

Fructose

Called *fruit sugar* because it occurs naturally in fruits, fructose, also known as levulose, is about 70 percent sweeter than common sucrose (table sugar) for the same amount of calories. It is made from cornstarch, taken from corn. An enzyme is used to rearrange glucose molecules to form fructose. Although fructose syrups are used frequently in the soft-drink industry, fructose is sold at the retail level in crystalline form.

If taken in large amounts, however, fructose is likely to cause diarrhea. Fructose works best with cold, slightly acidic beverages, which is why it is added so often by manufacturers to soft drinks; when hot, it has the same sweetening power as sugar.

Maple Sugar

Maple sugar is pure maple syrup that has been concentrated and crystallized to make a maple-flavored sugar. The syrup is obtained by drilling a small hole into a tree trunk and hammering in a tap onto which a 10-liter pail is hung to catch the sap; alternatively, the tap is attached to a pipe that feeds a central container. When the outside temperature is right, 28° to 40°F., the sap will run as soon as the taphole is made.

Maple sugar is made by boiling the sap until most of the water evaporates, so that it contains 95 percent solids and 5 percent water and has the consistency of a thick paste. This paste is pressed into forms and cooled into blocks; then it is sold as solid maple sugar. Sometimes it is evaporated even further to reach a 98 percent solids content, when it can be granulated to resemble brown sugar crystals. Canada is the largest producer of maple sugar, and Vermont is the second largest.

Maple sugar can be substituted cup for cup for white or brown sugar in a recipe. Both maple syrup and maple sugar are a bit sweeter than ordinary white sugar, although they both contain only 88 to 98 percent sucrose.

Natural Sweeteners

"Natural sweeteners" is a term used on many processed food labels that denotes any sweetener that occurs in nature: sucrose, dextrose, fructose, etc.; in other words, any variety of "sugar."

HANDLING AND STORAGE

If stored in an airtight container, in a cool, dry place, sugar will last indefinitely. Bacteria will not grow in sugar, which is why it is so often used for canning and preserving.

Brown sugar, which has such a high moisture content, can be stored in an airtight container in the refrigerator, which should prevent it from becoming hard, dry, and lumpy. If it has become dry, it may be softened if put into the microwave at a low setting for a very short time, or by putting it into an airtight container with a moist paper towel or a slice of apple.

Molasses can be stored in a cool pantry after opening; it does not need to be refrigerated.

COOKING WITH SUGAR

Aside from its flavor, sugar is used in cooking for many purposes. Sugar attracts water from the air to keep foods moist; it also enables cakes to rise higher by delaying the gluten in the flour from getting stiff too quickly. It lowers the freezing point of food; without it, ice cream would freeze so solidly that you wouldn't be able to eat it. Sugar adds bulk to food, especially to processed foods, where the taste of it is disguised by the spices and salt. It helps to tenderize meat and prevents ham and bacon from becoming too hard while being cured.

I decided to test the various characteristics of different sugars by baking a basic sugar cookie recipe several times, each time with another type of sugar.

I baked the cookies with white sugar, light brown sugar, dark brown sugar, maple sugar, and honey. For all the dry sugars, I simply substituted the sugar cup for cup for the white sugar in the recipe. The recipe worked well, technically, with every sugar. The only differences were in color and taste. The cookie with light brown sugar had a slight molasses flavor, the one made with dark brown sugar had more molasses flavor, the maple sugar cookie tasted strongly of maple. The colors of all of the other cookies were darker than the white sugar cookie, the depth of color depending on the original color of the sugar used.

All in all, this experiment led me to the conclusion that the decision to use one sugar over another in a recipe should be based on flavor more than anything else. My husband tried the cookies and characterized the differences in flavor in musical terms: The white sugar is preclassic; the light brown sugar cookie is Brahms; the dark brown sugar cookie is a slow movement of Tchaikovsky; and the maple sugar cookie is a Sousa march.

CHOCOLATE

Love, passion, guilt, indulgence, craving, sensuousness, addiction—these strong words are used to refer to chocolate, a food eaten almost every day by even the youngest among us. As one newspaper writer has said, "Does anyone in the whole wide world remember for sure the first taste of chocolate? Or is it, the knowledge of it, the instinct, printed into our little brains at birth?"

It is a culinary given, for many, an important part of our eating lives. Chocolate makes all those years of "finish your spinach" worthwhile.

The food industry recognizes our obsession and has been rewarded with growth. Godiva Chocolates, on the upscale end of the business and with more than 1,200 outlets nationwide, has had a 400 percent increase in sales since 1979. Others, such as Perugina and Lindt, have also grown tremendously.

Although the makers and importers of deluxe chocolates are experiencing the most dramatic increases in sales, Americans spent $4.4 billion on *all* kinds of chocolate in 1984. About 92 percent of that chocolate was made in the United States, which indicates an increase in imports from three years earlier, when about 97 percent of the chocolate Americans ate was made in the United States. Eighty percent of all of the chocolate eaten in this country is milk chocolate. One of the most popular forms of milk chocolate, Hershey's Kisses, are produced at the rate of 1,500 kisses every minute of every day.

Chocolate manufacturers are the second largest users of milk in the country, the first being the dairy industry, which uses milk for ice cream and yogurt, among other things. Milk chocolate uses 1.17 billion pounds of milk per year, or 3,500,000 pounds daily. Hershey alone uses enough milk in a day to supply a city the size of Philadelphia. Chocolate manufacturers use 20 percent of the total peanut production, 40 percent of the almonds, and 8 percent of the sugar.

Despite all of this growth coupled with the fact that the average American eats 11.2 pounds of chocolate per year (about 0.7 percent of all of the food consumed), we are far behind the average Swiss, who eats 19 pounds yearly. Added to that Swiss number, however, is the help they get from the American and other tourists who load up on chocolate during trips.

Chocolate has seasons: It doesn't sell as well in the summer as in the winter, which is logical, considering its perishability in warm weather. Also, no matter that some chocolate snobs feel that "dark is to milk chocolate what Dom Pérignon is to

Dr. Pepper," most of the country prefers milk chocolate. New Yorkers are the only exception; they prefer dark.

A DASH OF HISTORY

It's interesting to note that chocolate, coffee, and tea became popular in Europe within a hundred-year period, approximately between the turn of the sixteenth century and the turn of the seventeenth century.

Chocolate was first brought back to Spain from the New World by Christopher Columbus. (A Lindt advertisement remarks that chocolate was introduced to Europe by Christopher Columbus who, "incidentally, also discovered America.") But it was Hernando Cortez, who, in the early sixteenth century, made a significant finding when he observed how the Aztec Indians processed the bean to make a bitter drink. In fact, our word "chocolate" translates from the Indian meaning "bitter water." Cortez also reported that the Aztecs believed the beverage conferred energy, and that it was used as a nuptial aid by Montezuma, who was said to drink it before entering his harem.

The Spaniards wisely added sugar, plus cinnamon for good measure, and chocolate as a drink became a hit. It took 100 years for the fashion to reach other parts of Europe. Although shops that dispensed chocolate drink had cropped up throughout Europe by 1700, they were frequented only by the very rich, who wanted to see and be seen by their peers drinking such an expensive beverage. By the middle of the eighteenth century the heavy taxes were lifted from chocolate and the plainer folks were able to partake.

Chocolate manufacturing began in the American Colonies in 1765 when James Baker financed a plant in Dorchester, Massachusetts. Dr. Baker was the forefather of the familiar Baker's Chocolate (now a part of Philip Morris), sold in practically every supermarket in America.

In 1828, Coenraad van Houten, a Dutchman, invented a cocoa press that separated the cocoa butter from the beans, leaving behind cocoa powder that contained only a small amount of the fat. Thus a chocolate drink that wasn't greasy could be prepared. Van Houten also invented what was to be called *dutching,* a process still used today to treat the cocoa beans (before or after the removal of the cocoa butter) with an alkaline solution in order to remove some of their natural acidity. Chocolate that is "dutched" is darker in color and milder in flavor than ordinary chocolate, and blends more easily with water or milk.

The first chocolate bar, made of chocolate, extra cocoa butter, and sugar, was produced in England by Fry and Sons in 1847. This innovation made chocolate even more popular.

The Swiss tinkered with this latest form of chocolate and brought it to its ultimate level of sophistication. While searching for a cure to a milk-borne disease affecting children, Henri Nestlé, a Swiss chemist, developed a method for condensing milk. His next-door neighbor, Daniel Peter, was a manufacturer of semisweet chocolate. Peter worked for years to find a way to incorporate this condensed milk into chocolate, and was successful in 1875. He wrote at the time, "Since the Spaniards brought [chocolate] to Europe at the beginning of the seventeenth century, its use has increased continuously and now it is a normal article of diet like coffee, but with a high nutritive value." To this day the entire line of Nestlé wholesale 10-pound bars of chocolate bear the name "Peter" in honor of Daniel Peter.

Around the same time, another Swiss, Rudolph Lindt, further refined chocolate by devising a method called *conching* (see "How Chocolate Is Made," page 193), which took away the natural grainy texture and made it melt on the tongue.

The new chocolate technology was swept up into the Industrial Revolution and machines were made to manufacture chocolate, some of which were shown by a German entrepreneur at the World's Exposition in Chicago in 1893. With typical American enterprise, Milton Snavely Hershey, then a 36-year-old caramel maker in Lancaster, Pennsylvania, bought some of these machines and began to mass-produce chocolate candy bars in the United States for the first time in 1894. By 1911 he was selling $5 million worth of milk chocolate annually.

In the subsequent decades, chocolate, both the native and imported varieties, became enormously popular in the United States. As farfetched as it sounds, Swiss manufacturers felt that the $400,000 loss in trade with the United States in 1927 was due to the fact that many women who had begun to yearn to be fashionably thin stopped eating chocolate and started smoking cigarettes. Fortunately, the dip in consumption was only temporary.

The Swiss are getting back at us now, however. To counter declining sales at home and mounting competition in Europe, many high-priced Swiss, as well as French, Belgian, and other chocolate manufacturers are shipping their bonbons to their own boutiques throughout the United States. The reward is high prices, nearly $30 per pound in some cases, and big profits. The chocolates, made with fillings of cream and butter and, therefore, highly perishable, are flown here within a day or two of manufacture, and are meant to be eaten within a week. In 1982, the Swiss alone shipped 3,313 tons of chocolate to the United States, 22 percent more than the year before, pushing us ahead of Germany as their leading export market.

Some examples of this gourmet airlift: Namur (Luxembourg), Moreau (Switzerland), Corné Toison d'Or (Belgium), Teuscher (Switzerland). These purveyors are aiming for the luxury market. One of the ironies of this trend is that as the economy worsens chocolate sales increase. Psychologists might postulate that when people feel deprived because they can't afford life's big luxuries (cars, houses, vacations), they treat themselves to affordable indulgences, such as extremely expensive and beautifully presented chocolates.

HOW CHOCOLATE IS MADE

Cacao trees grow only within 20 degrees of the equator, so cacao-producing nations lie within a 40-degree band encircling the earth.

The three main types of cacao trees are *Forastero,* which produces an astringent bean and accounts for about 90 percent of the crop; *Trinitario,* used for good flavor; and *Criollo,* highly prized because of its scarcity (2 percent of the total crop) and outstanding flavor.

As with wine grapes and coffee beans, the quality and flavor of the finished chocolate depends largely on the type of cacao beans used as well as the growing conditions and the yearly variations in climate.

The cacao pod, which looks like a bumpy melon, contains cream-colored seeds, the cocoa beans, which begin to darken immediately upon exposure to the air. To begin fermentation, the pods are split by harvesters right in the field and the beans, 20 to 50 in a pod and 400 to a pound of finished chocolate, are exposed to the air for a period of 2 to 9 days.

This fermentation process is vital to the quality of the finished chocolate because it removes the raw taste of the cacao and develops essential oils in the beans, an enzymatic process that begins to produce the characteristic chocolate flavor. Amino acids, such as leucine and phenylalanine, are also formed during fermentation. At the same time, the fermentation process kills the germ of the bean.

Before shipping, the beans are dried in order to evaporate most of their moisture and consequently reduce their weight. When the beans arrive at the chocolate factory they are examined for quality and for proper fermentation. Those with purple centers have not fermented well and are rejected because chocolate made from improperly fermented beans will taste moldy.

The next step is cleaning of the beans, which takes place in machines that remove dirt, grit, and pulp; then the beans are shipped to the countries where they will eventually be consumed.

After manufacturers receive them, the beans are roasted in giant cylindrical ovens at from 250° to 400°F. for up to 2 hours. This makes them characteristically brown and develops a rich aroma. The roasting process also helps to determine the finished taste of the chocolate.

After that, in order to achieve an exact flavor, beans from different countries and of different qualities are then blended according to a proprietary formula of the manufacturer who uses his expertise and judgment, much in the same way that grapes are blended for wine.

Roasted cacao beans have been found to contain 369 volatile compounds that contribute to the flavor of chocolate. Each type of bean, however, has its own combination of these compounds, which means that different varieties of cocoa beans have different flavors, in the same way that different varieties of grapes have different flavors. Some of the characteristic smells of just a few of these compounds given off during roasting are toasted bread, violets, roses, caramel, lilac, burnt cheese.

The beans then proceed to a cracker and fanner machine, which breaks them down into small pieces called *nibs* and blows away the husks. At this point the nibs in their natural state contain about 55 percent cocoa butter, the cream-colored fat of the bean, and 45 percent cocoa, the brown substance that we think of as "chocolate."

The nibs are then milled in a heated environment, 100° to 180°F.; then they are passed through three sets of millstones to reduce their size, to liquefy the cocoa butter, and produce a paste called *chocolate liquor.* This has nothing to do with alcohol, but is the technical term for the chocolate in its most natural state, with no additives.

From this point, the chocolate liquor can be further processed in one of three ways:

• It can be poured into molds to cool and solidify and be sold as "baking" or "bitter" or "unsweetened" chocolate (different names for the same product).

• It can be pressed hydraulically to separate most of the cocoa butter from the chocolate liquor; what remains is known as *cocoa solids.* The solids are then pressed into a cake and pulverized to make cocoa powder. Most cocoa powder contains about 10 percent cocoa butter after this process.

• It can be sweetened and amplified with varying amounts of sugar, milk, sometimes vanilla, and more cocoa butter, depending on what kind of chocolate is being made (see "Varieties of Chocolate," page 195). Some manufacturers of milk chocolate also add 0.2 percent salt to round out the flavor.

If milk is to be added to chocolate, the milk must first be dehydrated, to reduce the water content and increase the level of milk solids from about 12 percent to 80 percent. This is because chocolate can only absorb a small amount of moisture, and milk is made up of 87 percent water.

If the chocolate is to be sweetened, the next two steps are among the most important in determining the degree of smoothness in the finished product:

To refine it, chocolate is sent through a set of 5 big steel rollers set on top of one another and reduced to a smooth paste to ready it for the next step, which is conching.

The conching process, so named because the original nineteenth-century machines were shaped like shells, is a sophisticated kneading technique. Large granite rollers push the chocolate back and forth in a vat across a corrugated granite floor. Milk chocolate is conched at 160°F. and nonmilk chocolate at 200°F. The fat globules in the milk act as a lubricant in the chocolate mixture, thus reducing the friction in the conching vat, effectively lowering the temperature in the vat. The best chocolates are conched for 72 hours or more; cheaper chocolates for less than that, as little as 12 hours or fewer. Not only is the duration of the conching important for the overall smoothness of the finished chocolate, but also the amount of agitation and aeration during the conching process makes a significant contribution in making the chocolate smooth.

Two methods for conching exist today: the *wet* method and the *dry* process. In the wet method, used primarily by Swiss manufacturers, such as Tobler, the cocoa butter is added to the chocolate at the beginning of the conching process. It takes longer than the dry conching method because it releases undesirable acids, etc., from the chocolate that have to be removed at the end of the conching process.

The dry conching process was invented by Belgian chocolate manufacturers about 30 years ago, and in this method the cocoa butter is added to the chocolate at the end of the conching process. Many experts feel it results in better-tasting chocolate than the wet method.

Among the purposes of conching is to rid the

chocolate of excess moisture and raw, acid flavor. But primarily, chocolate is conched in order to reduce the size of the solid cocoa and sugar particles and coat them with the cocoa butter. The more conching the chocolate receives, the smaller and rounder the particles become. Therefore, if chocolate has been conched well, the tongue will not detect any grittiness in the finished chocolate, and the chocolate will taste rich and suave.

Under a microscope, the particles of chocolate that have received very little conching are a miniature 12 to 15 microns in diameter, jagged and only sporadically coated with cocoa butter. The particles of chocolate that have been conched for a long time are 5 microns in diameter and perfectly round. This means the chocolate molecules will be evenly coated with cocoa butter and will taste very creamy. One's perception of creaminess contributes, to a large degree, to the quality of the taste.

Cheaper chocolate is sometimes emulsified so that it doesn't have to be conched so long. Giant egg beaters are used to mix the chocolate and make it smooth. Another money-saving device is to add up to 0.5 percent lecithin (the legal limit) to the chocolate during conching because lecithin is much less expensive than cocoa butter.

One of the last steps in chocolate manufacture is tempering. This is a process of stabilizing the cocoa butter crystals in the chocolate so that it won't melt easily; tempering also helps to give chocolate a glossy shine.

Tempering is accomplished by first melting the chocolate, then cooling it, then reheating it again, all at exact temperatures that will affect the cocoa butter in the desired way. Manufacturers who use cocoa butter must temper their chocolate before pouring it into molds, and conscientious home cooks, professional candy makers, and bakers should also temper chocolate that is to be used for dipping, glazing, or any other recipe in which it will be visible (see "Cooking with Chocolate," page 200).

Most chocolate is then aged by the manufacturer for at least a few weeks, up to 6 months for dark chocolate, in order to mellow its flavor.

How Chocolate Is Made by Retailers

Very few, if any, of the boutiques and stores that specialize in chocolate, both domestic- and foreign-based, make their own chocolate from beans.

These stores buy sweetened or unsweetened chocolate from wholesale suppliers. After combining it with perhaps more sugar, more cocoa butter, and some flavorings (or perhaps using it just as is), they use it to make their own signature candies, candy truffles, baked goods, and other confections. For example: Godiva buys its chocolate from Wilbur; Merckens supplies chocolate to Fanny Farmer and also makes the chocolate that goes into Oreos (Merckens is a division of Nabisco); Nestlé, under the Peter label, makes coatings for See's chocolates, as well as many others.

The companies that supply bulk chocolate to candy shops and bakeries around the country sell their chocolate, sweetened and unsweetened, in 10-pound bricks. They import and process cacao beans, blending the beans from various countries, roasting them, varying the cocoa butter and sugar content. The formula used by each company is proprietary and usually a closely guarded secret.

Nestlé, one of the biggest chocolate manufacturers in the world, makes 20 types of wholesale bulk real chocolate (sold under the Peter label): 10 milk chocolate, 6 semisweet dark chocolate, 1 bittersweet, and 3 unsweetened. A serious candy maker or baker would try many of these from several different companies and choose the chocolate flavor and sweetness level he prefers for his products—dusky, strong, mild, smoky, and on and on. Shopkeepers usually keep secret their choice of wholesale chocolate, preferring to place a veil of mystery over the process.

VARIETIES OF CHOCOLATE

The following definitions are based on the Federal Standards of Identity and industry labels for different types of chocolate. The government standards stipulate the minimum amount of chocolate liquor that must be present in each type. Keep in mind, however, that certain quality chocolate companies put much more than the minimum amount of chocolate liquor in their products.

Because of this variation in quality, a great deal of leeway, not to mention confusion, exists within each category, especially when trying to determine the sweetness level of different chocolates. For example, one company's bittersweet chocolate may well be sweeter than another company's semisweet. By the same token, a company could choose to label its bittersweet chocolate "sweet," even if it has much more than the specified minimum amount of chocolate liquor for that category, as is the case with German's Sweet Chocolate.

It is safe to say that different chocolates with the same brand name, all those bearing the Lindt label, for example, will become progressively sweeter when taken through the spectrum from extra-bittersweet to sweet, but not all brands of chocolate labeled semisweet will be of the same sweetness. Just about the only sure way to know is to taste. If the percentages are listed on the labels, as they sometimes are, it is safe to assume that the chocolate with the lowest amount of chocolate liquor will be sweeter than those with more chocolate liquor.

Unsweetened Chocolate

Unsweetened chocolate is also called *bitter chocolate, baking chocolate,* and *cooking chocolate.* It is pure chocolate liquor, the substance obtained when the beans are ground to a paste and then solidified; made up of about 45 percent cocoa solids and 55 percent cocoa butter (the fat of the bean).

Extra-Bittersweet Chocolate
Bittersweet Chocolate
Semisweet Chocolate

Extra-bittersweet, bittersweet, and semisweet chocolate are strong in flavor and comparatively low in sugar, more or less sweet, depending on the manufacturer and his labeling practices. Legally, they may not contain less than 35 percent chocolate liquor, the rest being made up almost completely of sugar.

Sweet Chocolate

Sweet chocolate is light in chocolate flavor and high in sugar. Legally, sweet chocolate contains less than 12 percent milk solids and not less than 15 percent chocolate liquor, the rest being made up almost completely of sugar.

Much of the commercial cooking chocolate labeled "sweet" is in fact bittersweet and marketed for the German Chocolate Cake made famous by the recipe on the Baker's German's Sweet Chocolate wrapper. The chocolate is not originally German, but named after Samual German, a nineteenth-century chocolate manufacturer who pioneered the German's Sweet formula. Other manufacturers have tried to cash in on the popularity of the German Chocolate Cake by making their own "sweet" chocolate bars to compete with Baker's.

Milk Chocolate

In milk chocolate, milk is substituted for a portion of the chocolate liquor, so the taste is less chocolaty and more sweet than nonmilk chocolate. It must legally contain at least 3.66 percent milkfat and at least 12 percent milk solids, and not less than 10 percent chocolate liquor, the rest being made up almost completely of sugar.

Couverture

Couverture is also called *chocolate coating;* it is sweetened bulk chocolate, so named because it is often used for dipping and coating. It generally contains a high level of cocoa butter. It can also be used in recipes calling for cooking chocolate.

The viscosity level of couverture chocolate is usually specified by the manufacturer so that a cook will know how runny it will be when melted. Those chocolates with a great deal of cocoa butter have a low viscosity rating and will be thinner; they are usually the European couvertures. Those chocolates with a high viscosity rating have less cocoa butter; examples include chocolate morsels and chips, which are often made with less cocoa butter in order to keep their shape better when baked.

Dark Chocolate

Dark chocolate is also called *vanilla chocolate,* and is chocolate made without any milk. "Vanilla" is an industry term that came about because dark chocolate was traditionally flavored with vanilla, while milk chocolate was flavored with vanillin, a synthetic vanilla flavoring (see "Vanilla Extract," page 215). Almost all chocolates today are flavored with vanillin because of the high price of real vanilla.

Cocoa Powder

When most of the cocoa butter is pressed from chocolate liquor, what remains is dry cocoa powder. "Breakfast cocoa" is the legal term for cocoa powder with at least 22 percent cacao fat; "cocoa powder" has between 10 and 22 percent fat; "lowfat cocoa" has less than 10 percent fat. The cocoa powder we see most often on our supermarket shelves is Hershey's, a medium-fat cocoa with between 14 and 15 percent fat.

Cocoa Butter

Cocoa butter is the natural fat contained in the cocoa bean. The melting point of cocoa butter is about 95°F., or about body temperature. The very best chocolate is made with all cocoa butter and not a substitute. Other fats, such as vegetable oils that have been chemically solidified, melt at a much higher temperature, and, therefore, do not "melt in your mouth" as does cocoa butter. This is one of the reasons that cocoa butter is so highly prized and thus expensive. Cocoa butter is also the flavor carrier in chocolate; it's the cocoa butter in a chocolate that makes it taste "chocolaty." After adding about 35 percent cocoa butter, however, the flavor of the chocolate doesn't improve but the chocolate will become thinner (and more costly!) when melted, and the chocolate flavor will be diluted. In the words of one manufacturer, "You can only add so much butter to a sauce."

Because cocoa butter is solid at room temperature and chocolate liquor is liquid at room temperature, the more cocoa butter in a chocolate, the harder it will be at room temperature. Manufacturers who want to save money remove the cocoa butter from their chocolate and sell it to other food manufacturers and cosmetics companies and substitute cheaper fats, such as solidified vegetable oils.

White "Chocolate"

By law, this is not allowed to be called *chocolate,* since it contains no cocoa solids, although popularly it is known as "white chocolate." It is made up of cocoa butter (although very often another fat is substituted), sugar, milk, and vanilla flavoring. Since by itself cocoa butter doesn't taste like chocolate but like the fat that it is, white chocolate has very little, if any, chocolate flavor.

Artificial Chocolate

Artificial chocolate is, by law, a product that does not contain any ingredients derived from cacao; it is made of artificial flavorings.

Chocolate-Flavored

Any food that is labeled "chocolate-flavored" contains some chocolate liquor, but not enough to conform to federal standards for chocolate.

Compound Chocolate

Compound chocolate is also called *summer coating;* both are terms used in the chocolate industry for a bulk chocolate product in which all or nearly all of the cocoa butter has been replaced by another fat. It is easier for confectioners to work with since it does not need tempering and is not affected by summer or tropical heat; it is also cheaper than chocolate with cocoa butter.

HANDLING AND STORAGE

Cocoa butter melts at temperatures above 78°F. If a piece of chocolate spends any time in temperatures above 78°F., it may develop a grayish-white discoloration known as "cocoa butter bloom." This means that some of the cocoa butter has melted and risen to the surface of the chocolate.

If sweetened chocolate is put into the refrigerator and then taken out and put into a very warm, humid environment, it may develop "sugar bloom." This means that condensation has formed, dissolved the sugar, and brought it to the surface of the chocolate. If the chocolate is only mildly affected by sugar bloom, it will become dull. In extreme cases, the sugar will crystallize and turn the chocolate gray. Sugar bloom will also occur if milk chocolate is stored in an environment of above 78 percent humidity, and to dark chocolate above 82 percent.

Because of the rise in popularity of elegant chocolate boutiques, chocolates are often displayed in elaborate open glass cases, some of which are refrigerated, which actually do harm to the candies because of the exposure to air and moisture. Unless there is a big turnover in these places, the chocolates will suffer.

Neither sugar bloom nor cocoa butter bloom is harmful, nor does either affect the taste of the chocolate. Each is just unsightly, and advanced sugar bloom can cause chocolate to become grainy, like sandpaper. Retempering (which, clearly, can be done only with unfilled chocolates) will remove the gray and make the chocolate shiny and bright again.

The best temperature environment for chocolate is between 60° and 72°F. and below 50 percent humidity. Under these conditions, plain dark chocolate will keep for at least 18 months or more, and milk chocolate for up to a year.

Chocolate connoisseurs feel that aged chocolate is richer, more mellow, and more suave than fresh. The head of one chocolate manufacturing company confessed to me that he has a 10-year-old block of chocolate in his desk drawer on which he nibbles from time to time; he compared its taste to that of a fine old red wine.

Well-wrapped plain dark chocolate (not milk chocolate) can be kept for years under the proper conditions. If you try keeping some around to age, you can monitor its flavor changes from year to year; it's likely to get better.

If you are storing chocolates with perishable fillings, you can refrigerate them, but they must be well wrapped in plastic wrap first, then in aluminum foil, to keep them completely airtight. This will prevent the cocoa butter in chocolate from absorbing nearby odors, as well as protecting the chocolate from absorbing moisture. To store these filled chocolates for longer than a couple of weeks, wrap tightly and freeze. To bring to room temperature, keep the package in the freezer wrapping and leave in a place that is not above 70°F. for at least 24 hours before unwrapping.

HOW TO JUDGE CHOCOLATE

Tasting Media

Each of the sweetened chocolates should be broken up into approximately 1-inch squares and these should be placed in numbered saucers.

Each of the unsweetened chocolates can be made into a mousse (using the same recipe for each, see page 202), so that the flavor of the chocolate itself can be gauged.

Color/Eye Appeal

Good chocolate should be smooth and glossy with even color. If a chocolate is not shiny, it may be either stale or not properly tempered. If there are streaks of gray throughout the chocolate, it has also not been tempered properly or it has suffered from "bloom" (see "Handling and Storage").

Chocolates that appear dark are not necessarily stronger-tasting than lighter chocolates; they may have been alkalized ("dutched"), which softens the flavor and darkens the color.

When a chocolate piece is broken into halves, the texture of the interior should look even and fine, the result of proper refining.

Taste/Aroma

Chocolate can smell heady and fragrant, or have very little smell at all. Depending on which beans were used to make it, a chocolate can smell nutty, malty, caramel, fudgy, or perfumed. As with a wine, the best chocolate has a rich, full, balanced bouquet.

Some defects in the taste of chocolate: *moldy,* from improperly fermented beans; *medicinal,* from beans that have not been stored properly; *bitter* or *sour,* from beans that have not been roasted enough; *smoky,* from overroasted beans; *burnt,* from overroasting; *tallowy, soapy, fishy,* or *metallic,* from mild rancidity; *flat,* from staleness, or from overconching; *artificial,* from chocolate made with fats other than cocoa butter, and from artificial vanilla; *dusty; chalky; musty; dry; overly sweet.*

Some desirable traits in the flavor of chocolate: *cheesy,* a tangy aftertaste that comes from aging milk chocolate; *nutty; coffee; citrus; wine.* Chocolate is a complex, individual food, and each well-made example will have a personality all its own.

All good chocolate should have a slight astringency and a well-rounded flavor.

Consistency

Professionals test consistency by placing the chocolate on their upper lip. Chocolate ranges from gritty and dry-tasting, to moist and smooth, to almost slippery; it all depends on the amount of conching and refining it has received. Chocolate can be conched so much that it is flat-tasting and slick. If it is underconched, and that is most often the case, it will be gritty. Chocolate should not feel sharp on your tongue, nor should it be waxy.

If a chocolate has a good amount of cocoa butter and is well refined and conched, it will "snap" sharply when broken into halves. Chocolate that splinters is too dry. If a chocolate is "friable" (crumbly), it has not been conched enough. Waxy chocolate and that made without cocoa butter will feel plastic and bend when broken, rather than snap.

Aftertaste

Some high-quality chocolate has a lilting, upbeat flavor after you've swallowed it; in some the flavor falls off quickly with no lingering taste. Poor chocolates have a bitter, raw, or sour aftertaste, or are overly sweet or sharp at the end.

CONCLUSIONS AND SUGGESTIONS

In general, most Americans don't like intensely flavored chocolate. The Swiss sacrifice flavor in their chocolate for superlative texture. The English prefer their chocolate very sweet. Belgians like a very heady, strong chocolate flavor. The French make and eat chocolate that is not up to the same quality as other European chocolates for an odd reason: The French are so nationalistic that they will buy cocoa beans only from former colonies, very few of which produce good beans. To compensate for the poor-quality cacao beans, they add a great deal of artificial vanillin to mask the flavor.

Americans often put down European chocolates as "too rich," when what they are objecting to is the degree of smoothness which is a result of conching. The ubiquitous American candy bar chocolate is conched for a minimum amount of time and thus tastes gritty or less "rich," but it's what we are used to.

On the other hand, the most popular American chocolate bar, Hershey's, is conched for a very long time. It also has what experts term "barnyard taste," which comes from the oxidation of the dairy butter it contains, meaning it is slightly "curdled" or "ripened" (see "Butter and Margarine," page 40). Many Europeans, used to a different style of chocolate, find this highly offensive. Americans, obviously, are fond of it.

The "too rich" complaint of Americans also comes from the fact that many European chocolates contain a great deal of cocoa butter, much more than the American standard. This cocoa-butter enhancement can dilute the chocolate "notes" in a chocolate, while at the same time giving it a rich cast.

These standards of national taste are very difficult to change, so European chocolate manufacturers sometimes alter their formulas for those chocolates that are destined for this country. Those made here, such as Godiva, a Belgian chocolate whose American division is owned by the Campbell Soup Company, often bear no resemblance to their European namesakes. Sometimes these European chocolate formulas change from country to country perforce, because of local laws and trade agreements requiring that a certain quality of cacao beans be used.

Chocolate and chocolate manufacture are often compared to wine and viticulture. When it comes to taste, the analogy bears extending: After the basic quality of a chocolate is determined, the flavor is purely subjective. You may like your chocolate strong and bitter, or sweet and milky, or somewhere in between (and maybe it coincides with the way you like your coffee!).

Assuming this to be the case, we divided the chocolates into categories, such as bittersweet, semisweet, and so on, using the manufacturers' label language, and bearing in mind the caveat outlined in the first paragraph under "Varieties of Chocolate" (see page 195). Each taster then concentrated on only one or two categories, rather than tackling the entire daunting spectrum.

Many experts feel that chocolate is one of those few foods to which applies the rule, "The more expensive, the better." We found out in our tasting that this is not true across the board. This could be because many of the really high-quality and appealing chocolates were wholesale *couvertures* and available at cheaper-than-retail prices, and thus you're not paying for advertising, packaging, and marketing. On the other hand, many were made more cheaply than others; those were generally the more commercial bars and it showed in our results. Chocolate *is* expensive to make, and some corners have to be cut to keep your favorite candy bar costing less than 75 cents.

"I never met a chocolate I didn't like," applies very well to this tasting. Few of the chocolates we sampled were actually so bad that a chocolate lover wouldn't eat them. (Of course a couple of exceptions landed in embarrassment at the very bottom of each of the lists!)

COOKING WITH AND EATING CHOCOLATE

The same rule of thumb that applies to wine applies to chocolate: You shouldn't cook with anything you wouldn't drink—or eat, in the case of chocolate. When considering chocolate that is not combined with nuts, fruit, cream fillings, and the like—plain chocolate, in other words—the reverse is also true: Anything you would eat you could theoretically also cook with.

Rose Levy Beranbaum, one of the country's foremost chocolate experts, points out, "Think of what happens when you use your favorite eating chocolate in your favorite chocolate dessert! A whole new level of pleasure becomes possible."

However, there are a couple of factors to keep in mind when choosing chocolate for cooking or for eating. Chocolate made specifically for baking is generally not refined and conched as much as chocolate for eating; the perception of smoothness is not as important when the chocolate is going to be combined with several ingredients. Therefore, if you were to eat a piece of sweetened baking chocolate, it might seem coarse, even if the flavor were pleasing.

Chocolate for eating, on the other hand, seems richer and creamier than the same chocolate which has not undergone the lengthy refining and conching. Assuming both pieces were made with the same proportion of chocolate liquor to cocoa butter and sugar, both would give the same result in the same baking recipe.

The choice between the two arises when you consider that many chocolates made for eating are of higher quality than chocolate made specifically for baking. Eating chocolate, aside from its further degree of refinement, is often made with better quality beans and more cocoa butter, and usually does not contain cocoa butter substitutes and emulsifiers.

An exception to these rules is cooking chocolate meant to go on the outside of candies and cakes, called *coating* chocolate or *couverture* chocolate (see "Varieties of Chocolate," page 195). It is conched and is ideal for cooking or for eating.

To substitute chocolates with different degrees

of sweetness for unsweetened chocolate—if you want to use a chocolate bar made for eating in a cake recipe, for example—see the chart below. The chocolate you ultimately choose for a recipe depends on its intrinsic flavor, not its sweetness level, and what you want to convey in your finished product. A simple American chocolate pudding, for example, might call for a straightforward, uncomplicated chocolate, such as Maillard Eagle Sweet, whereas a French *pot de crème* might require a more sophisticated chocolate, Tobler Tradition, perhaps.

Tempering

When you melt chocolate to use for coating, such as for coating truffles, glazing a cake, or dipping fruit, temper it so that the chocolate will be glossy and will set properly. Also, tempered chocolate will not develop bloom as readily as chocolate that has not been tempered.

The easiest way to temper chocolate is to put it into the top pan of a double boiler. The water in the lower pan of the double boiler should come to a simmer and should not touch the bottom of the top pan. Put the chocolate in the top pan and stir it constantly until it is melted and the temperature reaches 120°F. An accurate thermometer is essential for this operation.

At this point, replace the simmering water in the bottom pan with cold tap water. Stir the chocolate in the top pan until it reaches 80°F. Add hot tap water to the bottom pan of the double boiler and stir the chocolate again until it reaches 86°F. Now the chocolate is ready for dipping or glazing.

When melting chocolate for tempering or for any other purpose, make sure it does not come into contact with water, or it will stiffen. Even steam will do this to chocolate, which is why it should never be melted over boiling water. Some perfectionists feel that if you use a metal spoon to stir the chocolate while it is melting, the conden-

HOW TO SUBSTITUTE ONE KIND OF CHOCOLATE FOR ANOTHER

The following chart is the result of years of work with chocolate by Rose Levy Beranbaum, whose expertise was mentioned earlier in the chapter.

IF THE RECIPE CALLS FOR	YOU CAN SUBSTITUTE
1 ounce unsweetened chocolate	*2 ounces bittersweet chocolate if you subtract 2 tablespoons sugar for every 2 ounces chocolate and subtract 1/2 teaspoon shortening for every 2 ounces chocolate*
1 ounce unsweetened chocolate	*2 ounces semisweet chocolate if you subtract 2 tablespoons plus 2 teaspoons sugar for every 2 ounces chocolate and subtract 1/2 teaspoon shortening for every 2 ounces chocolate*
1 ounce unsweetened chocolate	*2 ounces* couverture *(also called coating chocolate) if you subtract 2 tablespoons sugar for every 2 ounces chocolate and subtract 1 1/2 teaspoons shortening for every 2 ounces chocolate*
1 ounce bittersweet chocolate	*2 ounces semisweet chocolate if you subtract 2 tablespoons sugar for every 2 ounces chocolate and subtract 1/2 teaspoon shortening for every 2 ounces chocolate*
1 ounce bittersweet chocolate	*3 tablespoons cocoa powder plus 1 tablespoon cocoa butter or shortening*

sation that forms on the spoon may fall into the chocolate and ruin it. Therefore, wooden spoons are recommended for stirring.

If your chocolate inadvertently stiffens (like a bad batch of fudge, very grainy and so dense that the spoon won't move in it), add 1 tablespoon of solid vegetable shortening, such as Crisco or Spry, for each 3 ounces of chocolate, and stir vigorously until the smooth texture returns. You should never add butter at this point, because its water content will also stiffen the chocolate.

To melt about 1 cup of chopped chocolate, which does not need tempering, in the microwave, process it on the high setting for 1 minute, stir the chocolate, and process it 1 minute more on high.

WHERE TO BUY CHOCOLATE

A number of chocolates are made for the wholesale trade, but because of the increasing seriousness about cooking in the last few years, they have been made available to the consumer through a variety of sources. See "Mail-Order Sources" for some of these.

In addition to these sources, many gourmet stores buy 10-pound bars of bulk wholesale chocolate and sell it by the pound as "break-up" cooking chocolate, in rough pieces in plastic bags. Although the brand name is usually not evident, you can ask your storekeeper to tell you what kind of chocolate he buys.

The bakery supply store in your area also sells bulk chocolate. In most cases they will be happy to sell you their minimum amount, which is usually $50, about enough to buy 10 to 20 pounds of chocolate.

RECIPES

Chocolate Mousse

The following recipe for chocolate mousse is simply a miracle. Designed by the Nestlé Company for their chocolate chips, it can be made with any sweetened chocolate chopped into chip-size pieces, in a food processor or by hand. (Makes 8 servings)

2 cups chocolate pieces
1/2 cup sugar
3 whole eggs
2–4 tablespoons brandy or rum
1 cup boiling milk

1. Place in a blender container, in the order in which they are listed, the chocolate pieces, sugar, eggs, brandy or rum, and boiling milk. Blend until smooth, about 30 seconds.

2. Pour liquid mousse mixture into 8 demitasse cups or dessert dishes and chill until ready to serve, at least 1 hour. This mousse is best topped with real whipped cream.

Rose Levy Beranbaum's Chocolate Oblivion Truffle Torte

Rose calls this her "best recipe," and I think it's one of the best I've ever had. It's like eating one big giant truffle. (One 9-inch torte)

18 ounces semisweet chocolate
9 ounces butter (18 tablespoons or 2 sticks plus 2 tablespoons)
6 large eggs

1. Unwrap butter and chocolate and put together in a bowl. Put the eggs, still in their shells, into another bowl. Place the 2 bowls in the oven (without turning the oven on) overnight. The warmth of the pilot light will melt the chocolate and butter together and warm the eggs.

If you don't have a gas oven, you can also melt the chocolate and butter together at the time of baking the cake; in that case, the eggs should be at room temperature.

2. Break the eggs into the bowl of a mixer and beat at high speed until tripled in volume. Stir melted butter and chocolate together. Fold chocolate mixture into beaten eggs, just until ingredients are blended together.

3. Spray the inside of a 9-inch springform pan

with a nonstick spray. Cover outer sides and bottom of pan with 2 layers of heavy-duty aluminum foil (this is to protect the pan so water doesn't seep into it during baking). Pour batter into prepared pan and set it into a larger baking pan. Place pans in a preheated 425°F. oven. Pour water into the larger pan so level of water comes halfway up the sides of the springform pan. Cover top of springform pan loosely with foil. Bake for 17 minutes.

4. After baking time, remove the springform pan from the water bath and place on a rack to cool; leave foil on top of the pan, tightening it around the edges of the pan. Cool for 30 minutes. Put springform pan into the refrigerator until it unmolds easily, at least 2 hours. Take cake out of the refrigerator at least an hour before serving, so it can come to room temperature. Serve with sweetened, softly whipped cream and raspberry purée, if you wish.

The "Original" Original Nestlé Toll House® Cookies

Under the terms of the agreement with the Toll House Inn, the Nestlé company was required to run the original recipe intact for 40 years, at which time it could, and did, change. The baking experts at Nestlé decided that with modern ingredients and baking practices, it would be a good idea to make the recipe easier. So, in 1979, they made a few significant changes in the Original Toll House® Cookies recipe. First, they decreed that the flour no longer needed to be sifted; they eliminated the 1/4 (or 1/2, for larger batches) teaspoon water; they reduced the baking time by 2 minutes, and finally they decided that the cookie sheet no longer needed to be greased.

After much testing of my own, I have found that the old Original Toll House® Cookies recipe makes a better cookie than the new one. Since the old recipe can no longer be found on the back of the chocolate chip package, I am reprinting it here, for old times' sake.

You can make these or any chocolate chip cookies softer by reducing the baking time further by 2 minutes and using vegetable shortening instead of butter. (Makes fifty 2-inch cookies)

1 cup plus 2 tablespoons sifted flour
1/2 teaspoon baking soda
1/2 teaspoon salt
1/2 cup butter, softened
6 tablespoons granulated sugar
6 tablespoons packed brown sugar
1/2 teaspoon vanilla extract
1/4 teaspoon water
1 egg
1 package (6 ounces, 1 cup) Nestlé Toll House® Semi-Sweet Chocolate Morsels
1/2 cup coarsely chopped nuts

1. Sift together flour, baking soda, and salt; set aside.

2. Combine butter, sugars, vanilla, and water; beat until creamy. Beat in egg. Add flour mixture; mix well. Stir in Nestlé Toll House® Semi-Sweet Chocolate Morsels and nuts.

3. Drop by well-rounded half teaspoons onto greased cookie sheets. Bake at 375°F. for 10 to 12 minutes.

PEANUT BUTTER

n the last few years, adults have rediscovered peanut butter, perhaps in a desire to recall the happy culinary moments of their childhood. The Reese's Peanut Butter Cup made by Hershey, for example, now outsells the classic Hershey chocolate bar. And peanut-butter-and-jelly sandwiches can be found on the menus of popular restaurants, such as America in New York City.

For decades, peanut butter has nourished generations of tiny Americans. Even today, the biggest users of peanut butter are children between the ages of 6 and 8; 33 percent of them eat it at least once every three days. Six percent of the people who consume peanut butter are African-American. Overall, Americans consume a total of about 700 million pounds of peanut butter yearly, which is the equivalent of 11.2 billion average-size peanut-butter-and-jelly sandwiches. Over eight hundred million dollars' worth of peanut butter was sold in 1984. Seventy-five percent of this total is consumed by children between the ages of 4 and 14.

These children are most likely to be found in families where the average income is between $20,000 and $34,999.

Not surprisingly, 73 percent of the peanut butter used in the United States is made into sandwiches; 43 percent of those sandwiches are made with jelly. Twelve percent of the peanut butter consumed in this country is eaten on crackers, and 10 percent is used as a cooking ingredient, mostly for peanut butter cookies. The remaining 5 percent of the peanut butter eaten falls into a mysterious "miscellaneous" category, since manufacturers are not sure how it is used.

People on the West Coast generally like crunchy peanut butter, while those on the East Coast prefer smooth peanut butter; no matter where they live, smooth peanut butter is most preferred by children, while crunchy is the favorite of adults. (An exception to both of these rules is Frank Sinatra, who requests that smooth peanut butter be put into every hotel room he stays in.) Smooth peanut butter draws 60 percent of sales and crunchy 40 percent, although the balance is moving toward 50-50. Those Americans who live in the Midwest eat the most peanut butter per capita, while those in the Southwest eat the least. The two top-selling brands are Jif, with 23 percent of the U.S. market, and Skippy, with 22.7 percent.

Curiously, the sale of peanut butter has seasons: Yearly sales reach a low point in the second half of June and pick up again in the fall, perhaps reflecting the end and the beginning of the school year. These days, 10 percent of the peanut butter consumed in the United States is eaten at breakfast, an increase from only 2 percent in

1976. Anyone over the age of 25, by the way, is likely to eat his or her peanut butter spread on toast rather than on untoasted bread.

To answer that age-old question, why does peanut butter stick to the roof of your mouth? Fred Kurasiewicz, the manager of technical services for Best Foods, which makes Skippy, explains that peanut butter has a "sticky mouth feel" because of the "hydration of the peanut protein." In other words, the high protein level of peanut butter draws moisture away from your mouth when you eat it, in much the same way that a sponge soaks up water. For the record, "arachibutyrophobia" is the psychological term given to an irrational fear of peanut butter sticking to the roof of your mouth.

A DASH OF HISTORY

Peanuts originally were found in South America and Mexico in the sixteenth century by exploring Spaniards. The explorers took peanuts back to Spain, and from there peanuts were introduced to Africa and Asia. Portuguese slave traders used peanuts as a cheap food for the Africans they carried to the Colonies, and by that route, peanuts made their way back to the New World. Until around 1800, peanuts were called *groundnuts,* which is still the name for them in Great Britain. The word for peanut in the Bantu language is *nguba,* which was pronounced "goober" by black slaves in America.

Peanuts were grown commercially as early as 1800 in South Carolina, but they weren't grown to a great extent in this country until about 100 years later, when harvesting equipment was modernized.

Around that time, at the turn of the twentieth century, the botanist George Washington Carver proposed that peanuts be grown as an alternative to the faltering cotton crops in the South; he also championed peanuts as a cheap source of protein for poor people. Through his support, peanuts emerged as an important part of southern agriculture.

It is believed that peanut *butter* was first invented by a doctor in St. Louis around 1890, who devised it as a healthy food for sick people; no one remembers the doctor's name, however. Coincidentally, records show that in 1903 Ambrose W. Straub, another native of St. Louis, patented a machine to make peanut butter. Peanut butter sandwiches were first made in the late 1920s, but it wasn't until the 1940s that homogenized peanut butter was invented.

The happy and benign course of peanut growing was sidetracked during the Great Depression. At that time, to bolster failing American agriculture, the federal government designated that certain crops could be grown only on specifically allotted acres. More than a million acres were earmarked as peanut-growing land, and those who owned the land were given acreage allotments—10 acres to this farmer, 100 acres to that one, and so on. The most recent allotments were set in 1954 and they still stand, most often owned by the descendants of the original holders. Anyone who wants to grow peanuts today has to rent the land from one of these allotment holders, at a cost of about $300 to $400 per acre per year, about four times the price for renting land for other crops.

If this wasn't enough to make peanut growing a cutthroat business, the crop failure of 1981 finished the job. This drove up the price of peanuts and in the process drove several peanut processors and peanut-butter makers out of business. It also doubled the price of peanut butter to consumers.

HOW PEANUT BUTTER IS MADE

Contrary to popular belief, the peanut is not a nut. Botanically speaking, it is a legume, more closely related to the pea. The name *groundnut* refers to the fact that the plant's fruit, the peanut in the shell, grows under the ground, although the "nut" is not part of the roots of the plant. Peanuts begin to grow beneath the soil when the flowers of the plant drop off and the vines on which the flowers once grew drop down to the ground. The tips of the vines implant themselves in the soil and the peanuts grow on these tips underground.

Only 10 percent of the world's crop of peanuts grows in the United States, mainly in Georgia, where 44 percent of this country's peanuts grow. The other peanut-growing states are Alabama, Texas, North Carolina, Oklahoma, Virginia, Florida, and South Carolina. The world's largest producers of peanuts are India and China.

When peanuts are harvested, they contain 25 to 50 percent moisture. In order to store them without spoiling, they are dried for about 2 days until they contain 10 percent moisture or less.

Only 10 percent of an entire crop of peanuts is sold in the shell. The rest of the peanuts are shelled, which is accomplished by putting the peanuts into giant drums which rotate. The friction of the nuts rubbing against one another forces the shells to separate from the nuts.

Half of all of the peanuts grown in this country is made into peanut butter. In making peanut butter, the shelled peanuts are first roasted and then, in some cases, the skins are rubbed off. At this point, some manufacturers remove the germ, the little knob at the top of the two halves of every peanut, which might otherwise cause the peanut to turn rancid too quickly. Unfortunately, it is the germ, together with the skin of the peanut, which contains many of the nutrients. However, the germ and the skin are usually used later to make peanut oil.

The roasted nuts are then ground, usually twice. For crunchy peanut butter, the manufacturer will stir in some chopped peanuts after all the other nuts are ground smooth. Altogether, it takes 540 peanuts to make a 12-ounce jar of peanut butter.

During the grinding process, the peanuts are heated to 170°F. At that point, emulsifiers in the form of hydrogenated fat are added, and then the peanut butter is cooled rapidly to 120°F. The high heat of the grinding liquefies the hydrogenated fat. When the mixture is cooled, the fat becomes solid again, trapping the oil in the peanut butter so it cannot separate out. The added fat is a solid at room temperature, much like Crisco, and not only keeps the peanut butter emulsified, but also makes it smooth and spreadable.

At the same time the emulsifier is added, other additives, such as salt, sugar, and/or other sweeteners, are mixed into the peanut butter. The peanut butter is then packed in jars. Emulsifiers are not added to old-fashioned peanut butter (see "Varieties of Peanuts and Peanut Butter," this page), which means that the peanut butter and oil separate in the jar, leaving a rather thick layer of oil at the top which can easily be stirred back into the peanut butter.

The federal government stipulates that the additives in peanut butter must not exceed 10 percent of the total volume. Artificial flavorings, artificial sweeteners, chemical preservatives, vitamins, and coloring are forbidden by law.

At the same time, manufacturers are permitted to add hydrogenated fat as an emulsifier, as long as the total fat content of this peanut butter does not exceed 55 percent. Peanuts naturally contain between 40 and 50 percent oil, so there isn't far to go when adding this additional fat.

If a peanut butter is made with unblanched peanuts, peanuts with the skins left on, the label must indicate this fact, in letters half the size of the words "peanut butter." In fact, many health-food manufacturers proudly state this inclusion, in order to highlight the nutritional and flavor advantages of the skins.

VARIETIES OF PEANUTS AND PEANUT BUTTER

Four types of peanuts are cultivated in the United States; from largest to smallest, they are *Virginia, Runner, Spanish,* and *Valencia.* Being the biggest and the most attractive, the Virginia peanut is often sold in the shell or as a cocktail nut, while Runner is the most widely grown variety.

All four varieties are used for making peanut butter, often mixed together to get different flavors. As often as not, however, logistics determine which varieties of peanuts are used for a brand of peanut butter. Deaf Smith Arrowhead Mills proudly states on its label, "100% Valencia peanuts," making the consumer think that Valencia are better-quality peanuts, which may or may not be true. The fact of the matter is that the company packs its peanut butter on the West Coast, closest to where that peanut variety is grown.

There are two main kinds of peanut butter: *old-fashioned* (or *natural*) and *regular.* Old-fashioned peanut butter is made simply from peanuts and salt; regular peanut butter is made from blanched peanuts, additional hydrogenated fat, sweetener, and salt. In each of these categories, both *crunchy* (or *chunky*) and *smooth* (or *creamy*) types are produced. Crunchy peanut butter has a slightly grainy texture and little pieces of nuts throughout; smooth has a very fine, even texture with no pieces of nuts. As with some other packaged foods, low- and no-sodium peanut butters are also available; all of the above varieties can be found without added salt.

HANDLING AND STORAGE

An unopened jar of regular peanut butter will last from 2 to 4 years if it is kept in a dry place where the temperature is lower than 70°F. The higher the temperature, the faster the peanut butter will turn rancid. An opened jar of peanut butter will go rancid after about 3 months. Refrigeration will stall the deterioration process somewhat, but it will make the peanut butter more difficult to spread.

Since old-fashioned peanut butter is made without hydrogenated fat, a layer of oil will separate and appear on the top of the peanut butter. Before using it, simply stir the oil back into the peanut butter, then place the jar in the refrigerator and the oil should not separate again. Because it is not emulsified, old-fashioned peanut butter is more susceptible to spoilage than regular and should be refrigerated, but, once opened, it should last at least 2 months in the refrigerator.

Rancid peanut butter will have the same distinctive odor and flavor of rancid oil.

HOW TO JUDGE PEANUT BUTTER

Tasting Media

Taste peanut butter from shallow glass bowls with spoons and fingers. Lukewarm water should be sipped between tastes to clear the oil from the mouths of the tasters. All of the peanut butters should be tasted at a temperature of between 70° and 80°F., in order best to gauge their flavors and spreadability.

Professional peanut-butter tasters rinse their palates three times with 100°F. water and wait exactly 30 seconds between samples. The 1 tablespoon samples of peanut butter are pulled with a special device which brings a plug of peanut butter from the exact center of the jar, not from the sides nor too close to the bottom or the top, assuring the tasters of a perfect sample.

Color/Eye Appeal

The best peanut butter has a light to medium-brown color. If the nuts were ground with the skins left on, there will be little flecks of dark brown in the peanut butter. Color defects include a dullness and/or a gray pallor, which may be the result of improper roasting techniques.

Taste/Aroma

Good peanut butter should smell and taste like freshly roasted peanuts, not rancid, musty, stale, or soapy. Many peanut butters are made with too much sugar or sweetener, making them attractive to children, but robbing them of the natural peanut flavor. The peanuts should have been roasted to the proper degree, so good peanut butter does not taste either like raw nuts ("beany") or bitter and burned from overroasting. Although too much bitterness and astringency are defects in peanut butter, some of these characteristics should be present in a good peanut butter to give it character. Peanut butter that is not fresh will smell and taste rancid, reflecting the oil that has gone bad.

Consistency

Good peanut butter should not be unpleasantly stiff or sticky, or overly oily. Smooth regular peanut butter should be creamy and not grainy; no dark particles should be apparent. The nuts in crunchy peanut butter should be crisp, with no large or sharp pieces, and the nuts should be evenly distributed throughout. The peanut butter should not look or taste sandy or mealy.

Old-fashioned peanut butter should look and taste more grainy than regular peanut butter, and will not appear ultrasmooth and buttery like regular peanut butter. With old-fashioned peanut butter, the consistency should not be too thin to spread well on a piece of bread and the oil separation should not be so great that the peanut butter on the bottom of the jar becomes too dry. It should also be relatively easy to mix the oil back into the peanut butter.

Aftertaste

The taste of a good peanut butter should stay in your mouth and not fall off to quickly. It should not have a chemical aftertaste.

CONCLUSIONS AND SUGGESTIONS

Surprisingly, peanut butter was one of the foods I found most difficult to taste. For such a seemingly mundane food, its various characteristics proved to be quite a challenge to discern; it is a very complex food. In the words of one of my fellow tasters, "This is a much more aggressive food than one imagines, especially considering that it is eaten mostly by children." One peanut butter professional explains: It is a food that is almost completely natural rather than being highly processed, which makes it more complex and sophisticated than a food structured in a laboratory.

A happy conclusion of my tasting is that peanut butter is one of those foods that does not suffer if the salt is taken out. On the whole, the salt-free peanut butters are quite delicious. In fact, the absence of salt seems to heighten the peanut flavor.

Another surprising conclusion of my tasting was that the one peanut butter with the most additives, including sugar, salt, molasses, hardened vegetable oil, and mono- and di-glycerides—Jif Creamy—placed very high, in spite of the fact that the idea of eating solid white vegetable shortening as a part of my peanut butter is repulsive.

The old-fashioned peanut butters taste better than the regular types, but the texture of the old-fashioned peanut butters is not very smooth or spreadable, even after they were thoroughly mixed.

The very best peanut butter, for my money, is Deaf Smith Arrowhead Mills.

COOKING WITH PEANUT BUTTER

Most of the world does not spread a purée of peanuts onto bread with jelly as Americans do. Peanuts and peanut butter are important foods around the world, especially in the cuisines of Indonesia and West Africa. Many stews and sauces from these areas combine peanuts and peanut butters with pork, beef, and chicken.

For a switch on the old p.b.&j., try a *nouvelle* Monte Cristo sandwich: dense rich bread spread with peanut butter and filled with boiled ham and mango chutney, dipped into beaten egg and sautéed in butter until crisp and golden brown.

When cooking, it's helpful to know that 12 ounces of peanut butter equals 1 cup.

For cooking or for eating, it's very easy to make your own peanut butter by putting shelled peanuts into a food processor or blender and processing until the peanut butter reaches the proper consistency. If you *do* grind your own, keep in mind that 5 ounces of shelled peanuts equal 1 cup of peanuts, which will make a little less than 1/2 cup peanut butter.

If you find yourself with a batch of peanuts in or out of the shell that need the red papery skins removed, put the shelled nuts into the freezer overnight, and in the morning the skins will pinch off easily with your fingers.

RECIPE

Cariucho Sauce

This is an Ecuadorian sauce served on roasted flank steak and boiled potatoes. It is also delicious served with any grilled, broiled, or sautéed meat (particularly lamb chops), poultry, or strongly flavored fish. (Makes $2^1/_2$ cups)

2 tablespoons lard
1 cup minced onion
1/2 teaspoon minced garlic
1 cup tomato purée
1/4 cup smooth peanut butter
1 cup light cream or milk
1 cup chicken stock
3 tablespoons Louisiana hot pepper sauce, or to taste (see NOTE)
4 teaspoons freshly squeezed lime juice
salt and pepper

1. Melt the lard in a medium-size frying pan and sauté the onion and garlic over low heat for 10 to 15 minutes, or until the onion is golden brown.

2. Add the tomato purée and the peanut butter to the frying pan. Stir and simmer until smooth and well blended. Add the light cream or milk, chicken stock, hot pepper sauce, lime juice, and salt and pepper to taste. Simmer, stirring occasionally, for 10 minutes.

NOTE: If you are using Tabasco, halve the amount and taste before adding more; it is at least twice as hot as other Louisiana hot pepper sauces.

JAMS AND PRESERVES

Izaak Walton, in *The Compleat Angler,* writes, "Indeed, my good scholar, we may say of Angling, as Dr. Boteler said of strawberries: 'Doubtless God could have made a better berry, but doubtless God never did.' " A lot of Americans agree with this statement, because strawberry is by far the most popular jam and preserve flavor sold in America, by some reports accounting for up to 40 percent of total jam and preserve sales, and about 15 percent of packaged food sales in specialty-food stores. The next most popular flavors are grape jelly, raspberry, orange marmalade, and apricot. Yet, at the same time strawberry is the most difficult jam flavor to make successfully; when it is good it is very, very good, but when it is bad it is horrid.

Nevertheless, a boom market has occurred in the jam and preserve business in the last few years, and it has been due partly to fallout from the change in American supermarkets. As more and more supermarkets have upgraded their foods, gourmet stores have had to seek out newer and better product lines to retain their specialty-store status.

Americans buy more than $500 million worth of premium jams and preserves yearly. New Englanders buy more jams and preserves than Americans in other regions, probably because of their English heritage and the connection to the tradition of tea and pastries with jam.

If the figures for the more prosaic side of the market are added in, the total spent on jam jumps to over a billion dollars. Jams and preserves, as a selling group, is one of the three most important categories for gourmet and specialty-food stores, the other two being chocolate and cookies (including crackers). As one retailer explained to me, "Everyone can use another jar of jam or preserve, whereas raspberry vinegar might be only a once- or twice-yearly purchase." About half of these jams and preserves purchases are made for gift-giving, and manufacturers are catering to those needs by packing their products in beautiful jars with artistic labels.

This chapter is more concerned with manufacturing than with a particular flavor of jam or preserve. I chose to use strawberry as an example of the industry because it is the largest-selling flavor in this country.

A DASH OF HISTORY

The method of preserving fruit as a jam was only perfected in the early nineteenth century. In 1775, the French government offered a prize of 12,000 francs to anyone who could invent a way to preserve food so it could travel with the army without spoiling. After much work, a French confectioner named François Appert in 1810 patented a process that was a rudimentary predecessor of today's mason-jar method—boiling the food in the container to set up a vacuum seal. Later in the century, another Frenchman, Louis Pasteur, identified the reasons why Appert's invention worked so well—it killed the microorganisms in the food. It didn't take long for home cooks and commercial manufacturers to realize that fruit was an ideal food for preserving in this manner.

American housewives regularly made their own fruit jams and preserves through the beginning of this century. At first the jars were sealed by tying a headpiece of paper over the top; later, liquid paraffin was poured on top of the contents of the jar to make an airtight seal.

Smucker's, which makes 27 percent of the jams and preserves in America today, began operation in 1897, making commercially prepared jams and preserves available to American households for the first time.

HOW STRAWBERRY JAMS AND PRESERVES ARE MADE

In the eyes of the Food and Drug Administration, the terms "jam" and "preserves" are interchangeable. In accepted usage, however, preserves are supposed to contain whole pieces of fruit, while jams are a more homogenous purée of fruit. These distinctions are not entirely clear in the marketplace; therefore, for practical purposes, jams and preserves are grouped together. Some manufacturers, however, make both a jam and a preserve, in which case (although not always) the preserves are puréed to make them smooth and labeled as "jam."

Although none of these foods is considered in this chapter, for the sake of clarity, here are the definitions of related products: A *conserve* is a jam that contains more than one kind of fruit; a *marmalade* is a preserve made of a citrus fruit containing pieces of the rind; and a *jelly* is the thickened juice of a fruit. (These days, however, the term "conserves" is used by some manufacturers for products that don't conform to federal standards for jam or preserves.)

Ingredients

Four ingredients are essential for making jams and preserves, whether you are making them at home or in commercial quantities: fruit, sugar, acid, and pectin.

Almost all the fruit used to make commercial jams and preserves is frozen; one of the few exceptions I have discovered is the American Spoon brand, which, interestingly, placed first in my tasting. This is because the harvesting and shipping of the frozen fruit can be controlled easily, and jams and preserves can be made all year round instead of only at harvest time.

The sugar content of jams and preserves is for purposes of preserving as well as flavoring, as bacteria cannot grow in a mixture that contains 50 to 55 percent sugar. Sugar is added to the naturally occurring sugar in the fruit to bring the total content up to that level. Cane sugar, or simple white granulated sugar, has the best flavor, but it crystallizes during long cooking and storage and is expensive as well. So, in many cases, corn syrup is added to commercial jams and preserves instead of, or in addition to, cane sugar.

Proper jams and preserves should taste slightly acidic instead of completely sweet. Since strawberries do not naturally contain much acid, citric acid, extracted from lemons or produced synthetically from fungi grown on sugar solutions, is usually added to strawberry jams and preserves.

Pectin is a carbohydrate that occurs naturally in most fruits, and provides natural thickening for jams and preserves. Strawberries, however, do not contain much natural pectin, so pectin extracted from citrus peel or apples is often added to commercial jams and preserves to help them obtain the proper consistency.

Although long cooking will thicken most fruit jams, many fine European and American jam manufacturers choose to add natural pectin to their products and cook them less; cooking fruit for a long time often dissipates its natural flavor and deadens the color.

Manufacturing

As if all of these impediments weren't sufficiently problematical for the manufacture of good strawberry jam, the delicate flavor of strawberries does not survive extensive boiling. The famous nineteenth-century French writer Grimod de La Reynière said in his *Almanach des Gourmands:* "We have tried to make [strawberry] compotes, jams, etc., but until now without success. The fire removes almost all its bouquet."

The cooking process for strawberry jams and preserves varies widely from one manufacturer to another. The American Spoon Company, which is an example of a small jam manufacturer, uses fresh, hand-picked local strawberries that are first washed in cold water whirlpool baths, 10 pounds at a time. The berries are then hand-chopped into about three pieces each. Thirty-two pound batches of the berries are put into a copper kettle, and sugar and lemon juice are added. This mixture is cooked at a high temperature for about 45 minutes to 1 hour, hand-stirred with a wooden paddle. The berries have finished cooking when the fruit to sugar ratio reaches 7 to 4. The cook at the American Spoon Company determines this state by using his judgment, as well as with a *refractometer,* which is a device made of prisms that measures the soluble solids content of the jam: the amount of dissolved solids in suspension in the liquid. The jam is put into a filling machine, which fills the jars one by one; the jars are then sterilized.

Clearbrook Farms is a medium-size jam manufacturer, and the process to make their jams begins with frozen whole berries. The berries and sugar are put into a vacuum kettle, which works on the same principle as a pressure cooker. The berries are stirred in the kettle to make them burst. A natural pectin solution is added, and the mixture, which totals about 450 pounds, is cooked under pressure at approximately 160°F. for about half an hour. After the cooking, citric acid is added to the jam. A refractometer is used to check the soluble solids content. While the jam is still hot, it is put into jars, then the jars are sterilized and cooled.

Knott's Berry Farm, an example of a large jam manufacturer, uses frozen whole berries that are packed in 55-gallon drums. The berries are put into the vacuum kettle with sugar and corn syrup; the mixture, which is equal to 3,000 pounds, is heated to 130°F. After 25 minutes of cooking, the pectin is added, then the temperature is raised to 190°F. for filling the jars; jars are filled at the rate of 300 per minute.

Those jams and preserves that are made without the addition of pectin are often cooked for a longer time to thicken through reduction; this sometimes results in tough fruit and an underlying bitter caramel taste that comes from the overcooked sugar. In addition, the strawberry flavor may cook away in the process. One of the ways to get around the long cooking time is to add the sugar in the form of a syrup so the granules don't have to be dissolved.

Although the government doesn't require that a manufacturer list ingredients on the label of a jam or preserve, it is stipulated that the fruit content be at least 45 percent, and that the sugar content be not more than 55 percent. The soluble solids content, a measure of the thickness, for jam and preserves must be at least 64 percent of the total, which means that the liquid content can equal as much as 35 percent.

As with all processed foods, a manufacturer must list ingredients on the label of strawberry jam or preserves in descending order of predominance. In other words, if the first ingredient on a label of strawberry jam or preserve is *strawberries,* then there are more strawberries than anything else in the product. If the first ingredient is *sugar,* then there is more sugar than fruit. Generally, the best jams and preserves are those made with more fruit than sugar; however, you have to read labels carefully to determine the truth. Smucker's, for example, lists strawberries as the first ingredient on its label, but the next three ingredients are three different forms of sugar (high fructose corn syrup, corn syrup, and sugar), which, when added together, amount to a greater volume of sugar than the strawberries.

HANDLING AND STORAGE

Jams and preserves will last for at least a year if unopened and kept in a cool, dark place. After opening, jams and preserves should be refrigerated and will last about 2 months. After long storage in the refrigerator (over 2 months) sugar crystals and mold may form on the top of the jar of jam or preserves. Although they are unappetizing, they are harmless.

HOW TO JUDGE STRAWBERRY JAM AND PRESERVES

Tasting Media

Place jams and preserves in clear plastic cups and taste with plastic spoons.

Color/Eye Appeal

A good strawberry jam or preserve should have a bright, clear, natural red color. In other words, it should look like strawberries. Age and overcooking can darken the berries, making an unappetizing brown or muddy jam or preserve. Artificial color is sometimes added to heighten the color of a jam or preserve, making it an unnatural, neon pink color.

Taste/Aroma

A good strawberry jam or preserve should taste like strawberries. As I've said, it is more difficult to make a strawberry jam or preserve than almost any other flavor, and so it is not surprising to discover that most of the jams and preserves I have tasted did not achieve this goal. The main flaw in almost all of them is that they are too sweet, tasting of sugar and not fruit.

An unnatural, chemical flavor can result when jams or preserves are made with too many additives. A burned, caramelized flavor can come from overcooking the sugar in the jam or preserve.

Consistency

This seems to be the most problematical aspect of commercial strawberry jams and preserves. Ideally, jams and preserves should be thin enough to spread easily on a piece of bread or toast, but they should not be runny. They should be thick enough to mound on a spoon, but not so thick that the preserve stands up by itself when taken from the jar.

If the product is jam, it should be a smooth purée of fruit. If it is a preserve, then it should contain whole berries within a substance of jam-like consistency. Many of the jams and preserves I have tasted were alternately runny, pasty, gelatinous, lumpy, soupy, syrupy, stiff. Some of the products labeled "jam" or "preserve" should rightfully have been labeled "sauces," since they consisted of pieces of fruit in a syrup base.

In many cases, the fruit in the jam and preserve is hardened and sugary and has no strawberry taste. Some jams and preserves contain so many seeds that they detracted from the flavor of the products.

Aftertaste

The most prevalent negative aftertaste in strawberry jam and preserve is a lingering artificial flavor, which results from the use of additives.

CONCLUSIONS AND SUGGESTIONS

One of the most annoying aspects of this tasting is discovering how many jam and preserve manufacturers play fast and loose with the language. One company's jam might contain larger pieces of fruit than another one's preserve, when technically it should be the other way around. To cite the most obvious example, Smucker's Jam contains whole strawberries, while Smucker's Preserves has almost a jellylike smooth consistency.

Since most people have strong feelings about the consistency of their strawberry jam and preserve, the same way that everyone has a preference for either a 3-, 4-, or 5-minute soft-boiled egg, it's frustrating to know that you can't rely on labels to guide you to your favorite type of jam or preserve.

Another obfuscation about label language on jams and preserves is that some manufacturers have begun to call their products *confiture* or *conserves,* which means they don't have to conform to government regulations for jams and preserves. Government regulations exist only for fruit butter, fruit jelly, fruit preserves, and jam. By referring to his product as confiture, a manufacturer may vary the solids content (the thickness) and/or the sugar level, making them lower or higher than regulation. Many times, this also means these manufacturers produce jams and preserves that are not consistent from one batch to the next.

Also, in none of the other tastings held for this book did I find such a disappointing range of quality among the foods we tasted. There were very few really terrific jams or preserves, even among the top-ranked brands in the tasting; many were simply adequate and most were clearly unacceptable. Part of the problem is that strawberry is a very difficult jam to make, and cooking often dissipates the delicate flavor, leaving a cloying sweetness. Those manufacturers that make a *good* strawberry jam or preserve, however, generally make *excellent* jams or preserves out of other fruits.

The results of this tasting made me realize that perhaps it might be a good idea for a conscientious cook to make his or her own jam or preserve, in a simplified way, to get a truly high-quality product. A long-winded canning process doesn't suit my cooking style, with bushels of fresh fruit and a day-long stint at the stove. Thus, I prefer something much easier, and include my Simple Jam recipe below. The best store-bought strawberry jam I've ever had is made by American Spoon.

COOKING WITH JAMS AND PRESERVES

Jam is a complete food in itself and doesn't usually lend itself to cooking. However, the English use jam as a filling for tart shells, and the Russians put spoonfuls of jam into their tea. I use a French method for jam: Heat it and strain it and brush it on fruit fillings in pastry, to make a shiny and delicious glaze that hardens when it cools. I also make a delicious and simple sauce by boiling strawberry jam with a little white wine, straining it, and serving it warm with toasted pound cake.

RECIPE

Simple Jam

1½ cups fresh fruit, such as strawberries, blueberries, or raspberries
3 tablespoons sugar or honey (more or less, depending on the sweetness of the fruit)
a few drops of fresh lemon juice (more or less, depending on the acidity of the fruit)

1. In a heavy saucepan, mix fruit with the sugar or honey and lemon juice. Boil for 15 to 20 minutes, until slightly thickened.

2. Put into a screw-top jar or one of those French glass canning jars with the pry-top wire closure. This "jam" lasts for a couple of weeks in the refrigerator, just about long enough for you to use it up on your toast every morning.

VANILLA

anilla is the world's most popular flavor. It scents tea in China, flavors pastry and custards and other sweets all over the globe, gives English pipe tobacco a lift, and is, as Carson McCullers wrote in *The Heart Is a Lonely Hunter,* sometimes used by young American girls as a perfume.

The Coca-Cola company buys almost one third of the world's vanilla crop to use in its soft drink. According to an article in the *Wall Street Journal* written during the Old Coke/New Coke fiasco in the summer of 1985, demand for vanilla from the island of Madagascar (the world's largest producer of vanilla) fell drastically when New Coke was introduced, which led industry experts to surmise that Old Coke (aka Classic Coke) contains vanilla and New Coke does not. The shift to the New Coke formula was enough to affect the economy of Madagascar adversely, until Old Coke was reintroduced and the vanilla connection to the soft drink reestablished.

The flavor of vanilla is so strong that if you mix a teaspoon of it into a gallon of paint, the strong smell will dissipate more quickly than usual after you've painted. In order to scent the house nicely for prospective buyers, anxious homeowners have been known to pour a bottle of vanilla into a pot and put it over low heat on the stove.

According to linguist William Safire, in the days of soda fountains, when a jerk called, "Vanilla!" he meant "Come out of the kitchen, there's a chick just walked in that'll knock your eye out!" Slang definition of the term "vanilla" used to mean "exaggeration," but now it means boring, plain, "tasteless."

Vanilla extract is so popular that many tourists bring it back from Mexico, thinking they are getting a great bargain in the country where the flavoring originated. However, much of the vanilla for sale in Mexico contains coumarin, an active ingredient in rat poison, which has been banned by the United States Food and Drug Administration since 1954. If someone ingests as little as the contents of one small bottle (1.65 ounces), it could be fatal. Smaller amounts can severely damage internal organs. Pure vanilla is not cheap in any country, so if you see a quart of vanilla for sale in Mexico for $1.50 (the same amount as an ounce in the United States), beware!

A DASH OF HISTORY

The flavor of the vanilla bean is so enticing that it's not surprising it was always highly prized.

While exploring Mexico for Spain around 1520, Hernando Cortez visited the court of the Aztec chief Montezuma and was offered a drink called *xoco-latl.* This bitter drink was made from the powdered cocoa beans (see "A Dash of History" in "Chocolate") and from a black pod called *thilxochitl,* or vanilla. The Aztecs used vanilla as a medium of exchange, as a perfume, and as medicine.

Cortez returned to Spain with most of Montezuma's treasure, including samples of cocoa and vanilla. Vanilla was first named *vainilla* by the Spaniards, meaning "small scabbard" or "small pod," which comes from the Latin *vagina,* meaning "sheath, pod, encasement." Vanilla mixed with chocolate was immediately popular in Spain, and soon throughout Europe. In 1602, none other than Hugh Morgan, the apothecary to Queen Elizabeth of England, recommended that vanilla be used as a flavoring by itself. Within a few decades, vanilla was used in France, and subsequently all over Europe, as a popular flavor.

For more than 300 years after it was brought from the New World to the Old, vanilla was obtained only from Mexico, because Europeans could not discover the secret of its cultivation. The orchid plant from which vanilla is harvested was planted in Java, India, and other tropical locations, but the fruit, the vanilla bean, refused to appear. In the nineteenth century, a Frenchman found that a tiny bee native to Mexico pollinated the orchid blossoms there, and by simulating this process by hand, he was able to coerce the vanilla orchid to bear fruit. The same method is used today.

Today vanilla is grown in Indonesia, Mexico, Tahiti, Uganda, the Seychelles, and Madagascar. Ninety percent of the vanilla used in the United States comes from Madagascar, an island along the eastern coast of Africa, and the remaining 10 percent comes from Indonesia. Ironically, even though it is where vanilla originated, Mexico no longer exports the vanilla it grows. The vanilla crop from all the other countries is very small and is entirely consumed in Europe.

HOW VANILLA IS MADE

Because it was a Frenchman who discovered how to hand-pollinate the vanilla orchid, the first plants to bear fruit outside of Mexico were planted in French colonies, including Madagascar. These French vanilla beans are called *Bourbon,* because the island of Réunion, in the same island group as Mauritius, is where this successful cultivation started, and it used to be called Bourbon.

The vanilla orchid, a species of the same plant that produces the familiar decorative corsage flowers, grows on a vine that attaches itself to the side of a tree in a dense forest. The vine is pruned to prevent it from growing so high that the pods can't be harvested. After 2 years, flowers appear on the vine, and after 3 years, as a result of hand-pollination, the flowers produce the pods that will become vanilla beans.

About 9 months after pollination, the green vanilla pods are ready to be harvested. At this point, they look like a string bean, about the thickness of a man's finger. To make this green, tasteless pod into the familiar vanilla bean requires a curing process much like the procedure that turns a plum into a prune.

To cure vanilla, in Mexico the green pods are first put into ovens for a day or two, until they start to shrivel; in Madagascar and Tahiti this first step is to immerse the green pods in hot water. Then, in all growing areas, the pods are placed side by side in the sun to bake for hours. When the sun goes down, the warm beans are put into airtight containers, where they sweat all night.

This baking/sweating process continues for a few weeks, until the beans turn dark brown and pliable. After this the beans are dried for several weeks. This curing process produces in the vanilla beans a white crystallized substance called *vanillin,* which is the most important flavor component in vanilla. The shriveled, mahogany-brown beans are then tied into bundles of 50 to 90 each, and packed in boxes to be shipped. The curing process reduces 5 pounds of green pods to 1 pound of brown beans. Indonesian and Ugandan vanilla is cured much more quickly: The pods are dried over wood fires for 2 or 3 weeks, but the result is vanilla that doesn't taste as good as that from other parts of the world.

Once the vanilla beans are shipped to the manufacturers, the vanilla extract is made. The inside of a vanilla bean contains lots of tiny black seeds imbedded in a sticky liquid. To expose these flavorful seeds, the beans are chopped into small pieces, and then put into stainless-steel baskets that are lowered into large vats. At that point, warm alcohol and water are poured several times over the vanilla in the baskets until all of the flavor is extracted. When the process has finished, the water and alcohol mixture has become a carrier for the vanilla flavor, just as the water in a coffee percolator becomes a carrier for the flavor of the ground coffee after it has brewed.

The liquid is then filtered and usually sugar or corn syrup is added for a sweet flavor and to keep the liquid from becoming cloudy. At this point some companies allow the liquid to mellow for a few weeks before it is bottled.

Alcohol is used in the manufacturing process to extract all of the flavor from the vanilla and to preserve the flavor in the bottle. When vanilla extract is heated or exposed to the air, the alcohol evaporates and the vanilla flavor remains.

Because the natural vanillin content of vanilla beans varies from crop to crop and country to country, each batch of vanilla extract is tested and blended to produce a standard strength and flavor. This consistency is one of the advantages of using liquid vanilla extract over vanilla beans in cooking.

Imitation vanilla flavorings (see below) are made with synthetic vanillin, which is obtained from the wood pulp by-product of the paper industry. Being the predominant flavor in the vanilla bean, vanillin has a characteristic flavor of the real thing; however, there are at least 25 other identifiable components of the vanilla bean that contribute to its complex flavor, such as various gums, oils, and resins.

VARIETIES OF VANILLA

Pure Vanilla

• *Extract* Extract is made with at least 13.5 ounces vanilla bean (called a *fold*) to each gallon of liquid and contains at least 35 percent alcohol. This is the strongest pure vanilla flavoring available to the consumer.

Some extracts used by professional bakers are more concentrated than those available in supermarkets; they are called *two fold* (26.7 ounces of vanilla beans to a gallon of liquid), *three fold* (40.05 ounces of vanilla beans to a gallon of liquid), and so on.

• *Flavor* Vanilla flavor (sometimes called *flavoring*) contains less than 35 percent alcohol and thus has a less-concentrated vanilla flavor because fewer vanilla beans are required.

Vanilla-Vanillin Extract

Vanilla-vanillin extract is the same as pure extract, except that as much as 1 ounce of synthetic vanillin can be added for every fold of vanilla beans.

Imitation Vanilla

In imitation vanilla, the basic flavoring agent is synthetic as opposed to natural—either vanillin and/or ethyl vanillin, which is a coal tar derivative and three times as strong as ordinary vanillin. Technically, imitation vanilla is any extract to which more than 1 ounce of vanillin has been added for every fold of vanilla. Synthetic vanillin is a chemically pure substance that lacks the minor flavor constituents in natural vanilla; therefore, it is harsh and bitter, to varying degrees depending on the brand.

HANDLING AND STORAGE

Theoretically, vanilla extract will last at least 3 years if it's kept in a tightly capped bottle in a cool, dry place away from light. Practically, however, vanilla will last much longer and may even improve with age. A small amount of sediment may appear in the bottom of a bottle of vanilla after a while, but it's harmless—simply the suspended pieces of the vanilla bean settling out of the liquid; you can mix it back into the vanilla by shaking the bottle.

HOW TO JUDGE VANILLA

Tasting Media

Myriad ways exist to taste vanilla flavoring; each manufacturer seems to have his own system, including mixing vanilla with any one of the following: distilled water, milk, heavy cream, sugar and cream, and so on. Many of the methods seem to be attempts to simulate an ice-cream mixture, a common use for commercial vanilla.

The simplest method is to pour a few drops of a brand of vanilla onto a cube of sugar and suck the sugar to detect the flavor.

Color/Eye Appeal

A good vanilla should be clear brown and not cloudy or murky. If a vanilla extract is clear white, it has been made with synthetic ingredients and is not natural and pure (see "Varieties of Vanilla").

Taste/Aroma

A whiff of vanilla flavoring will tell you almost everything you need to know about its flavor and strength. When smelling vanilla you should make a few short sniffs rather than one big one; this will give you a more accurate impression.

Some of the words that characterize the taste of good vanilla flavoring are *leathery, beany, resinous, sickly sweet* (like marshmallows or cotton candy), *pruney, fruity, woody* (like a freshly sharpened pencil), *bourbon/rum.*

Consistency

Vanilla flavoring should have a watery consistency; if it is thicker than that, it is probably old and the alcohol has evaporated somewhat.

Aftertaste

A bourbon/rum aftertaste in vanilla flavoring is considered good.

CONCLUSIONS AND SUGGESTIONS

The top vanilla in my tasting is far better than all of the other contenders. This is a case when a so-called gourmet product is actually far superior to prosaic foods.

Nielsen-Massey is a company that until recently sold their vanilla exclusively to food manufacturers, such as ice-cream companies, willing to pay the high price for top quality. It's a family-owned company that believes in making the best.

In general, the variation among brands of vanilla can be compared to the variation among brands of Scotch; each brand is quite different from the next. Since smell is a good indication of the flavor of vanilla, you might sneak off the cap of a bottle the next time you are in a supermarket trying to decide between two brands. A good vanilla can really make a difference in your baking. In fact, one baker I know claims she wins many prizes with her outstanding cakes, not because of her recipes ("a yellow cake is a yellow cake," she says), but because her vanilla is so superior.

The difference between imitation vanilla and pure vanilla is enormous. Even though the imitation is one third as expensive as the real thing, the price difference is only pennies per portion (12 cents per half teaspoon of real vanilla versus 5 cents for imitation). Imitation vanilla tastes heavy, and the flavor components are separate and distinct, as opposed to real vanilla, which is subtle and complex and mellow. The overriding flavor of imitation vanilla is grassiness, and the alcohol seems to predominate. Imitation vanilla also often has a bitter aftertaste. To my mind, there is no choice but to use the real thing. When I have been stuck with a bottle of imitation vanilla, however, I put a piece of vanilla bean into it, and after a few weeks the flavor improves considerably.

You can also make your own vanilla extract by cutting a whole vanilla bean lengthwise into halves and putting them into 1/2 cup of vodka; store in a tightly capped jar for at least a month. Taste it first to determine the strength, then use as you would commercial vanilla extract.

COOKING WITH VANILLA EXTRACT AND BEANS

It's easier to cook with liquid vanilla extract than with vanilla beans, but each has some distinct uses. I keep a large glass jar (such as a mayonnaise jar) filled with sugar in which I have buried a split whole vanilla bean. Whenever the sugar in the jar gets low, I simply fill it up again. The vanilla bean continues to lend its flavor to sugar for at least a year. I use this sugar in all sorts of baking recipes, and in custards, puddings, and so on, in addition to the vanilla extract called for in the recipe.

Whole vanilla beans can be used to make custards and dessert sauces. Cut the bean in half and cook with the liquid mixture you are making. Rinse it off after you've used it and reuse it several more times. The rule of thumb for using whole vanilla beans is to use about 1 inch of the bean in place of 1 teaspoon of extract.

When using liquid vanilla, allow 1 teaspoon of extract for each pint or pound of food. One mistake consumers often make, says one manufacturer, is to use too much vanilla, which results in a harsh taste.

When using vanilla in a dough with shortening and sugar, it's best to add the vanilla with the shortening so it is dispersed evenly. If adding vanilla to hot foods, wait until they cool slightly (for example, when making a custard take the pot off the stove before adding vanilla) so that the flavor doesn't dissipate too readily.

Be sure to add a little bit of vanilla to recipes that call for other flavorings as well (such as almond flavoring); the vanilla will heighten the other flavoring in the dish.

RECIPE

Vanilla-Coffee Liqueur

This recipe is courtesy of the Vanilla Information Bureau and makes a delicious after-dinner drink, ice-cream topping, or milk flavoring; it has kind of a Kahlúa flavor. (Makes 5 cups)

- **1 1/2 cups light brown sugar or granulated brown sugar**
- **1 cup granulated sugar**
- **2 cups water**
- **1/2 cup instant coffee powder**
- **3 cups vodka**
- **1 vanilla bean, split, or 2 tablespoons pure vanilla extract**

1. Combine sugars with water. Bring to a boil and boil for 5 minutes. Gradually stir in instant coffee. Cool.

2. Add vodka and vanilla to the coffee mixture and mix thoroughly. Pour into a decorative decanter or an empty liquor bottle. Cover tightly and let stand for at least 2 weeks.

LUXURY FOODS

CAVIAR

There is more simplicity in the man who eats caviar on impulse than in the man who eats grapenuts on principle.—G. K. Chesterton.

This simple man must have a few extra rubles in the bank to afford such an impulse. But barring these financial limitations, eating caviar is one of the few indulgences that ties us to the lost world of nineteenth-century Russian aristocracy, for whom caviar was the equivalent of our prosaic tuna fish.

We should eat fast, however, if we want to taste Iranian or Russian caviar, which comes from the body of water on which both countries border, the Caspian Sea. It is this inland saltwater lake that has long been considered the best source in the world for caviar. Many experts predicted that the Caspian sturgeon would be extinct by now, due to industrial pollution and overfishing. In 1965, however, the Russians and Iranians cooperated to stock the Caspian Sea with six and a half million baby sturgeon, which are just now coming into their breeding period. Nature and the act of man has granted us a reprieve, and Caspian caviar is still being harvested and shipped all over the world.

Since the fall of Communism, we have entered a new era in Caspian caviar production. Caviar from the Russian side of the Caspian Sea now comes from several republics, rather than the U.S.S.R., and many of them don't follow previous rules of fishing and production. Therefore, in the past few years, the Caspian was overfished, which resulted in a glut in the caviar market and lower prices. Now, however, there is a shortage of Caspian caviar and the prices are going up. The production of Russian caviar fell from a high of 2,000 tons per year in 1990 to 800 tons per year in 1994.

Doomsayers are further predicting that in 10 to 12 years, pollution from oil-drilling in the Caspian Sea will affect the supply of caviar adversely and "There is not much hope," in the words of one distributor.

Since 1987 there has been an embargo on Caspian caviar from the Iranian side; all Iranian caviar is sold in Europe.

The Russians are the largest consumers of caviar (which they call *ikra*) in the world. The next largest consumers are Americans, who eat approximately 130,000 pounds of caviar each year, and that number is growing, in part because we have rediscovered the fact that our own sturgeons produce caviar and we are eating this homegrown product in greater amounts. Several forward-thinking leaders of the caviar business in this country, predicting the eventual demise of Iranian-Russian caviar production, have seen to it that we will have plenty of native caviar to satisfy our newly awakened taste buds.

The French, from whom we might have adopted the habit of using caviar for celebrations, are the largest consumers of caviar after the Americans, followed by West Germans and the English. The rest of the (free) world eats so little, even when compared with these figures, that it's not worth tabulating.

The world's largest caviar buyer is the *QE2* luxury liner, where passengers consume 4 tons each year.

The word "caviar," from the Turkish *havyar,* refers to the roe of sturgeon; and this is the sort of caviar we are addressing here. Other fish roe can be called caviar legally, but only if that word is preceded by the name of the fish, e.g., *salmon caviar* or *lumpfish caviar.*

A DASH OF HISTORY

Throughout history, in every country where it was known, sturgeon and the roe that came from it were the property of those in power, whether it was a king or a dictator. An ancient English ditty describes this:

The sturgeon belongs to the King
So, if in some desolate chasm
You catch one or two on a string,
Make sure that His Majesty has 'em.

More recently, the very best Caspian caviar, called *golden caviar,* was always delivered to the czar of Russia and to the shah of Iran. Some experts say it used to go directly to the Kremlin. There is even a record of Teddy Roosevelt happily receiving a prize sturgeon from American fishermen.

The exact time when our ancestors became aware that the roe of a fish could be delicious to eat is obscure; however, Rabelais mentions caviar in 1533. Shakespeare also mentions caviar, in *Hamlet* (II, ii) ". . . 'twas caviare to the general." But caviar can't have been a well-known food in Shakespeare's time, since a 1618 reference to it in *The Court and Country* by Nicholas Breton reveals that a great lady had sent the writer's father a barrel of caviar and it was no sooner opened than it was fastened down again to be returned to the donor with a respectful message that his servant had enough black soap!

Before the revolution, the Cossacks were traditionally the group that fished for sturgeon in Russia, probably as emissaries of the czar, to whom they paid tribute each year with enough caviar to supply every royal meal.

The American caviar industry got started in the last half of the nineteenth century, when Henry Schacht, a German immigrant, opened a business catching sturgeon on the Delaware River. He treated his caviar with German salt and exported a great deal of it to Europe. At around the same time, sturgeon was fished from the Columbia River in the West, also supplying caviar. For a couple of decades in the late nineteenth century, American caviar was so plentiful that it was given away at bars for the same reason modern bars give away peanuts—to make patrons thirsty. In the heyday of the last century's native caviar industry, 150,000 pounds were produced annually.

Around the turn of the century, the production of American caviar slowed almost to a halt, largely because of the lack of controls on the fishing of sturgeon, which seriously depleted the supply of fish.

The next important event in the history of caviar was the Russian Revolution. The influx of immigrants from Russia brought the love of Caspian caviar to Western Europe. Even after the caviar industry had been nationalized in Russia, exports began to supply the craving for Caspian caviar.

In 1893, the Iranians allowed the Russians to franchise their caviar production. The Russians didn't want to give up this lucrative agreement, but in 1953, in the face of Iranian discontent about the inequity of the situation, the Russians magnanimously gave back the Iranians' rights to their own caviar industry. Over the years before this time, the Iranians had learned from the Russians how to process their caviar. Nevertheless, some experts claim that the quality of the Iranian caviar has never been quite as good nor as consistent as when it was harvested by the Russians, perhaps because the Russians eat a great deal of caviar themselves and the Iranians do not.

The universal demand for the best caviar caused a mild panic a few years ago when the overthrow of the shah threatened the supply of Iranian caviar. President Carter then imposed a boycott on Iranian goods pending the release of the American hostages taken in 1979. The Russian invasion of Afghanistan and subsequent boycott of Russian goods heightened the panic. Relief followed the lifting of both the Iranian and Russian boycotts. Subsequently, the market became flooded with Caspian caviar and prices dropped accordingly. The next big shift in the caviar market, which is probably a few years down the road, is expected to take the form of drastically diminished supply from the Caspian, with a concurrent further increase of sales and consumption of American caviar.

If it weren't for the political upheavals that have affected the supply of caviar, the modern American caviar industry might never have gotten off the ground. Arnold Hansen-Sturm, the fifth generation of an illustrious caviar-producing family that has worked on both sides of the Atlantic, compared the emergence of American caviar to the emergence of American wines; both industries were cultivated in response to a dearth of supplies from Europe.

HOW FRESH CAVIAR IS MADE

One could say that caviar is not made, it is born. But two important steps occur in the processing of sturgeon eggs after they are taken from the fish that create the differences among brands of fresh caviar.

The first of these steps is the salting of the roe. The amount of salt used and the way it is applied to the roe are decisions that must be made in the field by expert caviar handlers. Caviar handlers require years of experience and are held in high regard within the industry, much like the respect applied to renowned wine experts, or the "noses" who blend perfume.

The second significant step that affects the overall quality of caviar is a more general one—storage. Since most of us won't be lucky enough to go to the Caspian Sea and stand poised with a spoon over a just-caught sturgeon, we are subject to the way a batch of caviar is held between the time it is harvested and its arrival on the table. The storage of caviar has a great deal to do with its overall quality.

Sturgeons return each year to spawn in the same rivers in which they were born. Fishermen lie in wait for them at the mouths of these rivers, and when a fish is caught and determined to be a female containing roe, processing begins as quickly as possible.

In Russia, after a promising fish is caught, it is stunned by a blow to the head and the fishing boat immediately sails toward a processing center on shore, where the eggs are removed. In Iran, the fish is not taken in for processing until a few hours after it is caught and killed. According to a spokesperson for the Petrossian company, which handles only Russian caviar, the fish should be alive when the roe is removed from its belly, otherwise the fish sprays a bitter-tasting substance over its eggs as it expires. Other experts disagree with this assessment, however.

About 20 percent of the weight of a female sturgeon is made up of roe. The first step in removing this potential caviar is to slit open the fish with a sharp knife. The hands of an expert pull out the roe and push it through a strong cotton sieve to free the eggs from the membrane that encases them. Then the roe is rinsed, drained, and mixed by hand with salt, the amount of which is determined by the quality of the roe and its eventual destination. If the roe is of the highest grade and will be sold in America, it is designated *malossol* (see "Varieties of Caviar," this page), and salt amounting to less than 5 percent of its net weight is mixed into it. The best roe that is to be sold in Europe is also called *malossol,* but it is treated with a (less-than-5-percent) mixture of salt and borax, a preservative that is outlawed in this country. Many people who have tasted Caspian caviar in Europe have noticed that it tastes sweeter than the same caviar in this country, because of the addition of borax in place of some of the salt.

The purpose of adding salt to sturgeon roe is not only to preserve it, but also to "cook" the eggs so that they become firm and tasty. Gerald Stein, president of the Iron Gate company, has witnessed caviar processing on the Russian side of the Caspian, and reports that before salt is added, the roe is soft and tasteless, and the eggs have no "separateness." The sturgeon roe does not become caviar, in fact, until the salt is added. But if too much salt is added, the caviar grains will turn tough. If too little is added, the caviar stays too soft and mushy. This difficult decision is made on the spot, by an experienced eye, a man or woman who can properly assess the age, quality, and condition of the sturgeon roe. The age of the roe in question is an important consideration in deciding how much salt to add. If the eggs are mature when they are taken from the fish, they need less salt; if the eggs are more underripe, they need more salt.

After the roe is removed from the fish and mixed with the salt, a procedure that takes only 15 minutes, it is weighed and packed into tins and placed in a refrigerator that is between 28° and 32°F. In order to stay in pristine condition, the caviar must remain within this narrow temperature range until it is consumed. If it gets colder, the caviar may freeze and become a mush when thawed. If it is warmed above 32°F., it will spoil. The reason the caviar does not freeze below 32°F. is that the salt content lowers its freezing point. The best importers "baby-sit" an expensive shipment of caviar throughout its journey so the temperature can be closely monitored.

VARIETIES OF CAVIAR

The following terms refer to Caspian caviar, except where noted.

Beluga

This is the largest of the species of sturgeon in the Caspian Sea. The beluga grow up to about 2,000 pounds and yield the largest "berries" (as the caviar grains are called) of all the species; beluga do not begin to bear eggs until they are about 20 years old. For this reason, and perhaps because it has the mildest flavor, beluga is the most highly prized of all caviar, and, therefore, also the most expensive.

The color of beluga caviar is designated by *000* for the lightest gray, *00* for a medium gray, and *0* for the darkest black berries. The lightest color beluga, almost the color of polished pewter, is the most sought after, even though color has nothing whatsoever to do with the flavor of caviar.

Osetra

This is spelled many other ways, including *ossetra, oestrova,* and *osietr.*

This is the second-largest species of Caspian sturgeon, weighing up to about 600 pounds, and it produces slightly smaller caviar berries than beluga sturgeon; osetra begin to bear eggs when they are about 12 to 15 years old. The color of osetra eggs ranges from golden yellow to brown and the flavor is more intense than beluga.

Sevruga

This fish, which grows to weigh about 80 pounds, is the smallest and most abundant of all the Caspian sturgeon. The eggs are also the smallest of the three main species and taste the strongest; the sevruga begin to bear eggs when they are about 7 years old. The color of the eggs is usually dark gray to black. Many experts and gourmets consider sevruga to be the most delicious of all caviar.

Sterlet

This species of Caspian sturgeon is almost extinct. From this fish comes the legendary "golden caviar" that, in times past, was required by law to go to the shah if found on the Iranian side and to the czar if found on the Russian side. It is safe to say that today few of us will ever have access to this kind of caviar. I was lucky enough to have some recently at a private party in the Dorchester Hotel in London when the Sultan of Brunei, the hotel's owner, was in residence; it was quite exquisite, slightly smoky with a firm texture.

Malossol

The term "malossol" is derived from the Russian words *malo,* meaning "little," and *ssoleny,* "salted," or "lightly salted" in English. When the name is applied to one of the three main types of caviar listed above it means the caviar contains less than 5 percent salt, making it of a higher quality than that to which more salt was added. However, the limited salt also makes it more fragile and prone to spoilage.

Pressed

This is called *pausnaya* in Russian. It is lesser-quality caviar, or in some cases high-quality caviar that is left over after tins are packed and weighed, which is made into a dense cake by pressing out most of the moisture. It takes 5 pounds of regular caviar to make 1 pound of pressed caviar. The concentrated, salty flavor and pasty texture is favored by many connoisseurs, who, in my opinion, may do so out of reverse snobbism. I find pressed caviar to be somewhat like black shoe polish with a fishy taste.

Pressed caviar is traditionally used as a filling for Russian *blini,* or pancakes, where the look of the caviar is not important. It is generally much cheaper than whole-grain caviar.

Pasteurized

Lesser grades of caviar are mixed with about 6 percent salt and pasteurized, either at the time of processing or after shipping. This is accomplished by packing the caviar in glass jars or tins and processing these containers at 140°F. for a length of time that depends on the size of the containers. Pasteurized caviar is not prone to spoilage from extreme temperatures and will last for years if unopened.

When caviar is pasteurized, the berries become slightly hardened, which can improve a lower-grade mushy caviar. In fact, many unscrupulous importers pasteurize their fresh caviar when its 6-month shelf life comes to an end and it is too mushy to sell it as fresh. Pasteurizing most often takes away from the quality of good caviar, however, because the berries become hard and dry from the extra processing.

The law does not require that pasteurized caviar be marked as such. One sure way to recognize caviar that has been pasteurized is that it requires a church key to open it, as opposed to being pried open with the back of a spoon, and sounds a "thwack" when the vacuum seal is broken.

Chinese Beluga

A variety of large sturgeon (up to 2,000 pounds) that swims in the Amur River of northern Manchuria has recently been harvested. It is processed "malossol," with little salt, by experts from the West, and its size is closest to beluga caviar from the Caspian Sea. Its quality is excellent, almost as high as Caspian beluga, and the price is almost as high, too. If the price comes down in the future, as it might when the Chinese gain further experience, then it will be an excellent buy and alternative to Caspian beluga.

American

Although seven species of sturgeon swim in rivers all over the United States, none of the species indigenous to the Caspian Sea is among them. Two of our native sturgeons are considered the best for caviar, Pacific Coast white beluga and East Coast Atlantic sturgeon. Our American sturgeon caviar berries are similar in size to Caspian sevruga, but the taste is disappointing when compared to high-quality imports.

Lumpfish Caviar

This is the edible roe of the lumpfish, but only the uninitiated would mistake it for sturgeon caviar. It can be found, among other places, in Chesapeake Bay and off the coasts of Greenland and Iceland. The natural color of lumpfish ranges from yellow to dark green; it is dyed black or red for marketing purposes, sometimes resulting in a curious stain on the diner's mouth. It is almost always pasteurized and vacuum-packed.

Lumpfish is the kind of caviar we see most often gathering dust in the "gourmet" sections of our supermarkets and delicatessens. It is the first kind of caviar many of us try, and on occasion, it gives caviar a bad name among neophytes. It is *much* cheaper than "real" caviar, however, and if it is used judiciously it can be decorative and tasty. For instance, Scandinavian cuisines use *fresh* lumpfish caviar on their open sandwiches with great success.

If rinsed gently with cold water in a mesh strainer (to remove most of the saltiness) and served with lemon, minced onion, and minced hard-cooked egg (something you would never do with sturgeon caviar), it can be a delightful low-cost alternative to the real thing. When my husband was a very young impecunious bachelor, he tells me he used to serve lumpfish caviar this way to his less knowledgeable girl friends, who were always impressed.

HANDLING AND STORAGE

It's important to determine whether the caviar you have in hand is fresh or vacuum-packed (see "Pasteurized," above). This is not as simple as it sounds. The law does not require that "pasteurized" be written on the label. If the label says "keep refrigerated," then the caviar is fresh. Another clue for fresh caviar is that it is often packed in a tin with a wide (about 1½-inch) rubber band as a seal. However, many stores repack their fresh caviar in straight-sided glass jars with screw tops or in tins with snap-on lids that can be pried off with the back of a spoon. Pasteurized caviar requires a church key to open and sounds a "thwack" when the vacuum seal is broken.

Fresh caviar must be kept in your refrigerator (never the freezer) and eaten within one week after you've brought it home. Once fresh caviar is opened it should be eaten within 2 or 3 days, that's assuming there are any leftovers. Before putting away a tin of fresh caviar, smooth out the top to minimize the exposure to air and cover with a piece of clear plastic wrap before replacing the lid.

If it says "keep in a cool place" or "chill before serving," then chances are the caviar is vacuum-packed. If it's kept in a cool, dry place, like any canned goods, it will remain edible for up to a year. After it is opened it should be refrigerated and eaten within a week. Pasteurized, vacuum-packed caviar sometimes develops white specks that are little pieces of crystallized protein and are completely harmless. You might also see a cloudy liquid surrounding the caviar through the glass of the jar; this is simply the caviar's natural fat settling around the berries and it is also harmless.

If you have a choice, you should buy caviar from a store that has a lot of turnover. The chances are that the product didn't have an opportunity to sit around and get stale. Also, this will tell you that the purveyor probably has made an effort to know a little bit about the caviar he carries, and that the caviar may have been well handled.

The surest way to buy the most pristine fresh caviar is to go to a store that orders the caviar from the importer only when you request it. Many importers are handling their caviar this way now, and it means that it is kept in the optimum condition and constantly monitored until it is air-freighted, usually overnight, directly to the consumer. This does away with storage by a middleman, the storekeeper, who may not know how, or have the facilities, to keep his or her caviar in the best condition.

Two catches take place in the Caspian each year, the spring catch in March and the fall catch in October; it takes at least a month for the importer to get his caviar from each of these catches, meaning that we see a fresh batch of caviar beginning in April or May, and again in November, just before Christmas.

If caviar has been handled extremely well throughout its journey from the fish to you, if it has been kept constantly in the narrow range between 28° to 32°F., it will last for 6 months, just in time for the next catch to arrive. So you can feel extra safe buying caviar in June-July and at the Christmas season, and a little leery of it just before these periods.

One last caveat about buying caviar, which has been repeated to me again and again by experts: Don't look for bargains. If a special rock-bottom price has been placed on caviar, chances are good that it is over the hill and the storekeeper is trying to get rid of it. One major exception to this rule is the caviar price war between Macy's Cellar and Zabar's in New York City, which has happened several years in a row. The caviar consumer was the victor in the battles between these two major stores, as prices for the best Caspian caviar went below wholesale, causing importers to marvel at the retail price of their own products. Alas, these border skirmishes are not repeated too often.

Should you expect to taste the caviar you are about to buy? It depends on your relationship with the storekeeper. He or she should give you a look at the caviar, however, and if it seems to be swimming in oil (which indicates that the tins were not turned during storage and all of the natural oil in the caviar has risen to the top), looks dry, or if the berries are crushed, the caviar has seen better days.

HOW TO JUDGE CAVIAR

Tasting Media

I tasted American sturgeon caviars all together, and then beluga caviars together as a separate group.

Some Russian experts taste caviar by spreading it on the back of their hands and licking it off.

Color/Eye Appeal

The berries of beluga caviar should be plump and full, with a bright surface; the grains should also be whole and separate. Each grain should be coated with its own fat and should not look dry. No milky liquid or pieces of stringy membrane between the grains should be evident.

The color of good beluga caviar ranges from light gray to dark gray; never black, which indicates the presence of dye.

Although each batch of beluga caviar receives a numerical designation (see "Beluga," page 225), the color of caviar has little to do with its overall quality. Nevertheless, the 000 caviar (light gray) is the most highly prized.

The grains of the best caviar should be of uniform size and color, neither too compact and small nor too well developed.

Taste/Aroma

Caviar should not smell fishy, but should have an elegant seacoast aroma; the best caviar is reminiscent of the best fresh fish. Fresh caviar has a clean, oyster quality, with a slightly briny odor.

The best caviar should taste delicate but definite without a heavy taste of salt. Good caviar is often slightly nutty with a refined salinity. The flavor of any caviar should be very fresh and not at all fishy.

Consistency

When eating caviar, take it into your mouth and gently compress the berries between your tongue and the roof of your mouth. Good caviar should briefly resist, followed by a rewarding release of sweet flavor.

Each individual egg should be fresh, moist, and softly intact. If caviar is too soft, then it has not been cured enough. If a soft caviar is too salty, it has been treated by the processors in an effort to compensate for the soft eggs by putting in an extra amount of salt. If the eggs are too soft or fatty, they may have been overripe.

Aftertaste

Some caviars, notably the ones from the American species of sturgeon, have a bitter, almost chemical aftertaste, which detracts enormously from the overall flavor.

CONCLUSIONS AND SUGGESTIONS

Caviar is a tricky subject for a tasting because each batch is from a separate fish and tasting caviar from the same fish twice is unlikely. To underscore this fact, when a sturgeon is caught in the Caspian Sea it is given a number, and all tins of caviar taken from that fish are marked with this particular number, so that each tin represents caviar from the same source. This is done partly for cosmetic reasons, so the eggs in a tin are all of one color.

Nevertheless, tasting caviar is useful to help determine the quality of the handling the caviar receives from each of the importers. I bought the caviar directly from each importer. My tasting took place in June, and some importers had not yet received the caviar from the spring catch; thus some of the beluga caviar I tasted was up to 6 months old and, therefore, I could judge the condition of the eggs the importers considered salable. I believe the age of the caviar accounts for the fact that some highly regarded importers' caviars did not show as well as expected; Petrossian is but one example. The highest-quality caviar, as well as the most consistent over the years, is from Caviar Direct.

I have vowed, since this tasting, to control my urges to splurge on caviar to those months when I can be sure of getting it as fresh as possible: July, August, December, and January. It makes a big difference in the firmness of the eggs and the freshness of flavor.

With regard to flavor, I am suspicious of much of the caviar I have encountered since this tasting. I believe caviar is one of those foods that would surprise us if we could eat it at the source. The very best, freshest caviar, if we are lucky enough to get it, is sweet and very mild, *not at all* fishy. I am afraid that much of the caviar available to us, even from the best sources, is a little bit over the hill, still edible, but strong-tasting.

Another maddening thing about caviar is the fact that the labels are so unclear. If caviar is fresh beluga or osetra or sevruga, it should say so. More and more importers are changing their labeling policies, thus greater clarity should result in the future.

To address the American caviar issue: When it first became widely available a few years ago, American caviar was a revelation—fresh sturgeon caviar at about half the cost of the high-priced spread! The comparatively low price of American caviar is one of the reasons it is served more and more in American restaurants, garnishing other native ingredients on fussy plates.

Before my tasting, however, I had never eaten American and Caspian caviar at the same sitting. This tasting proved to be enlightening, because it demonstrated that no matter how good American caviar is, and it can be *good,* it will never measure up to even the lowest-rated Caspian caviar. The main reason for its inferiority is the bitter aftertaste that all American caviars seem to have. This acidic and sometimes too strong aftertaste won't prevent me from buying American caviar in the future, especially for use as a garnish; unlike lumpfish caviar, American caviar won't bleed. But it will make me think about saving up a little more money in order to afford the Caspian caviar, if I have a choice.

The prices for the caviar, by the way, are very close to one another, all brands governed by the same vagaries on the international market. However, from time to time, retail marketing wars, such as the one between Zabar's and Macy's in New York City every year around the Christmas holidays, depress caviar prices considerably.

COOKING AND EATING CAVIAR

One word applies when considering cooking with caviar: Don't! It is much too delicate to be exposed to heat, even for a moment. Nevertheless, it can be added successfully just before serving to a variety of dishes.

Traditionally, caviar should not be eaten with a metal utensil, such as a sterling silver spoon, because the metal interferes with the taste of the berries. Many gourmet shops sell elegant horn, bone, or ivory spoons for caviar, but a prosaic plastic spoon accomplishes the same purpose just as well.

The flavor of good caviar is marred by any garnish other than a squeeze of fresh lemon juice, if that, but second-rate (and still wonderful) caviar can be stretched by minced onion, chopped egg yolk and egg white, sour cream, and chopped parsley.

My favorite ways to eat caviar, other than straight out of the tin, are as a topping for a baked potato (with lots of sour cream, though unorthodox), or stirred into a potato salad made with a very subtle olive oil and just a hint of lemon juice. I've used Caspian and lumpfish caviars for these dishes and both are delicious.

Barry Wine, the former owner-chef of the The Quilted Giraffe Restaurant in Manhattan, makes a caviar appetizer named "Beggar's Pouches," which is another example of caviar in a successful combination with other foods. Very thin crêpes are filled with a touch of crème fraîche, chives, and sevruga caviar and the tops of the crêpes are tied with tiny strings cut from leek greens. This dish not only tastes wonderful, but is beautiful.

I've also used caviar in a dish named "Hobo Salad" that I have made for years; unfortunately, I don't know where the recipe originated, so I extend apologies here to its creator.

RECIPE

Hobo Salad

(Makes 2 servings)

1 can (20 ounces) white beans, drained
4 ounces caviar, the best you can afford
3 tablespoons extra-virgin olive oil
juice of 1/2 lemon
1/2 head of radicchio or red-leaf lettuce (optional)

Mix together all ingredients except radicchio or lettuce and adjust for seasoning; add more oil or lemon juice, if you wish. Serve immediately on a bed of finely shredded radicchio or red-leaf lettuce, if you wish.

TRUFFLES

If we could buy truffles as cheaply as turnips, would they have the same allure? Unfortunately, we will never get the chance to find out, because at hundreds of dollars a pound and rising, good truffles will always be expensive and rare.

Truffles have always been scarce, but now they are even more so. As demand increases for truffles, supply diminishes. In 1892, France, the world's largest supplier, produced 2,000 tons of truffles. Today the annual French truffle crop is below 12 tons. This dramatic change is largely due to the fact that during World War I, the truffle grounds in the Périgord region were plowed under and destroyed. Today, less than 3 tons of truffles are imported annually into the United States from Spain, France and Italy.

A DASH OF HISTORY

Truffles were known in the days of the Roman Empire, but after the fall of Rome they were ignored until the fourteenth century, when they were prized by the nobility of Italy and France. Louis XIV, who was a great gourmand, is said to have eaten a pound of truffles a day, and his chefs invented many elaborate dishes with truffles as the main ingredient.

Since the nineteenth century, truffles have been more sought after than at any other time in history. A couple of generations ago, the best tables in Europe and America were considered inferior unless truffles were on the menu. Today, to offer virtually any amount of truffles to guests is a sure sign of lavish generosity. This is a gift not experienced by too many lucky people these days.

HOW TRUFFLES ARE GROWN AND HARVESTED

A truffle is a fungus (in the same family as mushrooms) that grows a foot or two underground, usually at the base of a tree. Its size ranges from as small as a big marble to as big as a cantaloupe, and most of the ones we see in this country are about the size of Ping-Pong balls. Although more than 30 species of truffles grow around the world, the best come from France and Italy.

Even in this age of scientific advancement, how truffles grow remains a mystery, a legacy from a prehistoric past that refused to conform to the laws of modern agribusiness. No one knows what causes a truffle to materialize under a tree root, nor can one be induced to do so. Truffles appear to need chalky soil, a hot summer, and plenty of rain. Thunderstorms do them good, and one old myth claims that they are the product of lightning and an invention of the devil. Truffles are apt to grow under scrub oak trees. Although luck remains a large part of a good truffle harvest, most of the truffles produced in France today grow in plantations that have been seeded with oak trees expressly to try to stimulate truffle growth. Nevertheless, when a truffle is discovered in one spot, there is no reason to believe that another truffle will develop in the same spot again. Even if it does, as sometimes happens, it takes 5 to 10 years for a truffle to ripen enough to be harvested and eaten.

A truffle absorbs nourishment from the soil and vegetation surrounding it. The ground above where a truffle is growing is strangely bare. Another clue to the location of a truffle is a swarm of "truffle flies" just above the ground. Just as bees play a part in the reproductive cycle of flowers, these flies burrow into the dirt and lay eggs in the truffle itself, and by carrying spores to other locations encourage truffles to grow elsewhere.

Harvest time for truffles, in France and Italy, is in cold December and January. Harvesters have no way of sighting their quarry, so they use dogs, hogs, and even goats to sniff out the fungi, as bloodhounds might be used to sniff out fugitives. The animals' keen sense of smell detects the whereabouts of the truffles beneath the ground. They are trained not to eat the truffles once they have discovered them. The harvester must excavate with the greatest care to avoid bruising his find. Highly perishable, the truffle must be transported quickly to market; fresh truffles exported to the United States market arrive by air. If the climate has been less than perfect, the crop may be sparse. Thus, for many reasons, the truffle harvester is more of a gambler than most farmers, and it is no wonder that he and the middlemen are forced to extract a premium price for their product.

Truffles that are to be canned are sometimes peeled (the peels are sold separately for a cheaper price) and then put into cans of different sizes. The cans are sterilized under steam pressure, which cooks and shrinks the truffles by as much as 30 percent.

VARIETIES OF TRUFFLES

Black

One of the two most prized truffle varieties is the Périgord black truffle (*Tuber melanosporum*), which grows in the Périgord, Quercy, and Vaucluse areas in southern France. Although the same variety of black truffle is harvested in Spain, and some also come from Italy, they are not quite as good as the French black truffles.

Since truffles are in the same family as mushrooms, it is not surprising that their texture is similar, but sometimes truffles are as dense as potatoes, without being watery. Fresh black truffles have an earthy, heady flavor, usually subtle. Black truffles are usually quite misshapen and bumpy; an average-size black truffle is about 3/4 inch in diameter.

White

The second of the two most prized varieties of truffles is the Italian white truffle (*Tuber magnatum*) which grows in Piedmont in northern Italy.

White truffles are not really white but grayish, and they are a little larger than the black French ones, with a stronger, musky flavor, sometimes said to taste faintly of garlic. The texture of the white truffle is also very much like a mushroom, although sometimes firmer with a little more crispness.

Summer

The so-called summer truffle (*Tuber aestivum*), which grows in France, costs about one quarter the price of the black truffle and is often pawned off as the real thing in America. Summer truffles look like black truffles, but they are whitish inside instead of black all the way through, and have hardly any smell or taste. The season for summer truffles is June and July, and so, keeping that in mind, if a fresh truffle is on sale in those months, it is likely to be the inferior summer variety. A suspiciously low price, anything less than about $30 per pound is another clue that the truffle might not be the desirable Périgord type.

Desert

The desert truffle (*Terfezia leonis*) grows in northern Africa and is of a very poor quality.

Violet

The violet truffle (*Tuber brumale*) is found throughout Europe, and is also of a very poor quality.

American

The American truffle (*Tuber gibbosum*) is harvested in Oregon, and, according to Barry Wine, the former chef-owner of The Quilted Giraffe Restaurant in New York City, "The quality is so variable that sometimes I'm not sure if they're actually edible." Their characteristic piny flavor can sometimes be overwhelming.

HOW TRUFFLES ARE SOLD

Fresh

The season for white Italian truffles is late October until late January. Black truffles from France are also gathered during roughly the same period: from the beginning of December through the end of January. Black truffles from Spain and Italy are gathered from January through the middle of March.

Cans and Jars

Black and white truffles can be put up in both cans and glass jars. Those in glass jars are 15 percent more expensive than canned ones, partly because of the expense of the glass, which also allows you to see what you're getting. The truffles thus preserved are packed in either salt water or in truffle juice, extracted by pressing other truffles, which are then used in tubes of purée. Most people have the opportunity to taste only canned truffles in their lifetime, and then they wonder what all the fuss is about. In my opinion, the canning process takes away all of the ephemeral, special flavor of fresh truffles.

Following are the grades of packaged truffles:

- *Extra Brushed or Extra Grade* This is the best grade of preserved truffles, usually put up in glass jars rather than cans, carefully brushed and selected to be completely dirt-free and in good condition.

- *First Choice* This is the second-best grade of preserved truffles, put up in cans and jars, not up to the standard of "Extra Brushed," and usually slightly irregular in shape.

- *First Cooking* If a producer doesn't have a buyer for his whole black truffles, he sometimes cooks them in large batches, which preserves them for about 6 months. Then, as importers request truffles from him, he puts up the cooked truffles in small cans and cooks them again. Of course, as a result of being twice cooked, the quality of the truffles suffers. Some cans have the words "First Cooked" on the label, indicating that the truffles have only been cooked once. It is important to note, however, that not all truffles that have been cooked only once will state this fact on the label, but by the same token all truffles that have been cooked twice will not be so marked.

- *Bits and Pieces* Tiny pieces of truffles are sometimes put up in cans, and cost much less than whole ones. For a sauce that requires the truffles to be cut up into pieces, these canned truffles are ideal. Truffle peelings are also sometimes canned; they are the leftovers from the truffles that are peeled to put into commercially prepared pâtés. Peelings have very little flavor and, even though they are sold at bargain prices, are not a very good value.

Frozen

Freezing is a new method for preserving black Périgord truffles. They are flash-frozen using liquid nitrogen. Although they are not cheaper than fresh, their shelf life is much longer, up to a year, if they are kept at –10°F., and the quality is surprisingly good, much better than canned and surprisingly almost as good as fresh.

Purée

These truffles are pressed to extract their juice, which is then used to pack whole truffles in cans or jars. Once all their juice is extracted, these truffles are puréed in a vegetable oil base and put in tubes. The purée can be used to amplify sauces and add a slightly exotic, somewhat oaky flavor.

Imitation

Sometimes called *trufflettes,* these are made of vegetables and dyed black; they are used in professional kitchens for decoration and garnishing. They remind me of bicycle tires; I prefer to use a piece of black olive as a faux truffle instead.

HANDLING AND STORAGE

As one truffle professional told me, buying truffles is like buying diamonds: You have to trust your purveyor, because it is so difficult for the untrained eye to judge the product. A couple of tips, however, will help you choose a fresh truffle that is in good condition. Ask to see the truffle, of course, before you buy it, and give it a gentle squeeze. If it is not as firm as an unripe apple, it's probably too old. Also, it should have a very strong musky smell. If the truffle you're considering has *no* smell, it has been around too long. The smell of a fresh truffle, white or black, is so strong and pervasive that if one is cut into halves its odor will fill a room within minutes.

Fresh black truffles will last about 2 weeks at the most from the time they are taken from the ground. Considering how much time is taken up to get the truffle from Europe to the United States, it's best to eat the truffle as soon as possible after you get it. If you have to keep it for a day or two, you can wrap it in a damp cloth and keep it in the refrigerator. Another method is to submerge the truffle in water in the refrigerator overnight, taking it out of the water during the daytime so it doesn't spoil. If you plan to keep one longer than a couple of days, put it into a small container and cover with white wine; then the truffle with last about 4 weeks altogether, although it won't be nearly as good as when it was fresh. French chef Paul Bocuse recommends immersing a black truffle in a container of lard or melted goose fat to keep it for a couple of weeks, but this sounds like more trouble than it's worth.

Once it's time to use your black truffle, inspect it for dirt. If necessary, you can gently scrub it with a brush, using the point of a paring knife to pry out stubborn particles. There is no need to peel truffles. Sometimes a fine white moss will develop around the outside of a black truffle. Simply scrub it off and the truffle is safe to eat.

Fresh white truffles are more delicate than black, and will last only about 1 week at the most after you've purchased them. Many purveyors keep them buried in a container of white rice, although some chefs feel this dries out the truffles too much. I think the method is fine, as long as the truffle is used within a day or two after it has been put in the rice. When you do use the truffle, be sure to save the rice, which will have been permeated with the truffle's aroma; it will make a superb risotto or pilaf.

In the areas in the south of France where truffles are harvested, natives keep fresh black truffles in a covered bowl with a few fresh eggs. After just a few hours, the eggs will absorb the aroma and flavor of the truffles—through their shells!—and can be used to make the best scrambled eggs in the world. This trick can be used for white truffles as well.

Truffles in cans or jars should last for about 1 year. Ignore the advice of numerous cookbooks that suggest you pour Cognac or Madeira onto a fresh or canned truffle to preserve it. Although professional chefs have been using that technique for generations, the liquor is so strong that it takes over the flavor of the truffle, and you might as well be preserving a piece of rubber tire, as far as the taste is concerned. If you open a can of truffles and have some left over, transfer the truffle to a glass container and pour dry white wine into the container; use the remainder of the truffle within a week.

COOKING WITH TRUFFLES

Certain dishes in the classical French repertory require truffles. Any dish identified as *à la périgourdine* on a menu will have truffles in it, because it is named after the district in France which has long been known to produce the most and the best truffles.

Eggs Benedict are traditionally expected to be garnished with a piece of black truffle. To be sure, you don't run into too many truffles on this dish at the typical Sunday brunch, and to my mind it is a waste of good money to use any kind of truffle for this garnish. Some chefs use a piece of black olive for this and other dishes when the appearance but not the taste of the truffle is required.

Another waste of good money is *pâté de foie gras* studded with tiny black pieces that are supposed to be truffles. I would rather dispense with them altogether than use them just for this kind of show.

For my money, the only way to eat truffles is fresh. Unless there are enough truffles to detect the subtle flavor, it's not worth the extravagance. A slice of truffle, like one grain of caviar, is worse than none at all.

If one is lucky enough to get a fresh white or black truffle in good condition, it is best eaten immediately, grated right on top of a dish of mild-flavored food, such as certain salads, or perhaps steak tartare or pasta in a cream or butter sauce (without cheese), so that the taste of the truffle dominates. One medium-size truffle (about the size of a Ping-Pong ball) is just enough for two people to enjoy thoroughly. Black truffles can also be cooked in a sauce, where they will add a distinctly musky flavor.

Larry Forgione, chef-proprietor of An American Place Restaurant in New York City, shaves fresh black truffles onto fillets of sole, rolls up the fillets, and poaches them in a seasoned mixture of half white wine and half water (10 minutes of poaching for every inch of thickness of the fish before it's rolled up).

The best tool to use for shaving paper-thin slices of truffles is a truffle slicer, which looks like a single-edged razor blade embedded in a 6-inch metal holder. If you don't happen to have one lying around your kitchen, use a vegetable peeler. If you try to slice a truffle with a knife, the slices are likely to be too coarse and thick.

You can order a truffle slicer from Zabar's, 2245 Broadway, New York, NY 10024; telephone: (800) 221-3347.

CONCLUSIONS AND SUGGESTIONS

I was skeptical of truffles, thinking that they were prized simply because they were expensive, until I had my fill (lucky for me) on more than one occasion. The first time was when my family was living in Spoleto, Italy. Since some of the best white truffles in the world come from that region, the local restaurants feature them on the menu. At one festive dinner, with my five siblings around the table and a half dozen or so close friends, a waiter hovered over everyone's plate of pasta and shaved in so many white truffle slices that we couldn't see the noodles—about the equivalent of a golf-ball-size truffle for each plate. I so enjoyed this truffles-with-a-little-bit-of-pasta dish, with its heady, earthy flavor, that I admit to reaching over and grabbing the unfinished portions of my unsuspecting younger brother and sister.

The next time was when my husband and I went to Coriolano Restaurant in Rome. This small family-owned restaurant has an enclosed foyer so miniature that you have to close the outside door before you can open the door leading into the dining room. In this foyer on that October night was a platter piled high with a stack of about 75 white truffles. In that tiny enclosure the aroma of the truffles was so musky and sexy that I was almost embarrassed to be seen enjoying it in front of strangers. Of course, we had a new-potato-size white truffle with our buttered taglierini (a kind of fettuccine), first weighed on a little scale by a careful waiter.

Perhaps the best truffle dish I have ever eaten was prepared by Barry Wine, the gifted former chef-owner of The Quilted Giraffe Restaurant in New York City. He takes a 1/2-inch-thick oval slice of warm dark pumpernickel bread and covers it with a 1/4-inch-thick slice of cold sweet butter exactly the same size and shape as the bread. Then he shaves on top of the butter about 4 layers of gently warmed black or white truffles. As I ate this open-faced sandwich, the warmth of the truffles melted the butter and the flavors combined to make one of the best dishes I have ever eaten in my life. I plan to duplicate the experience as soon as my bank account allows for it.

These experiences have led me to the same conclusion as the great nineteenth-century gourmet Curnonsky, to whom is attributed the following story: When asked by his hostess, "How do you prefer your truffles?", he replied, "In great quantity, madame, in great quantity!" Truffles have a subtle flavor, and one should eat enough at one sitting to appreciate it fully.

Are they worth the money? As much as any luxury, I would say, but only if they're fresh and in good condition. Because truffles are so expensive to procure, and they spoil so quickly, some purveyors are not totally honest with their customers about the provenance and condition of the truffles they sell. Many purveyors themselves don't know that fresh black truffles available after the beginning of February are from Spain or Italy, and of decidedly inferior quality to those from France. Also, many truffles are weeks old by the time they end up in a home kitchen, and a cook is often disappointed with a mushy specimen with little or no flavor.

Flash-frozen truffles may be an answer to the freshness problem. As I stated earlier, they are not quite as good as just-harvested fresh truffles, but Paul Urbani, who is head of one of the most respected truffle-importing firms, finds them "85 percent as good as fresh," which makes them a lot better than fresh truffles that were harvested three weeks previously and have suffered in the meantime.

All in all, it's probably best to eat truffles as close to their source as possible, in France and Italy, and flash-frozen truffles (from a reputable dealer) in the United States.

RECIPE

Truffles in Cream Puffs

Recently I enjoyed this truffle dish, which is both witty and delicious, at the fiftieth birthday party of Warner LeRoy, the restaurateur-entrepreneur (and child of the glamor days of Hollywood—his father was the famous movie director Mervyn LeRoy). The dish replaced a cheese course and it was the perfect thing to precede a dessert of fresh berries. (Makes 8 servings)

1 cup water
1/2 cup unsalted butter
1/2 teaspoon salt
1 cup sifted all-purpose flour
4 eggs
1 egg yolk, mixed with 1 teaspoon water (for glaze)
1/2 pound cream cheese
1/2 pound blue cheese
1/4 cup heavy cream
8 fresh or flash-frozen black truffles, about 8 ounces

1. In a saucepan, bring the water, butter, and salt to a boil. Off the heat, add all of the flour at once, stirring vigorously with a wooden spoon until the ingredients are completely mixed. Put this mixture into the bowl of an electric mixer and begin to beat at medium speed. With the mixer running, add the whole eggs, one at a time, making sure each egg is completely incorporated before you add the next.

2. Drop this mixture by tablespoons onto an ungreased cookie sheet, making 8 even-size mounds. Brush the top of each one with a little of the egg-yolk glaze. Bake at 400°F. for 50 minutes, or until cooked through. Cool on a wire rack.

3. Mix together the cream cheese, blue cheese, and heavy cream to make a soft paste; add more cream if necessary. When cool, cut each puff into halves and put the bottom half of each one on a salad plate. Spread it with a couple of teaspoons of the cheese mixture. Shave slices of 1 whole black truffle onto the cheese spread (it's okay if a few truffle slices fall off the puff onto the plate). Spread underside of the top half of the puff with a teaspoon of the cheese mixture and place gently on top of the trufle slices. Serve immediately.

SOURCES

GOOD OVERALL SELECTION

Assouline and Ting
314 Brown Street
Philadelphia, PA 19123
(800) 521-4491

Balducci's
424 Avenue of the Americas
New York, NY 10011
(212) 673-2600 or (800)BALDUCCI

Bloomingdale's: Food Division
1000 Third Avenue
New York, NY 10021
(212) 355-5900

The Chef's Catalogue
3215 Commercial Ave
Northbrook, IL 60092
(708) 480-9400

Convito Italiano
1515 Sheridan Road
Willmet, IL 60091
(708) 988-7377

Corti Brothers
5810 Folsom Boulevard
Sacramento, CA 95819
(916) 736-3800

Dean and Deluca
560 Broadway
New York, NY 10012
(212) 431-1691

DeLaurenti Food Market
1435 First Avenue
Seattle, WA 98101
(206) 340-1498

E.A.T.
1062 Madison Avenue
New York, NY 10028
(212) 861-2544

Fraser Morris
1264 Third Avenue
New York, NY 10021
(212) 288-2727 or (800) 754-5331

Macy's
Attention: Food Department
170 O'Farrell Street
San Francisco, CA 94102
(415) 290-4439 or 4436

Maison Glass
111 East 58th Street
New York, NY 10022
(212) 755-3316 or (800) 822-5564

Marty's
3316 Oak Lawn Avenue
Dallas, TX 75219
(214) 526-4070

Merchant of Vino
29525 Northwestern Highway
Southfield, MI 48034
(810) 354-6505

Neiman-Marcus
P.O. Box 2968
Dallas, TX 75221-2968
(800) NEIMANS

Oakville Grocery
7856 St. Helena Highway
P.O. Box 86
Oakville, CA 94562
(707) 944-8802

Panache
2802 East Imperial Highway
Fullerton, CA 92621
(714) 870-8900

The Pasta Shop
5655 College Ave
Oakland, CA 94618
(510) 547-4005

Piret's
902 W. Washington Street
San Diego, CA 92103
(619) 297-2993

Provender
Tiverton Four Corners
3883 Main Road
Tiverton, RI 02878
(401) 624-8084

Ratto's
821 Washington Street
Oakland, CA 94501
(510) 832-6503

A Southern Season
Eastgate Shopping Center
Chapel Hill, NC 27514
(919) 929-7133

Sutton Place Gourmet
3201 New Mexico Avenue NW
Washington, DC 20016
(202) 363-5800

Todaro Brothers
557 Second Avenue
New York, NY 10016
(212) 679-7766

The Whip and Spoon
161 Commercial Street
Portland, ME 04101
(207) 744-4020

Zabar's
249 W. 80th Street
New York, NY 10024
(212) 787-2002

COCOA

Williams-Sonoma
Mail Order Department
San Francisco, CA 94120-7456
(415) 421-2033
Perngotti and Jersey Cocoa.

MUSTARDS AND KETCHUPS

Beaverton Foods
P.O. Box 687
Beaverton, OR 97075-0687
(503) 646-8138
Produces mustards, sauces, dressings and condiments and sells variety packs.

Beverly Hills Confection
Chalif, INC
5900 Noble Avenue
Van Nuys, CA 91411
(800) 828-3444

Jasmine and Bread
RR2
Box 256
South Royalton, VT 05068
(802) 763-7115
Two of their specialties are Beyond Ketchup, a blend of tomato, apples and vegetables; and Beyond Belief, a tomato-pear-chili-pepper condiment.

Norman Bishop
P.O. Box 2451
San Jose, CA 95113
(408) 292-1089
Mustards.

Blanchard and Blanchard
P.O. Box 1080
Norwich, VT 05055-1080
(800) 334-0268
Mustards.

Fox Hollow Farm
10 Old Lyme Road
Hanover, NH 03755
(603) 643-6002
Gourmet mustard called More Than a Mustard, flavored with balsamic vinegar and chopped garlic.

Mount Horeb Mustard Museum
P.O. Box 468
Mount Horeb, WI 53572
(800)GET-MUST
Sells over 400 different kinds of mustard, as well as other specialty foods.

PASTA

Al Dente
9815 Main Street
Whitmore Lake, MI 48189
(313) 449-8522

Bel Canto Foods
555 Second Avenue
New York, NY 10016
(212) 689-4433

Gaston Dupre
7904 Hopi Place
Tampa, FL 33634
(813) 885-9445

Rossi Pasta Factory
P.O. Box 759
Marietta, OH 45750
(800) 227-6774

PEANUT BUTTER

Arrowhead Mills
P.O. Box 259
Hereford, Texas 79045
(806) 364-0730

Sun Burst Farms
352 Paul Sumner Road
Omega, GA 31775
(800) 358-9412 or (912) 528-6692

Trader Joe's
P.O. Box 3270
South Pasadena, CA 91031
(818) 441-1177

RICE

Aromatic Rice

Ellis Stansel's Rice
P.O. Box 206
Gueydan, LA 70542
(318) 536-6140

Konriko Wild Pecan Rice
P.O. Box 10640
New Iberia, LA 70560
(318) 364-7242

Living Farms
Box 50
Tracey, MN 56175
(800) 533-5320

Lundberg Farms
P.O. Box 369
Richvale, CA 95974
(916) 882-4551

Northern Lakes
Wild Rice Company
P.O. Box 592
Teton Village, WY 83025
(307) 733-7192

Southern Brown Rice
P.O. Box 185
Weiner, AK 72479
(800) 421-7423

Italian Rice

Manganaro's
492 Ninth Avenue
New York, NY 10018
(212) 947-7325

Basmati Rice

Dean and Deluca
560 Broadway
New York, NY 10012
(212) 431-1691

SPECIALTY FLOURS

Arrowhead Mills
P.O. Box 2059
Hereford, TX 79045
(809) 364-0730

Bread Alone
P.O. Box 65
Burnt Cabins, PA 17215
800-BRT-Mill

Birkett Mills
P.O. Box 440
Penn Yan, NY 14527
(315) 536-3311

Giusto's
241 East Harris Avenue
South San Francisco, CA 94080
(415) 873-6566

Gray's Mill
P.O. Box 422
Adamsville, RI 02801
(508) 636-6075

Kenyon's
West Kingston
Usquepaugh, RI 02892
(401) 783-4054

Moore's Flour Mill
1605 Shasta Street
Redding, CA 96001
(916) 241-9245

Paprikas Weiss
1572 Second Avenue
New York, NY 10021
(212) 288-6117

Shiloh Farms
P.O. Box 97
Sulphur Springs, AK 72768
(501) 298-3297

Tuthilltown Griest Mill
1020 Albany Post Road
Gardiner, NY 12525
(914) 255-5695

Vermont Country Store
P.O. Box 128
Weston, VT 05161
(802) 824-3184

Walnut Acres
Penns Creek, PA 17862
(800) 344-9025

White Lily Flour Company
Box 871
Knoxville, TN 37901
(615) 546-5511

OLIVE OIL

Corti Brothers
5810 Folsom Boulevard
Sacremento, CA 95819
(916) 736-3800

Dean and Deluca
560 Broadway
New York, NY 10012
(212) 431-1691

ASIAN PRODUCTS

Eden Foods
701 Tecumseh
Clinton, MI 49236
(517) 456-7424

Kam Mam Food Products
200 Canal Street
New York, NY 10013
(212) 571-0330

Katagiri (Japanese)
224 East 59th Street
New York, NY 10022
(212) 755-3566

Kazy's Food Mart
8989 Forest Lane
Dallas, TX 75343
(214) 235-4831

Orient Delight Market
1024 Stockton Street
San Francisco, CA 94108
(415) 781-4650

The Oriental Market
2002 S. Wentworth Avenue
Chicago, IL 60616
(312) 949-1060

Santos Market
245 East Taylor Street
San Jose, CA 95112
(408) 295-5406

Uwajimaya
P.O. Box 3003
Seattle, WA 98114
(206) 624-6248

IMPORTED CANNED TUNA

Dean and Deluca
560 Broadway
New York, NY 10012
(212) 431-1691

E.A.T.
1062 Madison Avenue
New York, NY 10028
(212) 861-2544

Macy's Cellar
Herald Square
New York, NY 10001
(212) 971-6000

HERBS AND SPICES

Aphrodisia
282 Bleecker Street
New York, NY 10014
(212) 989-6440

The Chili Shop
190 East Water Street
Santa Fe, NM 87501
(505) 983-6080

Dean and Deluca
560 Broadway
New York, NY 10012
(212) 431-1691

The Ethnic Pantry
P.O. Box 798
Grayslake, IL 60030
(312) 223-6660

Frontier Cooperative Herbs
P.O. Box 299
Norway, IA 52318
(800) 669-3275

Fox Hill
Box 7
Parma, MI 49269
(517) 531-3179

GNS Spices
P.O. Box 90
Walnut, CA 91788-0090
(909) 594-9505
Only sells habanero peppers in all forms.

Stearns and Lehman
P.O. Box 1748
52 Surrey Road
Mansfield, OH 44901
(419) 522-2722

The Spice Hunter
254 Granada Drive
San Luis Obispo, CA 93401
(805) 544-4466

United Society of Shakers
Sabbathday Lake
Poland Springs, ME 04274
(207) 926-4597
All herbs are grown without pesticides.

INDIAN SPICES

Antone's Import Co.
4234 Harry Hines Boulevard
Dallas, TX 75219
(214) 528-5291

Bazaar of India
1131 University Avenue
Berkeley, CA 94702
(415) 548-4110

The El Paso Chile Company
100 Ruhlin Court
El Paso, TX 79922
(915) 544-3434

India Groceries
2610 West Devon
Chicago, IL 60659
(312) 334-3351

Little India Store
128 East 28th Street
New York, NY 10016
(212) 683-1691

Hungarian Paprika

Spiceco
900 Passaic Avenue
East Newark, NJ 07029
(201) 484-3726
They sell the Szeged brand of Hungarian paprika to the wholesale trade only, but they will tell consumers which stores around the United States carry their products.

Specialty Peppercorns

Flavorbank
4710 Eisenhower E-8
Tampa, FL 33614
(813) 885-1797

Stearns and Lehman
P.O. Box 1748
52 Surrey Road
Mansfield, OH 44901
(419) 522-2722

COFFEE

The Beverly Hills Coffee Company
369 S. Doheny Drive
Beverly Hills, CA 90211
(800) 576-1674

Cafe La Semeuse
P.O. Box 429
Brooklyn, NY 11222
(800) 242-6333

Coffee Drop Shop
12 North 3rd Street
St Charles, IL 60174
(708) 584-7989
Offers samplers that consist of 1/4-pound quantities of your choice.

Community Coffee
The Art Food Plaza
Ridgely, MD 21685
(800) 535-9901

Don Francisco Coffee Traders
P.O. Box 58371
Los Angeles, CA 90058
(800) 697-5282

Gevalia Kaffe
P.O. Box 11046
Des Moines, IA 50336
(800) 678-2687

Kobricks Coffee Company
693 Henderson Street
Jersey City, NJ 07302
(201) 656-6313

Luzianne Blue Plate Foods
Raleigh Foods
Box 60296
New Orleans, LA 70160
(800) 692-7895
Coffee and chicory blends available.

McNulty's Tea and Coffee Company
109 Christopher Street
New York, NY 10014
(212) 242-5351 or (800) 356-5200

Oregon Coffee Roaster
P.O. Box 223
North Plains, OR 97133
(800) 526-9940

Schapira's
117 West 10th Street
New York, NY 10011
(212) 675-3733

Starbucks Coffee and Teas
2010 Airport Way South
Seattle, WA 98124-1510
(800) 445-3428

The following coffee purveyors sell to the wholesale trade only, but they will tell consumers which retail outlets carry their products:

First Colony
204 W. 22nd Street
Norfolk, VA 23517
(800) 446-8555

Hena
383 Third Avenue
Brooklyn, NY 11215
(718) 596-7649

White Coffee Corp.
18-35 38th Street
Long Island City, NY 11105
(718) 204-7900

TEA

Barrows Tea Company
142 Arnold Street
New Bedford, MA 02740
508-990-2745
Darjeeling tea from this company is imported from a single estate in northern India.

Coffee Drop Shop
12 North 3rd Street
St. Charles, IL 60174
(708) 584-7989
They offer a nice variety of teas such as clove and elderberry.

Dean and Deluca
560 Broadway
New York, NY 10012
(212) 431-1691

G.H. Ford Tea Co.
110 Dutchess Turnpike
P.O. Box 3407
Poughkeepsie, NY 12603
(914) 471-1160
Sole manufacturers of the tea ball.

Grace Tea Company
80 Fifth Avenue
New York, NY 10011
(212) 255-2935

Harney and Sons Limited Fine Teas
Salisbury, CT 06068
(203) 435-5050

McNulty's Tea and Coffee Company
109 Christopher Street
New York, NY 10014
(212) 242-5351 or (800) 356-5200

Neiman-Marcus
P.O. Box 2968
Dallas, TX 75221-2961
(800) NEIMANS

Schapira's
117 West 10th Street
New York, NY 10011
(212) 675-3733

Simpson and Vail, Inc.
P.O. Box 309
Pleasantville, NY 10570-0309
(914) 747-1336

Stash Tea Co.
P.O. Box 610 R
Portland, OR 97207
(800) 826-4218

SUGAR AND SWEETENERS

Maasdam Sorghum Mill
Rural Route 1
Box 165
Lynville, IA 50153
(515) 594-4369

Specialty Sugars

Dean and Deluca
560 Broadway
New York, NY 10012
(212) 431-1691

Fraser Morris
1263 Third Avenue
New York, NY
(212) 288-2727

Maison Glass
111 East 58th Street
New York, NY 10022
(212) 755-3316

Stearns and Lehman
P.O. Box 1748
52 Surrey Road
Mansfield, OH 44901
(419) 522-2722

Cane Syrup

C.S. Steen Mill Inc
Abbeville, LA 70510
(318) 893-1654

Maple Syrup and Maple Sugar

American Spoon Foods
P.O. Box 566
Petoskey, MI 49770-566
(800) 222-5886

Auger's Sugar Mill Farm
Rt. 16
Box 26
Barton, VT 05822
(800) 688-7978

Butternut Mountain Farm
P.O. Box 381
Johnson, VT 05656
(800) 828-2376

Green Mountain Sugar House
Box 346
Ludlow, VT 05149
(802) 228-7151

Dan Johnson
70 Ingalls Road
Jaffrey, NH 03452
(603) 532-7379

Everett and Kathryn Palmer
Box 246
Waitsfield, VT 05673
(802) 496-3696

CHOCOLATE

Chocolate Lace
14 Clark Circle
Bethel, CT 06801
(203) 792-1234

Dean and Deluca
560 Broadway
New York, NY 10012
(212) 431-1691

Ghirardelli Chocolate Shop
Ghirardelli Square
San Francisco, CA 94109
(415) 474-3938

Hauser Chocolate
18 Taylor Avenue
Bethel, CT 06801
(203) 794-1861

Kron Chocolate
5 Bond Street
Great Neck, NY 11021
(800) 564-5766

Neuhaus
97-45 Queens Boulevard
Rego Park, NY 11374
(212) 518-5590
(800) 223-9001

Perugina
520 Madison Avenue
New York, NY 10022
(212) 688-2490

Plumbridge
30 East 67th Street
New York, NY 10021
(212) 744-6640

Stearns and Lehman
P.O. Box 1748
52 Surrey Road
Mansfield, OH 44901
(419) 522-2722

Williams-Sonoma
The Westin Hotel
Fountain Square South
21 East Fifth Street
San Francisco, CA 45202
(800) 541-1262

Zabar's
249 West 80th Street
New York, NY 10024
(212) 787-2002

The following chocolate purveyors sell to the wholesale trade only, but they will tell consumers which retail outlets carry their products:

Albert Uster
9211 Gaithers Road
Gaithersberg, MD 20877
(301) 258-7350

DeChoix and Amazon Specialty Foods
58-25 52nd Avenue
Woodside, New York 11377
(718) 507-8080
Callebaut and Van Halen.

Merckens
818 Main Street
Cambridge, MA 02139

Nestlé
(800) 258-6728

Universal Foods Corporation
400 Lyster Avenue
Saddlebrook, NJ 07663

Wilbur Chocolate Company, Inc
48 N. Broad Street
Lititz, PA 17543
(717) 626-1131

HONEY, JAMS AND PRESERVES

American Marketing Team
300 Broadacres Drive
Bloomfield, NJ 07003
(201) 256-7333

Champlain Valley Apiaries
P.O. Box 127
Middlebury, VT 05753
(802) 388-7724

Glory Bee Honey and Supplies
P.O. Box 2744
Eugene, OR 97402
(503) 689-0913

Hanna's Honey
P.O. Box 17353
Salem, OR 97305
(503) 393-2945

Marilyn Douglas Jam
Mendocino Jams and Jellies
Box 781
Mendocino, CA 95460
(707) 937-1037

Sarabeth's Kitchen
423 Amsterdam
New York, NY 10024
(212) 496-6280

Zabar's
249 West 80th Street
New York, NY 10024
(212) 787-2000

VANILLA

Dean and Deluca
560 Broadway
New York, NY 10012
(212) 431-1691

KCJ Vanilla Company
RD 1, Box 184
Pittstown, PA 18643
Stocks vanilla extracts from Tahiti, Madagascar, and Mexico, including single and double strength.

La Cuisine
323 Cameron Street
Alexandria, VA 22314-3295
(800) 521-1176
Vanilla essence.

The Spice House
Old World Third Street
Milwaukee, WI 53203
(414) 258-7787
They place a whole vanilla bean in every bottle of pure vanilla; made from Madagascar-Bourbon beans.

Stearns and Lehman
P.O. Box 1748
52 Surrey Road
Mansfield, OH 44901
(419) 522-2722
Neilson-Massey vanilla extract.

CAVIAR

Assouline and Ting
314 Brown Street
Philadelphia, PA 19123
(800) 521-4491

Balducci's
Mail Order Division
42-25 12th Street
Long Island City, NY 11101-4908
(800) 822-1444
(800) 247-2450 (in NY State)

Boyajian Inc.
385 California Street
Newton, MA 02160
(617) 527-6677

California Sunshine
144 King Street
San Francisco, CA 945107
(415) 543-3007

Caviar and Caviar
12307 Washington Avenue
Rockville, MD 20852
(800) 472-4456

Caviar Direct
Trump Tower
725 Fifth Avenue
New York, NY 10022
(800) 650-2828

Hansen Caviar
93 D.S. Railroad Avenue
Bergenfeld, NJ
(800) 735-0441

J and K Trading Comp.
10808 Garland Drive
Culver City, CA 90230
(310) 836-3334

Pana Caviar
1 Times Square
New York, NY 10036
(212) 581-7118

Poriloff (Purepak) Foods
47-39 49th Street
Woodside, NY 11377
(718) 784-3344

Petrossian
182 W. 58th Street
New York, NY 10019
(212) 245-0303

Russ and Daughters
179 E. Houston
New York, NY 10002
(212) 475-4880

Walter's Caviar
Howell and Bertha Boone
P.O. Box 263
Darien, GA 31305
(912) 437-6560
American caviar.

TRUFFLES

Aux Delices des Bois
4 Leonard Street
New York, NY 10018
(212) 334-1230

Gourmand
2575B Shirlington Road
Arlington, VA 22206
(703) 836-1670

Urbani
29-24 40th Avenue
Long Island City, NY 11101
(718) 392-5050 or (800)5-URBANI

INDEX

Page numbers in **boldface** refer to recipes.